SHAKESPEARE
STUDIES

SHAKESPEARE
STUDIES
Volume XLIV

EDITED BY

JAMES R. SIEMON
Boston University

and

DIANA E. HENDERSON
Massachusetts Institute of Technology

ASSISTANT TO THE EDITORS
DEVIN BYKER
Boston University

Madison • Teaneck
Fairleigh Dickinson University Press

Associated University Presses
10 Schalks Crossing Road
Suite 501–330
Plainsboro, NJ 08536

The paper used in this publication meets the requirements of the American National Standard for Permanence of Paper for Printed Library Materials Z39.48-1984.

International Standard Book Number 978-0-8386-4480-5
International Standard Serial Number: 0-0582-9399

Essays may be submitted for consideration at the journal web site: http://sites.bu.edu/shakespearestudies/. All other editorial correspondence concerning *Shakespeare Studies* should be addressed to the Editorial Office, *Shakespeare Studies*, English Department, Boston University, Boston, MA 02215 or by email to sstudies@bu.edu.

Orders and subscription inquiries should be sent to Associated University Presses at the address shown above.

Shakespeare Studies disclaims responsibility for statements, either of fact or opinion, made by contributors.

PRINTED IN THE UNITED STATES OF AMERICA

Contents

6   CONTENTS

Next Gen Plen

Articles

Reviews

Contributors

CRYSTAL BARTOLOVICH is Associate Professor of English at Syracuse University. Her current book project considers responses to *Utopia*—especially to More's foregrounding of the "common" as a problem.

CAROLINE BICKS is Associate Professor of English at Boston College. She is the author of *Midwiving Subjects in Shakespeare's England* and is completing a book on adolescent girls' minds in early modern England.

LINDA CHARNES is Professor of English at Indiana University, Bloomington. She is currently working on a monograph on intention, agency, and contingency.

JULIE CRAWFORD is Professor of English and Comparative Literature at Columbia University. The author, most recently, of *Mediatrix: Women, Politics and Literary Production in Early Modern England* (Oxford, 2014), she is currently completing a book on Margaret Cavendish.

CARLA DELLA GATTA is Assistant Professor of Critical Studies—Theatre at the University of Southern California. She is currently working on her first monograph on Shakespeare and Latinidad, and the staging of intracultural theatre.

JOHN DRAKAKIS is Professor Emeritus at the University of Stirling and a Visiting Professor at the University of Lincoln. He is the general and contributory editor to the forthcoming revision of Geoffrey Bullough's *Narrative and Dramatic Sources of Shakespeare.*

KATHERINE GILLEN is Assistant Professor of English at Texas A&M University—San Antonio. She is currently completing a book on the economic resonances of chastity tropes in early modern drama.

HUW GRIFFITHS is a senior lecturer in Early Modern English Literature at The University of Sydney, Australia. He is currently writing a book that will be called *Shakespeare's Body Parts.*

MATTHEW HARRISON is a visiting assistant professor at Albion College. He is currently working on a book project about representations of bad poetry in early modern England.

JOHN HARTLEY is John Curtin Distinguished Professor at Curtin University, Western Australia; and professor of journalism, media, and cultural studies at Cardiff University, Wales. His latest book is *Creative Economy and Culture* (with Wen Wen and Henry Siling Li, Sage Publications, 2015).

DIANA E. HENDERSON, Professor of Literature at MIT and author of *Collaborations with the Past: Reshaping Shakespeare Across Time and Media,* is currently involved in both online and performance projects, including MIT's Global Shakespeares curricular and archival initiatives.

ALLISON P. HOBGOOD is Associate Professor of English and Women's and Gender Studies at Willamette University in Salem, Oregon. She is currently working on a new book on disability in early modern England.

MICHAEL INGHAM is a Professor in the Department of English Studies at Lingnan University, Hong Kong, and a founding member of the Theatre Action drama company in Hong Kong. His contribution on Shakespeare and Jazz is included in the *Cambridge Guide to the Worlds of Shakespeare,* and his monograph on Intermediality in Film and Theatre will be published by Routledge in 2016.

DANIEL L. KEEGAN received his PhD from the University of California, Irvine and is Visiting Assistant Professor of English at the University of Wyoming. His current research concerns the relationship between prophetic and dramatic language in early modern England.

LAURA KOLB is Assistant Professor of English at Baruch College, CUNY. She is at work on a book about representations of economic credit in early modern plays and practical literature.

PAUL A. KOTTMAN is Associate Professor of Comparative Literature at the New School for Social Research. He is the author, most
recently, of *Love as Human Freedom* (Stanford UP, forthcoming)
and the editor of *The Insistence of Art: Aesthetic Philosophy and
Early Modernity* (Fordham UP, forthcoming).

JAMES N. LOEHLIN is the Shakespeare at Winedale Regents Professor of English at the University of Texas at Austin, and Director
of the Shakespeare at Winedale program. He has written books on
Shakespeare, Chekhov, and Marlowe in performance, including,
most recently, the volume on *Doctor Faustus* in the Palgrave series
on Shakespeare's Contemporaries.

KATHLEEN McLUSKIE, author of books on *Renaissance Dramatists, Dekker and Heywood, Macbeth,* and *Cultural Value,* retired
from the Directorship of the Shakespeare Institute in 2011. She is
currently making a garden in the Cotswolds and writing now and
then about Shakespeare and time.

CHRISTOPHER NORRIS is Distinguished Research Professor in
Philosophy at the University of Cardiff, Wales. He has written more
than thirty books on aspects of philosophy and literary theory, as
well as a collection of verse-essays, *The Cardinal's Dog and Other
Poems.* Two further such collections, *The Winnowing Fan* and *For
the Tempus Fugitives,* will be published later this year.

KARA J. NORTHWAY is Associate Professor of English at Kansas
State University, where she is currently working on a project on
early modern letters and theater history. Her research has been published in venues such as *Comparative Drama, Shakespeare Bulletin,* and *Renaissance Papers.*

LAUREN ROBERTSON received her Ph.D. from Washington University in St. Louis. Her book-in-progress examines the affective
experiences of uncertainty the early modern English theater created for its spectators.

TIFFANY STERN is Professor of Early Modern Drama at the University of Oxford. She is currently writing two books: one on Documents Beyond Performance and one on fairgrounds.

ROBERT TITTLER is Distinguished Professor of History Emeritus at Montreal's Concordia University, and has written extensively on the interaction between the visual arts and their social context in Early Modern England.

DEANNE WILLIAMS is Professor of English at York University. She is the author of *The French Fetish from Chaucer to Shakespeare* (Cambridge, 2004) and *Shakespeare and the Performance of Girlhood* (Palgrave, 2014).

ELIZABETH WILLIAMSON teaches at The Evergreen State College, and is the author of *The Materiality of Religion in Early Modern English Drama* (Ashgate, 2009), and co-editor (with Jane Hwang Degenhardt) of *Religion and Drama in Early Modern England* (Ashgate, 2011). Her current book project deals with Shakespeare and the politics of martyrdom.

DEBORAH WILLIS is Associate Professor of English at the University of California, Riverside. Author of *Malevolent Nurture: Witch-Hunting and Maternal Power in Early Modern England,* she is currently working on a book about early modern addiction, demonology, and Shakespeare.

JESSICA WINSTON is Professor of English at Idaho State University. Her most recent book, *Lawyers at Play: Literature, Law, and Politics at the Early Modern Inns of Court, 1558–1581,* was published by Oxford University Press in 2016.

JENNIFER LINHART WOOD is an Associate Editor at *Shakespeare Quarterly.* Her scholarship on uncanny sonic encounters between different early modern cultures was awarded Honorable Mention in the 2013 Shakespeare Association of America's J. Leeds Barroll Dissertation Prize competition. Her work has appeared in the collection *Gender and Song in Early Modern England* (Ashgate, 2014) and in the *Journal for Early Modern Cultural Studies.*

MARION WYNNE-DAVIES is Professor of English Literature at the University of Surrey. She has published extensively on women's writing in the Renaissance and is currently working on a history of PEN, the organization that champions freedom of expression.

SHAKESPEARE STUDIES

FORUM:

The Importance of Being Hawkes

For Ann, and David too

Introduction

DIANA E. HENDERSON

Honoring terence hawkes is a paradoxical enterprise. For one thing, it requires his absence: if he were around, he'd be scathing about any lapses into "wind," skeptical as he was about all forms of complacent rhetoric or conventions substituting for thought and action.

The enemy was often us, and right up until the end, he was having no truck with invocations of the "bloated 'wonder' called Shakespeare."[1] Any other such accomplished scholar, editor, writer, and teacher might have celebrated the signs of his theoretical and political agenda's success—the major paradigm shift that he had done so much to launch and sustain—but that was not Terry's way. In the late essay "Band of Brothers," he was still uncovering corrosive legacies of Anglocentric privilege (racial, linguistic, economic) even in seemingly progressive attempts at internationalizing performance. While others during the past decade began celebrating—and branding—"Global Shakespeares" and "Complete Works" festivals in the lead-up to round-numbered anniversaries of birth and death, Hawkes ferreted out signs of "nostalgic memory" and an "Undead" Bard sucking "the life-blood from any and all cultures . . . for these transfusions guarantee his 'truly global reach,' " leading him, Bartleby-like, to the wry conclusion: "It might be better not to drink the water."[2]

Not the water, perhaps, but the wine—for this was vintage Hawkes: the bravura connections among disparate moments and texts (beginning with the American philanthropist's gift of a water fountain to Victorian Stratford, quoting *Timon of Athens* and *Henry VIII,* and moving on through Henry Irving and Bram Stoker's *Dracula,* Karl Marx and Allardyce Nicoll, the formation of the ISC, the Cold War, and Barry Jackson's modern dress *Timon* on his merry way to the one-line zinger that finds its end in its beginning); resur-

17

recting the material realities of a bardbiz then and now but never "above politics"; and ultimately, yet playfully, refusing late capitalism's enchantments.

Probably he would refuse the wine analogy as well, preferring his pint at the pub and a football match; yet his essays never resembled workaday prose. The jazz stylings of his drumming provided the backbeat for riffs that were so much more—although the humility and collaborativeness of his book acknowledgments may have misled a few of those early reviewers whose ears had been muted by conventional scholarship. Some of them (returning years later to the ever-fresh essays in *Shakespeare's Talking Animals, That Shakespeherian Rag* or *Meaning by Shakespeare*) must have sheepishly realized that they had been "outplayed," while a tin-eared few may continue to miss the music that animated the politics and perspicacity which Hawkes was more inclined to attribute to others. But nobody could miss his main points, or the barbed wit that tried to keep us honest.

The Importance of Being Hawkes follows upon and complements several print forms of professional tribute, including essays in *Critical Practice* (Britain's first journal of literary theory, of which he was founding editor), *The International Journal of Cultural Studies,* and a special issue of *Critical Survey.* Consisting of nine diverse pieces that reflect variously on a multifaceted and transformative career, this forum serves as a further reminder of Terry's great scope and influence, of Hawkes's labors won. In the forum's most extensive contribution, John Drakakis helpfully traces the arc and through-lines of Hawkes's scholarly writing over the course of six decades, beginning with *Coleridge's Writings on Shakespeare* (1959) and *Shakespeare and the Reason* (1964) and emphasizing how the famed mid-career books anticipated the full blossoming of "presentism." Recalling for Shakespeareans Terence Hawkes's central role in the introduction and dissemination of poststructuralism, theory, and cultural studies, transcending—though as John Hartley reminds us, including—Shakespeare studies, philosopher and writer Christopher Norris provides a suitably inventive form of poetic tribute, an enlightened "Terza Rima for Terry (Meaning by Hawkes)."

The essays that follow retrace and develop patterns along some of the many paths Hawkes trod. Kathleen McLuskie reflects upon the role of Terry's British generational history in shaping his critical practices and emphases, as juxtaposed with those of another leading figure in making Shakespeare (and the bardbiz) pertinent in the "here and now": the very differently located European Jan Kott. John Hartley shifts the geographical and historical landscape by comparing Hawkes with an earlier trans-Atlantic visitor to America, Alexis de Tocqueville, and uses a cultural studies methodology (developed with Hawkes's guidance) to enrich our understanding of the Astor Place Riots as a sadly resonant form of Shakespearean class warfare. Such reconnection of Terry's work with theater history is especially apt given Marion Wynne-Davies's recollection of how deeply enmeshed with the materiality of performance his teaching had always been. Conversely, his emphasis on listening—in theater, in the classroom—allowed students such as Wynne-Davies to become collaborators even before they became professional colleagues.

In addition to mentoring (and mentoring the independence of) his own students, Hawkes became famous as a savvy volunteer advisor to many rising scholars across the profession and the world, as Linda Charnes attests. She reflects upon his contributions (and challenges) as an editor, as well as his iconoclastic importance in providing those coming up through the profession in the late twentieth century with a model for "cheeky" writing of a profound sort. Huw Griffiths also reflects upon Hawkes's writing as a beacon and provocation for those who have followed, in a piece that echoes the meaningful errancy of Terry's compositional style in "Hank Cinq." Punning to overthrow the orderly social control of proper names, playing in the mire and throb of preliterate society's margins (from bearbaiting to theatricality to Welshness), Hawkes dismantled forms of "literary" institutionalization that may no longer matter so much to the twenty-first-century's multinational robber barons, as both McLuskie and Griffiths observe; each sees work yet to be done, changes of focus needed in order to extend the Hawkesian spirit and legacy of meaningful contestation.

From the rhythms of the pun to those of song: Mike Ingham leads us away from the academy and critique into cross-media adaptation and the form of music Terry both loved and performed, focusing on jazz renditions of Shakespeare's sonnets by Cleo Laine and Johnny Dankworth as well as more recently by Belgian Carroll Vanwelden. Although the words of Mercury may yet sound harsh after the songs of Apollo, my epilogue builds on the imperative set out in many of these essays as well as in *Presentist Shakespeares:* that Shakespeare criticism "deliberately begin with the material present and allow that to set its interpretive agenda.'"[3] I do so with a requisitely provocative twist, calling into question the utility of the entire historicist/presentist debate strategy.

Taken as a whole these writings capture much (though far from all) of a remarkable life. The whirligig of time does indeed bring in his revenges: it attests that, among many other things, Terence Hawkes became an eminent Shakespearean himself. But the ways in which he undercut (indeed, skewered) that category and created new ones will endure much longer than the particular readings of so many others who have been awarded that honorific title—as will many of those artful Hawkes essays, and his unmatched editorial legacy. His full professional life as well as writings have provided a model for opening ourselves up to change, to a future that is all the stronger because of its differences from the past. For without a doubt, Terry always looked forward, and seized every opportunity to bring—even push—the world along with him.

Consider longtime, deeply respected Methuen editor Janice Price's account of the founding of the *New Accents* series:

> New Accents was invented by Terry Hawkes as the result of conversations with me and John Jump, general editor of the Critical Idiom Series, about the future of literary studies. New Accents fitted the Methuen publishing strategy which had, for many years, and in many subject areas, sought to engage with innovative research and teaching. *Alternative Shakespeares* was part of that programme. We published a range of works in Elizabethan and Jacobean drama including the Arden Shakespeare—a very different project to the first volume of *Alternative Shakespeares,* but one which had earned Methuen the respect of scholars worldwide.[4]

It was indeed a very different project, especially in the days of Arden 2. As Terry himself recalled thirty years later, in the third General Editor's preface that accompanied (among other volumes) *Alternative Shakespeares 3, "New Accents* deliberately took sides."[5] Addressing "the newly perplexed world of academic literary studies, where hectic monsters called 'Theory,' 'Linguistics,' and 'Politics' ranged," "it aimed itself at those undergraduates or beginning postgraduate students who were either learning to come to terms with the new developments or were being sternly warned against them."

> If mystification (or downright demonization) was the enemy, lucidity (with a nod to the compromises inevitably at stake there) became a

friend. If a 'distinctive discourse of the future' beckoned, we wanted at least to be able to understand it.[6]

Typically, Terry aimed to teach and learn, alongside his students, and gave them credit for wanting to understand what their elders considered alien, abstruse and esoteric forms of thought. Fair enough: but what combined with this impulse to make *New Accents* truly remarkable was the percipience of his choices and the accessibility of the wide-ranging list—much of which he personally composed or edited. In other words, Hawkes put his money (and time and talents and values) where his mouth was. From his own *Structuralism and Semiotics* and editing of *Alternative Shakespeares, Volume 2,* to *Deconstruction: Theory and Practice, Reading Television,* and the other two volumes in the *Alternative Shakespeares* series (all written or edited by contributors to this forum), to formative collections in emergent fields, such as *Making a Difference: Feminist Literary Criticism* and *Post-Colonial Shakespeares,* the *New Accents* list did not just make new developments "understandable": it reshaped and expanded the field of literary studies itself.

Similarly, when he spun off another lively sub-list of *Accents on Shakespeare,* he emphasized the dynamic temporality of scholarly work: "The fact that each book in the series promises a Shakespeare inflected in terms of a specific urgency should ensure that, in the present as in the recent past, the accent will be on change."[7] The world did not stop moving, and neither did Hawkes. *Hic et ubique?* Then we'll shift our ground. It was we the fortunate protégés who struggled to keep up with him, not vice versa.

Rest, rest, perturbèd spirit. Restless in life, relentless in your energy and good humor, your desire for political change, and your unbounded wit, you have done our state some service and we know it: no more of that. And no more of this apostrophizing ventriloquy, with which you would have no patience. Why should we be Shakespeare's dummies? The only properly improper way to honor Terry Hawkes, ultimately, is to bury him alongside that Undead Bard and all Ghostly fathers in our imaginations, and let the old mole burrow there (well said, old mole—always well said). And then, get back to the work at hand, the work he modeled and demanded of us. And so, we will "not only yearn to speak with the dead. [We] will aim, in the end, to talk to the living"—critically, without complacency, and with, as he demanded, our "cards on the table."[8] Every poem an epitaph. Let the games begin.

Notes

1. Terence Hawkes, "Band of Brothers," in *Presentist Shakespeares,* eds. Hugh Grady and Terence Hawkes (London: Routledge, 2007), 6–26; 20.

2. Ibid., 21, 24.

3. Grady and Hawkes, "Presenting presentism," in *Presentist Shakespeares,* 1–5; 4.

4. Personal email correspondence, September 11, 2015. My sincere thanks to Ms. Price for her willingness to clarify the origins of the series she played so vital a role in creating.

5. Terence Hawkes, "General Editor's Preface" to the *New Accents* series, cited from *Alternative Shakespeares 3,* ed. Diana E. Henderson (London: Routledge, 2008), vii.

6. Ibid.

7. Terence Hawkes, "General Editor's Preface" to the *Accents on Shakespeare* series, cited from *Presentist Shakespeare,* xi–xii.

8. Grady and Hawkes, *Presentist Shakespeare,* 4.

The Critical Process of Terence Hawkes

John Drakakis

I

THERE ARE FEW Shakespearean scholars of the post-Second World War generation who can match the range, the adventurousness, and the exciting unpredictability of Terence Hawkes. His academic journey began within the comparatively orthodox framework of an edition of selections from Coleridge's writings on Shakespeare in the Penguin Shakespeare Library in 1959, followed in 1964 by a major contribution both to Shakespeare criticism and the history of ideas in his book *Shakespeare and the Reason.* The range of Hawkes's interests was beginning to emerge by the early 1970s when he was the European editor for the journal *Language and Style,* and was evidenced in his short book in the original Critical Idiom series on *Metaphor* (1972). In 1973 he published *Shakespeare's Talking Animals,* a groundbreaking book that was well in advance of its time, and that launched a series of connections between the "historical" Shakespeare and what was then current popular culture. The full extent of that range was to emerge some five years later when he edited the volume on *Twentieth Century Interpretations of "Macbeth"* (1977), selecting relevant essays from the 1930s to the 1970s. In the same year the four initial volumes in the New Accents series, including his own *Structuralism and Semiotics* (1977), appeared. There were clear signs in the Introduction to the *Macbeth* collection, and more so in *Shakespeare's Talking Animals,* that Hawkes was uneasy with the dominant tradition of Shakespeare scholarship, and with the state of Literary Studies more generally. But his general editorship of the New Accents series and his commitment to presenting, in accessible form and for the first time, new linguistic and literary models that owed much to European "theory" served to change significantly the trajectory of literary studies—in British higher education and beyond. At the same time, Terence Hawkes was well on the way to becoming an accomplished jazz drummer, an interest and an expertise that was to filter into his own scholarly practice as the boundaries between academic disciplines and popular culture were beginning to dissolve.

That Shakespeherian Rag, published in 1986, borrows its title from T. S. Eliot's *The Waste Land* (1922) which itself conflates two temporally distinct articulations of popular culture—Shakespeare and popular music—as part of the fabric of a canonical modernist text. Eliot's backward glance to a heavily mythologized organic Renaissance culture is historicist insofar as it seeks consolation for the fragmentations of the present in the shards of the past that return as symptoms of a now defunct hierarchy. Hawkes's "essays," written at various stages during the early years of the government of Margaret Thatcher, are subtitled: "essays on a critical process," and refuse the ethos implied in the nostalgia of *The Waste Land.* Indeed, they embrace the "present" in a dynamic dialogue with the "past" and in ways that foreground the shaping "process" of the critic as deeply and consciously enmeshed in what is ostensibly his object of inquiry. The first essay, "Playhouse—Workhouse," initially *situates* the critic in a quotidian reality, in a manner that later became characteristic of Hawkes's general approach:

> I am eating fish and chips in Stratford-upon-Avon. To be precise, I am doing so while leaning on a lock-gate at the point where the Stratford canal flows into the river Avon. Slightly to my left is the Royal Shakespeare Theatre where I have just attended a performance of *The Tempest.* Slightly to my right is a fish-and-chip shop.[1]

This unusually candid positioning is the point of convergence of a number of forces: "canal [Culture] . . . river [Nature] . . . the Royal Shakespeare Theatre . . . fish-and-chip shop [Englishness]" open onto a terrain of constitutive differences whose "broad and potent distinctions" the observant critic simply "fails to allay."[2] The arresting stubbornness of these contiguous discursive frames, their capacity to resist an easy narrative homogenization, *appears* to be a consequence of their being an inseparable part of a larger, variegated but identifiably historical, context that functions to expand meaning. This process of generating meaning is exemplified, initially at any rate, in the ensuing gloss of the experience of seeing the "text" of *The Tempest,* performed in the theater. Except that the issue is clearly not one of according primacy to an allegedly accurate retrospection set against a description of an actual cultural practice that simply presents a fragmented reality (modernism), but rather one of the critic's acknowledging and recognizing in the present a "processing," an inevitable and irreducible processing, of the disparate elements of the past.

This startling recognition, permits, on the one hand, the allusion to a series of contemporary Renaissance texts that might have *informed* Shakespeare's play. However, at the same time, it also compels the critic to acknowledge both the continuities and the discontinuities that result from this surprising collision of textual materials. Situating what follows in Stratford circa 1986, the critic is able to filter through his own consciousness—a consciousness of the manner in which we receive the past, a consciousness of the primacy of language along with the problem raised by the assumed referential power of words—an awareness of the position that "Shakespeare" currently occupies in late 20th-century British culture. The additional awareness of the cultural status of the RSC *and* of the wider social and political climate within which this particular performance is taking place acts as a supplement to the intrinsic suggestive power of the text of *The Tempest.* This manifestation of Hawkes's interpretive practice is part of a complex process that is able to take in the historic investment that Shakespeare's play makes in the business of "colonisation," and what it might mean in terms of the wider issues of land ownership and "labour," for which the unequal relation between Prospero and Caliban serves as one of a number of structural models. Indeed, the binaries within which the critic is inscribed find echoes in *The Tempest* to the extent that it discloses "a major contradiction" that threatens "to dislocate the bars of the discourse which cage it in the play," and that "centres on the familiar paradox of work" that "traditionally represents a punishment inflicted on human beings as a penalty for Adam's sin." Lifting this burden impels a vision of utopia, but it also paradoxically invokes an implicitly moral resistance emanating from the claim that "work is good" because "it restrains carnal appetite and channels human energy to useful, moral and socially supportive ends."[3] The play may produce a pastoral politics, but the operation of power also produces a subversive reaction. Indeed, the interruption to the pastoral masque that Prospero has mounted for the benefit of the young lovers, Ferdinand and Miranda, is described in the Folio's stage direction as "a strange, hollow and confused noise," and emanated in the production from the rebellious Caliban. But the noise is heard differently in the modern world: "To twentieth-century ears, it might, for all the world, be a shop steward's whistle or a police siren."[4] These are the recognizable modern symbols of the larger dynamic of resistance and coercion in the "world" as currently experienced by Western capitalist democracies. And what has occurred here in Hawkes's reading is technically a "translation," the reformulation of a social relation that the text of *The Tempest* can only glimpse from its own partisan perspective. At one level the allusion to these sounds occupies the status of a parapraxis, but it is nonetheless a "translation." The critic is caught in the very act of "making meaning," while, at the same time, resisting the temptation to conflate the past and the present into a timeless continuum.

This instance is emphatically not a matter of the intrusion of an anachronism into Hawkes's critical vocabulary, nor is it a free-wheeling association of ideas. Rather, it is the returning of the critic to a position where what is, on the surface, an "objective" account, documented and legitimized by a fully professionalized discourse, is shown to be in and of itself partial, if not partisan. It is Hawkes's contention that we can only derive meaning from the perspective that we occupy in relation to an object or a text, that this is something that as readers we do "naturally," and hence the ensuing enlargement of the text's particular focus upon "work," "employment," and "unemployment" arises directly out of the critic's own engagement with a text that traverses similar issues but from an unfamiliar local perspective. The argument moves incrementally to engage historical topics such as land "enclosure," and the extent to which the uneven relations it produced gave rise to the structural binary of "employment/unemployment," issues that shortly before the publication of *That Shakespeherian Rag* were of crucial contemporary national importance to a country caught in the grip of a Thatcherite revolution that saw the smashing of trade unionism and massive increases in unemployment and homelessness. The contemporary political context is not so much a key to an understanding of Hawkes's argument as an element that is already factored into it. Thus the familiar traditional practice of excavating and recognizing historically overdetermined allegorical meaning gives way here to a dialectical operation that seeks to understand how it is possible, from the unavoidable standpoint of the present, to generate meanings from texts of the past.

In an earlier book, *Shakespeare's Talking Animals* (1973), the "process" was sketched out in a preliminary way through the juxtaposition of close reading of exemplary Shakespearean texts within the framework of a dialectical comparative encounter between the "pre-literate" world of the Shakespearean theatre and the "post-literate" world of electronic communication on the basis of what appears initially to be a shared nomenclature. Shakespeare's Globe and McLuhan's "global village" share an emblem in common that seized the avant-garde critical imagination of the late 1960s. Looking through the lens of the present at an institution of the past uncovers, both at a thematic and formal level, new readings and generates new perspectives in such a way that it displaces the ontological privileging of the past over the present as a gateway to the future. The thesis of *Shakespeare's Talking Animals* is thus, prophetically, an account of the various transmutations that an ephemeral institution such as Shakespeare's Globe Theatre underwent in the protracted process leading up to its ultimate emergence as an electronic global phenomenon. Indeed, if *Shakespeare's Talking Animals* were to be rewritten from the perspective of the beginning of the twenty-first century, it would need to re-situate Shakespeare within a framework of the radically democratic potential of the present-day social media as an element in a competitive struggle for ownership and control of public discourse, with all of the politics that that struggle implies.

It must be emphasized that Terence Hawkes's "presentism," which emerges fully in his *Shakespeare in the Present* (2002), is no simple ontological privileging of the present at the expense of the past. Nor is it, as in New Historicism, a belated acknowledgment that in order to speak with the dead and/or with the "voice of the other" the critic must hear his own voice.[5] Indeed, it constitutes a symptomatic *reading* of what had become, for New Historicists such as Stephen Greenblatt in 1988, when *Shakespearean Negotiations* appeared, an abiding "dream": to disentangle the critic's own voice from the voice of the "other." Fully embracing "theory" and the critic's own "situatedness," and in opposition to this persuasive fantasy, Hawkes argues:

> All restorations face one major problem. Reaching backwards they can't afford to examine the position in the present from which that manoeu-

vre is undertaken. As a result they discount the nature of the choosing
and the omission, the selections and suppressions that determine it. Yet
to avoid the pitfall by taking one's present situation fully into account
seems inevitably to compromise the project. Genuinely to capture, or
repeat, the past is of course fundamentally impossible for a variety of
other reasons.[6]

However, this symptomatic reading is predicated upon a series of
convictions: that meaning is produced differentially, that "original" meaning is fundamentally irrecoverable, and that there must
inevitably be a discrepancy between, say, Shakespeare's meanings,
and those we generate as readers and spectators from what we read
or see.

The substratum of *Shakespeare in the Present* is an earlier book,
Meaning by Shakespeare (1992), that follows on directly in terms
of its methodology from *That Shakespeherian Rag* (1986) but
makes much more explicit its own theoretical co-ordinates as part
of an evolving "process." Coming some two years before Greenblatt's *Shakespearean Negotiations* (1988), although some time
after Greenblatt's first (and in the final analysis, unsatisfactory)
foray into this terrain in *Renaissance Self-Fashioning from More to
Shakespeare* (1980), *That Shakespeherian Rag* sought to question
"whether we could have any genuine access to final, authoritative
or essential meanings in respect of Shakespeare's plays." Moreover, and in addition, Hawkes deliberately rejected the formal considerations of aesthetics, and with them those implicit, or even
unconscious, political assumptions that lay behind a persistently
dominant familiar tradition of Shakespeare criticism, offering
instead the candid revelation that "like it or not, all we can ever
do is use Shakespeare as a powerful element in specific ideological
strategies."[7] *Meaning by Shakespeare* now posed explicitly what
had been strongly implicit throughout Hawkes's own critical
lexicon, the question of the consequences of the transition from
Shakespeare to "Shakespeare," from the dramatist working in an
institution at a particular place and time, to the status of a timeless
"oracle" whose "lucubrations" are accorded the status of universal
truths: "the masterpiece of a poet-philosopher replete with transcendent wisdom about the way things are, always have been, and
presumably always will be."[8] There is, of course, a question here
that we will need to come back to, concerning the relations
between universals and particulars and between continuity and

change that is central to any discussion of literary, as distinct from philosophical, "presentism."[9]

II

The ontological privileging of the "present" may, from one per-spective, look like a pragmatic strategy for dealing with the facti-tious elements of history; that is to say with what in philosophical presentism is sometimes referred to as "the change in truth-value of tensed propositions over time."[10] Hawkes is fully aware of the *differences* that emerge when the process of generating "truths" in the present comes into contact with "facts" of the past that are the result of careful selection and representation. But he also situates his approach within the framework of a post-structuralism that extends well beyond familiar and limited invocations of Foucault as the theorist of power. Unlike those historicists who persist, despite the historical evidence that they amass to the contrary, to hold on to an illusion of both the author's and their own autono-mous identities,[11] Hawkes accepts the full consequences of the post-structuralist

> subversion of a central ideological commitment to the idea of the indi-vidual, sovereign self, the human "subject", as the fundamental unit of existence and the main negotiable instrument of meaning. In conse-quence, the notion of the text as the direct expression of the subject's innermost thoughts and feelings has been undermined. And amongst the first casualties of that development is the supposed 'authenticity' of the text as a document whose final "meaning" includes unmediated access to its author's intimate being.[12]

Moreover, he makes a crucial political distinction between a long European tradition of "making meaning" as a form of participation, and the essentialist alternative that is a "spectator theory of soci-ety" and that "is a recipe for, as well as a consequence of, totalitari-anism."[13] Although some fifteen years earlier Hawkes had devoted a book to explaining the evolution of structuralism,[14] the emer-gence of his own thinking in *Meaning by Shakespeare* demon-strates the distance he had traveled by 1992 from what Derrida had identified as the metaphysical, idealizing core of Saussurian struc-turalism, without forsaking altogether a theory of binaries or the principles of constitutive difference.[15] New Historicism had, for the most part, given ontological primacy to the past as a determinant of meaning, and even then within a particular, implicitly "present" conceptualization of the Foucauldian account of the operations of "power" in which "containment" was privileged over "resistance" as part of a structural whole. In contrast, and as a means of avoiding rhetorically seductive but conceptually glib formulations of the entanglement of the past and the present, Hawkes firmly rejects the ontological privileging of the past as the final determinant of a text's meaning or as the determining element in an unproblemati- cally heuristic process.[16] His is not so much a rejection of the past *per se* but a stern refusal to privilege those elements of the interpre- tation of the past that might generate universal and ahistorical statements; hence his initial acknowledgement of the influence of what he calls "anti-essentialist" philosophers such as William James, Richard Rorty, Nietzsche, Heidegger, and the later Witt- genstein.[17] At issue is the question of a text's "final" or stable mean- ing, and Hawkes is unequivocal in his statement of the problem:

> Such a position [pragmatism] does not of course imply that a text's meaning is finally determined by the historical context in which it ini- tially appears. That limited notion of historicism must always yield to the view that human beings are permanently involved in a continuing process of meaning-making, one to which all texts, as aspects of human culture, are always subject, and beyond which they may be conceivable but will remain ungraspable. To attempt to grasp them at all, as the essay on *A Midsummer Night's Dream* will show, is inevitably to become involved in the making of meaning in a particular context.[18]

The question here does not involve the formal pedagogically fueled protocols of what constitutes a text as such, so much as what hap- pens when the critic tries to make sense of a text ostensibly from the past. Moreover, the issue of the text's *referential* status emerges from this inquiry as deeply problematical; for example, is what underpins this approach a *realist* philosophy, or is there no "real- ity" outside the discourses of the text that can be made to mean? Of course, it is possible to argue that the phrase "continuing process" retains a residual universal appeal: "human beings are *perma- nently* involved in a *continuing process* of meaning-making" (my emphasis), and we might also say the same about the (ideological) business of producing narratives.[19] In addition, we might also legit- imately ask what the process of making plausible meanings entails. Alan Sinfield, whose *Faultlines: Cultural Materialism and the Poli-*

tics of Dissident Reading (1992) appeared in the same year as *Meaning by Shakespeare,* proposes a genuinely dialectical account of how cultures apprehend "the world." He argues that:

> As the world shapes itself around and through us, certain interpretations of experience strike us as plausible: they fit with what we have experienced already, and are confirmed by others around us. So we complete what Colin Sumner calls "a circle of social reality": "understanding produces its own social reality at the same time as social reality produces its own understanding." This is apparent when we observe how people in other cultures than our own make good sense of the world in ways that seem strange to us: their outlook is supported by their social context. For them, those frameworks of perception, maps of meaning, work.[20]

"The world" is a reciprocally produced reality involving the interaction of subject and object in a mutually determining "social reality," one that deeply involves the mechanisms of language as well as a politics of difference that, for Sinfield, permits the possibility of "dissident reading." But whereas Sinfield's "dissident reading" proceeds speedily from text to "plausible" narrative to a collective politics of dissidence, Hawkes slows down the process to concentrate on the investments made in the actual process of producing meanings, and he is careful not to project his own meanings onto what, in the terms of translation theory, we might for convenience label his "source text(s)."[21] Thus, Hawkes's "realism" includes language as a phenomenon that has material effects, within a social context that is riven with competing political claims, rather than the un-problematical expression of an organic reality. It emphasizes the *process* of meaning-making as a necessary precondition both to an understanding of the conditions under which certain texts come to acquire a talismanic status, as well as to the often occluded motivation for giving them a particular politico-cultural emphasis. Whereas Sinfield retains an orthodox historicist emphasis in his identification of the "frameworks of perception, [and] maps of meaning" and in the prospect of their recovery as a necessary precondition of effecting political change, Hawkes inserts a further element into the process with the insistence that this identification is always already tainted by the critic's own subjectivity, a subjectivity that, as Sinfield himself recognizes, *cannot* be reduced to the perception of the "free" autonomous individual who recognises in a writer like Shakespeare a mirror of her/his own freedom.

III

The present cannot be avoided, and the past does not of itself hold a key to a full understanding. The issue for Hawkes's particular version of "presentism" is the way in which past and present relate to each other given the investment, in particular on the Left, in the explanatory power of the former, and the logic of causality that this investment has generated. We have become accustomed to associating accounts of the present with causally connected narratives of the past, and on the surface of it, to invest in a pure "presentism" would be to sacrifice the explanatory concept of temporality altogether in favour of endless and undifferentiated repetition. Failure to link past, present, and future would mean effectively a capitulation to a full-blown post-modernism, what Susan Watkins, in another context, has described as "a changeless now, from horizon to horizon, and a presentist politics reduced to the mindless repetition of the words 'Yes we can.'"[22] Hawkes's "presentism" attempts to square this difficult circle insofar as he refuses to submit to the nihilism that the kind of presentist "politics" Watkins alludes to implies. Although he is prepared to use the resources of post-structuralism as part of a critical armoury, he manages to avoid the political error of New Historicism in its implicit counsel of despair and its inadvertent capitulation to the textual mechanisms of containment that chafe uneasily with its occasional desire to hang on to an autonomous identity no matter how self-consciously "fictional" it might be. For Hawkes, causality remains a key issue, although its polarities are reversed: it is the patterns of causality that the present imposes on the past, its impositions of periodization, its decisions of which literary texts to revive, which to discard, its decisions of which literary figures to lionize, which to mythologize, and of what stimulates the desire to generate meanings from texts from earlier historical conjunctures, that now assume primary importance. In one sense this is a dialectical and historical materialism *after* Theory, a methodology that emanates from the position of the overdetermined critical human subject, rather than a simple return to a *status quo ante* and to an old-fashioned historical criticism.

To take an example from *Meaning by Shakespeare,* the chapter on "Shakespeare and the General Strike" begins with the identification in the title of "a contradiction of a radical kind."[23] Hawkes continues, "Art and politics, in our culture, are not just opposites,

they rank as the organising epicentres of two quite contrary discourses." Nor is this a value-free binary opposition, since there
appears to be a deep cultural resistance to linking the two:

> To propose that such a possibility exists is almost to sanction some
> illicit act of transgression in which a grubby "Politics" may be
> "dragged" across a threshold to sully the otherwise sacrosanct shrine of
> Art. Worse, reversing the process, Shakespeare himself might even be
> "dragged into politics."[24]

Not to challenge this "common sense" approach, which would
affirm Shakespeare's "unsullied transcendence over the everyday
sphere of profit margins, market forces, redundancies and wage-
settlements," is to succumb to "the trap of essentialism" that
refuses to accept that "Any work can be *read* in an oppositional
mode."[25] To this extent Hawkes shares what has become a familiar
theoretically informed political platform with other oppositional
modes of "reading against the grain," from Marxism and feminism
through to postcolonialism. But the refinement he introduces is that
it is not the text *in itself* that is oppositional; rather Hawkes claims
that "Art" that has been hijacked by a tradition founded upon one
tacit, but deeply ideological consensus—"common sense"—can be
reclaimed for a different, deeply subversive consensus that derives
its energies from the "real" relations that inform the present
moment. This is neither an *identification* with the past nor an
appropriation of it, but the acknowledgement of a contiguity of
interests motivated by the complex over-determinations of a critical
subjectivity situated within its own network of cause and effect. In
a witty reversal of a conservative status quo, Hawkes calls for "a
strike against common sense," as part of a campaign against a complacent Establishment, with a view to securing a range of oppositional meanings whose origins derive from those sections of society
that are usually excluded from participating fully in the traditionally anodyne discourses of "Art." Nor is this so much an assertion
of identity, as a bid to re-align rather than appropriate or adapt what
was once a "popular" art, for those who, located in the social formation of late capitalism, are excluded from judgments that have
become the preserve of a cultural elite. At issue is also a critique
and a contestation of the operations of an ideology whose power
resides in "common-sense" assumptions about Art, about Shakespeare and about "life."

Thus far the argument of "Shakespeare and the General Strike" is clear and combative, with wit and excoriating analysis combining to disarm an adversary that, within the British academic establishment particularly, has not been accustomed to accounting for its privileges. What still remains problematical, however, is the issue of whether it is the *text* of *Coriolanus* that "so provocatively . . . connect(s) with political events outside the text" or whether it is primarily a *reading* of the text that is responsible for establishing these connections. In other words, can we treat the text as an independent signifying object in its own right, with its own inherently "presentist" commitment to an early-seventeenth-century process of cause and effect, or are we simply *appropriating* it for a series of contingent events that we recognize as our own? The answer to this crucial question lies in the historical evolution of critical approaches to *Coriolanus* and to a cultural history that points repeatedly to that text's resilience in the face of attempts to affirm "the boundaries of that 'Art' category to which common sense so earnestly wants to consign it."[26] In short, Hawkes's account points to a trans-historical existence for the text that stops short of a full-blown universalism, while allowing the critic to bypass an ontological privileging of the text in its original setting. Or, to put the matter a little differently, subject to editorial emendation the text remains a constant insofar as it comprises a particular order of words, but its *meanings* change. In this way, Hawkes resists firmly what we might call the "tenselessness" of presentism *per se* in favor of an implied theory of temporality that allows the past to occupy an equivalent, rather than a crudely determinist or privileged, position in relation to the present, so that explanatory force is distributed dialectically between the two. Although he does not abandon altogether historical materialism as a method, it occupies a place within an irreducibly dialectical materialism that fully acknowledges the complexity of the text's own "original" context, which must always remain speculative, and the vantage point of the critic, whose own social, cultural, and historical perspective drives the inquiry. We might also note in passing that while the focus of Hawkes's "materialism" is, in part, historical, it also provides the critic with an opportunity for occasional energetically Bakhtinian eruptions of expository verbal wit and improvisation. Notwithstanding these exuberant vitalist (almost spontaneous) eruptions of a material energy, Hawkes's presentism is future orientated in that is seeks to challenge the *status quo* in the interests of providing fuller, more nuanced explanations with important ethical implications. Indeed, his exposure of the investments of the Establishment in the "Art" of Shakespeare furnishes an indispensable pre-condition for a campaign dedicated to the liberation of the "text" from those who would limit the processes of signification by means of a restricted definition of "Art."

"Shakespeare and The General Strike" begins by situating the critic in Cardiff's civic center before the statue of the nineteenth-century "Coal-owner and Philanthropist" John Cory (1828–1910). This setting provides a context for a series of binaries in which Shakespeare's *Coriolanus* is implicated as part of a proliferating but densely woven tapestry of connections, at the center of which is the critic's campaign to dislodge "Shakespeare" from his ideological incarceration in the penitentiary of "Art." In political terms "the strike" constitutes the laborer's weapon of last resort against the manifold injustices of the employer—we can see from the outset why the epithet "Coal-owner and Philanthropist" might in such circumstances "offer a text suitable for the most stringent critical analysis"[27]—and the "general strike" is a truly oppositional, if not revolutionary, gesture. The year 1926 saw an event in what was to become one of a series of major crises of capitalism, and writing in the last years of the Thatcher governments (1992) Hawkes's own emphasis on what we now know to have been the beginning of just such another crisis was, and still is, nothing if not prescient.

At the epicentre of the essay's ingeniously woven tapestry of historical contingencies is the performance, following the Shakespeare birthday celebrations, of *Coriolanus*—not in the Shakespeare Memorial Theatre at Stratford but in a cinema, and, in 1926, at a time of impending political and social disorder. The argument proceeds to probe with some queasiness the "political unconscious" of the Stratford Establishment, and in particular the activities of the wife of the Vicar of Stratford, a Mrs. Melville, whose extraordinary sympathies with an emergent Fascism are carefully teased out. On the anniversary of Shakespeare's birth the prime minister of the day, Stanley Baldwin, met coal owners and miners in London, while in Stratford the traditional toast to "the Immortal Memory of the Bard" was delivered by James Montgomery Beck, a former US Attorney General, "an apostle of extreme individualism [who] would later resign from one of Roosevelt's New Deal committees, aghast at what he saw as its radical tendencies."[28] There then followed the performance of *Coriolanus*.

It is the rich texture of these associations, uncovered during the effective re-insertion of "Art" into a complex political situation in which some of the key participants appear to be caught in the act of behaving ideologically—that is to say, without being fully aware of the motives for, or the consequences of, their actions—that Hawkes exposes to view. "Of all his plays, *Coriolanus* seems," Hawkes readily admits, "so regularly and so provocatively to connect with political events outside the text that it immediately offers to undermine the common-sense separation with which we began."[29] For a presentism that refuses to privilege the past, the claim that the play is able "provocatively to connect with political events outside the text" appears deeply problematical, especially if we consider the frequently claimed association of *Coriolanus* with the Midlands grain riots of 1607. What in 1926 were obviously the effects of the withdrawal of labor—political disorder, and possible starvation—are, compared with the anxieties of the Roman populace in Shakespeare's play, cast in a different political register. But taken together, both situations also allude, by implication, to the dramatist's own "presentist" practice in resurrecting a series of episodes from the history of the Roman Republic that early Jacobean audiences might readily have endowed with contemporary meaning. For the nuanced "presentism" that Hawkes espouses the play can be "of its time," but also its resonances can have a trans-historical appeal that resists collapse into an unproblematical universalism:

> *Coriolanus* of course has its own "political unconscious," and perhaps bears the marks of its own social tensions surrounding its origins in 1607/8. In 1926 other pressures were certainly at work and the very choice of the play—perhaps the first move in an attempt, putting it baldly, to leap the Art-Politics divide and to hijack Shakespeare for a right-wing cause—could not help but make it seem "strangely up to date."[30]

Moreover, the hesitancy involved in attempting to reassemble the "facts" of a remote past (as evidenced in, for example, Hawkes's cautious "seems" and "perhaps") indicates a plethora of contemporary historical nuances that must inevitably be beyond recovery, even for the objectively minded historical scholar. But it is here that "presentism's" investment in a poststructuralist theory of textuality is equipped to offer a convincing response. If in 1926 *Coriolanus* seemed "strangely up to date" then a further manipulation of what we might describe as the plenitude of the text would be required to make it so. Indeed, Hawkes notes that for the play "to function as the ideological weapon its promoters presumably wanted, then in the name of integrity and coherence specific aspects of the text would, in the event, have to be fore-grounded at the expense of others."[31] In other words, the selection—even one guided by a "political unconscious"—of a particular focus subjects the plenitude of Shakespeare's text, with its own presentist agenda, to a limited reading, especially in the case of a play that appears to resist all attempts to shackle its concerns to "a specific party-political position."

The example Hawkes selects to illustrate the point precedes the events of 1926, and exposes the ideological assumptions that have guided successive generations of textual editors from the Third Folio onwards in their responses to the play: "like an eagle in a dovecote, I / Flutter'd (Flatter'd) your Volscians in Corioles. / Alone I did it" (5.6.114–16). The elimination of "Flatter'd," a rejection of what Hawkes describes as "a much more complex interactive engagement with the Volscians than the imperiously defensive 'flutter'd'," closes down one of the many unstable elements that underpin the argument that this text, or indeed any text, "can't be coherently read in any single way" without suppressing elements of meaning.[32] The critic does not simply restore originary readings where they are clearly not the result of compositorial error, but rather, he endows them with modern meanings that can then enter into dialogue with the words on the page under the signature of "Shakespeare": Hawkes thereby recovers "indeterminacy" and "multiplicity" that are, he insists, "fostered by the First Folio text," but that have no objective "meanings" in themselves.[33] Rather, they are invitations to the critic to enter into dialogue with the text, to engage in the process of contesting meanings, but from an ontological perspective that can only be the "present" of the observer. This is not a "presentism" that collapses past and present into a transcendent tenselessness or timelessness, but one that acknowledges the process and the practice of what dialogue with the past actually entails. To this extent *Meaning by Shakespeare* is a demonstration of process rather than a theoretical manifesto, a series of gestures, effected with the full rhetorical resources of wit and irony, that allows the critic to lay his cards on the table, while at the same time showing in surprising ways—far beyond the plausibilities of any fiction—how "the political unconscious" works in particular situations. Indeed, "making meaning" is the active preserve of the scholarly critic, alive to contemporary social, political and cultural concerns that extend far beyond the restricted and restrictive ideological business of mobilizing literary "judgement."

The project that began with *That Shakespeherian Rag* and *Meaning by Shakespeare* reaches its fully fledged expression in *Shakespeare in the Present* (2002) and the collaboratively edited *Presentist Shakespeares* (2007). *Shakespeare in the Present* begins by reiterating in forthright terms the issues broached in the earlier volumes. For example, the links among "fact," "value" and "meaning" are re-emphasized in the following terms:

> Facts do not speak for themselves. Nor do texts. This doesn't mean that facts or texts don't exist. It does mean that all of them are capable of genuinely contradictory meanings, none of which has any independent, "given," undeniable, or self-evident status. Indeed, they don't speak at all unless and until they are inserted into and perceived as part of specific discourses which impose their own shaping requirements and agendas. We choose the facts. We choose the texts. We do the inserting. We do the perceiving. Facts and texts, that is to say, don't simply speak, don't merely mean. *We* speak, *we* mean, *by* them.[34]

This amounts to something much more than the perception that "history" and the fabrication of historical narrative is itself a deeply rhetorical exercise. Some years ago Hayden White raised this issue in his claim that "the historical text" was, a "literary artefact," and he set out to address issues such as "What is the structure of a peculiarly *historical* consciousness? What is the epistemological status of historical *explanations,* as compared with other kinds of explanations that might be offered to account for the materials with which historians ordinarily deal? What are the possible *forms* of historical representation and what are their bases?" At stake was what White regarded as the "authority" claimed by "historical accounts . . . as contributions to a secured knowledge of reality in general and to the human sciences in particular."[35] Hawkes is similarly concerned with the "authority" claimed for "facts" but in the literary domain, just as he seeks to examine the professional rhetorics that sustain that authority. Whereas White was concerned to investigate the formal "literary" elements encountered in the writing of "history," Hawkes is concerned to address the "historical" elements that are frequently used to sustain literary discourse, and to challenge the partisan way in which they are often deployed.

The challenge amounts to an assault on the fetishization of the text, the displacement of a particular form of subjective "belief" into the realm of an objective reality. These are terms that have very recently been deployed by Bruno Latour in the claim that the distinction between "constructivism" and "realism" is a false one.[36] Latour uses "the label *factish* for the robust certainty that allows practice to pass into action without the practitioner ever believing in the difference between construction and reality, immanence and transcendence."[37] Hawkes's account, though not ethnological in the way that Latour's is, anticipates this dilemma, in his emphasis upon a literary discourse that is also a form of political intervention while at the same time acknowledging that "reality" itself cannot escape from the allegation that it is, indeed, constructed. What for Latour is exposed as a contradiction that lies at the root of the practice of the demystifying enquirer after knowledge is avoided by Hawkes's deft manoeuvre in drawing the critical observer into a contestatory process of making meaning—in effect, a competition for the possession of the linguistic sign. If Latour's "factish" names the product of a delusion that is equal to that of the fetish, then Hawkes navigates around that contradiction by situating the literary critic *inside* the process of making meaning. From a purely historical perspective, this move looks like a turn to cultural relativism. Except that, recast in a "present" that is accorded an empirical ontological superiority to the past, the resultant clash of meanings (both within the perspective of the present *and* in the engagement with an estranged history) is accorded an absolute analytical value. Thus, a text from the past càn be treated as a transhistorical document available to the process of each successive culture's practice of "making meaning," but its primary existence as a text that first appears at a particular historical conjuncture can have little "authority" *in its own right.*

This tension between the "fact" of a text's historical appearance and its subsequent reception as a cultural document is clearly what Hawkes "means" when he says that "The present ranks, not as an obstacle to be avoided nor a prison to be escaped from . . . it's a factor actively to be sought out, grasped and perhaps, as a result, understood." Engagement with the "present" is, in other words, a mode of action. It comprises nothing less than "an intrusive shaping awareness of ourselves, *alive and active* in our own world, [that] defines us" and that "deserves our closest attention" (my emphasis).[38] This strategy is very different from that which simply

endows the past with allegorical significance in relation to the present; rather it is a vital, and Hawkes would insist, indispensable,
means of talking "to the living."[39] Such criticism is not a quasi-
anthropological, or indeed, ethnological exercise, in which each
essay can be reduced to the status of an "anecdote," but a series of
investigations, to which the essay form is admirably suited, into the
various ways in which individual "presents," including the critic's
own, have shaped and continue to shape the emphases that are
placed on documents, literary or otherwise, from the past. In short,
Hawkes offers a root and branch recasting of the way in which "historical" study of literary texts has been conducted since the beginning of the twentieth century. Once the fetishistic literary cat has
been let out of the bag, then the full armoury of "theory" can be
made to serve as a means of "close reading," which itself develops
into an ethical form of "action" that is, in the final analysis a genuinely democratic and inclusive humanism.[40] Nowhere more than in
the present, and with the Humanities under siege, is this activist
message welcome.

IV

However, this assessment does not mean that presentism can
sweep the board, or that it should be regarded as something of a
new "fad" that might replace New Historicism, Cultural Materialism, Feminism, or Psychoanalysis. Although it is nervous about
"universals," the one universal that can be convincingly applied to
presentism is that it is the preserve of all cultures and at all times,
no matter how its concerns are expressed. In other words, what
may seem at a distance to be an indication of cultural naiveté turns
out to be no less conceptually, if not technologically, sophisticated
the more the enquirer subjects his or her own perspective to close
examination. That realization is both a humbling *and* an empower-
ing experience in that it recognizes investments in the present,
while at the same time acknowledging the strangeness of the past
and thus furthering the work of understanding as a precondition
for action in the future. Indeed, it is on the battleground of the present, with all of its subterfuges, its deviations, its conflicts and its
resolutions, that the future will ultimately be secured. Inherent in
the activities of the version of presentism formulated by Hawkes is
a manifesto for future action that challenges both the mystifications

to which literary texts have been subjected *and* many of those demystifications that have claimed to liberate both it and us.

At a political level *Shakespeare in the Present* represents the culmination of a long campaign to change the ways in which we view literary texts, especially those of Shakespeare. *Presentist Shakespeares* (2007) offers a much fuller context for the debate, whereby certain of the "problems" of presentism are examined. The emphasis upon signification would appear, on the surface, to locate literary presentism firmly within the orbit of post-structuralism: the radical instability of texts, the mechanisms of signification, and the problematization of the "we" "who *mean* by these texts." Is literary presentism, then, a kind of "realism"? While post-structuralism is generally thought to transform quotidian reality into a series of constantly receding "texts," there still remains a bridge to be built between what in crude terms may be referred to as "the text" and "the world." This involves an acknowledgment, indeed, an awareness, that while any form of textual study must concern itself primarily with the processes of signification, there is ultimately a "reality" that in some shape or form the literary or theatrical text *represents*. But more than that, Hawkes recognizes that between "the text" and "the world" there is a critical consciousness (and an implicitly political unconscious) that overdetermines, often in very surprising ways, how both are *read.*

To put the matter in this way is to issue a provocation, since the "we" who *mean* are ourselves located in time, whereas the ostensible object of our inquiry has been unavoidably dislocated from its own time. To be sure, we may look at a quarto or a folio text of the early seventeenth century and make certain deductions about the range of discourses (literary, cultural, social, bibliographical) that we can identify as being inscribed within its boundaries. But it must be emphasized that "we" determine the boundaries, the protocols, indeed, the entire methodology for making such texts mean. Nor, indeed, do "we" ourselves function as autonomous origins of meaning, since it is the material reality that language *represents,* which overdetermines both our own subjectivities *and* our approach to the object of our inquiry. Hawkes, of course, lightens this dour constructivist model by means of a witty inventiveness that discloses surprising detail that is then enclosed within an explanatory narrative of the critic's own carefully judged and historically responsible fabrication. Hawkes's binaries are far from constricting, and they are transported from one location to another in order to reveal some hitherto unrecognized synergies. However, what ultimately produces an obstacle to an otherwise convincing argument that sustains presentism is the possibility that in ontologically prioritising the "present," some of the formal properties of a Shakespearean text might be lost. Even more problematically than that, what happens when the critic identifies the text as being both "of its time" *and* also prophetic in the sense that despite its allegedly historical ideological constraints it can point to an alternative, ostensibly "modern" reality that is clearly beyond the boundaries of its own temporal location? Hitherto, for example, within the discursive field of a radical politically informed criticism, signs of a utopianism secreted, it is usually claimed, within the *form* of the text, have been regarded as part of the work that the critic undertakes, in the process of excavating rather than constructing meanings. This approach has usually assumed a conceptual baggage of origins and authorial intentions. To take one example, if there is a utopian core identifiable within, say, Shakespeare's *Troilus and Cressida,* is it a property of the text itself, a recognizable thematic trajectory, or does it amount to a political projection of the critical intelligence that claims to identify and position it?[41] In his essay on the play, Kiernan Ryan observes that:

> There is no escaping the stark truth that *Troilus and Cressida* presses upon us. The presentist dramatic practice that first produced *Troilus* itself, and the presentist critical practice that makes Shakespeare's *Iliade travestie* speak directly to us today, are symptoms of the very malaise the play lays bare.[42]

There are two points to be made here; firstly, the recognition that *Troilus and Cressida* is deeply imbricated in a presentism whereby an ancient literary text is given a modern, early seventeenth-century gloss, and secondly that in Shakespeare's presentism we find an echo of our own times that enables his texts to "speak to us." The evidence for a Shakespearean presentism is overwhelming, and can be detected in a range of plays: Histories, Roman Plays, Comedies, Tragedies, and late Romances, not as allegories for the critic to unpick, but as possible ways of engaging in a dialogue between past and present. This shift of perspective does not, of course, challenge the view that the historical material from which these plays are fashioned "spoke" to Shakespeare and his audiences. Rather, it is a matter of a particular kind of critical engagement that, in the words of Dominic LaCapra, comprises a dialogic relation between the historian or the historical text and the "object" of study [that] raises the question of the role of selection, judgement, stylisation, irony, parody, self-parody and polemic in the historian's own use of language—in brief, the question of how the historian's use of language is mediated by critical factors that cannot be reduced to factual predication or direct authorial assertion about historical "reality."[43]

At issue is the nature of that dialogue and the problematical status accorded to the " 'object' of study"; the diminution of the rhetorical impact of historical discourse inadvertently produces a temporal foreshortening that has the effect of relegating the constitutive elements of the process of recognition, at best, to a subordinate position. This in turn diminishes the dialogic impact of the discourse, and in the process distorts the rhetorical purchase that the present has upon the past. Recognizing and isolating a thematic synergy between elements of *Troilus and Cressida* as a direct consequence of an evaluation of the present, and then projecting that recognition back onto an acknowledged " 'object' of study," would, in Hawkes's terms, involve an obfuscation of the very processes in and through which genuine and dynamic dialogue between past and present takes place.

Of course, no critical practice can avoid the business of "factual predication," and literary presentism emphatically does not rule out the phenomenological existence of an historical reality. Rather, it goes out of its way to acknowledge it as one side of a dialogue, but one that is subject to the heuristic protocols the critic brings to it. What is perhaps more difficult to negotiate is the danger, within post-structuralism, of collapsing the text into a series of irreducible linguistic indeterminacies that cumulatively put in question all issues of temporality. Hawkes is able to acknowledge textual instability in terms of a contest for "meanings" but he is committed to a philosophy of language that harnesses constitutive difference to a deeply political contest for the "meanings" of the linguistic sign. The result is emphatically not a dialogue between, on the one hand, texts from the past that are assumed to possess their own independent ontological integrity, and, on the other hand, critics from the present who excavate them; rather, it is a matter of a perspective that endlessly renews texts by endowing them with meanings generated from within the present inhabited by the critic. To return to *Troilus and Cressida,* what could we say of the critic who refuses to recognize, or who dismisses, out of hand, as a fantasy, a utopian strain that may be excavated from the text, preferring a more conservative acknowledgment of the play's manifest emphasis on the dangers of disorder? The difference between a "conservative" and a progressive "radical" reading of the play brings us back to the investment and the perspective of the observer, and this is precisely Hawkes's point.

The problem arises when it is argued by Dominic LaCapra that texts make claims "on us as readers," in effect, reversing the prioritization that gives ontological preference to the present.[44] To privilege the practice of "making meaning" is to acknowledge an empirical reality that any student who has not "learned how to read" a Shakespearean text, especially one as complex as *Troilus and Cressida,* encounters in any attempt to make sense of the sequence of marks on the page with which he or she is confronted. In certain respects, of course, Shakespearean texts (some more than others) have become familiar just as Shakespeare has become "Shakespeare." In the process of interrogating that "familiarity" presentism performs, in Hawkes's own deeply ironic self-deprecatory language borrowed in part from Freud, a "Heimlich maneuver"; in Hawkes's own words, it seeks to promote "what are, by traditional standards, bogus connections and parallels of the sort that I have been shamelessly deploying" in order to expand "the possibilities of our *use* of criticism as a material intervention into history, rather than the prosecution of what we misguidedly think of as scholarly 'facts' or 'truth.'" [45] In an audacious reversal, Hawkes contends that "the *Heimlich* appears almost as a sub-species of the *unheimlich* and we begin to face the possibility that 'home' is only the tamed and taming doll's house we construct as a poor bulwark against the apparitions that permanently haunt us."[46] A close reading of the "present" with its attempts to neutralize those disturbing repressed energies that are now, once again, providing the fuel for political change, is designed to deliver a shock to the settled domestic professional complacencies of a criticism that has habitually turned away from "a prospect that is genuinely frightening, because truly known of old, and though long repressed, long familiar." That anxiety, in our time ratcheted up to near hysterical proportions as "art" falls prey to a rapacious capitalist managerialism, is precisely what the literary presentism of Terence Hawkes addresses, and his wit, irony and self-parody are vehicles that force us to confront what we prefer not to acknowledge:

The appalling possibility that home is where the art is: that in terms of the *unheimlich* critical vision, what we think of as home and what we think of as art are in some way shockingly coterminous in their role as mere vehicles for the most paltry of human comforts.[47]

Notes

1. Terence Hawkes, *That Shakespeherian Rag* (London: Methuen, 1986), 1.
2. Ibid.
3. Ibid., 5.
4. Ibid., 7.
5. Cf. Stephen Greenblatt, *Shakespearean Negotiations* (Oxford: Oxford University Press, 1988), 1, 20.
6. Terence Hawkes, *Shakespeare in the Present* (London: Routledge, 2002), 2.
7. Terence Hawkes, *Meaning by Shakespeare* (London: Routledge, 1992), 3.
8. Ibid., 4.
9. For an account of the philosophical theory of "presentism," and for the larger questions and implications of the persistence of "truth" claims through time, see Craig Bourne, *A Future for Presentism* (Oxford: Oxford University Press, 2006), 39ff.
10. Ibid., 77.
11. See Stephen Greenblatt, "Epilogue" in *Renaissance Self-fashioning from More to Shakespeare* (Chicago: University of Chicago Press, 1980), 255–57. But see also, Stephen Greenblatt, *Shakespeare's Freedom* (Chicago: University of Chicago Press, 2010), 95ff.
12. Hawkes, *Meaning by Shakespeare,* 5–6.
13. Ibid., 7.
14. Terence Hawkes, *Structuralism and Semiotics,* New Accents series (London: Methuen, 1977).
15. 15. Cf. Jacques Derrida, "Structure, Sign and Play in the Discourse of the Human Sciences," *Writing and Difference,* trans. Alan Bass (London: Routledge, 1981), 278–80.
16. Hawkes, *Meaning by Shakespeare,* 7.
17. Ibid., 6.
18. Ibid., 7.
19. Cf. Alan Sinfield, *Faultlines: Cultural Materialism and the Politics of Dissident Reading* (Berkeley: University of California Press, 1992), 29ff., and esp. 37 and 47: "All stories comprise within themselves the ghosts of the alternative stories they are trying to exclude."
20. Ibid., 32. Sinfield's reference to Sumner is from Colin Sumner, *Reading Ideologies* (London: Academic Press, 1979), 288.
21. Set against this nuanced account, we might place Stephen Greenblatt's curiously a-historical pronouncement that "Shakespeare as a writer is the embodiment of human freedom. He seems to have been able to fashion language to say anything he imagined, to conjure up any character, to express any emotion, to explore any idea." Greenblatt, *Shakespeare's Freedom,* 1.

22. Susan Watkins, "Presentism? A Reply to T.J.Clark," *New Left Review* 74 (March-April, 2012): 85–86.

23. Terence Hawkes, *Meaning by Shakespeare,* 43 and *passim.*

24. Ibid., 43.

25. Ibid.

26. Ibid., 44.

27. Ibid., 42.

28. Ibid., 50.

29. Ibid., 43.

30. Ibid., 51.

31. Ibid.

32. Ibid., 55.

33. Ibid., 56.

34. Terence Hawkes, *Shakespeare in the Present* (London: Routledge, 2002), 3.

35. Cf. Hayden White, *Tropics of Discourse: Essays in Cultural Criticism* (Baltimore: Johns Hopkins University Press, 1978), 81ff.

36. Cf. Bruno Latour, *On the Modern Cult of the Factish Gods* (Durham: Duke University Press, 2010), 21.

37. Ibid., 22.

38. Hawkes, *Shakespeare in the Present,* 3.

39. Ibid., 4.

40. Cf. Andy Mousley, *Re-humanising Shakespeare: Literary Humanism, Wisdom and Modernity* (Edinburgh: Edinburgh University Press 2007), 27ff., which makes a convincing case in the wake of arguments such as Hawkes's for a "literary humanism" that takes the argument into a future "use" and "value" for literary texts.

41. Cf. Kiernan Ryan, "*Troilus and Cressida:* The Perils of Presentism," *Presentist Shakespeares,* ed. Hugh Grady and Terence Hawkes (London: Routledge, 2007), 164ff.

42. Ibid., 179–80.

43. Dominic LaCapra, *Rethinking Intellectual History: Texts, Contexts, Language* (Ithaca, NY: Cornell University Press, 1983), 25.

44. Cf. Ryan, citing LaCapra: "presentist Shakespeare criticism must not commit the historicist's error of evading 'the claims texts make on us as readers' " (Ryan, "Troilus," 174).

45. Hawkes, *Shakespeare in the Present,* 20.

46. Ibid., 21.

47. Ibid.

Terza Rima for Terry
(Meaning by Hawkes)

CHRISTOPHER NORRIS

Note

TERRY HAWKES was my mentor, colleague in Cardiff, good friend, and regular Saturday-night drinking companion for more than three decades, so his death in January 2014 left me wishing we had remained more closely in touch during the past few years. When Diana Henderson asked me to write something for this commemorative number of *Shakespeare Studies* I had two main reasons for choosing what might seem the quaint or distinctly eighteenth-century genre of verse-essay or verse-epistle. One was our last exchange of emails when Terry had said some typically acute and generous things about previous ventures of mine in a similar mode. The second was my feeling that the style and ethos of that period were close to what Terry most enjoyed about living in the crossover zone between academe, literary journalism, and critical theory where the gloves were apt to come off (at any rate in print) and a ready wit would often do vital service alongside critical acumen and depth of scholarship. He wouldn't have wanted solemn proceedings so I tried to evoke—rather than match or imitate—something of Terry's own cheerfully irreverent, unfailingly good-humored, verbally inventive, at times polemically hardhitting but never less than genial and magnanimous spirit.

The main topic is of course "theory" and the large—indeed central—role he played in propagating new ideas about literature, criticism, and culture through his editorship, from the early 1980s on, of the *New Accents* book series and the journal *Textual Practice*. The poem also talks a lot about Terry's truly groundbreaking essays in Shakespeare criticism, his frequent run-ins with hostile (anti-theory) reviewers and respondents, and his expert deployment of cultural-materialist readings as a natural extension of adversarial class politics within and beyond the academy.[1] These went along with his singular gift—or creative flair—for approaching issues of Shakespeare interpretation via some ingeniously reconstructed set of historical and/or personal circumstances as they bore on some particular scholar-critic at some especially salient or critical point in a play's reception history. Terry's essay on Dover Wilson's notably overdetermined relationship to *Hamlet* was (I think) the first of these exhilarating ventures and, for my money, the most inspirational, so it figures as the main point of reference here.[2]

What the poem tries to do in a more general way is make the case that opponents of literary theory—some teachers of creative writing among them—are getting it wrong when they posit a kind of inbuilt antagonism between it and the processes, whatever these may be, involved in writing poetry or fiction. One way to challenge that idea is to point out how many students at various levels choose to do both and manage to combine them with no signs of stress or cognitive/creative dissonance. Another—more prominent here—is the sheer self-evidence of literary as well as intellectual creativity in a critic/theorist like Terry and others who looked to literary theory as offering a welcome release from the strictures of mainstream academic discourse. Debunking the more arrogant or self-serving claims of creative writers was undoubtedly one of Terry's favorite pastimes and very likely has something to do with the kinds of ambivalence or creative-critical tension—if not the full-scale Bloomian "anxiety"—plainly legible in critics like Geoffrey Hartman and the Yale acolytes of deconstruction.[3] However, in Terry's case the creativity expressed itself far more directly and with no such agonized quasi-Freudian detours, displacements, or sublimations. Scholarship and criticism were creative activities for him and he did more than anyone since William Empson to show that writing about Shakespeare had better be criticism as "answerable style"—in Hartman's well-chosen phrase—if it was to have any claim on our receptive-responsive powers.

Anyway, I hope that some of this will come across in the poem which I dedicate not only to Terry's memory but also to that other eminent Shakespearean, John Drakakis. John did more than anyone over the past thirty years both to carry on the cultural-materialist project and, after Terry's first major illness, to put him back in touch with his colleagues and admirers around the world.

The Cardiff thing it was, plus things that went
   Much farther back—mum, dad, class stuff, and school,
In your case Handsworth Grammar, where they sent

Bright kids to learn the ropes in ways that you'll
   Soon learn to turn around against the bunch
Of snooty Oxbridge types. Nobody's fool

Unless, like Lear's, the one who had a hunch
   That speaking truth to power was something best
Done by convincing them you're out to lunch

On some wild anecdote or screwball jest
   Which then—before they notice it—turns out
A real game-changer. That was how you'd test

Those manor-born Shakespeareans who'd tout
   Their natural entitlement to tell
Us groundlings what the plays were all about,

Or how us dull provincials would do well
   To cultivate a decent reverence
For such transcendent genius. This should quell

All thought that common readers could dispense
   With mediation by the fit though few
Interpreters who'd properly make sense

Of things and help the hoi polloi construe
   What otherwise would surely stretch their poor
Resources past endurance. So when you

Came up with sundry items from the store
   Of odd Shakespeareana—all those tales
Retrieved from centuries of scholar-lore

Or followed back along the mazy trails
   Of critics' lives and times—it was to show
Bardolators what craziness prevails

When zealous champions of the status quo
    In Shakespeare studies, such as (let's recall)
J. Dover Wilson, pledged themselves to go

That extra step in striving to forestall
    The least suggestion that in truth their god
Might sometimes err or even *Hamlet* fall

To Greg's critique. Should its creator nod
    And it not hang together then (he wrote
In *Milestones on the Dover Road*) the squad

Of strikers up North might as well just vote
    To join the Soviets since, as well as Greg's
Outrageous article, he'd taken note

On his rail journey up to meet the dregs
    Of disaffected labor how the press
On that same day was putting all its eggs

In revolution's basket. Just to stress
    Him out yet further the war-effort now
Looked well-nigh certain to collapse unless

He won them over and contrived somehow,
    In this his current role, to get the strike-
Call lifted and persuade them to allow

Munitions through despite his strong dislike
    (Think Coriolanus) of the fawning role
This might require. You figured how he'd psych

Himself up and establish his control
    Over these looming crises by the choice,
From then on, more devoutly to extol

Great Shakespeare's genius, give that genius voice
    Through commentary, and so redeem its claim
Against all comers. Chiefly he'd rejoice

In giving back to *Hamlet* its good name
    Against the charge of playing fast and loose
With time-scales or enjoying unjust fame

Since the cracked plot gives Hamlet no excuse
    For his wild conduct.
                              Other critics caught
On soon enough and started to produce

More Shakespeare criticism of the sort
    You trail-blazed there, but didn't have the near-
Shakespearean dexterity of thought

Or—what enabled that—a poet's ear
    (There were some early poems, but you kept
The fact well hidden) for effects of sheer

Linguistic serendipity. These leapt,
    For you, right off the page or gave the cue
For jokes and puns unthinkable except

By way of those same language-paths that you,
    The signifier-sleuth, had tracked so far
Into Shakespearean country that the view

At times seemed quite *unheimlich.* If we are,
    In truth, all these years on still just a touch
Bewildered maybe it's because the star

We hitched our lumbering wagons to was such
    A dazzler that it left the common sky
Of scholarship a zone where nothing much

Stood out compared with how some pure *trouvaille,*
    Some chance encounter turned up in the course
Of (maybe) casual reading, by and by

Took on the unlikely role of vaulting-horse
    To scenes, real or imagined, that supplied
Through Prospero-like conjuring a source

Of critical perspectives from outside
   The goldfish-bowl they'd made of academe,
Those keepers of the flame. That's why you tried

To get them off that old imperial theme,
   To show them how the transcendental stuff
(Traversi and the like) ran out of steam

Once recognized as just a high-toned puff
   For fascism, to *épater* the kind
Of Oxbridge tone you caught when Graham Hough

Reviewed those first *New Accents* books ("please mind
   Your language—don't say that," they begged in vain,
Your publisher and everyone inclined

To smooth things over), and—surely a main
   Intent of all your work—to take a hint
From Marx, confront them on their own terrain,

The Eng Lit gentry, call them out in print,
   And give no quarter to the dozy heirs
Of scholar-privilege. To look asquint

At all the classic texts they took as theirs,
   As if by right, to annotate and gloss
Was your big strategy to kick upstairs

Your young "New Accents" crew and teach the boss-
   Class how their precious canon might emerge
Scrubbed up and sprightlier despite the loss

Of culture-capital. A very scourge,
   They thought, with new barbarians at the gate
And cultural materialists set to purge

The libraries till no vestige of the Great
   Works they'd long served now lingered to reproach
Them for their failure to avert the fate

Of literature once theory drove a coach
　　And horses through the delicate rapport
Of text and reader. Truth is, you could poach

The big game—even Shakespeare—right before
　　The big game-keepers' eyes because you'd read
The plays more often, better, and with more

Attention to what other critics said,
　　Or—just as relevantly—didn't say
But wrapped in secrecy, so that instead

It fell to you and those who knew a way
　　Of making silence speak to unconceal
The interests that required they not betray

Such less than noble truths. You had a feel
　　For just what hidden crux it was in this
Or that Shakespearean text that made them deal

With it so off-the-pointedly, or miss
　　The mark with such persistence that their lapse
Of insight brought the hermeneutic kiss

Of life to those you'd helped to see the gaps
　　In classic texts as not to be repaired
By some discreet re-drawing of the maps

To join them up. Rather it meant a shared
　　Re-cultivation of the common land
Long since enclosed by critics who declared

Themselves uniquely fit to take a stand
　　On matters that required the exercise
Of literary judgment, not the hand-

Me-down ideas that took the Theory prize
　　(They liked to joke) for ways of passing off
Some half-baked notion in the splendid guise

Of some new jargon coined by some new prof
   At the Sorbonne, or Yale, or any place
Except (as Leavisites were prone to scoff)

The kinds of native habitat by grace
   Of which the star-struck theorists might have learned
That well-trained readers didn't need to chase

After strange gods. Such jibes you shrewdly turned
   Around and batted back with perfect ease,
So that New Accents-bashers always earned

Not just another point-by-point reprise
   Of where they'd got it wrong but, lest they not
Quite cotton on, a joke or two to tease

Them into seeing how they'd lost the plot,
   Whether in reading Shakespeare or *That Shakes
Peherian Rag,* because of some blind-spot

Or (more like) ear that's deaf to what it takes
   To write in genial style about a text
Whose challenge to the keen-eared critic makes

That task the more demanding. This perplexed
   Those on the anti-theory side who took
For granted how the curse of theory hexed

Our language-sense, although the merest look
   At any page of yours would quickly serve
To knock that thought for six and cock a snook

At all those cloth-eared types. They had the nerve
   To set aside the awkward truth that yours,
Not theirs, is writing with the kind of verve

And creativity that's on all fours
   With how good poets (Shakespeare more than most)
Took every verbal chance to settle scores

With proto-puritans whose proudest boast,
   Back then as now, was to make doubly sure
That errant thought not conjure up a coast

For its Bohemia and thereby secure
   Full-scale poetic license.
                    There are some
Of your late essays where the marsh-light lure

Of wordplay—as, by Johnson's time, they'd come
   To think it—largely frees you from the rules
Of normal scholarship and lets you drum

Out syncopated readings where old tools
   Won't fill the bill since it's your jazz-inspired
Prosodic and thematic riffs when school's

Out, so to speak, that kept your prose live-wired
   And keeps the circuits humming when we read
You now. Most likely the same neurons fired

Each time an agent rang to say they'd need
   A trad-style drummer up to handling things
When some jazz legend came to town. Then we'd

Just happen by and think how your prose swings
   The accent phrase to phrase yet always keeps
In view the cunning denouement that springs

A shocker such as positively leaps
   To eye (take Armstrong/Fortinbras!) once sprung
But, on a first encounter, either sweeps

All scruples clean aside or seems far-flung,
   Like Shakespeare's puns to Johnson, way beyond
What mutual interests and a common tongue

Required to keep intact the vital bond
   Of civil concord. You had little use
For suchlike notions, thinking them *au fond*

Just means to reinforce or reproduce
  The same old deferential ways of talk
That education plus a bit of nous

Should get us over once we've learned to chalk
  Up every stage along the post-war road
As either one step in the lengthy walk

To social justice, since it breaks the code
  Of class-respect, or else a backward lurch
Since, like unthinking reverence bestowed

By rote on classic texts, it makes a church
  Where orthodoxy's prized at the expense
Of thought. Let's call your project not "research"—

A word you loathed, along with "excellence,"
  "Engagement," "impact," "added value," plus
"Empower" and "innovate"—but more a sense

Of what might do best service with least fuss
  To show those culture-rituals up as mere
"Keep off the classics" notices for us

"New Accents" types who'd best not interfere
  With matters that lay properly within
An altogether more exalted sphere

Of judgment. These include—lest we begin,
  Thus theory-primed, to get ideas above
Our station—asking why the critics pin

Transcendent value to the sorts of love-
  Intrigue that leave straight gender-roles intact,
Or why that preference goes hand-in-glove

With others, such as choosing who gets backed
  For all the fellowships, or qualifies
As "research-active" owing to the fact

Of having come up publication-wise
   With stuff in the right places.
                    There are those—
And were from early on—who say: "You guys,

The theorists, were the first ones to impose
   This periodic curse, the latest round
Of research-auditing, since you first chose

To publish all those theory-books they found
   Offensive, no doubt, but a ready-made
Excuse for telling everyone they're bound

Contractually to keep up the cascade
   Of four-star items or resign themselves
Either to have some bureaucrat degrade

Their post to 'teaching only,' or stack shelves
   In Tesco." More than that, the charge-sheet runs
To saying that the theory-stuff just delves

A little distance down so we're the ones,
   Us early converts, who kicked off the whole
Bad shooting-match by turning round the guns

Of critical dissent against the sole
   Resource that might just possibly avail
To dig us theorists out of this deep hole

We'd dug ourselves. Best reassess our scale
   Of values so as not to let the drive
For theory-centered projects so assail

Our judgment that no thoughts of ours survive
   Beyond the stage of critical review
By some internal censor set to strive

For maximum research-points with as few
   Hours spent in gaining them as might be spared
From writing research-grant proposals. You

Were quick to say, whenever someone aired
   This anti-theory charge, that what they missed
By such comparisons was just what scared

Both management and those recidivist
   Upholders of the canon whose real gripe
With each new book on the "New Accents" list

Involved their sense that talents of the type
   That went to make good theorists also went
To make the sorts of literature they'd hype,

Those canonists, as fit to represent
   The human mind at full creative stretch.
Yet then it seemed the speculative bent

Of theory worked, like poetry, to fetch
   Up thoughts, ideas, and images unknown
To those who gave the standard hostile sketch

Of its agenda in the standard tone
   Of high disdain. Your writing had a gift
For skewering those reviewers (all the clone-

Like Leavisites especially) who'd lift
   Their pen as if reluctantly compelled
To set you straight, then show themselves adrift

Or floundering when it came to concepts spelled
   Out as who runs may read in your precise,
Well-groomed, yet laid-back style that so excelled

In knowing just what joke might best suffice
   To make the point.
                 So really what we need's
Not some routine infusion of cut-price

Arnoldian high seriousness that bleeds
   Away into low posturing as soon
As tried, but more an attitude that heeds

Your "Twenty Hamlets" point: let's take the tune,
   The basic theme, then run as many riffs
On it as some jazz vocalist might croon

Or Shakespeare critic spin against the ifs-
   And-buts platoon of scholars set to wage
Their old campaign anew through endless tiffs

In *Notes & Queries.* Sounding off with sage
   Remarks, like Leavis, on the sorry state
Of things would get a laugh on Shakespeare's stage,

Or catcalls, or be heard at any rate
   As just the kind of talk that malcontents
Will typically come on and use to bait

A restive audience. Take their two cents'
   Worth, you'd advise, but see the other side,
Their comic aspect, since it best prevents

The sorts of finger-wagging talk you tried
   To show was just as out-of-place when used
By jazz-authenticists as when applied

By high-toned Shakespeare critics who accused
   You and your rebel crew of making light
Those themes that, weighed more carefully, refused

Such infra-dig recension. Yet despite
   That Brechtian or Bakhtinian readiness
To thumb your nose whenever you caught sight

Of pious posturing (the *TLS*
   Once ran a photo of you and referred
To your coiffure, and maybe style of dress,

As "a poor man's Jacques Derrida") you heard
   Far subtler nuances and finer shades
Of meaning in some long neglected word

Than ever struck the not-so-light brigades
    Of Shakespeare savants. They deplored the *lèse-
Majesté* of a writing that degrades,

So they suppose, the solemn offices
    Of scholarship—here taking the same line
As, long ago, l'Académie Française

On Shakespeare—yet in truth's a very mine
    Of senses lost on those with filters set
To block whatever readings they'd incline

To count as signs of how absurd things get
    When presentism bids our better part
Of judgment go to pot. For then we let

Anachronistic fancy trump the art
    Of balancing (they say) a due respect
For what's been made of Shakespeare's works by smart

Interpreters against—lest we neglect
    The scholar-critic's calling—a robust
Sense of how texts, like whole careers, are wrecked

By any too egregious breach of trust
    Between two basic items in the shrewd
Shakespearean's credo. These advise: adjust

To changing times but don't let them intrude
    Too much and drive your readings from the fold
Of civilized consensus among clued-

Up types who know how critically bold
    To be, or not to be.
                                    Not in the least
Your way, that canny ruse to put on hold

The scope for speculation that increased
    Apace through theory's liberating zest
And so make sure their boundary-pushing ceased

At just the point where commonsense deemed best
   To rein it in. We didn't know, back then,
How soon enough you'd stand out from the rest

As scourge of all like-thinkers, even when
   They thought like you. So, Terry, if I quote
"We shall not look upon your like again"

(Predictably, you'd say) as the right note
   To end on, please forgive this weak resort
To citing just the text you always wrote

About so well: the gesture sells you short.

Notes

1. Terence Hawkes, *That Shakespeherian Rag: essays on a critical process* (London: Methuen, 1986) and *Meaning by Shakespeare* (London: Routledge, 1992).

2. Hawkes, *That Shakespeherian Rag,* 92–119.

3. Geoffrey Hartman, "The Interpreter: A Self-Analysis," *New Literary History* 4, no. 2 (Winter 1973): 213–227.

Bardbiz and the Echoes of the Past

Kathleen McLuskie

Terry Hawkes is the only critic whose writing has made me laugh out loud. The occasion was reading (in *That Shakespeherian Rag*) his virtuoso deconstruction of the language of early twentieth-century bardolatry that culminated in the image of Shakespeare as "Phallus in Wonderland."[1] I had first encountered Terry at the summer conference at the Shakespeare Institute in Stratford-upon-Avon, a terrifying experience in which three generations of international scholars introduced their colleagues' lectures with clever buried quotations and a show-off display of recondite knowledge. The event represented an academic establishment certain of its own connection both to the revered elders, made famous by their work, and to the selected neophytes whose bustling assertiveness seemed to demonstrate assurance of their place in the procession of academic authority from one generation to another. In that environment, I had been especially grateful for Terry's kindness and generosity as well as being inspired by his serious sense that the business of Shakespeare criticism was on the point of change and that younger women might help to make that change occur.

My memories of Terry Hawkes seem in large measure to have been shared by many of the Shakespeare scholars who joined the profession in the 1970s and 1980s, as they are recounted in obituaries and essays that followed his death in 2014.[2] Those memorials for the most part communicate a sense that a good academic life, the right mix of the political and the personal, of academic achievement and shared conviviality had been lived by him and shared by them. They capture a moment that Catherine Belsey described in her recollection of the founding of *Textual Practice*:

> a world without research assessment, with no obligation to produce on demand, no panels to be appeased and no hesitation to peer over the parapet for fear of antagonising our judges.[3]

In the elegiac genre of the academic memorial, the memory of a distinguished colleague allows the scholars of a later but overlapping generation to identify themselves with an important moment as well as an important individual. It holds the remembered moment still and seldom acknowledges that, as Samuel Beckett reminds us, the time "would have passed anyway."

The scholars who memorialized their shared moment with Terry Hawkes more or less explicitly have agreed with him (and E. H. Carr) that "the historian . . . belongs not to the past but to the present"[4]—yet that axiom disguises the equally obvious fact that history itself recedes into the past, and the present in which it is written has a past of its own. Impressive and influential as Terry Hawkes's influence on subsequent generations may have been, he was himself part of a generation that was particularly concerned to identify itself with the present and the future. Born in 1932, Hawkes had grown up during the Second World War but was too young to be directly involved. He thus benefitted (as we all did) from both the sacrifice and the social imagination of those who brought about the innovations in health and education transacted by the postwar Labour government. He described himself as "a child of the Butler Education Act" and took a mischievous delight in the part he saw himself playing in fulfilling the worst fears of an outdated and reactionary establishment.[5] The spirit of utopian optimism that informed the postwar generation in England had given new confidence to those who could identify the enemies of progress not only in the former owners of now nationalized capital-intensive industries[6] but in a complacent intellectual establishment content to repeat the certainties of an earlier time. Raymond Williams, for example, a decade older than Hawkes, mocked his postwar Cambridge colleagues for their assumption that "when a particular history is completed, we can all be clear and relaxed about it."[7] Williams challenged their sense that history was a matter of settled meanings by re-examining the vocabulary of cultural criticism in *Keywords.* It was in a similar spirit that Hawkes put his editorial and intellectual weight behind the New Accents series of popularizing monographs that facilitated the dissemination of the innovations associated with critical theory.

Given that postwar social formation, it is hardly surprising that Hawkes's ethical instincts were inclusive and egalitarian, with a particular mocking scepticism for the pretensions of those he regarded as part of a complacent establishment. In his writing on the past, he championed the resistances of the powerless and the poor and was always alert to the humiliations of patronage and condescension. An ethical outrage, for example, runs through his virtuoso account of the multiple connections between the "playhouse" and the "workhouse" that form the texture of Shakespearean history in Stratford. His essay on the topic linked two distinct periods, the early modern production of *The Tempest* and the late nineteenth- and early twentieth-century social relations of the town of Stratford. Hawkes made the connection between the two periods via a series of gleeful raids on the local Stratford archives held in the library of the Shakespeare Birthplace Trust. He also examined the collections relating to the Shakespeare Memorial Theatre and a recently published memoir of living in poverty in Stratford that was being adapted for performance by the Royal Shakespeare Company. Those documents provided him with accounts of local resistance to early modern enclosure as well as vivid quotations from later court records that gave voice to much later recalcitrant individuals who refused to abide by the social norms imposed by the burghers of the town. The apparent synergies of recurring popular resistance, together with the random coincidence that one of the lowlife women was called Cal, allowed Hawkes to connect Prospero's maltreatment of Caliban both with Shakespeare's controversial role in the case of the Welcombe enclosures and with the hypocrisy of William Salt Brassington, rack-renting landlord and archivist of the Shakespeare Memorial Theatre. Terry's account of the evidently inhumane treatment of the Stratford poor across both historical periods created a bass note of sympathy that demanded assent to the overall proposition that the artistic power of Shakespeare's plays was no guarantor of ethical social relationships either in Shakespeare's own time or in later historical eras.

The effect of Hawkes's essay was less to provide an alternative historical analysis of the connection between the present and the past and more to provide an imaginative account of the recurring and continuously unethical relations between the powerful and the poor. The children in the Stratford alms house or the indigent cottager who could not pay his rent could have been the victims of all the poor laws enacted by Tudor or Victorian reformers and imagined in literary texts from *As You Like it* and *King Lear* to *Oliver Twist*.

For all their vivid particularity, the social relations that Hawkes describes were not specific to any particular historical moment either present or past. They were instead presented as exemplars of

> a discourse which precedes and generates all of them . . . rooted in and geared to long-embedded political notions familiar enough to all British citizens, including those who had never travelled further west than Stratford itself.[8]

He rejected the then commonplace readings of *The Tempest* that linked the play to contemporary accounts of new world exploration, preferring instead to insist that

> The roots of the Prospero-Caliban relationship extend beyond that of Planter to Slave to find their true nourishment in the ancient home-grown European relationships of master and servant, landlord and tenant.[9]

The structures of oppression were thus presented as transhistorical, an enduring feature of social relations untouched by industrialization, the extension of the governing franchise, or compulsory universal education. His emotionally evocative and essentially literary account of the injustice of the powerful toward the poor was less concerned to make a case for an alternative historical narrative or a set of specific references to the social order or the late twentieth century. Rather, it was addressed to a "larger enterprise . . . which involves our society's recuperation and sentimentalization of a moment in its own history of four hundred or so years ago."[10]

The idea that Shakespeare's plays were regularly and predictably "put to use" by reactionary forces in the twentieth century informs many of Hawkes's other accounts of conflicting readings of the plays. Many of those controversies had taken place in the academic generation that had preceded his time. Their work had formed the core of the Shakespeare criticism with which he had been educated in the 1950s and '60s and remained influential for the following generation. Hawkes's skill in offering the controversies in which they had been forged as exemplars for the "present" of the 1980s and 1990s lay in his ability to mine existing historical resources for literary anecdotes and to present his cast of characters engaged in familiar everyday activities. John Dover Wilson (author of *What Happens in Hamlet*), for example, is first seen on "a train proceeding from Leeds to Sunderland one Saturday evening in November 1917," though the issues that unravel as the essay proceeds concern the Bolshevik revolution, trade union conflict in the munitions industries, and fascinating insights into Dover Wilson's interests in contemporary Russia.[11] A more direct connection between present and past was teasingly offered in Hawkes's description of a divisive academic scandal that "involved clear and possibly radical social and political implications."[12] Such a description might have encouraged readers in 1986 to assume that the occasion under discussion was the still-notorious case of Colin MacCabe, whose teaching of structuralism had brought him into conflict with the Cambridge University English Faculty in 1981. The connection between past and present was created as much or more by the shapes of the narrative than the issues in conflict, since part of Hawkes's point was that the recurring round of intemperate argument and dismissal from academic posts was followed by intellectual innovation. The reactionaries could be defeated by the innovative upstarts. MacCabe went on from Cambridge to a distinguished career in film studies and cultural criticism while

> just over one hundred years ago, in Oxford, the subject involved was philosophy, the Master was Benjamin Jowett, the college Balliol. And most interesting of all, the name of the martyred young man whose career, apparently blighted, was then so decisively revived in a new field by everything that happened, was A.C. Bradley.[13]

Conflict in academic life, it appeared, could be more productive than merely supporting Shakespeare as "a pillar of the existing social and political order in Britain."[14]

In all of the conflicts discussed, Hawkes was clear whose side he was on. His emotional account of the recurring humiliations of the poor in "Playhouse-Workhouse" suggested the need for change in the traditional cultural role of Shakespeare (though it was not claimed that those changes would make a material difference to poor children); and his account of academic conflict whether in the present or the past aligned itself firmly with critical practice that emphasized the dynamic rather than the settled connection between language and meaning. Yet the battle appeared never to be won. His account of the intellectual differences between F. R. Leavis and L. C. Knights over *Measure for Measure* in 1942 was presented as a re-run of a similar disagreement between G. Wilson Knight and William Empson in 1929. The dates were not, of course, arbitrarily chosen. The storms in academic tea-cups were always articulated with more obviously "historical" events—the great crash, the Bolshevik revolution, the General Strike and the world wars—that had structured the late twentieth century's account of the turning points of modernity.

The connection between academic conflict and political events was all the more evocative for being inexplicit with no direct suggestion that academic differences over readings of, say, *Measure for Measure* could be causally linked to a major liquidity crisis in the global market or the international war against fascism. Hawkes's suggestion that the contested readings of Shakespeare provided a way to discuss more fundamental conflicts was instead merely hinted in his rhetorical denial:

> I shrink from the bald proposal that (L. C. Knights) saw himself as a compromised Claudio . . . And it may finally be not entirely mischievous to suggest that within the compass of Leavis's Angelo-like perception of the back-sliding Claudio . . . we might just glimpse the recalcitrant figure of Knights.

By taking the side of innovation in past conflicts, Hawkes suggested that the late twentieth-century resistance to new critical paradigms was particularly foolish in its view that the robust continuity of English letters was being undermined by "fashionable French and American ideas." As he had in the discussion of *The Tempest,* he insisted that

> the issues are much more deeply rooted in native soil, go back much further than a few years, and can be located in places much nearer home than Paris or New Haven. Here in Britain, in that year of crisis, 1929/30, when things have "broken down everywhere" certain familiar critical battle lines seem quite clearly drawn. And there is not a Frenchman in sight.[15]

From the perspective of 1980s and '90s Britain it seemed possible to suggest that academic dissension in Shakespeare studies was a re-run of older "familiar critical battle lines" rooted in the class structures of English intellectual life. However, the claim that Hawkes had made to link past struggles to "our own situation in respect of its cognate economic climate and its fruit" tended to restrict the discussion to an English politics of the Right and Left as they were played out in the relatively peaceful conditions of the postwar universities.[16] In spite of the inflamed rhetoric of revolu-

tion that occasionally attended the discussion of the social role of
the literary curriculum or the connection between Politics and Art,
significant change in access to higher education and changes in
curricula were achieved by committees and parliamentary reports
rather than storming the winter palace of Cambridge or Sunderland. Hawkes's impatience at the continuing British tendency to
meet national crisis with "green, alternative worlds of percipient
peasants, organic communities, festivals, folk art and absolute
monarchy" was shared by many reforming academics but their
objective in mounting an assault on tradition was curriculum
change, not complete social breakdown.[17]

The question of "tradition" and the sense that "things have broken down everywhere" might have been viewed differently by an
earlier generation who had had a more direct experience of the
1930s, particularly in Europe. One of the earliest presentations of
Hawkes's essay on the mid-century conflict over *Measure for Measure* was at a conference held at Humboldt University in East Berlin
in the early months of 1990. Literary scholars from the universities
of East and West Berlin who had been divided physically as much
as ideologically during the Cold War were invited by the British
Council to join a small group of British academics in their first joint
seminar since the fall of the Berlin Wall. The aim of the British
Council organizers was to resolve conflict through culture as they
had done in international venues many times before, often in ses-
sions led by Terry Hawkes. On this occasion, however, rather more
seemed to be at stake than a shared view of literature. In England,
in the 1980s, the catch phrase "don't mention the war" had become
a running joke from the *Fawlty Towers* comedy sketches; here it
took on much darker resonances as the exploration of the benign
continuities of literary critical debate were disrupted by angry rec-
ollections of "an earlier recantation" from Berlin scholars who
were of the generation that could recall discussions of the past during postwar de-Nazification.

For European intellectuals of the mid-century, managing the past
in order to make sense of the present was a project that was more
overdetermined and perhaps more tragic than it could ever have
been in Stratford or Cardiff. In her account of Walter Benjamin's
struggle to write literary history in the 1930s, Hannah Arendt
observed that he "knew that the break in tradition and loss of
authority which had occurred in his lifetime were irreparable."[18]
The rise of fascism had produced a break in tradition that involved

rather more than a rejection of a complacent, old-fashioned cultural discourse. Benjamin represented that separation of the present from the past through a bleak vision of the Angel of history whose

> face is turned to the past. Where we perceive a chain of events, he sees one single catastrophe which keeps piling wreckage upon wreckage and hurls it in front of his feet.[19]

Partly because it was inspired by a painting—Paul Klee's *Angelus Novus*—Benjamin's vision of history is represented by a single static image of a catastrophic past being blown backwards into an unknowable future with such force that the Angel cannot open its wings. The invisible past and future had been frozen into a traumatic and inescapable contemporary.

The idea of a traumatic "contemporary" encompassing past and present was given its application to Shakespeare in Jan Kott's 1956 essay "Shakespeare our Contemporary," first published in the Parisian journal *Les Temps Moderne.* Parisian readers, for whom the Nazi occupation of Paris was only a decade past, may have been persuaded by Kott's analogy between Shakespeare's history plays and an inescapable, endlessly repeated Grand Mechanism. Such a view might well have reflected the Polish people's experience of the cycles of tyranny under the Nazis and then under the post-1945 Soviet-backed communist regime. However, as John Elsom argues, this view of the connection between Shakespeare and the past was not only a reflection on personal or even national experience: it was also a sly inversion of the nineteenth-century German view of the "immortality" of Shakespeare: "suggesting that Shakespeare is *so* immortal, that he's actually living next door, alive and well in cold war Warsaw."[20]

Martin Esslin (a chronological contemporary of Jan Kott's and one who shared his experience of Eastern Europe) located the idea of the contemporary in the experience of a "daily proximity to civil war, brutality, ideological intolerance, conspiracy and its bloody repression" that, he said, "determined the life of Shakespeare's time . . . as it did and still does the atmosphere of mid-twentieth-century Europe."[21] When those connections were noted in England, they were more often realized by the experience of theater. Edmund Wilson's "Notes on England at the End of the War" remembered how

In the *Duchess of Malfi,* the scene where her doom is announced to the Duchess amidst the drivelling of the liberated madmen, at the moment of the exposé of the German concentration camps.[22]

A more direct link to the idea of Shakespeare as "Our Contemporary" came in the encounter between Kott and Peter Brook, who visited Warsaw on, as it happened, a British Council tour. Brook, of course, wrote the preface to the English edition of Kott's book and, famously, used Kott's essay on *"King Lear* and *Endgame"* to inform the bleak vision of his 1962 *King Lear.* The general rejection of an outmoded idea of Shakespeare was given a particular theatrical form that generated not only a new critical perspective but possibly the creative work both on *King Lear* and on the life of Shakespeare created by the younger playwright, Edward Bond. For creative practitioners and for many adaptors of Shakespeare's plays, it was new work as much as new analysis of the past that offered an exciting alternative to the reiteration of traditional versions of Shakespeare.

Moments of performance could present new images of Shakespeare with an immediacy that did not depend on the cogency of the argument that they upheld. Kott's analogies between the tyrannies of Nazi or Soviet power and Elizabethan kingship will not bear much historical or political pressure. As John Elsom wryly pointed out: "There may have been bullies in Shakespeare's time but they did not brandish nuclear weapons."[23] What made Kott's account persuasive was that it was communicated by a set of images that could be realized in the theatre and could be counted on to communicate an emotional and ethical, if not political, force:

A flash of the sword, the tramping of the guards; the applause of intimidated noblemen; a shout from the forcibly gathered crowd.[24]

It was less a style of argument than a style of theatre-making developed earlier in the twentieth century by Edward Gordon Craig and Komisarjevsky.

Whether one calls those images "contemporary" or "timeless" will depend on the particular style of the performance and the surrounding referents to which an audience member or reviewer connects them. That moment of connection, whether it takes place in the theatre or in reading is more likely to be remembered and understood if it can be communicated with a measure of affect. The images of Kott's description and the narrative form and wit of Terry Hawkes's made a considerable contribution to the impact that those two versions had on twentieth-century criticism. That impact was felt in both criticism and theater—and in the new critical disciplines of theater history and varying kinds of attention to history, and the present that emerged from them. In the case of Jan Kott, his legacy was the subject of a conference held in 1988, the year before his death and, coincidentally, the year before the collapse of Eastern European communism. The audience comprised more émigré and Eastern European critics and theater practitioners than university academics, and the final session tended to conclude that Shakespeare was not our contemporary but could be made so in theater and critical practice.

In 1989 Terry Hawkes wrote his own summary essay in mid-career. It began, with characteristic vigor, "Few things unhinge the British as much as doublet and hose" and goes on to a characteristically combative account of the building of the Globe Theatre on London's Bankside, together with the discovery of the Rose Theatre site a short distance away. His robust discussion of the problematics of authenticity and originality is followed by a generous and engaged review of new work whose detailed research in history does nothing to mitigate its engagement with the politics of popular representation and the use of Shakespeare for specific political purposes.

The essay, reprinted in his *Meaning by Shakespeare* in 1992, came to be called "Bardbiz" after the exchange of thirteen letters that followed its first publication in an early issue of the *London Review of Books.* The correspondence ran for over a year, perhaps partly because the *LRB* was a new journal and its editors may well have relished the appearance of a lively exchange in its early issues. Led by the then little known young critic James Wood, it went over the old ground of the aesthetic versus the political (or the universal versus the historical; or the traditional versus the contemporary Shakespeare). It was a spat to take its place alongside the rows so vividly described in Hawkes's essays but, looking back, it feels like a last hurrah of a cultural era that was already on the way out.

The *LRB*—now a successful London journal—had taken over the space left vacant by the absence of the *Times Literary Supplement.* All of the *Times* newspapers had ceased publication during a dispute with the National Union of Journalists over working practices, new technology, and the move of the newspaper offices to new developments downriver in Wapping. The dispute, angry and divisive though it was, was eventually resolved as new technologies of communication transformed print journalism and its relations of production into the myriad forms that exist today. The Globe Theatre, in spite of the cogent academic critique of its fundamental assumptions, was built and became one of the so-called anchor institutions in the redevelopment of the South Bank—a development based on arts institutions that could be seen as beginning with the Festival of Britain in 1951, and continuing through the Cultural Olympiad and Global Shakespeare Festivals of 2012.

Shakespeare, of course, continued to change too. The "doublet and hose" that Hawkes referred to has not often been seen in the English theatre since. The combination of increased Arts Council funding, commercial sponsorship and new funding models ensured that creative work continued while changes in university structures and curricula have ensured the supply not only of audiences but of creative practitioners (however underpaid and precariously employed) too.

Time moves on and with enduring generosity Terry recognized that his role in Shakespeare studies was changing too, as new generations in turn mock the monuments of the past. With good-natured self-mockery he made comic capital out of recognizing that

> Some wretched "white British Shakespearean scholar" scourged in half a paragraph [in Gary Taylor's *Re-inventing Shakespeare*] for a lifetime's imperception . . . bears my own name.[25]

His response to the Bardbiz controversy was also welcomed as a teacher might relish a dynamic graduate seminar. He found it "entirely apt that [its participants] should finally elbow me off the page."[26]

Terry of course, was not elbowed out of academic life for more than another three decades. Many scholars from those years will remember him more for the establishment of "presentism" as an academic sub-speciality. That generation will set up their own eras and periodizations, their own ways of creating the past out of the present. It is to be hoped that the circumstances in which they make that history will be as congenial as those that created the history between Terry Hawkes and those of us who came of age in the 1970s and '80s. The omens are not good. From the perspective of the twenty-first century, the relative calm and growing material prosperity of the period from 1945 to 1989 increasingly looks like a historical blip in a much darker history of economic uncertainty and an ever widening chasm of inequality that now presses more directly on the relative privilege of the Western world. Our, perhaps parochial, concern with the historical may need to be augmented with more attention to the global and our attention to discourse may need to be augmented with attention to institutions and structures. But that was not Terry Hawkes's job, and it is no longer mine.

Notes

1. Terence Hawkes, *That Shakespeherian Rag* (London: Routledge, 1986), 60.
2. *Special Issue: Radical Shakespeare; in memory of Terry Hawkes. Critical Survey* 26, no. 3 (2014).
3. Catherine Belsey, "The Legacy of Terence Hawkes," *Textual Practice* 29, no.1 (2015): 1–8; published online February16, 2015. http://dx.doi.org/10.1080/0950236X.2014.993525
4. Terence Hawkes, "Review of James Shapiro's *1599: A Year in the Life of William Shakespeare* (London: Faber, 2005)," *Shakespeare* 2, no. 2 (2006): 249–52, 249.
5. Terence Hawkes, "Lear's Maps," in *Meaning by Shakespeare* (Routledge: London, 1992), 75.
6. See his mockery of the idea of a coal owner being a philanthropist in the opening paragraph of "Shakespeare and the General Strike," in *Meaning by Shakespeare*, 42.
7. Raymond Williams, *Keywords: A Vocabulary of Culture and Society* (London: Fontana, 1976), 16.
8. 8. Ibid.
9. Hawkes, *That Shakespeherian Rag*, 3.
10. Hawkes, "Playhouse-Workhouse" in *That Shakespeherian Rag*, 23.
11. Hawkes, "Telmah" in *That Shakespeherian Rag*, 101.
12. Hawkes, "A Sea Shell" in *That Shakespeherian Rag*, 27–28.
13. Ibid.
14. Hawkes, *Meaning by Shakespeare*, 48.
15. Hawkes, "Take me to your Leda," in *Meaning by Shakespeare*, 64.
16. Hawkes, *That Shakespeherian Rag*, 13.
17. Ibid., 109.
18. Hannah Arendt, introduction to Walter Benjamin, *Illuminations* ed. Hannah Arendt, trans. Harry Zohn (New York: Harcourt, Brace and World, 1968), 38.
19. Walter Benjamin, "Theses on the philosophy of history ix," in *Illuminations*, 259.
20. John Elsom, introduction to *Is Shakespeare Still Our Contemporary?* (London: Routledge, 1989), 1.

21. Martin Esslin, introduction to Jan Kott, *Shakespeare Our Contemporary*, trans. Boleslaw Taborski (London: Methuen, 1964), xix.

22. Edmund Wilson, "Notes on London at the End of the War," in *Europe without Baedecker* (New York: Doubleday, 1947), 7.

23. Elsom, *Is Shakespeare Still Our Contemporary?*, 1.

24. Kott, *Shakespeare Our Contemporary*, 12.

25. Hawkes, "Bardbiz" in *Meaning by Shakespeare*, 149.

26. Hawkes, postscript, in *Meaning by Shakespeare*, 154.

"The pit has often laid down the law for the boxes": Terence Hawkes, Alexis de Tocqueville, and Shakespearean Class Struggle

JOHN HARTLEY

"Strange developments"

THE EDITORIAL BRIEFING FROM *Shakespeare Studies* was clear enough. As part of "an appraisal and appreciation" of Terence Hawkes's work, and "more broadly of the paradigm shift which he did so much to help advance," my task is to discuss "Terry's contributions in the world of cultural studies, theory, and politics beyond Shakespeare studies." What could be more straightforward than to demonstrate how these preoccupations follow his provocations, as indeed they do, well beyond the purview of Shakespeare studies? The trajectory of my own career illustrates the shift. Despite—and because of—being trained by Terry Hawkes, I have never worked in an English department, only in (you may say) increasingly *outré* interdisciplinary novelties, from communication, media, and cultural studies, via journalism and creative industries, to internet studies. Now I am professor of "cultural science" at a university in what has been called the most isolated capital city in the world (namely, Perth in Western Australia, where Curtin University is located). My observation throughout has been that Hawkes did indeed help to precipitate the "paradigm shift" we now call (among other things) cultural studies.[1]

Job done?

Not quite! Now, from my shifting paradigmatic, disciplinary, and geographical vantage point, I can cast a "backward glance o'er travel'd roads," as Walt Whitman did in order to proffer his own "definitive *carte visite* to the coming generations of the New World," where "these lines . . . will probably blend the weft of first purposes and speculations, with the warp of . . . experience afterwards, always bringing strange developments."[2] Indeed, the practice of "cultural studies, theory, and politics" took on a life of its own, amidst far-flung disciplines, outlandish ideas, and exotic destinations across the world. But such "strange developments" remained path-dependent experiences, meaning that no matter where they traveled, curious navigators rarely strayed far from the "first purposes and speculations" that Hawkes himself articulated in his long conversation, over five decades, with the "Old Bill" himself[3] and, through that now thoroughly defamiliarized (остранение) figure, with "Shakespeare's talking animals" at large.[4]

> Much have I seen and known; cities of men
> And manners, climates, councils, governments,
> Myself not least[.][5]

As I have acknowledged: It's a long way from Shakespeare to Kylie Minogue.[6] But Terry was with me every step of the way. What I have discovered out there in "the world . . . beyond" is that it is the same world, weft and warp. "Cultural studies, theory, politics" and "Shakespeare studies" are one and the same. One of Hawkes's enduring achievements has been to establish that fact. It would be tempting to sing his praises by showing how he has influenced ever more remote intellectual territories (as indeed he has, not least through his New Accents book series). But I do not want to suggest that the genesis of his ideas in Shakespeare studies was followed by an exodus to alien lands, such that Shakespeare studies is construed as one thing (original, pure, and sacred), and cultural studies as another (contaminated, worldly, profane). On the contrary: all the contaminated worldly profanity you might wish for is right there where you started.

Circumspice

Cultural studies emerged as a *mediating* discourse, literally acting as an intermediary agency between some hefty oppositions.[7] It was as much political as cultural; as much about everyday life (the ordinary, pop culture) as about intellectual traditions (theory, critical practice); as much about power as meaning; as much about sub-jectivity (formed in ideology) as identity (self-representation). Inevitably, thence, it was as much about how we know as what we value.[8] Indeed, it was not only Terence Hawkes who noticed that industrial-scale sense making (popular culture) was at odds with the cultural values carried in intellectual traditions and high cul-ture. As a movement, or what Raymond Williams once character-ized as an "open conspiracy," cultural studies set about the work of disrupting received notions of how (common) sense was made in language and other coded systems, including disciplinary knowledge systems, and subjecting inherited cultural evaluations to "creative destruction" (in Joseph Schumpeter's phrase) in order to open up the possibilities for cultural-political renewal.[9]

Thus, cultural studies quickly became about the class struggle in language, and cultural struggles around difference and power. It was good for mediating the new *political* social movements of the 1960s and '70s—youth (sub)cultures, feminism, anti-racism, identity politics, sexual liberation, the peace and environment movements—with the *theoretical* ferment engendered by a succes-sion of intellectual "isms" of the period: structuralism and post-structuralism, modernism and postmodernism, deconstruction, post-colonialism and the Marxist New Left.[10] Cultural studies investigated identity, ideology, meaning, social relationships, and media in order to analyze inequalities of power and the discursive stratagems used by different agencies and administrations in vari-ous struggles beyond the spheres of formal representative politics or canonical cultural forms.

But ah, there's the rub. This was not, in fact, the "world of cul-tural studies, theory, and politics *beyond Shakespeare studies,*" at least, not for Terence Hawkes, because mediation between popular and high culture, politics and theory, class struggle and cultural values, was already his characteristic mode of *studying Shake-speare.* Further, over an extended period, he analyzed not just Shakespeare but also "Shakespeare"—the product of Bardolatry, Bardbiz, and Shakesploitation—in Shakespeare *studies.* Any "appraisal and appreciation" of Hawkes's work is obliged to con-clude that he did not locate cultural studies, theory, and politics *"beyond* Shakespeare studies." He found these novelties right at the center of the Shakespeare enterprise. Indeed, you may say that what he did *within, to* and *as* Shakespeare studies was an exem-plary performance *of* cultural studies, theory, and politics, *avant la lettre.* Terry *mediated* that world and the world of Shakespeare studies.

Terry Tocqueville

Terence Hawkes was Tocquevillian in temper—astute, wry, literary, transatlantic, and worried. He was adept at using America to effect what Thorstein Veblen would have called "invidious comparison" with England.[11] What worried Hawkes in this comparative method was that neither side of the Atlantic provided a satisfactory solution to the problems that he wanted to figure out. But Americanness and Englishness might begin to explain one another.

Britain was the colonial Power from which the Americans had wrested their liberty. As Hawkes put it: "to fight free of Englishness by turning to things French has, after all, been a major transatlantic ploy since the eighteenth century."[12] Here, he is discussing Duke Ellington, jazz, and the future of literary criticism, but of course Alexis de Tocqueville's *De la démocratie en Amérique* was one of the "things French" towards which the Americans turned as soon as the two volumes were published (1835 and 1840).

Democracy in America was really about France. That is what worried Tocqueville. He thought it might be possible to "fight free" of the problems that bedevilled the French polity by turning to both England and America, the one for liberty, the other for democracy, despite their manifold shortcomings. Tocqueville's anglophile tendencies were unusual in French public life, which habitually shared with the Americans a desire to "fight free of Englishness."[13] Perhaps his motivations were not only political (he wanted to balance order and liberty, avoiding both dictatorship and revolution), but also personal. His own aristocratic Norman ancestors, so he thought, had introduced into England the conditions for *liberty* to develop, by *conquering* it (it is a long story).[14] His personal interest in English liberty may have been extended further by his marriage to an English Protestant commoner, Marie Mottley, six years his elder—against the grain of his nation, religion, and caste. By all accounts the marriage was a successful and lifelong union of opposites (something else that he shared with Terry, perhaps).

Terence Hawkes analyzed the condition of democracy through drama; he analyzed Britain by comparing it to America; and he ana-

lyzed Shakespearean drama through the lens of class, as did Tocqueville in *Democracy in America.* In a fascinating section on "the
influence of democracy on intellectual movement in the United
States," he devoted a chapter to "Some Observations on the Theater of Democratic Peoples."[15] He recommends:

> When the revolution that changed the social and political state of an
> aristocratic people begins to make itself felt in literature, it is generally
> in the theater that it is first produced, and it is there that it always
> remains visible. . . . If you want to judge in advance the literature of a
> people that is turning toward democracy, study its theater. (846)

On re-reading Tocqueville with Terry in mind (or turnabout)—a
pleasure I can recommend—it is remarkable how often Tocqueville's insights shine with a Hawkesian glint; a glint in the eye that
surprises, amuses, instructs, and illuminates all at once, revealing
previously unsuspected tensions about the state of reality at play.
Both of them employ (or enjoy) what one of Tocqueville's critics
describes as a "paradox-seeking tone," infuriating to some but
an efficient rhetorical vehicle for the "invidious comparison"
method.[16]

Postmodern Thunder

You may say that my suggestion of a Hawkesian glint in Tocqueville's text smacks of the ludicrous time-inversion of David Lodge's
Persse McGarrigle (in *Small World,* 1984), who studied "the influence of T.S. Eliot on Shakespeare" to general amusement in the
common room—until the Eliot scholar Jason Harding pointed out
that the fictional McGarrigle's paradoxical arrow of time was in fact
pointing the right way: "Had Persse been a more attentive student
of Eliot, he'd have known that the author of the dictum 'the past
should be altered by the present as much as the present is directed
by the past' anticipated his postmodern thunder by half a century."[17]

Now, then, may be a good moment to investigate Hawkes's influence on Tocqueville, since the burden of Hawkes's own later work
is that texts say what *we* mean, albeit with a sting in the tail of that
particular truth:[18]

Let's get it straight. It's not what the plays say that counts, but the uses
to which they are put. We wonder about what they "mean." But the
truth is much starker. We mean. Worse, we mean it by the plays.[19]

"We mean it by the plays" is "worse" because it is *our* "uses to
which *they* are put." They are an alibi. The same is true of Tocqueville. The uses to which he has been put include his status (up there
with Shakespeare) in the United States. Blithely, commentators
endlessly repeat: "*Democracy in America* is at once the best book
ever written on democracy and the best book ever written on
America."[20] Democracy and America become "convertible terms"
(as Whitman asserted in *Democratic Vistas*), no matter that Tocqueville had doubts about democracy as a system of government, or
that America may no longer practice the backwoods egalitarian version that he observed. In the name of Tocqueville, minority elites
and corporate raiders cloak undemocratic practices in democratic
theory, simply by invoking Americanness. It seems high time to
subject the uses of Tocqueville to some Hawkesian air-clearing
"postmodern thunder."

Totus Mundus Agit Prop

Both Hawkes and Tocqueville had something to say about Shakespeare. Tocqueville claimed him for the enterprise at hand, calling
him "the democratic author par excellence."[21] Even as America
was "struggling to fight free of Englishness," Shakespeare ruled its
public rostrum and log cabin alike:

> The literary genius of Great Britain still shines its light into the depths
> of the forests of the New World. There is scarcely a pioneer's cabin
> where you do not find a few odd volumes of Shakespeare. (803)

This may be characterized as the literary (read-only) or *pedagogical*
Shakespeare, rather than a *people's* Shakespeare. A more riotous
version was also to hand across America: a dialogic, dramatic one,
playing in the theaters. Tocqueville had a theory of the theater that
was straightforwardly political. In an early performance of Hawkesian cultural studies, Tocqueville subjects the theater of the 1830s
to class analysis:

> It is only in the theater that the upper classes have mingled with the middle and lower classes, and that they have agreed if not to accept the advice of the latter, at least to allow them to give it. It is in the theater that the learned and the lettered have always had the most difficulty making their taste prevail over that of the people, and keeping themselves from being carried away by the taste of the people. There the pit has often laid down the law for the boxes. (846–47)

Drama co-evolves with democracy, no matter that theaters themselves were class-divided between "the pit" and "the boxes."

> If it is difficult for an aristocracy not to allow the theater to be invaded by the people, you will easily understand that the people must rule there as a master once democratic principles have penetrated laws and mores, when ranks merge and minds like fortunes become more similar. . . (847)

Not only was this true for Shakespeare's own theaters (groundlings commingling with lords), as Alfred Harbage has noted at length, but it is also true for contemporary mediated societies.[22] The radical potential of the "popular dramatic tradition"—first noted by S. L. Bethell, one of Hawkes's own teachers—was also inherent in the popular drama of the current period, i.e., television, where, "once democratic principles have penetrated laws and mores," "the boxes" had been thoroughly "carried away by the tastes of the people."[23] This is of course where Terence Hawkes came in.[24]

"Overthrown by riots"

The riotous potential of the popular dramatic tradition was soon on spectacular—and lethal—display, in New York City, May 1849. Tocqueville had been prescient:

> the tastes and instincts natural to democratic peoples . . . will show themselves first in the theater, and you can predict that they will be introduced there with violence. In written works, the literary laws of the aristocracy will become modified little by little in a general and so to speak legal manner. In the theater, they will be overthrown by riots. (847)

The "Shakespeare Riots" duly ensued.[25] This fatal disturbance included a strong dose of anti-British sentiment, but one particular manifestation of Englishness—Shakespeare—was exempt. Indeed, as "the democratic author, par excellence," Shakespeare was appropriated, according to the logic of Whitman's "convertible terms," as the *American* author par excellence. No matter what the machinations of *la perfide Albion, "Shakespeare"* was henceforth "translated" as a universal soldier of the American way.

The crisis, which extended over several days, was ostensibly provoked by a dispute between two Shakespearean actors, the American Edwin Forrest and the Englishman William Charles Macready, who were appearing in different theaters in New York City. Both were playing the role of Macbeth. Forrest, who had genuine working class credentials and a loyal following in the New York "popular dramatic tradition," saw himself in the rugged individualist mold of the American pioneer (thereby creating the template for the film star). Apparently he had clashed previously with Macready, whom he now cast in the villainous role of English toff—an effete, simpering aristocratic fop, who had insulted him in London four years earlier. He was out for revenge.[26]

But the scale and violence of the showdown far exceeded the bounds of professional jealousy. Forrest had whipped up patriotic fervor among the Bowery Boys or B'hoys, an early spectacular sub-

LEFT: *Mr. Edwin Forrest as Macbeth.* RIGHT: *Mr. Macready as Macbeth.*[27]

culture of urban, alienated youth in a New York City that was undergoing the painful transformation from an artisanal to an industrial economy, and thus to a full-blown class distinction between workers and capitalists.[28]

The Bowery Boys were motivated by inequality, nationalism, class hatred, and urban subcultural swagger. They spilled out of "The Republic of the Bowery" in spectacular style, precursors of Martin Scorsese's *Gangs of New York* and Dick Hebdige's *Subculture:*

> dressed in outlandish manner, with slicked-down forelocks, gaudily colored suits, expensive walking sticks, high working boots, and tall beaver hats set at a jaunty, defiant angle. Avid drinkers, carousers, and battlers with rival gangs, the Bowery toughs comically asserted their place in the urban landscape, with stage plays devoted to their exploits and their aggressive aping of their betters.[29]

The Astor Place Opera House was associated with New York's well-to-do elite. That is where Macready was playing. The stage was set for three different provocations to civil war: the dramatic conflict unleashed by Macbeth with the murder of King Duncan in the Scottish Play; class war in a city newly marked by industrial inequality; and a continuing war of decolonization between American "Workingmen!" and "English Aristocrats And Foreign Rule," as an incendiary poster put it at the time, to inflame the disturbances.[30]

The climax was Shakespearean—bodies strewn everywhere. Except that these were the corpses of the audience, not the players. Before order was restored, the forces involved on both sides had glimpsed nothing less than revolution. Faced with an unarmed crowd estimated at between 15,000 and 20,000 people from "the pit," the Mayor called out the National Guard. For the first (but not the last) time in United States history the Republic's own soldiers "shot point blank at American citizens":[31]

> a crowd of Forrest's partisans gathered early in the evening before the theater, and waiting till the performance had begun, attempted to force a way inside and put a stop to it. The police were powerless and sent for the military; the Seventh Regiment (New York militia) came up, and was assailed by the mob with showers of brickbats and stones. Before the fray was ended, 34 rioters were killed, a great number wounded, and 141 of the regiment injured by the missiles.[32]

Confronted with their own fellow democrats, what motivated the National Guard to shoot so many of them down? Their theatrical

Riot at the Astor-Place Opera-House, New York 1849.[33]

excess? Not entirely, threatening though such visible "otherness" has seemed to security forces in American cities from that day to this. But here, at the "hated elite" Astor Opera Theater, it seems that class supremacy played a role. "The boxes" were shooting into "the pit":

> [National Guard] units had historically played a central role in the social and political lives of the localities, regions, and social communities in which they were based. The 7th Regiment of the New York National Guard, for example, carried on its muster rolls the names of so many scions of New York City's socially prominent families that it was commonly known as the "Silk Stocking" or "Blue-Blood" Regiment. The unit's strict peacetime entry requirements endowed it with the character of an exclusive club for New York City's patrician elite, the regiment's membership being limited only to recruits able to produce evidence of proper pedigree or social connections.[34]

Throughout the nineteenth century, these patrician scions of "proper pedigree" continued to keep order among unruly industrial workers: The Seventh Regiment was called out to support state or municipal authorities for one emblematic disturbance after another:

- Execution of James Reynolds, 1825
- Election Riots, 1834
- Abolition Riot, 1834
- Stevedore Riot, 1836
- Flour Riots, 1837
- Anti-rent War, 1839
- Croton Water Riot, 1840
- **Astor Place Riot, 1849 (the Shakespeare Riots)**
- Police Riot, 1857
- Dead Rabbits Riot, 1857
- Draft Riots, 1863
- Orange Riots, 1871
- Labor Riots, 1877
- Motormen's Strike, Brooklyn, 1895
- Strike, Croton Dam, 1900[35]

The Shakespeare Riots were provoked by feuding Shakespeare-ans; they ended as a modern tragedy of Shakespearean proportions. And *Macbeth* was just the play to use for thinking through such matters. As Terence Hawkes has pointed out:

Most modern critics agree that the play exhibits . . . concern with the diagnosis of evil in the modern world. . . . Macbeth's reduced world, its language, its politics, are instantly familiar to us. Yet that familiarity perhaps becomes the play's most complicating factor, making it difficult to "see" Macbeth as the self-damned wretch its structure demands. He looks too much like someone we know.[36]

For in the end, as Hawkes has been arguing all along, it is the uses to which the plays are put that counts. What *Macbeth* may say is no guarantor of what it may mean, but what it means certainly includes the politics of class, nation, and industrialization that played out in Manhattan in 1849.

"You might want to work on that little roar of yours, hmm?"

The face of evil as "someone we know" is the legacy of the Forrest-Macready feud. Springing from the craggy heights of tragedy, Shakespearean villainy ran quickly into the fertile alluvial plains of popular culture so beloved of cultural studies. For the American popular dramatic tradition has never quite recovered from the "model" of evil that presented itself on stage in New York in 1849. Hollywood's image of the bad guy is not Macbeth but *Englishmen.* The foppish but menacing caricature of Englishness exploited by Edwin Forrest has made William Charles Macready the unwitting archetype of stage malice; so much so that it keeps resurfacing in places where children may be present, just to remind Americans to stick to simple-and-strong, and not to fall for the wiles of the Old European intellectual, especially one speaking in suspicious "New Accents."

Take for instance Jeremy Irons's portrayal of Scar, the villain in *The Lion King,* that remake of the Forrest model of rugged individualist American pioneer, whose puritan self-realization is achieved not in the backwoods of the New World, or even in the rowdy mean streets of the Bowery Boys, but in a transplanted Africa-without-Africans, designed for the global marketplace where "a Shakespearean monster" can be recognised by his posh English accent:

> *The Lion King* offers viewers clear analogues for Hamlet and his father. But the film's best representation of the pleasures and grandeur of Shakespeare comes not in little Simba or martyred Mufasa, but in its villain: Scar, a Shakespearean monster par excellence.[37]

To Alfredo Michel Modenessi's sceptical and postcolonial ear, this is not so much Shakespeare as "Shakespeare"; little more than "leftovers of bardolatry freely circulating in ready-to-use packages," where "the British accented and Shakespeare-allusive" Scar of *The Lion King* represents the "sinister, un-American villain":

> Irons' voice and inflections stand in sharp contrast to [James Earl] Jones' "heroic" rendering of Mufasa: the gaunt, sometime RSC player delivers a depraved, decadent Old World counterpart to the New World's robust character, who is just as deeply voiced but "noble" and physically imposing.[38]

Modenessi asks of such "Shakesploitation": "how far should Shakespeare artists and scholars participate?" The answers to that question are of course also circulating in ready-to-use packages, in the Shakespearean criticism of Terence Hawkes. The objection to such characterization is his too. Once you have bolted the theater's doors *against* class, colonialism, politics and theory, to focus on "individual character" and "personality," you may be discomfited by what happens next out there on the street.

To avoid another "Shakespeare riot" along the hard road to

democratization, the reduction of Shakespearean drama to American individualism needs to be shown the door. The trick is not to *reduce* Shakespeare to a John Wayne movie or Disney cartoon, but to make these popular dramatic forms worthy of the mantle they have inherited. The alternative is too awful for Terry to contemplate:

> Forget [Shakespeare's plays'] complex concern with the issues of nationhood, governance and morality. Welcome to our modern, ingrowing, back-bedroom world, where individual personality and its discontents line up to be furtively probed, picked, squeezed and sniffed. . . . But this replaces the epic sweep of a 400-year-old drama with the comfiness of current soap opera prattle . . . bossily shooing us down that bleak *Coronation Street* of the soul where Hamlet, Juliet, and Othello turn out to be "people just like us" and where we are "as darkly ambitious as Lady Macbeth, as jubilantly lusty as Bottom, as embittered as Iago". Reduce the Bard, reduce his art.[39]

400 years after Shakespeare's death, here's the take-out message for "cultural studies, theory and politics." We need to find a way to investigate the Shakespearean in our societies, not to insert our personalities into the Shakespearean: to disturb, for our own uncomfortable good, "the scarcely penetrable world of engulfing violence, wholesale insecurity, and inexplicably mingled cruelty and sentimentality where our roots disturbingly lie."[40]

That is surely still an all-too-recognizable world, well "beyond Shakespeare studies." What a waste if the latter is merely "tamed . . . curbed . . . explained . . . made fit to appear on a syllabus near you." The responsibility for the required paradigm shift lies with the gathered forces of cultural studies, theory, politics—*and* Shakespeare studies. Terry Hawkes's Shakespearean and Tocquevillian contributions set the stage for an awkward question: what would it mean, and what would it take, for "the pit" of contemporary popular drama to "lay down the law" for the "boxes" where new-made antidemocratic evils lurk?

Notes

1. See John Hartley, *Tele-ology: Studies in Television* (London: Routledge, 1992); *A Short History of Cultural Studies* (London: Sage Publications, 2003), 51–55; and "Housing cultural studies: A memoir of Stuart Hall, Richard Hoggart

and Terence Hawkes," *International Journal of Cultural Studies* 18, no. 2 (2015): 185–207.

2. Walt Whitman, *Leaves of Grass,* The Walt Whitman Archive (<http://www.whitmanarchive.org/published/LG/1891/poems/399>).

3. Terence Hawkes, *Shakespeare in the Present* (London: Routledge, 2002), 66–82.

4. Terence Hawkes, *Shakespeare's Talking Animals: Language and Drama in Society* (London: Edward Arnold, 1973).

5. Alfred, Lord Tennyson, "Ulysses," (1833/42).

6. Hartley, *Tele-ology,* 3.

7. John Hartley, *A Short History of Cultural Studies.*

8. See R. E. Lee, *Life and Times of Cultural Studies: The Politics and Transformation of the Structures of Knowledge* (Durham, NC: Duke University Press, 2004) and *Knowledge Matters: The Structures of Knowledge and the Crisis of the Modern World System* (St. Lucia: University of Queensland Press, 2010). Also see J. Frow, *Cultural Studies and Cultural Value* (Oxford: The Clarendon Press, 1995).

9. Raymond Williams, "Communications as Cultural Science," *Journal of Communication* 24, no. 3 (1974): 17–25, at 25.

10. Terence Hawkes, *Structuralism and Semiotics* (London: Methuen/Routledge, 1977). Also see Niall Lucy, *A Dictionary of Postmodernism,* ed. J. Hartley (Oxford: Wiley-Blackwell, 2016).

11. See Thorstein Veblen, *Theory of the Leisure Class* (Oxford: Oxford University Press, 2009), 27–28. These shifting signifiers—"America"; "England"—are uncomfortable equivalents for the USA and UK. What each may have meant in Shakespeare's or Tocqueville's time, never mind Hawkes's, is indeterminate. Both carry imperial baggage, which Hawkes, an Englishman living in Wales, eventually confronted in his essays "Blyn Glas" and "Aberdaugleddyf." See Hawkes, *Shakespeare in the Present,* chapters 3 and 4.

12. Hawkes, *Shakespeare in the Present,* 125.

13. Hugh Brogan, *Alexis de Tocqueville: Prophet of Democracy in an Age of Revolution* (London: Profile Books, 2006), 399.

14. Cheryl Welch, *De Tocqueville* (Oxford: Oxford University Press, 2001), 128–29, 162 n. 11.

15. Alexis de Tocqueville, "Some Observations on the Theater of Democratic Peoples," *Democracy in America,* vol. 3, Historical-critical edition, ed. E. Nolla, trans. J. Schleifer (Indianapolis, IN: Freedom Fund, 2010), 845–52. (<http://classiques.uqac.ca/classiques/De_tocqueville_alexis/democracy_in_america_historical_critical_ed/democracy_in_america_vol_3.pdf>).

16. Christopher Caldwell, "Even God Quotes Tocqueville," *The New York Times,* July 8, 2007 (<http://www.nytimes.com/2007/07/08/books/review/Caldwell.html>).

17. J. Harding, "T.S. Eliot's Shakespeare," *Essays in Criticism* 62, no. 2 (2012): 160–77, at 160.

18. Hawkes, *Meaning by Shakespeare* (London: Routledge, 1999), and "*Coronation Street* of the Soul," *New Statesman,* April 7, 2003 (<http://www.newstatesman.com/node/157436>).

19. A post by Terence Hawkes on the *Shaksper* website, August 10, 2007 (<http://shaksper.net/archive/2007/256-august/25677-washpost-ourselves-in-shakespeare-sp-2088857046>). This comment was part of a short discussion

string in which the Shakespeare Riots (and Nigel Cliff's book) were mentioned in someone else's post, to which Hawkes's comment is a response. Also see Hawkes, *Shakespeare in the Present,* 2002.

20. H. Mansfield and D. Winthrop, "Editors' Introduction," in Tocqueville, *Democracy in America* (Chicago: University of Chicago Press, 2000).

21. Tocqueville, "Some Observations on the Theater of Democratic Peoples," 868 n.

22. See Alfred Harbage, *As They Liked It: An Essay on Shakespeare and Morality* (London: Macmillan, 1947).

23. S. L. Bethell, *Shakespeare and the Popular Dramatic Tradition* (London: Staples, 1944).

24. E.g. Hawkes, *Shakespeare's Talking Animals,* 215–41.

25. Nigel Cliff's book is the definitive account: *The Shakespeare Riots: Revenge, Drama, and Death in Nineteenth-Century America* (New York: Random House, 2007). Also see Michael Dobson, "Let him be Caesar!", *London Review of Books* 29.15 (2007): 15–7.

26. Cliff, *The Shakespeare Riots.*

27. LEFT: Forrest: R. Thew, engraving, 1856. Shelfmark ART File F728 no.17 (<http://www.shakespeareinamericanlife.org/lg_image/008973W5_.cfm>). RIGHT: Macready: T. Sherratt after H. Tracey, engraving, 19th century. Shelfmark ART File M174.4 no.20 copy 1 (<http://www.shakespeareinamericanlife.org/lg_image/009001W5_.cfm>). Folger Shakespeare Library. Illustrations used by permission of the Folger Shakespeare Library, Creative Commons Attribution-ShareAlike 4.0 International License (CC BY-SA 4.0).

28. P. Adams, *The Bowery Boys: Street Corner Radicals and the Politics of Rebellion* (Westport, CT: Praeger, 2005), 39–45; R. Zecker, *Metropolis: The American City in Popular Culture* (Westport, CT: Praeger, 2008), 25–26.

29. Zecker, *Metropolis,* 25–26. The parallels with Hebdige's *Subculture: The Meaning of Style* (1979)—one of the most influential of Hawkes's *New Accents* series—are clear.

30. Adams, *The Bowery Boys,* 42–43.

31. Ibid.

32. *Encyclopaedia Americana,* 1920. Archived at Wikisource: (<https://en.wikisource.org/wiki/The_Encyclopedia_Americana_(1920)/Astor_Place_Riot>).

33. Wood engraving. Shelfmark ART File N567.7 no.2 (<http://www.shakespeareinamericanlife.org/lg_image/008979_l.cfm>). Folger Shakespeare Library. Used by permission of the Folger Shakespeare Library, Creative Commons Attribution-ShareAlike 4.0 International License (CC BY-SA 4.0).

34. S. Lukasik, "Military Service, Combat, and American Identity in the Progressive Era," PhD Dissertation (Duke University, 2008), 84 (<http://dukespace.lib.duke.edu/dspace/bitstream/handle/10161/909/D_LUKASIK_SEBASTIAN_a_200812.pdf>).

35. "7th New York Militia," *Wikipedia.* <https://en.wikipedia.org/wiki/7th_New_York_Militia>

36. Editor's "Introduction", *Twentieth Century Interpretations of Macbeth,* edited by Terence Hawkes, Englewood Cliffs, NJ: Prentice-Hall (1977), 11.

37. I. Butler, "*The Tragedie of Scar, King of Pride Rock:* The Shakespearean grandeur of The Lion King's villain," *The Slate Culturebox,* 2014 (<http://www

.slate.com/articles/arts/culturebox/2014/06/the_lion_king_20th_anniversary_
scar_is_a_great_shakespearean_villain.html>).

38. Alfredo Michel Modenessi, "Disney's 'war efforts': *The Lion King* and Education for death, or Shakespeare made easy for your apocalyptic convenience." *Ilha do Desterro: Journal of English Language, Literature in English and Cultural Studies* 49 (2005), 397–415: 404–5. (<https://periodicos.ufsc.br/index.php/de sterro/issue/view/651>).

39. Terence Hawkes, "*Coronation Street* of the Soul." *New Statesman,* April 7, 2003: http://www.newstatesman.com/node/157436. This piece is Hawkes's review of Stephanie Nolen's *Shakespeare's Face* (London: Piatkus, 2003). The internal quotations are from the book under review.

40. Hawkes, "*Coronation Street* of the Soul."

"Theatre is a temple to memory": Terry Hawkes and the Cardiff School

MARION WYNNE-DAVIES

OCTOBER, 1976. It was the second week of the first-year Renaissance Drama course at Cardiff University and I was a conventional 17-year-old listening to my very unconventional professor, Terence Hawkes, as he explained that "theatre is a temple to memory."[1] As a conscientious student, I took detailed notes, including the direct quotation used in the title of this essay. However, it was not diligence that made me preserve those neatly penned transcripts for almost forty years; instead, it was Terry's innovative ideas, theoretically informed arguments and inspiring tone that made me realize, even as a callow student, how important his teaching was for me and for a whole generation of scholars. As such, this essay serves as a tribute to Terry Hawkes the teacher. It traces the ways in which Terry employed cutting-edge scholarship with regard to performance space; pioneered the use of theory when analyzing plays by a range of dramatists, including Shakespeare, Jonson, and Marlowe; and motivated his students. As such, this essay argues that Terry's teaching transformed early modern studies in universities across the United Kingdom and beyond, creating the vibrant and influential "Cardiff School."

In the 1970s, most British university professors were very traditional. In English studies many of them remained faithful to a certain brand of liberal humanism and, as such, they taught their students how to read texts in order to uncover universal truths and to impart moral values. Moreover, they never questioned issues of race, class, gender, or sexuality, since all differences could be dismissed as simply aspects of a timeless and universal human nature. From the very start, Terry was different. Instead of telling us what to think, he made sure that we understood the importance of both

"talking and listening," an argument that had been the cornerstone
of his second book, *Shakespeare's Talking Animals* (1973). This
concept was also essential to our understanding of early modern
plays in performance: drama that was "spoken" by the actors and
"heard" by the audience. But, his words also served as a timely
reminder that his students should be "listening" to him "speak"
because that was how we would learn to think differently. Indeed,
I'm not sure Terry would have approved of me writing down his
words so that they could be read so many years later. But I am glad
that I did, because they made me think then and, as I have reread
my notes for the purposes of this essay, I have learned afresh the
impact that those lectures had on my own teaching.

Overall, those first weeks of the Renaissance Drama course were
intended to challenge our presumptions about early modern theater and to introduce us to an array of theoretical approaches that
served to expose the political discourses underpinning our conventional expectations. This is why Terry foregrounded the importance
of memory, explaining to us that while we came from a world of
readers and writers, the Elizabethans were a semiliterate society, so
that for them "talking . . . listening . . . [and] remembering" were
the primary conveyors of signification. Recollection therefore had
a more potent role in oral cultures: the primarily non-literate early
modern audience relied upon memory; the actor presents "memory
as an artistic form"; and thus the "distracted globe" of the mind is
replicated in, and indivisibly linked to, the plays that were enacted
on the Globe's stage.

Therefore, before undertaking a close analysis of individual
plays, Terry provided us with an introduction to Elizabethan theater and to the concept of what he and experimental theatrical practitioners were then calling "theatre in the round." He demanded
that we recognize the difference between the solitary process of
reading and the communal activity of a live audience, especially
when confronted with a thrust stage in a circular house, allowing
the actors to move about, "turning from and towards an audience
as one does in actual conversation," rather than marching across
the rectangular rostrum like words printed across the page of a
book. Such observations seem conventional enough today, yet it is
important to recall that the Swan Theatre in Stratford-Upon-Avon
would not open until 1986 and the Globe in London until 1997.
Even looking beyond these "Shakespearean" examples, in 1976
very few theaters were able to replicate the participatory dynamic

of the early modern stage: Britain's first "theater in the round" was founded by Stephen Joseph on the first floor of the public library in Scarborough (1955); in 1969–70 the Cockpit Theatre opened in Marylebone in what was the first purpose-built theater in the round in London since the great fire of 1666; in 1971 what is now the Orange Tree Theatre was founded by Sam Walters above the Orange Tree Pub in Richmond. Which of these theaters had Terry visited and what productions had he seen by 1976? Perhaps he had seen an American production at one of the several venues that had developed along the guidelines drawn up by Margo Jones in her influential *Theatre in the Round* (1951); for example, Jones's own Theatre '47 in Dallas; theaters in Pasadena, New York, Seattle, and Washington, D.C.; as well as via Albert McCleery's television series Cameo Theatre. Whatever Terry had seen, few–if any–of the students listening to his 1976 lecture had any experience of the rediscovered staging pragmatics of early modern theater. At the same time, Terry had no intention of allowing us to believe that we could reconstruct for ourselves the experience of the late sixteenth- and early seventeenth-century audiences. Rather, it was essential that a new generation of scholars should be shocked out of their complacent proscenium stage sensibilities.

Imagine, then: it is our third lecture and already ten minutes past the hour, which leaves us, a group of bewildered undergraduates, gazing at an empty stage and wondering why our professor is late. Suddenly, we hear Terry's urgent summons coming from behind us and, as we crane around to see him at the back of the lecture hall, he explains how a circular theater was able to represent both the microcosm of the mind and the macrocosm of the world. Then, as he strolls down one of the side aisles, he explains that the movement of the actor in and about the audience denaturalized the play, demonstrating that any links between stage, mind, and world were constructed. After all, he reminds us, regaining the podium and raising his arms as if to draw two curtains together, on a stage with no drapes "dead players just had to get up and walk off" in full view of the audience. And that was a quintessential Hawkes lecture. There was no dry and methodical history of the theater. Rather, students were shocked out of their certainties through a combination of cutting-edge knowledge of production techniques, the rejection of realism and all the ideological certainties that it implied, and finally, by the material evidence provided by Terry's own "staging" of theater in the round. It was only week three, but

English students at Cardiff were already learning to question assumptions, to look for new and polemical ideas and to take nothing for granted.

Throughout the Elizabethan Drama course and the lectures Terry gave over the three years of our degree we continued to develop the methodologies necessary for questioning traditional assumptions about literature, art and, above all, early modern theater. As John Drakakis wrote in *The Guardian* obituary of Terry, "he championed the radical, oppositional potential of both high art and popular culture."[2] This opposition was transmitted to his students alongside a raft of theoretical perspectives: Marxism, structuralism and semiotics, feminism, postcolonial studies, queer theory, and Bakhtinian readings. Today such a list reads like the contents page of a theory reader, but in 1976, it proved a radical challenge to the conventions of academia.

Of all the theories employed by Terry in those 1970s lectures, Marxism was, unsurprisingly, the most prevalent. He drew our attention to the social upheavals of the early seventeenth century: the way Elizabethan society "felt itself pulled between two worlds" (*Hamlet*); "the rise of the mercantile middle class" (*The Alchemist*); "the conflict [embedded in] the Protestant religion and capitalism" (*Tamburlaine*); and the role of the "landlord and master" (*The Tempest*). But Hawkes made it clear that not all dramatists sought to question the dominant hierarchy and, if Marlowe was a "revolutionary," then Jonson's writing was "a statement of conservatism in the face of a great social upheaval." The lecture on *Tamburlaine* took as its premise that all Marlowe's protagonists are "revolutionaries who rise up against their society and are punished." This yearning for power represented the growing influence of individualism, Machiavellianism. and capitalism on Elizabethan society, although just as Tamburlaine's victories must be seen as successful advancement in monetary and class terms, they would also have been recognized as against God's will. Moreover, if Tamburlaine, like all Marlowe's protagonists, must suffer for his revolutionary zeal, Hawkes reminded us that, while the Scythian shepherd dies at the end of part II, this is "the only loss he can incur"—a tragic death that "places him outside the Christian framework." There can be no question that Terry reveled in the sheer audacity and virtuoso linguistic skill of Marlowe's plays. Indeed, perhaps that verbal sensitivity explains his carefully structured consideration of the more learned dramatist, Ben Jonson.

Although even in *The Alchemist* lecture Terry was—no other word for it—theatrical.

If we had been surprised by the lecture in week three, we were completely baffled by that in week seven. It began with Terry standing center stage, lighting a match, holding it up for all of us to see, and then allowing the flame to flare, dwindle, and go out. Such was the stuff of alchemy. How, like the Elizabethans before us, could we tell if it represented the bright light of "knowledge" or if it exposed a fast-fading fraud? For Ben Jonson, Terry argued, the alchemist was a charlatan who revealed the fraudulent nature of a money-based society, although a more complex reading suggested that the play conveyed more than the simple moral message, "it is bad to lust after money." In order to excavate further, Terry asked us to "translate it [alchemy] into human terms" because then—a pause—"we might believe in it." He pointed out:

> all human beings contain a quintessence [so] that if their outside elements can be reduced . . . everyone is the same as everyone else . . . Alchemy is education; the alchemist is the teacher. His raw material can be broken down and reassembled to produce gold. Noble metal. True nobility can be achieved by everyone.

Here was Marxism in action: not only a challenge to the class system, but a powerful endorsement of the postwar Labour government's commitment to expand educational opportunities, a validation of the role of universities and—perhaps best of all—the recognition of our own part in that drama. Terry had presented himself as the alchemist-teacher who brought the light of knowledge to his students so that our "raw material[s]" could be "broken down" and transmuted into "gold." Then, damning Jonson as a "conservative," we were told that the dramatist thought such ambitions to be "against nature . . . a disruptive force . . . new, modern and hateful . . . [because they] had democratic overtones." The allusion to twentieth-century British politics was hard to miss and, while those pre-Thatcher years hardly seemed to call for class warfare, young people were increasingly disillusioned and rebellious; after all, the Sex Pistols' debut single *Anarchy in the UK* was released on November 26, 1976, within weeks of lecture seven. This is important because Terry's lectures not only gave us a set of processes that could be used to deconstruct a literary text, they made those methodologies—and, so the works themselves—

sharply relevant to our own lives; we understood Tamburlaine because like him (and the Sex Pistols) we wanted "anarchy."

I hesitate here, since it would be wrong to suggest Terry was a hardline Marxist indoctrinating his students and working towards "the revolution." Indeed, Terry's teaching sought to dispel the idea that there was a single theory of literature, language, society, or human existence that could lay claim to be "the truth." For example, the lectures on Marlowe's *Edward II* used what we would now term queer theory to uncover the "potential revolutionary state" offered by a play in which the protagonist is seen both as "a threat to society" (homosexual) and yet, at the same time, as a figure of ultimate authority (the king). And, of course, since the body of the king must be both private (the individual) and public (the state), Edward's sexuality and subsequent suffering cannot be marginalized as "other." A similar focus upon difference was made in the lecture on *Othello,* where Terry chose again to emphasize how the protagonist and what he represents cannot easily be rejected by society. On one side, Othello is an ostracized character: his color makes him "different," and he is similarly "isolated . . . a stranger . . . [with] no family" in Venice. But it is important to remember that Othello chooses his role in life; he hasn't inherited his position, as does Hamlet, and so is simultaneously constrained by societal expectations and liberated by social mobility. Perhaps, Terry suggested, *Othello* explores the ways in which race is used not only to define identity, but also to show how appearance operates as a classifier that both encompasses and extends beyond the color of one's skin. A parallel reading informed Terry's lecture on *The Tempest,* although this time it also employed what we would come to recognize—post Stephen Greenblatt's 1980's *Renaissance Self-Fashioning*—as a new form of "historicism." In hindsight, it is important to recognize the divergences between the American school of New Historicism and the more politically radical British Cultural Materialism. In the 1980s Terry undoubtedly favored cultural materialism—as his 1976 lectures already indicate—since they encouraged his students to work for and believe in the possibility of social change. At the same time, his focus upon historical evidence allows us to identify the beginnings of both American and British historicist theory. As such, Prospero was identified as the landlord and master of plantations (both Ulster and Virginia), while Caliban was seen to characterize the aboriginal slave (tenant/ servant). Terry discussed Thomas Gates's adventure and William

Strachey's well-known 1609 account of it, as well as explaining how enclosures had increased, with the consequent rise in the number of beggars, thieves or, in present-day terms, the unemployed. Topping it off, we learned that Shakespeare, whose similarity to Prospero is usually based upon their artistic prowess, had on July 24, 1605 spent £440 on a half-interest in tithes from Old Stratford, Bishopston, and Welcombe, aligning him on the side of master rather than slave. In each instance, Terry was introducing us to theories—sexual, racial and postcolonial—well ahead of other scholars and, from the reaction of some of the other lecturers at Cardiff, we understood that our learning was both radical and controversial.

Yet, although we were Terry's students, we were not blind devotees. Nor would he have wished to school a band of acolytes, since arguing and welcoming difference of opinion was central to the Hawkesian approach. Indeed, he always appreciated a challenge and seemed delighted when I disagreed with the conclusion to the lecture on *Love's Labour's Lost*. The session began with useful reading material on comedy as a genre: this included Neville Coghill's essay "The Basis of Shakespearean Comedy" (1950), Northrop Frye's *Anatomy of Criticism* (1957), and Mikhail Bakhtin's *Rabelais and His World* (1968).[3] From these Terry drew strands that he would subsequently interweave into his own theoretical position: from Coghill came the focus upon the traditional oral comedy found in Shakespeare's plays, and from Frye, the importance of the "green world" that allows the action to move cyclically from the flawed innocence of the old world, through the confused experience of the present, to the possibility of a combined innocence and experience in the future, where problems are solved through marriage and the invocation of renewed fertility. But it was his use of Bakhtin that enthralled me, since Terry located Elizabethan comedy in the traditional folk festivals that allowed the power of carnival to overthrow the constraints of hierarchies—social, religious, and gendered. From these critical foundations, the lecture proceeded with a set of dualities:

court/city	country
nurture	nature
everyday	holiday
reason	intuition
literacy	orality

Yet, Terry argued, those columns could not do justice to the cyclical power of performance, since "theatre is the place, mode and scheme of renovation" and since it is an "oral artifact" it cannot help but bring about regeneration. We were encouraged to identify both Coghill's and Frye's definitions of comedy, and to see that the literacy and learning of the gentlemen from the court appear to be set against, and transformed by, the orality and intuitive under-standing of love demonstrated by the ladies. As such, Terry argued, the irony of *Love's Labour's Lost* is that "the men who study books are eventually caught out by the reality they assume they have been reading about," and that the play enacts a "comic reversal" in that "women first usurp and then become the books they have usurped." These are almost direct quotes from *Shakespeare's Talking Animals:*

> The fundamental irony the play explores is that those who confine themselves to books, and to book-language, end up by being paradoxi-cally and wittily "caught out" by ordinary human language in its wid-est sense . . . It also leads, inevitably and naturally, to the comic "reversal" at the play's core, in which women first usurp, and then met-aphorically *become* the books which the "book-men" admire.[4]

There is a certain slippage caused perhaps by Terry's rephrasing or my own inadequate note taking, but the central argument hinges on the male scholars coming to appreciate that book learning is no substitute for the regenerative—and "fertile"—interaction with women. What I disagreed with then, and still disagree with now, is the way in which Terry interpreted the play as objectifying women as books—even if they are *metaphorical* books—and apparently presenting an uncomplicated link between women and nature. Although it was only six years since the first UK WLM (Women's Liberation Movement) conference had been held in Oxford, by 1976 young women considered themselves feminists, campaigned for equal pay and abortion on demand, read *Spare Rib* and, yes, really did call one another "sister." One of the most powerful argu-ments of 1970s feminism was that women's roles were constructed and that so-called feminine attributes needed to be challenged. It is hardly surprising, therefore, that I found it difficult to agree whole-heartedly with Terry's lecture. In particular, I was uncomfortable with a reading that seemed to base its argument on the association of women with nature and yet did not complicate that interpretation. Perhaps I am being unfair, but it seemed to me then that Terry was more than ready to countenance social change if it related to class, but that he was not as familiar with emerging feminist criticism. Unsurprisingly, therefore, when the lecture supported political transformation Terry used Bakhtinian theory in demonstrating how the old hierarchies could be overthrown through comic inversion; he had not used the Russian theorist's work in *Shakespeare's Talking Animals,* which was published in 1973, but would go on to use Bakhtin in *That Shakespeherian Rag* in 1986. So, while I still disagree with that 1976 lecture, I admire how Terry allowed research to inform his teaching, how he treated first-years on a par with his fellow academics and, primarily, how he refused to stop thinking and revising his ideas. If it was Frye who had caught his attention in 1973, then we can judge, from his lectures, that by 1976 he was already working with Bakhtinian theories—again well ahead of the scholarship of his day. From theater in the round, through Marxism, theories on sexuality and race, postcolonialism, new historicism and, yes, eventually, feminism, Terry "spoke" to his students about new ways to think, see, understand and "listen."

Indeed, those of us who went on to become university teachers not only listened: we also remembered. When I look at my own lecture notes, now prepared on Powerpoint slides, Terry's inspiration is manifest. Let me give an example: *Hamlet and the Bucket.* "What," I ask at the start of the lecture, "can a simple bucket have to do with one of the most complex plays ever written?" At this point, I pass around a plain metal bucket and ask the students to take one of the sheets of paper from inside and read out what they have: madness, death, revenge, corpse, murder, incest, and so forth. I ask them to keep the slips safe and then proceed with a reading of the play informed by psychoanalytic theory (Judith Butler), performance (Doran's 2008 version for the RSC) and history (the sad tale of Katherine Hamlet who drowned in the Avon). The answer to my first question is that if you go to a river with a bucket, as did Katherine Hamlet, and then drown, it will have been by accident—in other words you are not mad—because you were clearly intending to come back with a pale full of water. The bucket, therefore, represents rationality. At the end of the lecture I tell them that if they have "heard" me "speak" their word, then they should replace their slip of paper in the bucket as it is passed around. And, of course, if they have been listening carefully they *will* have heard me talk of all the key terms represented on the slips of paper. Then, as the last sheet drops into my aluminum pail, I remind my students that buckets are important since they symbolize what is rational and, therefore, stand between us and madness, or revenge, or murder and so on. As a last piece of advice, I suggest that if they intend to wander along a riverbank, even if they are searching for flowers or climbing trees, they would be well advised to take a bucket with them. As I give this lecture every autumn as part of the first-year Shakespeare module, I remember what inspired it—the famous "match lecture"—and, as I recall Terry's words, I hope that my students will similarly be motivated by the "bucket lecture."

To conclude here, however, I would like to quote Terry not from my lecture notes but from the Acknowledgements section in *Shakespeare's Talking Animals* (viii):

> Finally, I must thank my own students at Cardiff, their amiable scepticism ever the best antidote for overweening confidence. They will discover that they are still owed a book worthy of them.

It is the modest and not the overweening teacher who thanks his pupils and, more importantly, it is those students who owe Professor Terence Hawkes many thanks—and many more books that are worthy of him.

Notes

1. All quotations from Professor Terence Hawkes's lectures are taken from my own lecture notes.

2. John Drakakis, "Terence Hawkes obituary," *The Guardian,* February 21, 2014, http://www.theguardian.com/education/2014/feb/21/terence-hawkes

3. See Neville Coghill, "The Basis of Shakespearean Comedy," *Essays and Studies* 3 (1950): 1–28; Northrop Frye, *Anatomy of Criticism* (Princeton, NJ: Princeton University Press, 1957); and Mikhail Bakhtin, *Rabelais and His World,* trans. Helene Iswolsky (Cambridge MA: MIT Press, 1968). Although Iswolsky's translation of *Rabelais and His World* was published in 1968, it was only in 1975 that Francophone and English-speaking scholars began to use Bakhtinian theory.

4. Terence Hawkes, *Shakespeare's Talking Animals* (London: Edward Arnold, 1973), 62–63.

The Importance of Being Impudent

LINDA CHARNES

SOMETIME DURING THE 1980S AND EARLY 1990S (during my time "coming up" in the profession), it seemed as if much of the fun to be had in the enterprise of literary scholarship went missing. In what I have elsewhere referred to as "the Methodology wars," the agendas of various critical approaches were serious business.[1] Cheekiness in scholarly work was rarely encouraged and even more rarely embraced. Wit (of a sort) was permitted, in the way that, say, the Cavalier poets or John Donne used it: cerebrally and preferably wearing a cummerbund. Wit deployed in the context of vanquishing a critical opponent was especially prized. I suspect that few of us were entirely innocent of this kind of sparring (I certainly wasn't, as my early wit cracking against the always intelligent whipping boy of the "young Turks," Richard Levin, demonstrated). If one wanted to be cheeky it was most acceptable when showing how someone else, of a different theoretical stripe, was wrong-headed, a living dinosaur, or—heaven forfend—a Formalist or a *New Critic*. Wit for its own sake was usually (not always wrongly) dismissed as a substitute for careful critical thought, a privileging of attitude over substance. Throughout my years in graduate school, I worked hard to keep my impulse toward cheek in check, and to embed my critical writing in what I regarded as a different, more "serious" mental place. After all, I was doing my doctoral work at UC Berkeley, the early manse of what later came to be called "the New Historicism."

For scholars motivated by an Oedipal imperative to knock their critical forefathers off the mountaintop, establishing critical authority was paramount. At UC Berkeley in the late 1980s, Renaissance Studies was definitely serious business. Methodological boundaries and territories were being established and fiefdoms encouraged, directly or indirectly. In order to practice our critical

101

methods "responsibly," the boundaries of Period also had to be reinforced, since Geertzian synchronic cultural anthropology had been adopted by scholars such as Stephen Greenblatt and the categories of what could be considered a readable text expanded greatly. The fact that such widely synchronic reading worked perfectly well with the temporal categories organized in the Norton Anthology enabled the New Historicism to leave literary periodicity intact, even as it pushed the borders of "the literary" far into new textual hinterlands. I believe that these developments were overwhelmingly salutary. The notion that literary work of any kind existed solely within the bubble of an author's mind was definitively laid to rest—and rightly so. The Old Formalism (qualifier needed since a more theoretically astute version, known as the "new" Formalism, driven in part by a Lacanian notion of "dreamwork," has since emerged) made little sense in a scholarly environment that was making its first major forays into institutional interdisciplinarity.

That many bona fide historians balked at the New Historicism was irrelevant for most of us. History had the cultural imprimatur of being the most objective of humanist disciplines, and literary studies needed some of that caché to ward off an impression of elitism—of being an outmoded and impractical "gentleman's discipline." This was the best—not worst—of times for literary scholarship; the method wars revived a sense of the urgency and value of what we were doing. Cultural issues mattered and not merely as background. Alongside the protestors' shantytowns against South African apartheid springing up on college campuses were new programs that began to recognize the tremendous contributions of African-American scholars to the "canon" of western literature. Stakes were to be had in every form of cultural text and discourse; ideology critique reached well beyond Althusser and earlier forms of "crude Marxism," and literary criticism could be poststructuralist as well as post-Marxist.

In the United States, such scholarship broadly adopted a Foucauldian model of power, providing the means both of critiquing the master's house and of keeping its foundations and walls intact. For at least two decades thereafter, ideology critique mattered, as there were deep oppressive structures to be unmasked even in the most innocuous-seeming social and political norms, as well as in the obviously oppressive realms of gender, sexuality, race, and class. Representation became the primary field for mobilizing these critiques, at least within departments of English, Comparative Literature, and Art History. The work produced during these decades was exciting, frequently brilliant, and changed the trajectory of critical work in the future.

Even acknowledging the excitement of those decades bridging the end of the twentieth century, frequently sacrificed to the high-stakes seriousness in our critical enterprise was an awareness of the constitutive uses of "play": of self-satire, self-irony and most importantly, the sheer delight in a personal critical writing *style.* These took a back seat to the all-important imperatives to a) always historicize and b) always demystify. The idea of style as anything other than garnish was anathema, the privileging of the sensibilities of the author over the text. Stylish writing could be appreciated, but not as an *engine* of critique. There were of course, Roland Barthes and (slightly less fun) Derrida; but then there were the rest of us. In Renaissance Studies (a field that boasted Rabelais and Cervantes), subversive *humor*—a word both reductive and trivialized—was rarely encouraged.

Over time however, critical rebels grow older and often replace their former nemeses. Those who as young scholars wanted nothing more than to vanquish critical forefathers have ascended their thrones, and now look back anew at those they chafed against, rediscovering things of value. Case in point: Stephen Greenblatt succeeded M. H. Abrams as General Editor of the Norton Anthology. That Greenblatt himself, in 1982, would have scoffed at the idea that this would come to pass is immaterial. Time changes us all; and the awareness of our intellectual limitations sometimes curbs our hubris and situates us in a more straight line with our forebears. However, I come not to bury Caesar but to praise Diogenes of Synope. For if Shakespeare Studies ever had a Diogenes, he was without a doubt Terence Hawkes.

Hawkes (Terry to his friends and colleagues) taught me—a young graduate student when I first discovered his work—two invaluable things: how to read backwards, and the creative importance of being *impudent.* In Terry's brilliant work, reading in all temporal directions at once was intellectually valuable, professionally substantial, deeply learned and—most importantly—*fun.* Few of his peers in Renaissance literature and Shakespeare Studies wrote with his combination of political commitment and playful dynamism. Hawkes's work grew from an organic temperament composed of irreverence for received critical bromides, as well as a

Birmingham-grown gimlet-eyed view of the category of "English Literature" writ large. Add in the uses of Shakespeare in the "making of an English gentleman" and the socially disastrous Thatcher years, and Terry became a *sui generis* critical sensibility who was never afraid to challenge the pieties, either of British and American culture or the Academy.[2] How did he manage to maintain his unique critical voice while others seemed so pressed to follow the contemporary "rules of the road"? I believe his lack of fear was an inevitable byproduct of his lack of interest in setting himself up as a leader of any particular methodological school. The last thing that Terry Hawkes wanted was to be a proselytizer or an "institution" in himself and he resisted it during his long and distinguished career. To the contrary, the more distinguished Terry Hawkes became, the more he bent his efforts as a booster of others' work, especially that of new generations of scholars, as his General Editorship of Routledge's *New Accents* series and later, *Accents on Shakespeare* series during the late 1990s–2010 demonstrates. "Ax on Shax," as it came to be known among those of us who published in his series, showcased the unorthodox, the fresh, the irreverent, the *foudre,* and the cheeky. All the titles published in his series were learned and substantial works of scholarship; but they were also outliers, by people interested in exploring the interesting peripheries of the field with the aim of making them more central, or at least a crucial part of the bigger picture.

What can be said definitively is that Terry Hawkes was first, last, and always a cultural materialist: his post-Marxist sensibility permeated everything he wrote, and especially his awareness of the invidious—if not insidious—political uses of Bardolatry. The Hawkes difference was that even as he worked alongside his fellow cultural materialists—Jonathan Dollimore, Catherine Belsey, Alan Sinfield, and John Drakakis (among others), Terry never relinquished his sense that wit and wordplay could take critique to fresh places; that ideology critique without play could lead not only to boredom but eventually run out of things to demystify. His sensibility was prophetic; much critical writing in the 1990s did become formulaic and knee-jerk, the critical observations repetitive and moralistic.

In the first chapter of his recent book *Shakespeare in the Present,* entitled "The Heimlich Maneuvre," Terry doubles down on the form of criticism he had always practiced, dedicated to ferreting out the "unheimlich," the return of the very phenomena that historicism wished to embed in the past.[3] Urging the importance of reading texts of any period in the stark light of the present, Terry made a case for criticism as a "creative genre in its own right." He writes against the artificial separation of scholarly analysis and creative uses of the past—no matter how irreverent—in order to intervene in the here and now. He calls what he is doing a "homeless 'hooligan' criticism," one that "must eventually subscribe to a morality" that is not based on ultimate "true judgment, or worse, the soul-gelding aridity of *quellenforschung* (investigation of sources)"(20–21). This was the impulse that I channeled in the introduction to my first book, *Notorious Identity,* in 1993, in which I took on the imperative to choose one method over another and instead announced that I would be practicing a "Theory without Organs," or a "principled New Hystericism," a method that exploited the interstices of multiple theoretical frameworks.[4] Although it was frightening at the time for a newbie to make such a declaration, I regarded critical unorthodoxy as a creative response to textual analysis at a time when it seemed that even the best of literary criticism was in danger of calcifying. My approach at that time earned me a few knuckle rappings. One prominent senior colleague who reviewed my book in a major journal called my approach "impudent"—it was not meant positively. It would take some years before I learned to wear "impudence" as a badge of honor, as a kindred affiliation with Terry Hawkes.

But the "impudence" of a "hooligan' criticism" begs serious questions about how to generate work that is usable by, and transmissible to, other scholars, and especially to our graduate students. One answer to that question is that a cheeky attitude toward institutional methodologies was never meant as a *repudiation* of the historical conditions of textual production and reception, nor was it ever a privileging of any particular critics' artsy sensibility. Rather, it was about ferreting out the potential cheek in the work itself. After all, how many of us would dispute that most of Shakespeare's best plays are, in many ways, "impudent"?

Cheekiness in a grounded intellect becomes a philosophical disposition, an epistemological mode of exploration, a substantive form of analysis, one with a long tradition. In his landmark book *A Critique of Cynical Reason,* Peter Sloterdijk makes a central distinction between kynicism in the tradition of Diogenes of Synope, and the world weary, gimlet-eyed, shruggy cynicism that he argues underlay Enlightenment critiques. Cynicism, Sloterdijk writes, is "the universally widespread way in which enlightened people see to it that they are not taken for suckers."[5] We may not agree with his portrait of "present-day cynics" as "borderline melancholics"; but it would hard to gainsay him when he points out that today's enlightened cynics are among the most highly productive of the intellectual elite:

> The key social positions in boards, parliaments, commissions, executive counsels, *publishing companies,* practices, faculties, and lawyers' and editors' offices have long since become a part of this diffuse cynicism. A certain chic bitterness provides an undertone to its activity. . . . Their psychic apparatus has become elastic enough to incorporate as a survival factor a permanent doubt about their own activities.[6] (Italics his)

This ontological disposition Sloterdijk calls "enlightened false consciousness," the signal feature of contemporary cynicism. Although his critique was written at the end of the twentieth century, it is perhaps even more apropos today (although thankfully there are new investments in concerns with animal and human rights and global crises that cannot be characterized this way). I have written extensively about Sloterdijk elsewhere;[7] but in critical scholarship, at least in Renaissance studies, the turn of the century saw even the sharpest of ideology critiques arguably hit their walls. If everywhere one looks there is only power, masked and trussed up, there can only be demystifications and deconstructions, a disposition toward analysis that ultimately becomes boilerplate and leads us nowhere new.

The opposite of cynical practice (and I would argue that any work that aims *solely* to demystify partakes of Sloterdijk's particular use of the term) is not naiveté or idealism. The end of the century (and first decade of this one) made any brand of idealism impossible to endorse without making oneself a tool of structures that were still recalcitrant and ossified. So what would the opposite of an "enlightened" cynical ideology critique look like, and how would we know it? Perhaps precisely by its re-investment in *style,* one that Terry Hawkes modeled, one that offered a powerful "delivery device" for the content of any particular analysis he wrote. There is style as parody, style as camp, style as farce, and style as mere window dressing. But there is also what I would argue is *constitutive* style. Lacan deployed it, as did Derrida and Barthes, Sloterdijk and Žižek (admittedly with various degrees of success). In such writing, style is a mode of intervention, one that bypasses the limits of syllogistic argument and a purely didactic method.

Terry Hawkes's writing had precisely this constitutive style. It was simultaneously serious, learned, topical, often angry, yet usually playful and always cheeky. Cheekiness itself is a stylistic form of challenge. In his chapter called "In Search of Lost Cheek," Sloterdijk defines Diogenistic kynicism as the philosophical foundation of constructive (not destructive) cheek.[8] For Terry Hawkes, cheekiness was never cynical, nor did it ever "change sides." In a section in *Shakespeare in the Present,* titled "Easily Freudened," Terry argues that a "homeless" criticism can be an antidote to (quoting Edward Said) an "aggressive sense of nation, home, community, and belonging."[9] Only by writing from a position of "homelessness" can one uncover the uncanny, the place beyond established boundaries, whether of period, field, method, or even geographical place. What is the value of such an approach? It repudiates what Hawkes called "Michel Foucault's disingenuous statement that the hierarchical relationship primary/secondary, text/commentary is permanent, regardless of the nature of the documents that take on these functions."[10] This is a most serious criticism of Foucault's work, which although it recognized that such hieratic relations were often unstable, nonetheless usually returned to a differentiation between primary and secondary as a fundamental relationship of power and domination. To my mind (and I realize this is arguable), the eternal return to the structure of hierarchy was a serious flaw in Foucault's sensibility, no matter how much his work tried to dodge it; and the adoption of Foucault as central to new historicism left that method—which ruled in the United States academy from at least 1990–2005—subject to the same stasis, a predictable return of the same. It was this perpetual structural return that Terry worked to counter—that he *did* counter.

Impudence or cheekiness is, among other things, an irritant. It provokes: the questions it poses are potentially mocking of anyone unwilling to entertain questioning as the foundation of critical enterprise. Cheekiness is an intellectual disposition, one that sees through things but is not content to stop at anatomizing. The impulse to anatomize texts critically, to uncover and lay bare everything until a text is as dormant as anything on a coroner's table, was probably the inevitable result of several decades of *unmasking,* unmasking without remaking, uncreating without creating. Quite apart from the issue of how to engage texts creatively, the danger here was a critical methodology that also severely limited the reach and use of its own enterprise. I have written elsewhere about this problem, a failure to create critical futures to replace adherence to a largely factitious (as Terry often argued) fidelity to "period" or field "mastery."

The very notion of "mastering" a field of literary study was anathema to Terry Hawkes, symptomatic of an increasingly lifeless, futureless approach to texts that rendered them moribund for political and social intervention in the present. The term "Presentism" arose, after all, as a derogatory dismissal of work on earlier historical periods that superficially put texts to the service of the "here and now." The "ism" was an inherent dismissal of a new approach that insisted that "the past" is in fact always with us in some form: that perhaps four hundred years ago is not such a long time away from our own world, since neither cultures nor history move in lockstep and theories of uneven development have shown the ways things once considered atavistic (Roman Gladiator games) continue in the present in variable form (from football to the World Wrestling Federation). Deep cultural structures rarely disappear along with the fantasy of a march of "progress." The idea of the "unheimlich" is obviously central to this enterprise, because it connotes the unease with the "familiar," or the productively creepy—in that uncanny but also crab-like sense, that there is something not quite settled in its temporal relationship either to a particular time or place. Something, maybe, that refuses to "stay home."

Although Terry Hawkes was always first a Midlands Englishman of working-class background, he was also keenly aware of the political and cultural entanglements of being British. That he refused to subsume his entire critical identity into temporal "thick" description, while nonetheless always addressing historical events and their contemporary fallout, is indicative of the gadfly role he embraced over his entire career, from his profoundly cheeky and preposterous chapter on the importance of reading backwards —"Telmah"—in *That Shakespeherian Rag,* to the chapters in *Shakespeare in the Present,* which toggle seamlessly between contemporary events, historical instances, and textual anomalies. Not in the interests of asserting an ego or air of critical superiority but rather, in the interests of chronically, and diachronically, staying "fresh." That he did so while maintaining a constant stylistic critical voice is not merely to note someone who was a wonderful writer (although he was) but to point out the investment Terry had in style as intervention. To proffer a signature writerly voice during the early decades of the "death of the author" was an act of daring, one that few had the courage or commitment to maintain.

Cheekiness—the importance of being impudent—had serious literary and cultural consequences for Terry, as he tapped into the long intellectual history of satire and witty writing as a viable intellectual critique of existing society. For instance, the aforementioned chapter he called "Telmah." This essay, which explored both the links between Dover Wilson's scholarship and the social institutions of post-Weimar Europe, while also invoking jazz as his critical scaffolding, was a revelation: by reading the temporality of "events" in *Hamlet* backwards, Terry uncovered the deep structures of Thatcherite educational regimes in Britain. The cheeky title was a bait but not merely a bait; and it brought him from Fortinbras's takeover of a dying Denmark to the emergence of black Jazz on the American music scene. The end of the essay linked them through an outrageous pun: Fortinbras backwards is another way of saying (Louis) Armstrong. The main thrust of that essay was always toward his present cultural moment. Not just "clever" but funny; not just playful but impudent. He broke rules of critical engagement, yet ended up creating substantial new ground for analysis.

"Telmah" was a model of how to avoid stepping into the concrete overshoes of one "serious academic method" at the expense of all others. For me, a graduate student in 1986, reading *That Shakespeherian Rag* was a revelation. The performative work of his approach was proof of the intellectual value of wit and play and style and cheek, and his work offered an alternative to becoming someone's acolyte or adherent, to boxing oneself in to the point of being unable, as well as unwilling, to look at everything that refused to fit into temporal boxes. Terry's writing gave me the courage to draw from everything and everyone from whom I had learned and with whom I had studied, and to follow my own critical instincts to perform theoretical recombinations.

I entered graduate school searching for something; I graduated still searching, but for something different from what I had found there. Graduate school began with an initiation to the world of "expertise." My professional career began in search of lost cheekiness. It is no accident that my first book had a press that was code for "the experts" (Harvard University Press) but an acquisitions editor committed to fresh work: Lindsay Waters. Nor that my post-tenure book, *Hamlet's Heirs: Shakespeare and the Politics of a New*

Millennium was published and edited by Terence Hawkes. Not only was Terry a prolific scholar, but he was a daring and tireless editor and promoter of the work of others, especially if he felt they had something new and brave to say. First, as an editor of Routledge's New Accents Series, and later as General Editor of the series Accents on Shakespeare, Terry worked with both seasoned scholars and those newly coming up.

My own experience of Terry as editor was marked by my profound uncertainty about an argument I was making regarding the constitutive irrationality of American politics at the end of the millennium. I had begun the project in the late 1990s; then "Indecision 2000" changed the presidential outcome in a way no one could foresee. Followed hard upon by 9/11 and the unilateral invasion of Iraq in 2003, I was certain as 2004 approached that George W. Bush would *not* be re-elected to office. I put my work on hold, prepared if not to abandon then radically to shift my arguments about ideological fantasy and the American electorate. Periodically, Terry wrote me to ask about progress. I told him that I might have to scrap the project if America awoke from its national stupor and booted W. out of office. Terry's response was invariably kind and usually something along the lines of "Apply a pint of Guinness and consider it not so deeply." However, after the 2004 election (or "re-election") of Bush, I was able to complete my arguments about Hamlet and American revenge politics. At that point, Terry—his patience stretched by my delay—told me the book had better be decent since he had waited "so bloody long" for it. The feedback he gave me was bracing, astute, at times brutal; but it was never wrong. He was extraordinarily perceptive as a reader, and every sentence benefitted from his laser eye. Terry wanted me to call it something in keeping with the Accents on Shakespeare boilerplate of "Shakespeare and . . ."; I insisted the main title had to be *Hamlet's Heirs*. He made endless fun of this. "Omelettes Errs," "Hamlet's Hares," "Amleth's Hairs," were just a few of his pet names for the project as we went over the final details. Eventually he agreed that I could call it *Hamlet's Heirs* so long as I added a post-colon Ax-on-Shax subtitle: *Shakespeare and the Politics of a New Millennium.* I think he liked the book. He called it *foudre.* I think he forgave me for being late on the deadlines. I think he understood my dilemma after 9/11. But I don't think he ever entirely forgave me for my insistence on the title *Hamlet's Heirs*—for in the rest of our correspondence, and in every conversation thereafter, he referred to the book as "Omelettes Err," guaranteeing that whatever else the consequences of that book might be, taking myself too seriously would never be one of them.

Notes

1. See Linda Charnes, *Notorious Identity: Materializing the Subject in Shakespeare* (Cambridge, MA: Harvard University Press, 1993) Introduction *passim* and *Hamlet's Heirs, Shakespeare and the Politics of a New Millennium* (New York: Routledge, 2006), chapter two: "The Fetish of 'the Modern,'" *passim*.

2. See Terence Hawkes, *That Shakespeherian Rag: Essays on a Critical Process,* esp. chapter 3: "Swisser Swatter: Making a Man of English Letters" (London: Routledge, 1986).

3. Terence Hawkes, *Shakespeare in the Present* (London and New York: Routledge, 2002).

4. Linda Charnes, *Notorious Identity,* Introduction.

5. Peter Sloterdijk, *A Critique of Cynical Reason* (Minneapolis: University of Minnesota Press, 1987), 5.

6. Ibid.

7. Charnes, *Hamlet's Heirs,* Introduction *passim*.

8. Sloterdijk, *A Critique of Cynical Reason,* 101 ff.

9. Hawkes, *Shakespeare in the Present,* 10.

10. Ibid., 11.

Muted All WITH Hawkes

HUW GRIFFITHS

Publius's Hawks

IN HIS ESSAY, "Harry Hunks, Superstar," Terry Hawkes quotes one of John Davies's wonderfully witty and satirical epigrams from the mid-to-late 1590s. In the poem, a law student named Publius puts down his books and finds himself deep in the muck of Southwark, "down among the bears and dogs":

> Publius, student of the common law,
> Oft leaves his books, and for his recreation,
> To Paris Garden doth himself withdraw,
> Where he is ravished with such delectation,
> As down among the bears and dogs he goes;
> Where, whilst he skipping cries, 'To head! To head!',
> His satin doublet and his velvet hose
> Are all with spittle from above bespread:
> When he is like his father's country hall,
> Stinking with dogs and muted all with hawks;
> And rightly on him too this filth doth fall,
> With such filthy sports his books forsakes;
> Leaving old Ployden, Dyer, Brooke alone,
> To see old Harry Hunks and Sacarson. [1]

Publius exchanges one set of proper names for another: "Ployden" for Harry Hunks; books for bears. In scholarly work, assigning a proper name to a piece of writing is everything, whether that is Ployden [sic], Plowden, or Hawkes. Careers and reputations are made and lost; ideas are exchanged and circulated, or squandered and wasted, with the proper name as the unit of currency. Or, as Karen Newman writes, "The proper name is the commodity fetish of individualism, presumed indexical and historical."[2] In putting to one side his law books, fetishized as cultural capital through the

112

names of their authors and acting as the signifier of marketable knowledge ("Ployden, Dyer, Brooke"), Publius instead meets up with two well-known bears, "Harry Hunks and Sacarson." The poem's final couplet stages a confrontation between the world of academia and the world of entertainment. If the cultural capital of legal knowledge is stored up in the names of "Ployden" et al., then an incipient marketplace for celebrity is discernible in the naming of the two famous bears.

However, the other name in Davies's epigram renders its purported owner apparently anonymous. "Harry Hunks" and "Ployden" are famous and Davies trades on their differing reputations in the witty juxtaposition that closes the poem; Publius, however, is lost to us. Richard McCabe suggests that, in the satirical writings of the 1590s, "The use of fictitious names, whether Latin or Italian, gave no guarantee that a real person was not intended, or that the name itself was not a clue to the subject's identity."[3] In that febrile political world, such naming ensured that satire was treated with particular suspicion by the authorities. The fictional names invented by satirists may have provided them with a cover, but this cover was only likely to exacerbate the paranoia of the authorities, all too prepared to project their own fantasies of who might be a potential victim. However, as McCabe's awkward double negatives seem to indicate, even if the targets of this kind of satire might have been identifiable by their contemporaries, their identity is obliterated for us through a severing of the ties between the proper name and person. Structuring Davies's epigram is a subtext concerned with the relationship between authority and the proper name. Who gets to be called by their right name, by any name? What does it mean, within culture, to be assigned a name? What if we imagine that the different kinds of name present in the poem—"Ployden," "Publius," "Harry Hunks," "hawks"—are not as distinct from each other as the satirical intent of the epigram (to criticize Publius for slumming it with the bears) snobbishly seems to suggest?[4] Proper names are, of course, a persistent theme in Hawkes's work, not least in "Harry Hunks, Superstar" and the subsequent essay from *Shakespeare in the Present,* "Hank Cinq." In the wider context of the book within which this Davies epigraph is first published, this concern with names can be seen to have still broader ramifications.

Making use of the typical methods of satire, Davies uses generic rather than specific names for each of the targets of his cuttingly satirical epigrams: "Rufus the Courtier," "Quintus the Dancer,"

"Titus the brave and gallant gentleman." He also reminds his readers, in the first epigram of the printed collection, that an epigram, "taxeth under a particular name, / A general vice that warrants public blame" (sig A3r). The aliases that he deploys both identify individuals and subsume them under a general attack that excuses any personal assault. These verses had circulated widely in manuscript, chiefly among fellow Inns of Court men, as part of their culture of carnivalesque reveling and gulling, particularly associated with Christmastime, before their print publication in late 1598 or early 1599. Susannah Hop discerns in their printed form, oddly anthologized alongside the first printed version of Marlowe's translations of Ovid's *Elegies,* a reflection of "the structure, texture, and nature of the Middle Temple Revels."[5] By the time that they make their way into print, however, Davies does not put his own full name to the sequence, but uses just his initials. Hop speculates that Davies's overenthusiastic enjoyment of the Inns of Court's reveling culture, an enthusiasm that had led to him being expelled from the Middle Temple, lies behind the thinly veiled anonymity of the publication. He goes into print, she suggests, with, "the double purpose of getting his revenge, and regaining his dignity."[6] In June 1599, following the Bishops' Ban, the book is ordered to be destroyed. Both Hop and McCabe surmise that this is as much due to the satirical intent of Davies's poems as it is to the overt eroticism of Ovid in translation. Davies is named in the list for the Bishops' Ban, as is Marlowe.[7] Their advertised anonymity had fooled nobody.

Within this cultural set-up that links fame, authority, notoriety, and cultural capital to the proper name, to what does the name Publius refer then, if it is something different from either a famous bear or the author of a legal textbook? Who is this law student who skives off and takes a short boat trip across the Thames—from Middle Temple to Paris Garden—to watch some bear baiting, only to be reminded once he gets there of the squalor of his ancestral home? I assume he is a second or third son, sent off to the city so that he could train in a profession. The dilapidated country estate in which he grew up, "Stinking with dogs and muted all with hawks," has proven unable to sustain an extended family. Now that he is in London, he finds himself caught between the need to forge a professional career and a desire to make the most of the city's opportunities. His taste for low-brow entertainment, a distraction from his law books, could find a faint echo in the name that Davies gives him. "Publius" might refer to Ovid's full name, Publius Ovidius

Naso, especially in a book that also contains some scurrilously entertaining verse from the Latin poet in the form of Marlowe's translations. Elizabethan students had an affection for Ovidian erotica. In the St John's College entertainment, *The Return to Parnassus,* one character, a gull named Gullio, sleeps with a copy of Shakespeare's distinctly Ovidian *Venus and Adonis* in his bed: "I'll worship sweet Master Shakespeare," he says, "and to know him will lay his *Venus and Adonis* under my pillow."[8] *The Return* is the middle play in a trilogy, staged over a number of years, which in part dramatizes the difficulties of maintaining a scholarly career and the pitfalls that might await a student if he were distracted from his studies.

Davies himself falters at this moment of his legal and literary careers but later goes on to become a highly visible member of the political elite, whose portfolio includes working as Attorney General in Ireland under James VI and I.[9] By the end of his life, the youthful indiscretions of the *Epigrammes* were behind him. Hawkes's work, on the other hand, got bolder and more scurrilous as his career went on. And here, in this essay from his last single-authored collection, he briefly entertains a pun on his name that links his critical approach to the scatological satire of Davies. At the end of "Harry Hunks, Superstar," he reminds us of one of the constant refrains in his criticism: that in working with Shakespeare, we should pay attention to the sounds of words. We are dealing, he writes, with a "preliterate age" that "deepens and sophisticates its communication by means of the activity of punning, something that a literate society judges to be the lowest form of wit."[10] This allows him to bring together the seemingly opposed entertainments of the playhouse and the bear garden by means of a pun on "baiting" / "bating." Both activities stage scenes of torment and persecution ("baiting") as well as provide an opportunity for rest and relaxation ("bating"). Acknowledging that this link might appear scandalous, Hawkes writes, "It may be that, in making such a suggestion, this essay, like one of Publius's hawks, merely 'mutes' (i.e., defecates over) the pantheon of timeless masterpieces."[11]

Because of the impact of animal studies on early modern studies, recently the ideational, as well as physical and geographical, links between the bear garden and the playhouse have become more widely understood. Erica Fudge's work on bearbaiting, in particular, has traced the ambiguities of the spectacle, seeing it as both confirming and undermining man's apparent superiority over the animals that were forced to participate in the cruel sports. Apparent mastery ultimately manifests itself as an uncomfortably shared animality: "To watch a baiting," she writes, "is to reveal, not the stability of species status but the animal that lurks beneath the surface."[12] Hawkes's focus on the spectacle of bearbaiting, equally attuned to the cruelty of the practice, produces a slightly different picture. His concern is not so much to situate the bearbaiting within an emergent anthropocentrism as to use the similarity between the two practices—baiting and playing—to reveal the shared contingencies of both. He claims that, in the Davies epigram, we see that "the smell and the savagery" of the bear garden becomes "most fully and fruitfully meaningful in terms of an opposition" to the apparently rational world of Publius's law books.[13] Earlier in the essay, he writes that the two events share a sense of "play":

> at the centre of both spectacles, the focus of attention, there throbs a 'live', unpredictable quality of immediacy in the sense that both seem to frame, manage, and work with contingency, with unshaped, actual, 'here and now' experience, making that a fundamental part of what they have to offer. In this sense both events seem categorisable as 'games'— bear baiting's unpredictability makes it possible to 'play' or bet on the outcome—and that expanded sense of the concept must in turn be part of what is hinted at by the early modern term 'play.'[14]

This is a familiar theme from Hawkes's earlier work, particularly *Shakespeare's Talking Animals,* which, through an insistence on the emergence of Shakespeare's drama within a preliterate culture, sees it as resistant to integration within a literate, literary world. The improvised entertainments, the "play" of the bear garden, reveal their mirror image of the playhouse as nothing like a "pantheon of timeless masterpieces."[15] As the pun on hawks / Hawkes briefly swoops down and across the final paragraph of "Harry Hunks, Superstar," Hawkes aligns himself not only with the hawk that mutes Publius's ancestral home, but also the bears and dogs who make the poor student filthy during his visit to Paris Garden, and declares his affinity with Davies himself, through the scatological work of satire, and in the squandering of the cultural capital of the proper name that is entertained by the Publius epigram. The translation of Jesus Christ into a baited bear, in his title's echo of the Andrew Lloyd Webber and Tim Rice musical, *Jesus Christ, Superstar,* is another measure of the extent to which Hawkes is prepared to denigrate proper names as sites that might accumulate authority.

The King is Dead, Long Live the Pun

Karen Newman, writing about the growing cultures of memorialization in early modern London, points out Thomas Browne's wittily playful attitude towards his subject matter in *Urn-Burial,* where he substitutes the proper names of people and places with witty puns:

> Though we might expect proper names, linked as rigid designators to historical places and persons, . . . Browne's names are notoriously errant. Cremation urns are found—guess where—in the *Burnham* villages; an authority on burial sites and remains in Norway and Denmark is named *Wormius.*[16]

Commenting on this, she writes that, "Puns corrode, like death itself, the power of the name to mark and specify; they empty it of pathos."[17] Hawkes acknowledges, by implication, this corrosive work of the pun when he argues that the act of naming "offers to weld language to the world and the world to language and to use that impacted link as an instrument of control."[18] In the essay that follows "Harry Hunks, Superstar"—"Hank Cinq"—Hawkes extends his handling of puns further to "corrode" "the power of the name," bringing names to bear on kingship and sovereignty. Newman's argument that punning about death removes the possibility of pathos is pertinent. No figures have been treated with more pathos in their critical history than some of Shakespeare's kings and, in "Hank Cinq," it is the king to end all kings—Henry V—who comes under punning attack. Hawkes points out from the beginning that, "Of all Shakespeare's plays, *Henry V* is the one that most clearly explores and manipulates the early modern theatre's crucial duality."[19] Like Publius, it is a play that is self-consciously caught between the literary ambitions involved in memorializing the great king and the often-dirty exigencies of the playhouse. And, of course, his essay proceeds to take us deep into the mire in which Henry V's control over both his name and his country is lost to the improvisatory play of punning, playing, and animality.

In that, it picks up from "Bryn Glas," an earlier essay in the *Shakespeare in the Present* volume that uses Welshness as a means

to undermine claims that *Henry V* might be read only as a celebration of national triumph via the unifying force of the English monarchy. Here, although Hawkes agrees that the putatively "Welsh"
character of Fluellen is a "demeaning confection"[20] that mainly
serves to underwrite a colonizing position in which the English
monarchy insists that "To be 'English,' and a participant in that
world, is . . . simply to be human,"[21] he also offers a potential way
to read the play against this project. Again, he does this by means
of an animalistic change affected on a proper name. When Fluellen
compares his king to "Alexander the Pig"—the supposedly comic
substitution of "p" for "b" that is a feature of Robert Armin's stage-
Welsh—then Hawkes argues that naming "once more bursts the
boundaries of straightforward reference."[22] The Welshness that
Hawkes sees at work in *Henry V,* and that brings the "beastly transformations" at Bryn Glas (mentioned in *Henry IV, Part One*) to bear
on the supposed triumphs of Agincourt, is one that can be linked
to the improvisatory quality of performance to which his critical
practice always returns. Welshness and improvisation are linked
through the word "throb." In linking the playhouse to the bear garden, he argues that "there *throbs* a 'live', unpredictable quality of
immediacy" that they share.[23] Hawkes argues that Wales, and Welshness, should be brought into play against the militaristic Anglo-
centrism of the history plays, just as much as Ireland and Irishness
has been in the criticism of the later twentieth century, and in the
wake of the ongoing devolution of the "United Kingdom":

> For what must surely be sensed, in our own post-devolution present, is
> that Welshness and its concerns *throbs* with a no less powerful, if
> occluded, pulse in the vasty deep of these plays. And periodically, its
> muffled bear invades and disrupts the step by which they march.[24]

Hawkes advocates for, and demonstrates, a critical practice that
pays attention to this throbbing rhythm, a rhythm discernible in the
pun, and seeks to destabilize conservative claims on the name of
"Shakespeare" for literary élitism.

"Hank Cinq" is a bravura display of that practice, improvising
connections between Henry, Prince Hal, Harry Hunks the bear, and
Duke Ellington. The key critical move occurs in a passage in which
"Harry England," as the French king calls him, is translated into
Harry Hunks, the bear from the previous chapter. Already, dislocat-
ing the naming of Henry V, giving control of it to the French, starts

to corrode the hold the king has on his name. By the time Hawkes has finished muting him, he has become something else altogether:

> if we look closely at the blood-stained figure who confronts us here, and if we link with 'Harry England' the emblem of the 'warlike Harry' that the Chorus describes at the beginning of the play, with his three snarling dogs, named Famine, Sword and Fire who 'Crouch for employment' at his side, we begin to discern a familiar animal figure. It forces us to confront a serious question. If to give a bear the name 'Harry' undoubtedly lends it a disturbing power in the bear-baiting arena, what happens in the theatre next door, when you give the same name to a King?[25]

To answer that question is to discern, along with Hawkes, the outlines of a politics in Shakespeare's *Henry V* that refuses the sovereignty of the proper name as it is invested in the English monarchy, and in a version of "Shakespeare" that is allowed to underwrite that sovereignty.

Not content with turning Hal/Henry/Harry into a bear, Hawkes turns to jazz in order to mute Henry in a different sense. Duke Ellington's "Sonnet to Hank Cinq," from which Hawkes derives his title, is without words. Ellington's *Such Sweet Thunder,* from which "Hank Cinq" comes, is (as Stephen Buhler describes it) a suite of "twelve jazz instrumentals, ranging in length from about one-and-a-half minutes to just over four, each linked by its title and by the programmatic commentary supplied on the album sleeve of its first recording to various Shakespearean characters and works."[26] Hawkes foregrounds both the non-Englishness (American in origin; part-French in title) and the playfulness of Ellington's response to Shakespeare's king: a "racy irreverence in the face of the serried ranks of British monarchy" that "marks it as firmly republican."[27] Hawkes advocates a jazz-inspired approach to Shakespeare criticism in *That Shakespeherian Rag,* where he turns that archconservative monarchist, T. S. Eliot, into the inspiration for a playful engagement with the plays' anti-authoritarian playfulness, by means of what Hawkes sees as Eliot's jazz-like vocalizations in the poetry. Hawkes's translation of Shakespeare, via Eliot and Ellington, into an American republican with an ear for communal music making was already affected by Ellington himself, who wrote, "Somehow, I suspect that if Shakespeare were alive today, he might be a jazz fan himself—he'd appreciate the combination of team spirit and informality, of academic knowledge and humor, of all the elements that go into a great jazz performance."[28] By the close of

"Hank Cinq," Henry/Hal/Hank has come to figure that "throb" to which Hawkes's critical practice always attends, and that might variously be imagined through the pun, through turning animal, or turning Welsh and/or French and/or American. What he is turning his attention to is the potential for a scandalously noisy future in "English" literary criticism, what he calls "that 'rough beast', currently slouching towards the academy."[29]

Noisy Futures

Amidst the puns, the jazz, and all the beastly transformations and translations that Hawkes's criticism seeks to enact, one of the critical tropes that punctuates his work is the repetition of words that verge on the nonsensical. They burst through his prose, like puns, and instantiate the preliterate and communal nature of Shakespearean playing. From the reverse spelling of *Hamlet* in "Telmah," through the celebration of the phrase "Swisser swatter" as an orgasmic version of Sir Walter Raleigh, and the cheeky "willy nilly" in his account of Derrida's *Glas* in "Bryn Glas," these nonsense phrases present themselves as obdurately non-literate.[30] Looking at the pages in *Shakespeare in the Present,* as your eye moves from the end of "Harry Hunks, Superstar," with its concluding suggestion that the essay has been just so much satirical defecation (muting "the pantheon of timeless masterpieces),"[31] it should probably come as no surprise that the opening subheading for "Hank Cinq" is the equally scatological, "Poop-poop!"[32] What follows, however, is a different model for critical practice: not a Davies-like muting on the pretensions of those who would pretend to rescue Shakespeare studies for the world of the purely literate, but rather the "Poop! poop!" of Toad's joyous exclamation from *The Wind in the Willows,* as he sits in the middle of the road and dreams about driving his beloved motor car, propelling himself beyond the "material limits of the world," breaking "the bounds of humanity itself."[33] If Mole calls Toad an ass at this point, thus allowing Hawkes to see Toad as an avatar of Shakespeare's Bottom, then perhaps we are still on a scatological trajectory. But elsewhere in the essay, Hawkes continues to make a call for a propulsive jazz-like improvisatory critical practice that, like Toad's motorcar, can noisily usher in the future. This culminates in a breath-taking description of a possible future:

What will it [the future of Shakespeare criticism] look like? Of course, it won't be a bear, and its name won't be Harry. It'll be shadowy no doubt, but perhaps less compelling than shifty and inconclusive. Its arguments won't really seem to hang together. The connections it proposes will seem arch, tenuous, linked, if at all, in some rhapsodic, jazzy way that owes scandalously little to the procedures of traditional text-based scholarship.[34]

It sounds great. I can't wait. But I have a lingering doubt about the usefulness of Hawkes's work in the twenty-first century. The monuments against which his work has always tilted have already been dismantled. What Hawkes works against is, for the most part, that version of "English" as a scholarly discipline and associated pedagogy that Bill Readings describes:

Shakespearean drama . . . became for England what Greek philosophy was for Germany: the lost origin of authentic community to be rebuilt by means of rational communication between national subjects—a rational communication mediated through the institutions of the state.[35]

All of Hawkes's irrationalities (puns, etc.) work towards interrupting that state-sponsored communication. But, as Readings goes on to argue, with the dismantling of the nation-state, then we get a dismantling of the institutions of the state that support this self-actuating "rational communication," including the English department as a supporting pillar of the national university. As Karen Steigman elucidates, "the political purpose of the university—serving to effectuate the idea of a national culture—has become irrelevant in a techno-bureaucratic, and primarily economically driven, global moment." The corollary of this for literary studies, she continues, is a "loss of literary studies' own originary mission."[36] There is a sense in which, incubated through the political contexts of the 1970s and 1980s, Hawkes's brand of cultural materialism, even his later presentism, might be seen as ill-equipped to deal with a situation in which the national institutions of the "literary" have already been dismantled. Tied to the "cultural turn" in literary studies in which we are still caught, his critical practices might not be attuned to the possibilities of a future literary criticism where what constitutes "culture" is no longer linked either to the "literary" or to state institutions, such as the university.

But "Hank Cinq" hints at other possibilities for a noisy future, in which he seems to retune his critical ear to the "throb" at the heart of a new century:

> the challenge from the left for any post-capitalist criticism will surely lie in the proposal that, at work underneath that surface, there was always—and there remains—a just-discernible, non-textual, perhaps non-discursive and even non-human dimension, which requires fully to be confronted in the twenty-first century.[37]

The critical practice that Hawkes barely imagines here seems to have something in common with more positive critical responses to Bill Readings's influential depiction of the English department as the first casualty of a "ruined" national university. Diane Elam argues that, after Readings, we should now abandon a fruitless pursuit of the "literary *thing*," by which she means literature as a rarefied object, and instead pursue "the continuation of questioning, of thinking, that literature makes possible amongst the ruins of the university."[38] Steigman further elaborates what forms this thinking might take. In place of the citizen, contained within the institutions of the University, institutions still haunted by their idealist histories, Steigman would see "a citizen who gets articulated by and performs himself or herself as a linguistic, language-based subject, . . . a new concept of citizenship in language."[39] Literary study construed as a field of study that "expressly raises the question of language" and is "founded on a particular conception of language as cultural"[40] might have the Toad-like motility and the jazz-like improvisational skills to blast its way into the future. And Hawkes's criticism is, as I have suggested, everywhere concerned with this uncooperative relationship between language and culture: the irreducibly preliterate pun that corrodes any claim to sovereign presence and, of course, the muting of law students. The pun that he offers on his own name (hawks/Hawkes) hints at the kind of critical practice that he can barely see at the end of "Hank Cinq": "shadowy," "shifty and inconclusive."[41] If, in an era of research metrics, we can ill-afford to disavow ownership of our own proper names, we might still try to tune our ears to the "throb" of Hawkes's "rough beast," "slouching towards the academy."[42]

Notes

1. Quoted in Terence Hawkes, *Shakespeare in the Present* (London: Routledge, 2002): 91–92.

2. Karen Newman, *Cultural Capitals: Early Modern London and Paris* (Princeton, NJ: Princeton University Press, 2007), 132.

3. Richard McCabe, "Elizabethan Satire and the Bishops' Ban of 1599," *The Yearbook of English Studies* 11 (1981): 192.

4. Other examples from Davies's *Epigrammes* include "Rufus the Courtier" who is hypocritically fussy about slumming it with the hordes at the theater, but is quite happy to go to brothels, "Though all the world in troupes do thither runne" (sig A4r). "Severus the puritan" advocates a strong line against "vaine speeche" because "That thing defiles a man that doth proceed / From out the mouth, not that which enters in." This dictum, of course, does not prevent Severus from devouring, "more capons in a yeare / Then would suffise a hundredth protestants." (Sir John Davies, *Epigrammes and Elegies, by I.D and C.M.* [London, 1599], sig B2r).

5. Susanna Hop, " 'What Fame is This?': John Davies' *Epigrammes* in Late Elizabethan Culture," *Renaissance Journal* 2, no. 3 (January 2005): 40.

6. Ibid., 40.

7. McCabe, "Elizabethan Satire," 188.

8. Anonymous, *The Returne from Parnassus, or The Scourge of Simony* in *The Parnassus Plays,* ed. J. Leishman (Nicholson and Watson: London, 1949), III.i.1223–25.

9. See his entry in the *Dictionary of National Biography* for a condensed version of a very full literary and political career.

10. Hawkes, *Shakespeare in the Present,* 105.

11. Ibid., 106.

12. Erica Fudge, *Perceiving Animals: Humans and Beasts in Early Modern English Culture* (Chicago: University of Illinois Press, 2002), 15.

13. Hawkes, *Shakespeare in the Present,* 91.

14. Ibid., 89.

15. Ibid., 106.

16. Newman, *Cultural Capitals,* 131.

17. Ibid., 132.

18. Terence Hawkes, *That Shakespeherian Rag: Essays on a Critical Process* (London: Methuen, 1986), 47.

19. Hawkes, *Shakespeare in the Present,* 113.

20. Ibid., 45.

21. Ibid., 37.

22. Ibid., 42. Robert Armin would have played Fluellen, and this comic actor developed this accent into a bit of a trademark. See my chapter on "Listening to Welsh in Shakespeare and Armin" for an assessment of the cultural politics of Armin's comic performances of Welshness: Huw Griffiths, " 'O I am ignorance itself in this': Listening to Welsh in Shakespeare and Armin," in *Shakespeare and Wales: From the Marches to the Assembly,* eds. Willy Maley and Philip Schwyzer, (Farnham, UK: Ashgate, 2010), 111–26.

23. Ibid., 89; my italics.

24. Ibid., 44; my italics.

25. Ibid., 115–16.

26. Stephen Buhler, "Form and Character in Duke Ellington's and Billy Strayhorn's *Such Sweet Thunder,*" *Borrowers and Lenders: The Journal of Shakespeare and Appropriation* 1, no.1 (Spring / Summer 2005): http://www.borrowers.uga

.edu/781406/show. Buhler's essay is in a collection, introduced by Hawkes, for an online journal issue dedicated to Duke Ellington's adaptations from Shakespeare. The collection was instigated by the panel on Ellington, jazz, and Shakespeare at the 2004 SAA meeting in New Orleans. Buhler's essay contains sound clips of the twelve pieces.

27. Hawkes, *Shakespeare in the Present*, 125.

28. Quoted in Brent Hayes Edwards, "The Literary Ellington," *Representations* 77, no. 1 (Winter 2002): 6.

29. Hawkes, *Shakespeare in the Present*, 126.

30. In a gloriously extended pun throughout "Bryn Glas," Hawkes picks "willy" up again at the end. Having used it illustratively within his paraphrase of Derrida's argument regarding the proper name in *Glas* ("A proper name ought indeed to involve pure reference, but since it is part of language, it works like language, and always retains, willy-nilly, the capacity to signify" [Ibid., 131]), Hawkes closes the essay with an account of Wilde's Willy Hughes, as muse for the sonnets. Another Welsh presence making itself felt in the Shakespearean extended text, Hawkes offers him as a counterpoint to the anti-Welsh sentiment of the descriptions of Welsh women inserting penises into the mouths of their dead opponents in *Henry IV, Part One*: "a story which began with willies could also," he writes, "be said to end with one" (Ibid.,138).

31. Ibid., 106.

32. Ibid., 107.

33. Ibid., 108.

34. Ibid., 126.

35. Bill Readings, *The University in Ruins* (Harvard, MA: Harvard University Press, 1996), 79.

36. Karen Steigman, " 'The Student is a Far Stranger Figure': Managing Literary Studies' Anxiety in the Global University," *The Journal of the Midwest Modern Language Association* 37, no. 1 (Spring 2004): 24.

37. Hawkes, *Shakespeare in the Present*, 126.

38. Diane Elam, "Literary Remains," *Oxford Literary Review* 17 (1995): 154.

39. Steigman, " 'The Student is a Far Stranger Figure,' " 29.

40. Ibid., 27.

41. Hawkes, *Shakespeare in the Present*, 126.

42. Ibid., 126.

The "Stretchèd Metre of an Antique Song": Jazzin' the Food of Love

Mike Ingham

> Bill Shakespeare never knew
> Of ragtime in his days
> But the high-browed rhymes,
> Of his syncopated lines,
> You'll admit, surely fit,
> any song that's now a hit,
> So this rag I submit.
> —Gene Buck, Herman Ruby, and David Stamper,
> "That Shakespearian Rag" (1912)

Intro: It's a Jazzy Sonnet

THE TITLE OF MY PAPER is taken from the last quatrain of Sonnet 17 ("Who will believe my verse in time to come?")[1] and is chosen for its pertinence to the treatment of Shakespeare's verse in jazz vocal settings, notably those of the late Johnny Dankworth and his spouse Cleo Laine and more recently of Belgian female artiste Caroll Vanwelden. In fact, although the reference to "stretchèd metre" applies to both Dankworth's and Vanwelden's settings, it is Vanwelden's 2012 setting of Sonnet 17 that literally stretches the meter of this particular sonnet line, as well as many others. While some attention has been paid to the interaction of jazz, blues and ragtime forms with Shakespeare's work—notably Douglas Lanier's erudite article, "Minstrelsy, jazz, rap: African American music, and cultural legitimation"—jazz versions of the sonnets have been virtually ignored.[2] My paper begins to redress this lack of scholarly focus by assessing the assured legacy of Dankworth and Laine and the still-fresh contributions (2012 and 2014) of Vanwelden and her group.[3]

As Terence Hawkes pointed out in his influential 1977 essay "That Shakespeherian Rag" (echoing Eliot's whimsical and deliberately misquoted song citation from *The Waste Land*), ragtime music was essentially a more "genteel" and "intellectualized" form than the raucous, visceral jazz music that was starting to upstage it during the first decades of the twentieth century.[4] Hence the use of the words "intelligent" and "elegant" in the lyrics of Buck, Ruby, and Stamper's 1912 popular song as well as in Eliot's parodic allusion to it. Moreover, ragtime's orientation toward the written medium, by sharp contrast with jazz's proclivity for extemporization, offered a respectable and more serious veneer of cultural acceptability in keeping with Shakespeare's literary iconicity. Unlike the brash exuberance of upbeat New Orleans jazz and the raw emotion of downbeat jazz-blues, the moderated, largely piano-oriented sounds of ragtime could be juxtaposed more justifiably with the Bard's name.

In his essay Hawkes emphasizes the paralinguistic qualities and vocal semiotic connotations of Eliot's parodic interpolations to the song—the syllables "O, O, O, O" and the extra syllable in "Shakespeherian." He argues that, as in jazz music, it is the sound quality conveying meaning through emotion that is significant, using the example to reflect on the tendency to neglect the physical, oral-aural dimension of Shakespeare's world of drama, poetry, and song in favor of purely literary, written, and intellectual perspectives on his art. In the decades since Hawkes's insightful piece appeared, it may be argued that greater equilibrium between the oral, performative, and the literary has been achieved in Shakespeare scholarship. While this emphasis on emotion and the sensory is significant and chimes with Lanier's observations and arguments, there is nevertheless an intellectually rigorous quality at the level of both form and idea in the sonnets that make them more challenging to set than, for instance, the songs from Shakespeare's plays.

The latter are clearly designed for sung performance in terms of their metrical form —usually employing iambic or trochaic trimeter or tetrameter—and strophic arrangement.[5] They have the tendency to avoid regular, even-syllable ictic stress, which, prosodic variations notwithstanding, is the very heartbeat of the iambic pentameter sonnets. Furthermore, many Shakespeare songs are influenced by the ballad tradition and fall readily into a four-beat, two- or four-line structure sometimes with a refrain. Such characteristics are not present in the Shakespearean sonnet, despite the regularity of the end-stopped rhyme scheme of the three-quatrain structure. Nor does the final couplet of the Shakespearean sonnet approximate to a song refrain, as in his purpose-written lyrics. It is not surprising, therefore, that the sonnets do not appear to lend themselves to any pre-existent or "antique" song form. Having said that, the etymology of the word itself derives from the Italian for "sound" or "song"—"sonetto"—originally signifying a diminutive form, and it should be borne in mind that the distinction between a song and a poem becomes blurred the further back in time one goes.[6]

In a considerable number of instances the organization of the Shakespearean sonnet content resembles the Petrarchan sonnet in tenor and semantic structure, despite the surface adherence to the 3-quatrain sonnet form. This is because the discourse shift or transition—technically referred to as the "volta" (Italian) or "turn"—tends to occur at the beginning of the third quatrain, whether the shift is contrastive in mood or temporal reference, or rhetorically dramatic or intensifying. Sonnets 12 ("When I do count the clock that tells the time")—set by Vanwelden—and 18 ("Shall I compare thee to a summer's day")—set by Dankworth are good examples of this type. On the other hand, sonnets 53 ("What is your substance")—set by Vanwelden—and 147 ("My love is as a fever")—set by Dankworth—favor an incremental strategy. With this conceptual pattern the thematic conceit is progressively developed across the three quatrains and the final couplet acts as the "volta," expressing a resolution, paradox or epigrammatic comment that breaks with the tone of the preceding twelve lines.

In examples of the former type the first two quatrains form the first part of a binary division, thus linking the third quatrain with the closing couplet. They effectively constitute an octet (eight-line group) and a sestet (six-line group) as in the Italianate Petrarchan convention in accordance with what Anthony Hecht refers to as their "dramatic or rhetorical" rationale.[7] This quasi-Petrarchan effect of binary structural contrast can be extremely effective in facilitating a balanced but musically integrated song setting. It also enables the composer to reflect a mood change or rhetorical shift at the macro-text level without employing a bewildering range of tonal shifts and sonorities to follow each twist and nuance of micro-level meaning in every single phrase or line of the source text.

The recurrent themes and conceits of the sonnets also revolve around binary tropes —antitheses and paradoxes of night and day, body and soul, desire and abstinence, sexual and spiritual love, transience and permanence and, as David Schalkwyk has argued, the transformation of a "poetics of praise into the poetics of blame."[8] All of these antitheses are pertinent to sophisticated song-writing on the theme of love, even if the paradoxical motif in the Shakespearean sonnet presents challenges to the setter. These challenges, of course, arise out of the sonnets' cornucopia of intellectual and emotional subtleties and their accomplished interplay of standard iambic pentameter versification with metrical variation to create their particular fusion of thought and sound.

The sonnet settings that convey integral semantic and formal units most intelligibly are usually those that retain the integrity of half lines (pausing on the natural caesura in the respective line) or whole lines. Enjambments tend to complicate the musical metrics and not least the singer's breathing patterns, but Shakespeare's versification in the sonnets rarely involves the kind of dense syntactic run-on we find in much modern poetry. The motifs, arguments and counter-arguments are often delineated at line- or quatrain-level with a remarkable degree of balance and symmetry between these textual units. This formal regularity, predicated on units of four or two that correspond perfectly with musical form, enhances felicitous transposition.

As with classical or pop styles of sonnet settings, articulation, accentuation, phrasing and other aspects of prosody in the adaptation and the sung interpretation significantly affect the reception of the sonnet as transformed through the jazz genre. Given jazz music's predisposition toward syncopated, "ragged" rhythms and variations on a fixed underlying form—for example, the frequent deployment of the choriamb device[9] discernible in Shakespeare's verse that produces a "syncopated" effect—there do not, on the face of it, appear to be insoluble impediments to the marriage of the jazz form and the sonnet. Perhaps more vexed, though, is the question of interpretation and voice, specifically the homoerotic connotations generated by the majority of the poems. Appropriating the sonnets within a heterosexual frame of reference, female interpreters such as Cleo Laine and Caroll Vanwelden tend to elide the theme of taboo and transgression that underpins them. On the other hand, the jazz song canon, from which jazz singers draw inspiration, is necessarily open to multiple vocal interpretations and varying gender constructions.

Dankworth's and Laine's Interpretations

In *Shakespeare and Music: Afterlives and Borrowings,* Julie Sanders makes special mention of the Duke Ellington-inspired song settings of John Dankworth and Cleo Laine. "There is a sense of shared artistry here between performers and source text, which offers a rich reading of the poems themselves."[10] This is as true of their original Shakespearean song settings, including their jazz styling of "It was a lover and his lass," "O Mistress Mine" and "Winter—when icicles hang by the wall," and their skillful arrangements of well-known blank verse extracts, such as "If music be the food of love" and "All the world's a stage," as it is of the later sonnet transpositions. The clarity, wit and dazzling virtuosity of Laine's vocal lines and the subtle inventiveness of Dankworth's clarinet and alto sax playing, together with imaginative small-ensemble and occasional big-band accompaniment, serve the texts well. Their setting of sonnet 18 ("Shall I compare thee to a summer's day")—performed to great public acclaim in their 2007 Royal Albert Hall Proms concert—is a mellifluous jazz ballad in which the relationship between verbal and musical ideas coalesces perfectly. Laine's vocal control and sultry *colla voce* [11] delivery manages to make a sonnet so often adapted that it has almost become a musical adaptation cliché sound fresh and compelling.

To exemplify Dankworth's and Laine's craft I will discuss two settings based on Duke Ellington's instrumental compositions for the 1957 Shakespeare jazz suite, "Such Sweet Thunder," and two of Dankworth's entirely original compositions based on "a pair" of sonnets.[12] The twelve Ellington pieces comprising the suite are abstract evocations of character and situation in various Shakespeare plays, of which four are conceived according to a sonnet-like structure; this consists of an introductory four-bar line, followed by three uniform sections corresponding to quatrains, with a closing eight-bar coda representing the final couplet. Dankworth's sonnet settings tend to imitate this pattern of transposition established by Ellington. The latter's obvious influence leads him to deploy a similar ternary musical structure for the sung lines, offset by an instrumental introduction, break and coda —A (quatrain 1), B (quatrain 2), A (quatrain 3), C (closing couplet), combining melodic and rhythmic variation with a sense of reprise normally associated with song. Although the volta/turn of the sonnet, as discussed above, signifies a transition point in mood and meaning, the melodically repeated third stanza tends to recapitulate the musical motif of the opening, thereby promoting tighter cohesion in the musical theme than is requisite for the purely verbal element.

Dankworth's compositional prowess and sinuous instrumental fills and solos create a distinctive sound, one indebted to the swing era of jazz—as the jazz boom of the 1960s certainly was—but one that is equally conscious of the radical innovations of be-bop and the "cool" sound of Miles Davis, Charles Mingus and other exponents across the Atlantic. Equally important, Cleo Laine's limpid diction and utterly distinctive vocal timbre have distinguished her as an exceptional vocal performer in the popular jazz idiom. She has been fittingly described by Thomas Cunniffe in the website Jazz History Online as a "renaissance woman, both in their figurative and literal definitions," referring specifically to her performance on the album *Shakespeare and all that Jazz*.[13] Her vocal range of well over three octaves enables her to bridge note intervals with apparent effortlessness. In their creative partnership generally, and in their Shakespeare specifically, Dankworth and Laine succeeded in matching ideas and feelings of playfulness, melancholy, irony, exuberance and regret so evident in Shakespearean songs, sonnets and plays with jazz music's predilection for impulsive, wistful and often expansive emotional expression and spontaneity.

Dankworth's smoky version of sonnet 147 ("My love is as a fever") is based on the Ellington tune "Sonnet for Caesar" (number 2 in his suite). The original melody evokes Caesar's enigmatic mystique and, in its closing bars, hints at his tragic end within Shakespeare's play. However, Dankworth reconceptualizes the setting as an obsessive love-song. Laine's wide vocal range and *legato* delivery acts as a counterpoint to the spiky, plucked bass and unresolved dissonant chord sequences of the accompaniment. Added to this, the angular, brooding melody, with its altered tones, unconventional note intervals and alternative harmonic voicings, creates an underlying instability in the musical accompaniment that matches the mood of the sonnet text. It aptly conveys the mood swings and oscillations in temperature of the "patient" who is now "frantic-mad" and both "past cure" and "past care."

The setting of sonnet 40 ("Take all my loves") takes its alternately leaping and plunging melodic line from the amusingly titled "Sonnet for Hank Cinq" (number 3 in the suite). In his version Dankworth makes full use of Laine's exceptional *tessitura*[14] to substitute for the virtuosic solo trombone line written for Ellington's "sonnet." The up-tempo swing accompaniment, with swirling clarinet intro and a busy "walking bass" pulse, provides a distinctive blend of chromatic bluesy movement and angular leaps that plays off against Laine's bravura vocal; it reflects the mood of the sonnet text, which blends reasoned argument, paradox ("lascivious grace") and a tone of forgiving reproach. The mood swings of the first and third stanzas are contrasted with the more restrained ethos of the second, in which a sustained pedal effect promotes tension. Laine's rendition of the *colla voce* final couplet imitates the trombone's dizzying climactic phrase and builds to the high final note on "foes" as the accompanying music resumes its hectic pace. Ellington' s musical arrangement and Dankworth's vocal setting stretch Shakespeare's meter in this—probably more than in most other sonnet settings— well beyond the norm; but in the process they demonstrate the elasticity of both the form and Shakespeare's use of it.

A musically audacious and inventive approach to the formal and thematic dualism of Shakespeare's poetry can be heard in the juxtaposition of sonnets 23 ("As an unperfect actor on the stage") and 24 ("Mine eye hath played the painter"). This composition, *A Duet of Sonnets,* epitomizes the dialogue between the jazz ensemble and Laine's uniquely mellow voice, which seems to function both as lead instrument and as robust yet sensitive interpreter of the lyric. The virtuosity of both composition and performance is underlined by the prodigious feat of interweaving the pair of sonnets contrapuntally in a third concluding verse. Each sonnet is rendered individually, with the first, "As an unperfect actor," employing a higher range of notation, whilst the melodic line of sonnet 24 is at a generally lower pitch and written specifically to harmonize with the preceding setting. In a beautifully synchronized overdubbing where Laine's "two voices" play freely—but in precise phrasing, rhythm, and harmony—against each other, the duality inherent in the sonnets is imaginatively and excitingly explored in performance.

Dankworth's and Laine's ambitious setting of this sonnet pair, referencing (and combining) the respective arts of actor and painter, provides a potent aural metaphor for the synaesthesia of pictorial art, poetry, and, implicit in the song's performance pragmatics, jazz. Although acting and portraiture are the figurative devices for the respective sonnets, from the opening lines of both it is clear that the play of imagery and analogy—actors, books, portraits, windows—is evoking the sound and look of love, as well as the conventions and artifices of acting, painting, and writing. To these creative representations and conventions is added that most ancient of sung genres, the love song ("the perfect ceremony of love's rite"), albeit framed through the altered perception afforded by the jazz form.

Cleo Laine's voice is an instrument that fuses thought and emotion in a felicitous blend. She avoids the tendency for over-emoting that is common among contemporary pop-jazz and stage musical divas. Instead, her versatile vocal chords negotiate the contours of Dankworth's scoring of Shakespeare texts with the whimsy and playful detachment of her illustrious predecessors, particularly Ella Fitzgerald, or the timbre of husky melancholy derived from the Billie Holiday vocal technique. Essentially, Laine's judicious interpretations communicate that ambivalence between passion and reason, male and female, age and beauty, good love and bad love (sonnet 144's "Two loves I have of comfort and despair") that give the sonnets their continued appeal to song setters, listeners and readers alike.

Vanwelden's Interpretations

Caroll Vanwelden, by sharp contrast with Dankworth and Laine, is a jazz vocalist less influenced by swing and the mainstream tradition and much more by the modern, post-swing, hybrid jazz idiom. That said, her voice, though less adaptable and extensive than Laine's, proves an effective vehicle for interpreting the Shakespeare sonnet. Her vocal style has something in common with better-known jazz *chanteuses,* such as Stacey Kent and Diana Krall, and like them she articulates the lyrics with clarity and panache. Having released two albums dedicated entirely to sonnet settings in 2012 and 2014, her selection of sonnets is wider than Dankworth and Laine's. Laine's vocal influence is evident in the vocal style in some of Vanwelden's self-penned compositions, and in her best Shakespeare settings there is a similar facility in conveying "the highbrow rhymes of his syncopated lines."[15]

Vanwelden's up-tempo settings, where there is closer consonance between vocal line and musical accompaniment and a stronger jazz sensibility, are better structured and phrased than her ballad-style efforts to preserve the sense of the source text; the former group includes sonnet 116 ("The marriage of true minds"), sonnet 12 ('When I do count the clock"), sonnet 91 ("Some glory in their birth"), and sonnet 17 ("Who will believe my verse in time to come"). Her version of sonnet 93 ("So shall I live, supposing thou art true") provides a perfect example of transposition that reflects in musical terms the full effect of the sonnet turn or transition after the second quatrain. Her striking chord change and melodic lift in what is effectively a "middle eight"[16] in the third quatrain ("But heaven in thy creation did decree") mark the turn to the Petrarchan sestet before the song reprises the syncopated dotted figure of the opening quatrains.

By contrast with the more breezy settings, the phrasing and articulation of many of her slower-tempo jazz ballads "stretch the meter" beyond the extent at which the original sonnet prosody is readily discernible. The exception is her setting—very different in mood and style from Johnny Dankworth's—of sonnet 23 ("As an unperfect actor on the stage"). The singer's sincere and simple *a cappella* vocal on the opening quatrain expresses the tentative nature of the confession of love, while also evoking aspiration for "the perfect ceremony of love's rite." Here, as in other settings where his moody trumpet fills and solos complement Vanwelden's vocals, Thomas Siffling's pure, haunting flugelhorn "outro"[17] solo is resonant with implication; it represents a soulful, wordless appeal to the ear, but in the pure language of musical sound that deconstructs the original poem's intention to value the eye above the ear.

Vanwelden's interpretations of sonnet 17 ("Who will believe my verse in time to come") and sonnet 116 ("Let me not to the marriage of true minds") are among her finest settings, because they retain the flow of the verse, with a delicate rhythmic and melodic interweaving of voice and instruments. The syncopated loping bass accompaniment and spare percussion accompaniment to the sung verse of sonnet 17, together with the virtuosic trumpet solo between the first and second iterations of the 14 lines, combine to produce a thrilling jazz variation on Shakespeare's theme. In this artfully constructed version of the "antique song," the swung and syncopated rhythms are stretched and ragged, as in a ragtime or jazz transformation. Vanwelden's setting offsets this angularity with a mellifluous melodic construction and a felicitous phrasing which observes the integrity of meaning in the verse, fitting the caesuras, line endings and run-ons, and highlighting the poem's contrastive imagery, of age and beauty, contemporaneity and posterity.

Vanwelden's melismatic[18] delivery of the end-stopped words "song" and "rhyme" in lines 12 and 14 subtly but aptly stretch the meter of the original. Like the trumpet solo over the throbbing *ostinato*[19] bass figure, these anachronisms demonstrate how the sonnet lives twice—in its own rhymes, "yellowed with their age," and in the regenerative jazz rhythms of "the time to come."

Perhaps the most frequently set and recited of all sonnets (with the possible exception of sonnet 18), "Let me not to the marriage of true minds" is one of Vanwelden's strongest compositions in terms of the combination of melody, rhythm, style and word setting. This poem, as Dympna Callaghan and other critics have pointed out, is steeped in serious legal terminology and litigious rhetoric. In Vanwelden's adaptation it becomes a jauntily assertive foot-tapping shuffle with an irresistible melody. Listening, for example, to the musical phrasing in Vanwelden's slyly disarming rendition of "It is the star to every wand'ring bark" and the closing line "I never writ, nor no man ever loved," it is difficult to imagine a better fit between words and notes.

The harmonic shifts at lines 5 ("Oh no, it is an ever-fixèd mark") and 9 ("love's not time's fool") draw particular attention to the affirmative tenor of the texts, though, paradoxically, this affirmation of a love that transcends time is expressed through a series of negatives that are belied by the singer's optimistic interpretation of the text. An obvious cause for the breezy optimism of the jazz setting is that the poem has remained an "ever-fixèd mark" for love in Anglophone culture. The setting's lightness of tone and style can be seen as an appropriate counterpoint to the poem's rhetoric precisely because it has not been Time's fool. Nor are the poem's conceptual metaphors of a transcendent love altered by its alteration in the jazz mode, even when Vanwelden scat-sings "ba-dooby-doo" in the time-honored jazz tradition in the song's interlude and "outro."

Coda

The sonnets have been transposed as art song, and latterly have enjoyed considerable vogue in various pop/rock stylings. Jazz settings, by contrast, are much rarer, and have seldom been discussed in an academic context. Cleo Laine makes a dry and mocking reference to Shakespeare's inevitably close associations with academe in the course of her Royal Albert Hall concert. Despite her ironic self-deprecation, it is evident that these jazz sonnet settings engage in a dynamic dialogue with the sonnet texts, discovering reciprocity and suggestive musical imagery in the juxtaposition of Shakespeare and jazz.

The Dankworth-Laine versions are often playfully allusive about the generic possibilities of jazz Shakespeare; in this respect one might describe them as "meta-settings." Vanwelden's settings range more widely than the relatively popular, better-known selections of Dankworth and Laine. She tends to opt for many lesser-known sonnets, especially on her latest recording, *Caroll Vanwelden Sings Shakespeare Sonnets 2.* Neither Laine nor Vanwelden imbue the darker sentiments of the sonnets, of which there are many, with the melancholy inflections that are associated more closely with blues than with an ironic or breezy jazz mode. What both singers signally achieve is to highlight how jazz variations on "an antique song" can reproduce the sonnets' verbal music and take it in fresh directions.

Notes

1. All citations of Shakespeare's sonnets refer to the edition of Jonathan Bate and Eric Rasmussen, *William Shakespeare: The Sonnets and Other Poems,* RSC Shakespeare Series (New York: Modern Library, 2007).

2. Douglas Lanier, "Minstrelsy, Jazz, Rap: Shakespeare, African American Music, and Cultural Legitimation," *Borrowers and Lenders: The Journal of Shakespeare and Appropriation* 1, no. 1 (2005), <http://www.borrowers.uga.edu/782016/show>

3. The musical recordings discussed here are Cleo Laine and Johnny Dankworth, *Shakespeare and All that Jazz* (Universal Records, 1964) and *The Collection.* (Spectrum, 2002) 3154 47702; and Caroll Vanwelden, *Caroll Vanwelden Sings Shakespeare Sonnets* (Jazz 'n Arts, 2012), JNA6012 and *Caroll Vanwelden Sings Shakespeare Sonnets 2* (Jazz 'n Arts, 2014), JNA6014.

4. Terence Hawkes, *That Shakespeherian Rag: Essays on a critical process* (London: Methuen, 1977).

5. It is by no means certain that all songs in Shakespeare plays were designed to be sung and accompanied by music, although musical notation set to some lyrics is extant. Some of them could have been referential, or simply recited in the context of the performance.

6. For more on the sonnet's history and variety, see Anthony Cousins, ed., *The Cambridge Companion to the Sonnet* (Cambridge: Cambridge University Press. 2011).

7. Anthony Hecht, "introduction" in *The Sonnets,* ed. G. Blakemore Evans,

The New Cambridge Shakespeare (Cambridge: Cambridge University Press, 2006), 6–7.

8. David Schalkwyk, "Poetry and Performance," in P. Cheney, ed., *The Cambridge Companion to Shakespeare's Poetry* (Cambridge: Cambridge University Press, 2007), 249.

9. This is the technical term used in prosody to describe the rhythmic effect made by an initial trochee in the iambic pentameter line being followed by the more regular iamb. The foot is thus composed of two short unstressed inner syllables flanked by two long stressed syllables.

10. Julie Sanders, *Shakespeare and Music: Afterlives and Borrowings* (Cambridge: Polity, 2007), 22.

11. *Colla voce*—literally "with the voice" or follow the solo voice; flexibility of tempo for the solo vocalist which accompanying musicians need to follow to match the singer's freer tempo and rhythm.

12. Duke Ellington and his orchestra, *Such Sweet Thunder.* Columbia/Legacy, 1957/1999. CK65568.

13. Thomas Cunniffe, "Cleo Laine 'Shakespeare and All that Jazz' (Fontana 5209)," Retro-Review in *Jazz History Online,* <http://jazzhistoryonline.com/Cleo_Laine.html>

14. *Tessitura*—appropriate vocal range for a particular voice from the lowest note to the highest.

15. G. Buck, H. Ruby, and D. Stamper, "That Shakespearean Rag" 1912 song lyric.

16. "Middle eight" or "bridge" is a musical technical term to designate a transitional, contrasting section in which the melodic and harmonic structure evinces a distinct variation on the song's regular pattern. This is often indicated by a key change or temporary modulation, as in Vanwelden's setting of sonnet 93. "Middle eight" literally means eight bars of music, here eight in moderate tempo or sixteen in double time. At the end of third quatrain going into the final couplet the harmonic and melodic structure of the original two quatrains is resumed.

17. The "outro," or coda, of a song usually constitutes an instrumental figure, either fading out, or repeated. The term was coined as a symmetrical match for "intro," or introduction, which is an instrumental opening before the song vocals begin.

18. Melisma refers to the setting of a single syllable of a word in the text to more than one or multiple musical notes.

19. *Ostinato*—a continuously repeated phrase/figure/rhythm across a section or sequence of the music.

EPILOGUE

Star Wars and Shakespearean Spacetime: on Mentors and Our Collective Future

Diana E. Henderson

2015: IN SHAKESPEARE STUDIES, a year between birth and death remembrances. For me, a year of transition after nine years in administration back to focusing on our field and its possibilities. Converging with these facts, several opportunities to reflect upon professional mentors arose: one happily, in the form of a David Scott "Kastanfest" at Yale;[1] the other sadly, as Terence Hawkes's death early in 2014 sparked the creation of this forum. And in that juxtaposition, the shadow.

In order to understand the issues, and Terry's pivotal place in the argument that follows, some imaginative time travel is required. Thirty years ago one of my first graduate mentors, Bernard Beckerman, died at age 64. As the story in the *New York Times* Arts section stated, Professor Beckerman had "blended his practical knowledge of working theater with an intellectual curiosity about drama theory." He had served, uniquely, as both Columbia's Dean of the School of the Arts and as Chair of the Department of English and Comparative Literature, in which I was then a doctoral student. In addition to having been President of the SAA in 1981, Beckerman had "established . . . the program that enabled students to receive doctoral degrees in theater at Columbia"; this program had allowed me to take advanced theater history seminars with students who would go on to become distinguished dance historians, puppeteers, and film directors.[2] Most notably for this occasion, Terence Hawkes copiously thanked Beckerman in the acknowledgments to *Shakespeare's Talking Animals,* citing his role in calling attention to the performative dimensions of the plays. And Terry again acknowledged his debt in *That Shakespeherian Rag* (published soon after

Beckerman's passing), with typically self-deprecating generosity: "The kindness and keen percipience of the late Bernard Beckerman demands special mention and deserves a better memorial."[3] Only through preparing this forum did the connection between these two in other ways so different Shakespeareans fully register for me: there are many such critical genealogies and unexpected multigenerational collaborations yet to be explored.

As well as personal gratitude, the association between these scholars evokes the differences among our institutional locations and the critical interventions that follow from them. Beckerman was humble in a department not well known for that attribute; yet it was not only his kindness but what was then his seemingly unique refusal to oppose text *versus* performance that numbered among the reasons I was still in grad school, having entered with the overly optimistic belief that one could maintain involvement in professional theater while becoming a literature PhD. By 1985 I was instead channeling my performativity into the classroom and trying to keep up with a slew of exciting new essay collections that would become hallmarks of New Historicism, poststructuralist theory, and feminism as applied to Shakespeare, while searching for a full-time academic position.

The early to mid-1980s were both an exciting and appalling time to be a graduate student, as Columbia shifted tempestuously from an older model of Renaissance studies that had been led by American New Critics and European historians of ideas, to those new approaches that would reign, at least in the United States, for the next several decades. It was also a time when advancement through graduate school was competitively structured and entirely contingent on mentorship: 100 students were admitted each year to the Master's degree program, most taking out loans to pay their own way, and at the end of that year only 25 were allowed to continue into the PhD program, based on the decisions of a committee of professors within the department. From the first orientation meeting onward, the top-down message prompted individual competition: we were told to look to our right, look to our left, and realize that only one of us (on average) would be returning the next year. In fact, students bonded together out of resentment as well as shared interests, but this treatment generally fostered a sense of distance from larger institutional structures, depriving us of learning as much or contributing as effectively to the university as we might otherwise have done.

After making that first "cut," I witnessed a similar public competition take place at the level of a senior faculty hiring in what was then called the Renaissance, with fairly disastrous consequences: while students certainly benefited from hearing lectures and taking classes with a series of visiting eminences and emerging stars, the faculty's divisions over the paradigm shift in literary studies meant that each temporary "guest" eventually either turned down a job offer from Columbia or felt they had been ill-treated. And everyone knew it. By 1985, I thought I had found a way forward, shuttling between the Derridean historicist poetics of Professor Edward (Ted) Tayler, my primary advisor, and Professor Beckerman's more pragmatic performance approach. And then, without a chance to say thank you, Beckerman was gone.

Enter Kastan. Actually, the process by which David Scott Kastan became my second reader involved an unlikely convergence in Shakespearean spacetime, far from Columbia's New York campus. Within a few weeks of Beckerman's death I was receiving MLA interview requests, and by the academic year's end, I had a fulltime faculty position. Here we encounter another of those obvious yet remarkable changes in the profession over the past thirty years. It was not an easy job market then, but the percentage of positions earning a living wage was higher, and with a single forthcoming article in a good journal I was judged a credible candidate even without a completed dissertation. It was a mixed blessing: I moved to Vermont to become an overnight generalist with the expectation of an open-door policy to all comers. Those years were a blur of undergraduates and feeling as if I had been cast in a 1950s film pitched somewhere between a Kingsley Amis satire and *Mad Men.* To modify Doctor Johnson, the wonder is not that I completed my dissertation well, but that I completed it at all. Many people I knew did not.

Although his appointment to Columbia's faculty was in process, David Kastan was still teaching at Dartmouth when he kindly agreed to discuss my dissertation. I had an anxious two-hour drive over the mountains to meet him, but will never forget the deliberateness with which he searched for the words to describe my motley typescript. Finally, he ventured, "Well, it reads somewhat like a *palimpsest.* . . ." I do not think he had Genette in mind; I certainly recognized the pertinence of the word's traditional, material meaning. More to the point and surprisingly, David made clear that he did not expect me to erase and rewrite yet again to please him, but instead would assist my moving forward with my career. It was a deeply generous yet frank response, the kind to which I hope we all aspire. It was also far from the last such improbable and deeply humane encounter to transform my academic journey, at each stage involving valued mentors.

Fast forward up to 2003, when I fortuitously met Terence Hawkes at a conference on Shakespeare and European Politics in Utrecht, sponsored by the group that subsequently became ESRA (the European Shakespeare Research Association). Terry and I hit it off at the opening reception, discussing the history of United States foreign policy. Three days of the intensity, humor, and frustration that discussions of European unity (not to mention Shakespeare studies' role in that project) can certainly provoke, and we had established the professional friendship that eventuated in my editing *Alternative Shakespeares 3* for his *New Accents* list. This led to extensive correspondences, and many summer hours sitting outdoors at the International Shakespeare Conference—that odd remnant of the mid-twentieth century, the origins of which Terry unearths in "Band of Brothers."[4] Sometimes we worked, sometimes just chatted. But most often and vividly I found myself listening to his real-time rapier witticisms about certain dull, self-important, or to his mind inconsequential talks being amplified across the Shakespeare Institute's garden, as I tried to suppress outright laughter (I suspect that is one reason why the amplification practice was discontinued, forcing the invited attendees indoors). Typical Terry.

A tenuous job situation, an international conference: these are the not-*so*-serendipitous encounters in spacetime that spark Shakespearean collaborations and shape lives. Both Terry and David displayed a generosity disproportionate to the brevity of those initial encounters. Each also showed certain rare habits of mind, style, and community building.

However, putting these two relationships in dialogue also created a less comfortable feeling of professional dislocation, in some ways recalling the competitiveness and often unnecessary oppositions that plagued my graduate school days. For in latter years, these mentors seemed at odds, or rather, the profession chose to take up the gauntlet and enact a battle between what Hawkes and others called "presentism" and what Kastan and Peter Stallybrass dubbed, with self-deprecating humor, "the new boredom."[5] No doubt because of personal loyalties as well as a tendency toward intellectual synthesizing, I found myself unpersuaded that their differences rose to the level of a theory war, somewhat cynically thinking that its inflation by adherents testified instead to the impoverishment of our field, its baroque reenactment of residual academic protocols that habitually require new approaches and antagonisms. Rereading Terry's and David's books in tandem this year, I of course was reminded of the faultlines (to invoke yet another important cultural materialist, Alan Sinfield), but I also discerned a remarkable degree of commonality among the historically rooted claims each makes.

Take, for example, their shared departure not only from New Critics and New Bibliographers but also from certain contemporary New Historicists—Stephen Greenblatt, most famously—who have been perceived to emphasize social containment over the possibilities of subversion or, even more to the point, a *heterogeneity* of responses to Shakespeare's drama. Here is an illustration:

> But the play seems to me less coherent—not therefore less interesting or good, but less willing to organize its disparate voices into hierarchies—than . . . demonstrations of its putative unity would allow. The formal coherence that critics have demanded . . . can be achieved only by subordinating . . . commoners to aristocrats, comedy to history, by imposing, that is, the same hierarchies of privilege and power that exist in the state upon the play.

If the name were withheld, as in a Leavisite passage-identification test, one might be hard-pressed to know which critic to assign to it. In this instance, the paragraph comes from Kastan's 1991 essay on *Henry IV, Part One,* " 'The King hath many marching in his Coats,' or, What did you do in the War, Daddy?" as republished in 1999's *Shakespeare After Theory*—the work most roundly criticized in Grady and Hawkes's subsequent presentist attacks.[6]

Or consider the kinship between the textual arguments of Hawkes's classic "That Shakespeherian Rag" and Kastan's later "The Mechanics of Culture: Editing Shakespeare Today"—right down to their joint focus on deconstructing Fredson Bowers's metaphor of the "veil" of the text. The "Text" section of Hawkes's 1986 essay begins by quoting Bowers's goals to "strip the veil of print from a text" before commenting that:

> Such metaphors covertly map a familiar conceptual terrain. Buried treasure glints: here be dragons. The printed text "veils" an "underly-

ing" manuscript, its sacramental status guaranteed by the fact that it issues literally from the hand of the author.[7]

Then add Kastan's closing lines:

> The play exists in its materializations . . . It is always as text that litera-
> ture enters and acts in history, and a focus on the material and linguistic
> conditions of its textuality firmly locates it in the world in which and
> to which it is alive. Recognition of this may perhaps dull our desire to
> "strip the veil of print from a text," but it is, after all, the nineties.[8]

Even the shared, characteristic delight in humorous rhetorical play aligns these essays: they show a sense of style and an ability to wear learning lightly in order to allow more readers access—the same rationale that, Kastan has noted, undergirds the ubiquitous edito-rial practice of modernizing the spelling and punctuation of Shake-speare's playtexts themselves.

Furthermore, in each instance the writer turns his attention to the particulars of both a past and present moment, with con-sciousness of the role of our own priorities in sorting among interpretations—which, in an apt geometrical metaphor, Kastan likens to the unlimited number of differing lines that can pass through a single point.[9] Yes, he tends to focus his energies on the early modern materials, whereas Hawkes places as much or more emphasis on historicizing the politics of formative Shakespeare scholars alongside his readings of Shakespeare within an early modern frame. There are potential differences in the consistency and extent to which they take into account poststructuralist theo-ries disputing our access to certain forms of facticity. And the directness of Terry's connections between academic study and con-temporary British politics is definitely distinctive. But at least in their epistemological and ontological claims, the variance would seem to one outside early modern literary studies (and perhaps to some within it) insignificant.

So how do these resemblances become transmuted into a theory war? In part, perhaps, because of a perceived lack of adequate acknowledgment on Kastan's part regarding his predecessor, and in part as a result of the familiar debating habit of citing one passage to stand for the whole, in a way less generous than I hope I have just practiced: a pouncing on particulars, usually taking lines out of context from introductions, rather than considering the full texture of the readings that follow.[10] So, instead of modeling that form of abstraction, I want to gesture at another sort, building on Kastan's geometrical metaphor.

In an attempt to reposition this debate, and with a glancing nod to Sir Philip Sidney's continuum of the disciplines in the *Defense of Poesy,* I turned to contemporary philosophy. More specifically, I attended to the claims of *that* field's presentists, who believe we only have ontological access to the present, there being no "space" of the past. I also studied Bradford Skow's critique in his 2015 volume, *Objective Becoming,* which explores the possibility of a "robust" rather than "anemic" understanding of the "passage of time" (his adjectives) within alternative post-Einsteinian models that undo the separation of temporal from spatial dimensions, producing the useful concept of 4-dimensional spacetime itself.[11] I hoped to find some meaningful dialogue between what literary studies and philosophy call "presentism," but in this endeavor, as so often in looking across academic disciplines, I was disappointed. How sadly ironic, given the crucial importance of Terry's *New Accents* list and vision in having fostered cross-disciplinary understanding! This type of vocabulary dissonance may be why university administrators, who regularly interact with faculty across a range of fields that are not talking to one another, often speak of our "silos," and why at least US undergraduates, who move among professors trained in different disciplines in the course of their daily lives, are even now perplexed by our vocabularies.

So I have borrowed at least one useful concept from the philosophers: the 4-dimensional block universe model of spacetime, which fruitfully complicates the texture of historicist approaches by recognizing each point's indivisible combination of distinct matter, time, and space. This is not the place to elaborate upon the finer argument between the passage of time in a 4D block universe model of spacetime and the presentist or the moving spotlight theories of time that contest it. While there are linguistic and conceptual consequences to one's choice among them, I still would not be able to convey a sense of the stakes being more meaningful (perhaps less so) than in my churlish description of our subdiscipline's historicist/presentist debate. Indeed, the author of *Objective Becoming* recently told me as much. But I did come away from our conversation assured that I had some understanding of the basic terms of the philosophical debate. And my course of study thus provided a diagram for my own only slightly tongue-in-cheek version of a block universe of Shakespearean spacetime. It illustrates the synchronic closeness yet distinct lifelines of Kastan and Hawkes (Terry of course on the left), viewed not as positions we should choose *between* but rather as fellow travelers in spacetime, whom we, their audiences, triangulate and multiply, generating a larger, potentially more collaborative and capacious field. That, at least, is my hope and intention in projecting this one instance of Shakespearean star wars as reconceived in 4D spacetime.

And that is also the glory of literary studies' use of analogy, allegory and metaphor to popularize ideas. By contrast, Skow himself,

The block universe view of the passage of time

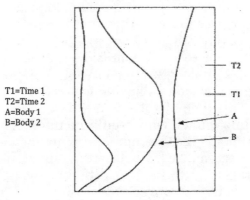

T1=Time 1
T2=Time 2
A=Body 1
B=Body 2

From Bradford Skow, *Objective Becoming* (Oxford: Oxford University Press, 2015). Key added.

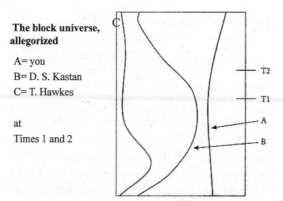

The block universe, allegorized

A= you
B= D. S. Kastan
C= T. Hawkes

at
Times 1 and 2

Shakespearean space time, partial view (A stands in for any number of distinct scholarly bodies, in dynamic relationship to lines B and C as well as each other). With apologies to Brad Skow.

despite participating in the temporality debate, considered his own philosophical work entirely "academic" in something close to the popularly dismissive use of that word. The silver lining I was left with was that some of the debates over the past thirty years in Shakespeare studies have at least inspired more sense of commitment, more passion and—here is the point that would matter to Terry—have had institutional effects (not the least of which involved improving the status of women in the professoriate, and beginning to address postcolonial and queer subject positions as well as, in some locations, race and class; I leave to others the evaluation of cultural materialism and theory's less identity-bound effects). But even so, I fear this will not be enough to guarantee a "robust passage of time" for the humanities, the kind that enables a vital future for Shakespearean collaborations, unless more of us shift our attention to the defense of our field in its entirety, in ways even outsiders can perceive as significant. Too often, in debates as typical as the Kastan/Hawkes example, we sound to the scientists like this philosopher sounded to me.

The world does and does not change quickly in the academic version of spacetime. Many of us shaped by the breakthrough work of Hawkes and company are still here, although the professional protocols that got us here have changed radically—for both good and ill. It has been well over a decade since Stephen Greenblatt called attention, as MLA President, to the need for a more diverse, generous definition of what "counts" as publication in our now-outlier discipline—yet there is little evidence that those securely positioned in the field have worked successfully to alter promotion criteria and practices in order to match those perceptions and publishing realities. Meanwhile, economics and "adjunctification" are certainly shaking up the academy, including our field. One other huge material change has taken place, even since Kastan wrote in 1999 that "most of us will for the foreseeable future continue to read Shakespeare's plays and teach them in edited versions, in book form rather than off a computer screen."[12] For many of us, *that* "foreseeable future" is now passing away. Despite what I ask, for my undergraduates, e-books, online streaming, and excessively marked-up rental copies have replaced creating a library of one's own, including a collected Shakespeare or even a few good-quality paperbacks. Campus bookstores will not resist this trajectory unless pressured by faculty (as we recently managed at MIT, albeit on a very small scale). The digital landscape of course offers more inviting possibilities that I can only gesture at here, including the ability to relocate plural Shakespeares beyond the Anglo-American axis (the differences within which remain a subtext in the Hawkes/ Kastan debate). But it is also true that, as more of us pursue what we call Global Shakespeares and the lucky ones with institutional access enjoy new JSTOR citation tools linked to the *Complete Works,* it becomes all the more important simultaneously to recall the pre-digital contributions that will otherwise disappear; ergo my recollection of Professor Beckerman's career, worries about the removal of legible paperbacks from college bookstores, and concern about *non-*JSTOR-catalogued citations. Our future involves negotiating among new worlds of online pedagogies and global markets of production and consumption that make many of our old distinctions trivial—at least beyond our personal or conference encounters, or our cherished, snatched hours in studies and libraries.

For me this means not only more online projects (for some of these are exciting indeed) and reading outside our areas of shared interest but also less theoretical effort spent on subtle differences among our methodologies and more on articulating spaces of alliance and their application. And in institutional, political collective action, based on whatever common ground we can achieve. At this historical juncture, I simply do not think literary studies can afford to advertise as focal our familiar models of inwardly focused competitive debate—unless we are content to be cast as the Aristotelian schoolmen of the twenty-first century, dancing on the head of a pin rather than (as feminists used to say) dancing through the minefields.[13]

How we talk about our work matters—to us, of course, but just as importantly to our students and the public, and those differing audiences demand attention urgently. Our location in institutions, as in Shakespearean spacetime itself, makes both individual and factional purity or perfection an illusion, even bad faith. Given that we live in an era when quantitative metrics are increasingly treated as the only or at least hegemonic standard of "real world" value, I continue to hope Shakespeareans will exchange economic metaphors such as "appropriation" for (uneasy) collaboration. Even "adaptation" is still too embedded in natural selection models of positivist science, a nineteenth-century perspective on temporality that the past century's rethinking of spacetime should help us counter, to the benefit of our historicist work. Collaboration lets us work with the past without effacing our own locations—which the presentist challenge in Hawkes's best formulations rightly demanded we keep visible.

Right now, it seems worth striving to make it easier for all humanities scholars (and certainly all Shakespeareans) to converse together without worrying quite so much about whether each person's ideas are smart enough individually and whether one school of thought's approach trumps another's: collaboratively, we know our field has much to offer. Those with secure jobs can surely help: in addition to advocating for a broader range of media forms as worthy scholarly credentials, many of us can stop presuming "work" necessarily translates to a book project. Indeed, we can stop publishing single-authored books unless there is a truly compelling reason to do so, in order to reserve those precious opportunities in a dwindling academic print culture for our younger colleagues and those facing oppressive institutional or governmental pressures. One alternative is to put more energy into creating projects that allow both individual and group opportunities. And *all* of us can work to improve the connections among our institutions and across our subfield by thinking more strategically about what work needs to be done and by whom, avoiding redundant labor. In a media-saturated world, the recurrent worry that an idea or project will be "scooped" by another scholar simply should not be happening any more.

I remain hopeful for our collective future if—and really *only* if—we swiftly modify many of the inherited practices described in this essay, and generate more and new collaborative models. Alongside our familiar work in the library and study we can indeed use a laboratory model, without having to share the bad hierarchical habits of many science labs, such as naming them after a single faculty member who gets most of the credit. Some younger scientists are already revising that model even if they still have to put their name on the door for funding reasons. Shakespeareans do not have to: we can create projects called A/S/I/A, or the Global Shakespeares Curriculum Initiative. By their very naming and structure, such projects help replace the competitive versions of scholarship with newer collaborative models truer to our stated ethics and the work itself. Let us share ideas and projects broadly whenever it is institutionally possible, rather than hoarding or protecting what nobody ever really "owned" in the first place. Perhaps in doing so, we can keep hope—and at least *some* of the remarkable spirit of Terence Hawkes—alive.

Notes

1. The official title was "The Futures of Historicism: A Symposium in Honor of David Scott Kastan," sponsored by the Yale Program in the History of the Book and the Department of English, New Haven, October 1–3, 2015.

2. Richard F. Shepard, "Bernard Beckerman, 64, Shakespeare Scholar," *The New York Times,* October 8, 1985; http://www.nytimes.com/1985/10/08/arts/bernard-beckerman-64-shakespeare-scholar.html. The students referenced included Susan Manning, Roman Paska, and Bill Condon.

3. Terence Hawkes, *That Shakespeherian Rag* (London: Methuen, 1986), x.

4. Terence Hawkes, in *Presentist Shakespeares,* eds. Hugh Grady and Terence Hawkes (London: Routledge, 2007), 12–13 ff.

5. Others share my concern, based on congenial responses including that of Ben Carson at October 2015's "The Futures of Historicism" conference at Yale; see also Jonathan P. Lamb, "Studies in Books and Their People or, the New Boredom 2.0" *Shakespeare Studies* 43 (Madison, NJ: Fairleigh Dickinson University Press, 2015), 211–34.

6. David Scott Kastan, *Shakespeare After Theory* (New York: Routledge, 1999), 132. See, for example, Grady and Hawkes, "Presenting presentism," in *Presentist Shakespeare,* 2.

7. Fredson Bowers, "Textual criticism," in O. J. Campbell and E. G. Quinn, eds., *The Reader's Encyclopedia of Shakespeare* (New York: Thomas Y. Crowell, 1966), 869, as cited in Terence Hawkes, *That Shakespeherian Rag,* 74.

8. Fredson Bowers, *On Editing Shakespeare* (Charlottesville: University Press of Virginia, 1966), 87, as cited in Kastan, *Shakespeare After Theory,* 69–70.

9. Kastan, *Shakespeare After Theory,* 196.

10. A footnote to *Coleridge's Writings on Shakespeare* constitutes the single reference to Hawkes's oeuvre in *Shakespeare After Theory,* 179n2; conversely, the attack in *Presentist Shakespeare* on Kastan's materialism as apolitical and not just "after" (or informed by) but "anti-" theory focuses primarily on a few passages in the introduction, i.e., Kastan, *Shakespeare After Theory,* 17, 38.

11. Bradford Skow, *Objective Becoming* (Oxford: Oxford University Press, 2015), *passim,* though in relation to presentism especially 32–34ff.

12. Ibid., 69.

13. The reference derives from Annette Kolodny's "Dancing Through the Minefield: Some Observations on the Theory, Practice, and Politics of a Feminist Literary Criticism," first published in *Feminist Studies* 6, no. 1 (1980) and often debated and reprinted since. My point here obviously resonates with Bruno Latour's critique of critique, though in another context I would call more attention to our differences.

NEXT GENERATION PLENARY

Introduction

W<small>E ARE DELIGHTED</small> to include in this volume five papers by distinguished young scholars that were chosen for delivery at the inaugural session of the Shakespeare Association of America's Next Generation Plenary, which took place at the SAA's April 2015 annual meeting in Vancouver. It is a pleasure and a privilege to share with our readers the work of these young Shakespeareans, and we hope that this collection of essays from the *Next Gen Plen* will be only the first of many to appear in *Shakespeare Studies* in the years to come.

The Editors

From *West Side Story* to *Hamlet, Prince of Cuba:* Shakespeare and Latinidad in the United States

Carla Della Gatta

In this short paper I hope to introduce a brief history of Shakespeare and Latinidad[1] and the questions that this rapidly growing field raises for theater making, as well as for performance analysis. I use the umbrella term of "Latino Shakespeares" to describe a textual adaptation or a performance in which Shakespearean plays, plots, or characters are *made Latino.* Latino Shakespeares are booming; there have been over forty Latino Shakespearean productions in the United States, most of which were produced in the last ten years, and a quarter of which occurred in the last two years. They range geographically across the country, from regional to repertory theaters, from Shakespeare festivals to universities. Examples include productions such as Edit Villarreal's 1991 *The Language of Flowers,* a *Romeo and Juliet* adaptation set during Day of the Dead festivities; Yale Repertory's 2002 all-male, all-Latino *The Taming of the Shrew;* the 2004 Los Angeles musical *Zoot Suit Romeo and Juliet;* the 2009 bilingual Broadway revival of *West Side Story* in which the Sharks sang and spoke in Spanish and the Jets in English; Oregon Shakespeare's 2011 *Measure for Measure* set in a border town with a mariachi band as the Chorus; and the 2014 post-apocalyptic *Henry IV* adaptation entitled *El Henry* funded through La Jolla Playhouse and staged in the streets of San Diego.

Latino Shakespeares did not surface through the agitprop Teatro Campesino from the 1960s or with the birth of contemporary Latino theater in the 1980s, but rather resulted from two concurrent but distinct genealogies. They were developed both by Latino directors and playwrights who adapted Shakespeare for Latino audiences, and as outreach initiatives by white practitioners (who are Jewish, gay, Anglo but foreign-born, or a combination of the three) who sought to tell their stories of acculturation through a different ethnic group. Latino Shakespeares vary in the quantity and usage of the English and Spanish languages, in the ratio of Latino and non-Latino actors and directors, and in their dramaturgical strategies for conveying Latinidad. Latino Shakespeares destabilize the binaries that classify productions as concept or traditional, Shakespearean or Latino, adaptation or translation. These productions are not "intercultural," or demonstrative of cultural exchange, but "intracultural," indicative of current American culture and Shakespeare's position in it. Thus they should be understood as a new development in American theater.

The intersection of American Shakespeare production and Latino culture can be traced back to September 1957 to two unrelated theatrical events in New York. That month, Joseph Papp of the New York Shakespeare Festival (now the Public Theater) mounted his first Mobile Theater production in an effort to bring Shakespeare to the people of the diverse boroughs and many neighborhoods of New York. Nearby, *West Side Story* opened in the well-established Broadway theater district. *West Side Story* changed the trajectory of musical theater, but not just that: it would become the most significant theatrical construction of Latinidad on Broadway and film for the next fifty years. The musical offers a highly contested depiction of Latinos set in opposition to a gang of border whites[2] and is mediated through an ethnicized adaptation of a Shakespearean play, shifting Shakespeare's households that are "both alike in dignity" to ethnically different ones.

The multiple legacies of *West Side Story* to the "Latino-ization" of Shakespeare cannot be overstated. It is the subtext, intertext and übertext with which Latino Shakespeares continue to be in fraught dialogue today. Reverberations of *West Side Story* are numerous, but here I will address two of them, both of which suggest that one value of Latino Shakespeares lies in their aptness to move outside racial categories still largely conceived of as binary and remarked for the most part visually.

The first is what I term "The *West Side Story* Effect." It involves the re-inscribing of Shakespearean representations of difference of various kinds—class, locale, familial—as a cultural-linguistic difference. This is seen now not just in Latinoized productions and adaptations of *Romeo and Juliet* or limited to Latino Shakespeares, but in non-Latino *Romeo and Juliet*s and other Shakespearean productions.

The second has to do with the trajectory of *West Side Story*, which moved from monolingual in its original inception and initial revivals, to bilingual in 2009, to semi-bilingual from 2009–12 when the Broadway run and subsequent touring production removed much of the Spanish to cater to monolingual English-speaking audiences. This path elevates the role of aurality in depicting a cultural division. Casting white actors as Jets and Latino actors as Sharks was not sufficient for conveying ethnicity to today's audiences; the Spanish language was incorporated and then changed as the show moved geographically to various cities with different cast members, audience expectations, and demographics. *West Side Story*'s legacy, clearly evidenced in Latino Shakespeares, is that white skin color is not a reliable marker of whiteness nor is it the theatrical counterpoint to Latinidad—monolingualism is.

The influx of Latino Shakespeares signals the growing desire to represent Latinidad onstage in productions and theaters not historically designated for Latinos or Latino Theater, and it also signals an ongoing reevaluation of American whiteness that is constructed through opposition to an auditory, rather than a visual, Other. Although casting choices and elements of the mise-en-scène contribute to cultural construction, dramaturgically, the Spanish voice (or the Spanish language) is a key signifier used to convey Latino culture. Spanish is used to overcome the challenge of recognizing an "authentic" Latino body onstage. The liminal figure of a Latino presents a way of imagining a visually diverse group of people whose heritage ranges from California to Texas, Puerto Rico to Cuba, Spain, Argentina, and so forth. Because Spanish dialects, accents, and slang vary just as widely, frequently the musical soundscape is used to specify a particular Latino culture where other auditory markers do not.

In twenty-first century Latino Shakespeares, oftentimes bilingual Latino actors who speak English without a Spanish accent are cast in lead roles,[3] and secondary characters are played by a range of brown-haired actors, who are white, Latino, and sometimes black, who use a Spanish inflection to signal their characters' ethnicity. This structure asks the audience to recognize ethnicity aurally for some characters and visually for others. Ultimately, Latino Shakespeares make clear that the performance of ethnicity places greater value on aural signifiers and requires a model of analysis that prioritizes language and sound.

What audiences finally see (and hear) onstage is only a small portion of what occurs in the process of the theater making of Latino Shakespeares, which includes the politics of the rehearsal room. As Latino Shakespeares mix practitioners and roles that are Latino and non-Latino, Spanish speaking and non-Spanish speaking, challenges arise for monolingual directors to coach monolingual and bilingual actors in bilingual roles. Asolo Repertory's 2012 *Hamlet, Prince of Cuba,* was performed in Shakespearean English for one month and then entirely in Spanish for one weekend by the same cast, although some of the cast, and the director, did not speak Spanish. The director employed Pulitzer Prize-winning playwright Nilo Cruz to do the translation and a bilingual Latino voice instructor, who was the first person to translate the Linklater voice method into Spanish, to work with the actors. This voice instructor, Antonio Ocampo-Guzmán, first recognized the need for both bilingual and Spanish voice methods when he directed Florida Shakespeare's bilingual *Romeo and Juliet* in 2005, and he has since trained other bilingual and Spanish-speaking coaches. In this way, Latino Shakespeares expand not just the reception of ethnicity, but the directorial strategies and acting methods for producing it.

The field of Latino Shakespeares demands new tools for theater making, and it does for performance analysis as well. Viewers of, and listeners to, Latino Shakespeares hear modern-day Spanish, perhaps in a variety of regional accents, together with Elizabethan/ Jacobean English, and see a bevy of racial and ethnic bodies onstage. This lack of temporal, linguistic, and cultural cohesion calls into question—which is more foreign to today's audience: Modern-day Spanish or Elizabethan/Jacobean English? This cross-temporal code switching, the movement between languages from different time periods, can facilitate understanding for people who do not speak either language. For example, in Chicago Shakespeare's 2008 bilingual staged reading of *Romeo and Juliet,* Benvolio's first greeting to Romeo, "Good morrow, cousin" became "Buenos días cousin,"[4] translating the greeting to a familiar phrase that eased comprehension for even non-Spanish-speaking audience members.

Funding initiatives specifically for what many would consider to be "cultural adaptations" are all but non-existent. Larger grants and corporate funding such as Shakespeare for a New Generation and funding from the Ford Foundation has assisted the production of Latino Shakespeares, but mostly in larger, established Shakespeare theaters. The National Association of Latino Arts and Cultures (NALAC) offers a substantial grant that is open to Latino artists and organizations that "demonstrate artistic excellence in pursuit of social justice through the arts,"[5] which makes Latino Shakespeares less likely to be funded. Without consistent financial support, most theaters that have produced a Latino Shakespeare have not produced a second one.

Programming strategies have also affected productions in larger theaters that have staged more than one Latino Shakespeares. At the Oregon Shakespeare Festival (OSF), a theater whose commitment to diversity has been exemplary for years, when Latino Shakespeares are staged, new works by Latino playwrights are not. For example, in 2009 the Festival staged an adaptation of *Don Quijote* penned by a Latino playwright, in 2010 a new play by a Latino playwright, in 2011 and 2012 they offered Latino Shakespeares, and in 2013 and 2014 new plays by Latina playwrights. But plays written by or about Latinos are not mounted in the same year as Latino Shakespeares; the Hispanic/Latino diversity box is fulfilled by either one or the other.[6]

This could be viewed as either a positive or negative consequence of Latino Shakespeares, but I argue that it clearly signals that Shakespeare is now part of the Latino Theatre canon, and similarly, other Latinoized classics are becoming so as well. Adaptations of works from the Spanish Golden Age such as Carlos Morton's *Johnny Tenorio* (*El Burlador de Sevilla*) and Octavio Solis's *Dreamlandia* (*Life is a Dream*) and of classical Greek drama such as Luis Alfaro's *Oedipus El Rey* (*Oedipus the King*) and *Electricidad* (*Electra*) are making their way onto prominent stages. But Latino Shakespeares have gained the greatest traction. Indeed, in the October 2014 Encuentro in Los Angeles, an unprecedented one-month Latino Theatre festival with seventeen productions, there was only one work by a non-Latino playwright: a production of *Julius Caesar.*

Latinos are the fastest growing American minority group, and by 2050, the United States will be "the third largest Latin American nation, behind Brazil and Mexico."[7] As scholars of Shakespearean performance, if we do not talk about Latinos onstage, or why they are not onstage, or how Latino culture is being portrayed or being ignored, we are not talking about American Shakespearean performance.

Notes

1. "Latinidad" is a term that translates directly to "Latinity." Latinos are typically defined as Americans or people living in the United States who are of Latin and South American descent. To note, "Hispanic" includes people of Spanish origin and is a term predicated on the Spanish language as the unifier across nations of people.

2. *West Side Story* does not present a group of ideal whites in contrast to Latinos, but rather a version of whiteness that deviates from the model citizen. Neither gang is presented as aspirational, and division in *West Side Story* has as much to do with all of youth culture as outsiders as it does with Puerto Ricans. "Whiteness on the border" is a term used by scholar Lee Bebout to describe the relationship between "whiteness and the Aztlán-reconquista narrative" ("The Nativist Aztlán: Fantasies and Anxieties of Whiteness on the Border," *Latino Studies* 10, no. 3 (2012): 298), but here I use the term "border whites" to designate the Jets' precarious position as whites who are not accepted by other more assimilated and middle-class whites. The Jets are unified through their position in society, their gang identity, and their white skin, but not through a shared national or cultural background or an ancestral language like the Sharks.

3. This is the common construct in Latino Shakespeares. By contrast, Shakespearean productions with Latinos in lead roles but without a Latino theme (e.g., much of Raul Juliá's body of work at the Public Theater) often allow Latino actors to retain their accents, especially if they are well-known or celebrity actors.

4. Henry Godinez and Karen Zacarías, *Romeo y Julieta* (Unpublished Script, 19 July 2008, MS), 3.

5. "NALAC Fund for the Arts (NFA)." NALAC (National Association for Latino Arts and Cultures). Nalac.org. http://www.nalac.org/nfa Web. 5 Oct. 2014.

6. Although OSF's season includes only one Spanish or Latino play per year, they offer additional events and support the development and staging of works by Latino playwrights. When Bill Rauch became the artistic director in 2007, he established a commitment to diversity in casting, staffing, and programming that has expanded each year. In summer 2008, OSF hosted a Festival Latino, and due to the success of the event, it morphed into CultureFest in 2010, which is now a biannual event that is inclusive of other cultures. In 2013, OSF hosted a Latina/o Play Project that became an annual initiative, and by 2015, OSF's Web site included synopses in both English and Spanish of all productions.

7. Antonio Viego, *Dead Subjects: Toward a Politics of Loss in Latino Studies* (Durham, NC: Duke University Press, 2007), 108.

Chaste Exchanges and Theatrical Legitimacy in *Measure for Measure*

KATHERINE GILLEN

IN THIS PAPER, I want to suggest that plays such as *Measure for Measure* invoke female chastity in response to widespread anti-theatrical discourse linking the theater with the brothel. As I hope to show, I believe that we could learn a great deal about the theater's reflexive interrogation of its own legitimacy if we attend to depictions of chastity in this light.

According to anti-theatrical logic, the theater, like the brothel, commoditizes people and seduces audiences with deceptive artifice and cheap, corrupt wares. As Stephen Gosson warns in *The School Of Abuse,* plays feature "melody to tickle the eare; costly apparel, to flatter the sight; effeminate gesture, to rauish the sence; and wanton speache, to whet desire too inordinate lust."[1] In addition to emphasizing actors' troubling sexuality, anti-theatricalists objected to the commercial exchange underlying both theater and prostitution. As Joseph Lenz explains, "Prostitution emblematizes, all too vividly, the worldliness of trade, the mercenary nature of all commerce," and depictions of the theater as a brothel reflect "the 'base' nature of any exchange or transaction, whether sexual, economic, or aesthetic."[2] As a result, the theater came to be seen, in Gosson's memorable phrase, as a "generall Market of Bawdrie," trafficking in human bodies and illicit representation.[3] Invoking this paradigm themselves, many early modern plays feature prostitution as a means of interrogating the theater's reliance on exchange, both mimetic, within the drama, and commercial, as actors were incorporated into early capitalist networks of labor, debt, and profit creation.[4] Shakespeare engages with these concerns most directly in *Measure for Measure,* in which Angelo bans the "merriest" of the "two usuries" (3.2.6–7), causing trouble for the bawd

Mistress Overdone and initiating the play's interrogation of sexual, economic, and representational exchange.[5]

Female chastity, in *Measure* and elsewhere, proves integral to the stage's response to anti-theatrical attacks and to its reflexive theorization of the ethics of theatrical exchange. In contrast to the prostitute's presumed artifice, the chaste woman is inscribed with representational stability to match her sexual purity.[6] Like the prostitute, however, her commodity status is foregrounded, first as a prize on the marriage market, where according to Luce Irigaray she is figured as "pure exchange value," and later as the possession of her husband.[7] In *Measure for Measure,* I suggest, Shakespeare offers this sanctioned, though still problematic, sexual exchange in place of prostitution as a metaphor for the theater. While Isabella's displacement from the convent into sexual traffic illuminates the violence of exchange, her marriage to the Duke reflects the uneasy process by which playwrights invoked female chastity to legitimize the theater, associating theatricality not with prostitution but with the normative exchange of marriage and the mimetic authenticity of the chaste woman.

As a novice in the Poor Clares, Isabella is initially defined by her resistance to sexual exchange, which in turn informs her objection to the legalistic exchanges proposed by Angelo after he arrests Claudio on charges of adultery. Drawing on Christian theology, Isabella rejects Angelo's conception of the law as an abstract series of exchanges in which transgressions are repaid with lives, pleading instead for Claudio's "free pardon" (2.4.111). She reacts even more forcefully to Angelo's extralegal proposition that she "fetch [her] brother from the manacles / Of the all-binding law" (2.4.93–94) by "lay[ing] down the treasures of [her] body" (2.4.96), a logic that adequates her chastity, now objectified as treasure, with her brother's life. Isabella appeals instead to the unequal exchange of Christian salvation, reminding Angelo that "all the souls that were, were forfeit once, / And He that might the vantage best have took / Found out the remedy" (2.2.73–75). In keeping with this outlook, Isabella refuses to bribe Angelo with "fond sickles of the tested gold, / Or stones whose rate are either rich or poor / As fancy values them" (2.2.150–52) and instead offers him prayers "From fasting maids, whose minds are dedicate / To nothing temporal" (2.2.155–56). Isabella regards her own chastity, like these virginal prayers, as operating outside the realm of commercial—and legalistic—evaluation, and she seeks to preserve its absolute value.

Isabella's Christian stance is compromised, however, by her fetishization of chastity as the sole entity that should remain exempt from exchange. While she claims that she would "throw . . . down" her life for Claudio's "deliverance / As frankly as a pin" (3.1.103–5), she refuses to submit her chastity, stating, "Better it were a brother died at once, / Than that a sister, by redeeming him, / Should die for ever" (2.4.106–8). Isabella ultimately accepts Angelo's quantifying logic but, believing that she will be damned eternally, contends that her chastity is of greater worth than Claudio's life. She even imagines her chastity to be twenty times more valuable in her supposition that, had Claudio "twenty heads to tender down / On twenty bloody blocks, he'd yield them up / Before his sister should her body stoop / To such abhorr'd pollution" (2.4.179–82). When Claudio fails to meet her expectations, Isabella compares him to a bawd who "take[s] life" (3.1.139) from sinful sexual exchange, claiming that his "sin's not accidental, but a trade" (3.1.148). Although Isabella's militant virginity is morally questionable in Shakespeare's Protestant England, her critique of the dehumanizing aspects of exchange is substantiated in the play both in the bed trick, where Angelo's fiancée Mariana substitutes for Isabella, and in the head trick, where the head of the prisoner Barnardine is swapped for Claudio's. Although these transactions facilitate the plot's comic resolution, they remain uncomfortably similar to those advocated by Angelo, and they expose the particularity that is forfeited when people are submitted to mechanisms of exchange.

The Duke connects these tricks to the mimetic exchanges of the theater, calling attention to actors' substitutions and transformations. Averring that "disguise shall by th'disguised / Pay with falsehood false exacting, / And perform an old contracting" (3.2.273–75), he attempts to recuperate sexual and theatrical exchange in the interests of the state, and he marshals Isabella's chastity to authorize his project. Though associated with representational purity, Isabella agrees to the Duke's plans and even turns to the language of the theater to justify her role in revealing Angelo's crimes. She explains to Mariana, "To speak so indirectly I am loth; / I would say the truth, but to accuse him so / That is your part" (4.6.1–3), conceding that the women have different "parts" to play and must temporarily "veil full purpose" (4.6.4). Isabella adheres to her faith in absolute truth, however, attesting that, in a larger sense, her claim "is ten times true, for truth is truth / To th'end of reck'ning"

(5.1.48–49). For Isabella, truth, like chastity, cannot be reckoned or exchanged, even if its representation is slightly unreliable.

Thus reconciling truth and spectacle, Isabella offers the play's most convincing vision of ethical theatricality when she affirms the audience's interpretive abilities, asking them to "let your reason serve / To make the truth appear where it seems hid, / And hide the false seems true" (5.1.68–70). Like a theatrical practitioner, Isabella relies on the audience to discern truth from the mimetic exchanges they see before them. Theatricality, heretofore associated with the artifice and commoditization of prostitution, is thus partially redeemed by Isabella's chaste presence. This shift registers in Isabella's discourse of gifts, as she claims that Angelo asked her to submit the "gift of my chaste body / To his concupiscible intemperate lust" (5.1.100–101). Although her wording does little to mitigate the nature of the proposition, it gestures toward an alternate framework in which exchange, theatrical as well as sexual, can be understood in terms of gift giving rather than dehumanizing transactions.

The Duke appropriates Isabella's emphasis on the gift in his efforts to reassert authority over his subjects. Even as he displays his prerogative to evaluate personal worth in the multiple marriages he arranges, he reveals that his power rests ultimately in his ability to transcend legalistic systems of exchange by granting mercy. Before pardoning Angelo, he articulates the logic that would demand his life in exchange for Claudio's presumed death: "An Angelo for Claudio; death for death. / Haste still pays haste, and leisure answers leisure; / Like doth quit like, and Measure still for Measure" (5.1.407–9). After Isabella forgives Angelo and pleads for him on Mariana's behalf, the Duke reveals that he has in fact preserved Claudio's life and pardoned Barnardine. The Duke's culminating spectacle thus showcases his mastery of theatrical exchange while simultaneously demonstrating his willingness to deploy the power of the gift, a power intimately associated with Isabella's chastity. The biopolitical violence underlying this authorization of exchange, however, is revealed in the Duke's famously troubling marriage proposal to Isabella. The Duke's statement "What's mine is yours, and what is yours is mine" (5.1.533) highlights the transactional nature of the exchange, while Isabella's silence indicates its coercive nature.

In *Measure for Measure,* then, Shakespeare gestures toward a model—later developed, I would argue, in *Pericles,* when Marina reforms the theater-like brothel—in which the exchanges of the theater are validated through their association with female chastity. Although *Measure* remains wary of theatricality, never fully abandoning the association of theater with prostitution, Isabella's participation in the final scene points toward a potentially redemptive, socially ameliorative theatrical ethic. Whereas the Duke uses spectacle to mystify his power, Isabella's plea to "let your reason serve / To make the truth appear where it seems hid, / And hide the false seems true" (5.1.68–70) offers a greater interpretive role to the audience, conjuring a more consensual model of theatrical "intercourse." Despite this overture, however, chastity retains its resistant quality in *Measure*. Isabella's silent response to the Duke, it seems, reflects residual discomfort not only with his display of biopolitical power but also with those defenses of the theater that rely on the traffic in women inherent to normative ideals of Protestant marriage.

Notes

1. Stephen Gosson, *The Schoole of Abuse [August ?] 1579 and A Short Apologie of the Schoole of Abuse [November?] 1579,* ed. Edward Arber (London: Southgate, 1868), 32.

2. Joseph Lenz, "Base Trade: Theatre as Prostitution," *ELH* 60 (1993): 833–55, esp. 842, 834.

3. Stephen Gossen, *The Schoole of Abuse,* 35.

4. For an analysis of the brothel's significance within the theater's negotiation of commerce, see Jean Howard, "(W)holesaling: Bawdy Houses and Whore Plots in the Drama's Staging of London," in *Theater of a City: The Places of London Comedy, 1598–1642* (Philadelphia: University of Pennsylvania Press, 2007), 114–61.

5. All citations from *Measure for Measure* refer to the Arden Shakespeare, ed. J. W. Lever (London: Methuen, 1965; reprint 1997).

6. For further discussions of chastity and representation, see Kathryn Schwarz, "Chastity, Militant and Married: Cavendish's Romance, Milton's Masque," *PMLA* 118, no. 2 (March 2003): 270–85.

7. Luce Irigaray, *This Sex Which is Not One,* trans. Catherine Porter with Carolyn Burke (Ithaca, NY: Cornell University Press, 1985), 186.

Glitches and Green Worlds
in the *Sonnets*

Matthew Harrison

In his edition of the sonnets, David West writes that the "key" to Shakespeare's sonnet 32 is "that it is totally insincere" (110).[1] In that poem, you'll remember, the speaker imagines a moment after his death when his beloved comes across his poems. They have not aged well: whether by the vicissitudes of taste or the steady development of poetic technique, they now seem "outstripped by every pen," "Exceeded by the height of happier men" (32.6, 32.8). The solution, offered twice, is to read "for . . . love" rather than for "rhyme" or "style" (32.14, 32.7, 32.14).[2]

West's point echoes through the criticism, not only of this moment but of the many similar moments in which Renaissance poetic speakers malign their own poems. We read failure as insincere mastery. Thus West refers this instance to "the convention of an ironic personal depreciation or mock modesty in the sonnet tradition." Likewise, Hyder Rollins reminds us of "the Elizabethan convention of pretended humility" (in Atkins 101), Atkins of the reader's "difficulty accepting the humility as genuine" (100), and Vendler of the "modesty topos" (174).[3] But notice that these four accounts (of irony, convention, disbelief, and topos) all locate the problem slightly differently: in the sonnet tradition, in Elizabethan culture, in readerly reaction, or in that long tradition of writerly self-deprecation. Even in calling the sonnet's sense of its own failures conventional, we disagree on what convention is being invoked.

I want to suggest that insincerity is this poem's key without being its claim. That this is a poem we are locked out of, and insincerity is one way of getting in. We *cannot* read the poem the way it asks to be read, for "my love." Note, by the way, how that phrase oscillates between "for love of me" and "in remembrance of my love of you"—and how painful the gap between those two can be in the *Sonnets.* In both cases, the poem begs for an intimate, specific, embodied love that we, separated by time and so much else from speaker and beloved, cannot offer.

So we take the readings our instruments allow, not only here but throughout the literary tradition. We systematically decode moments of doubt, confusion, relinquishment, and failure into signs of mastery over stylistic traditions.[4] In the brief time I have, I want to think through another way into such poems. And I want to do so by thinking about failure.

So: one mode of thinking about failure is what I will call "comic failure." We find this kind of failure laid out in self-help books and entrepreneurial culture, in advice to "fail better," "fail faster," "fail forward," and so on. Comic failure recuperates unpleasant feelings by incorporating them into narratives that (allegedly) move towards success. Such accounts are ideologically potent: they turn moments of abjection, rejection, dismay, or bad luck into reaffirmations of dominant values.[5]

I call this comic failure because it is the movement of so much comedy: a structural blockage becomes a series of personal mistakes—misconceptions, misrecognitions, blunders—that lead into a reaffirmation of a more-or-less existing order. At least for certain members of the cast. (We might think, for instance, about how *As You Like It* turns problems of capital—inheritance—into problems of *cultural* capital that can be resolved with a little "education," a show of valor in rescuing his brother, and a friendship with the Duke.)

The Sidneyan sonnet, in particular, often deploys this kind of comic failure. A structural problem (Stella's refusal, the conflict between virtue and desire) turns psychological and is then revised through wit. The sonnet "Grammar Rules" is exemplary for the ways wit reinterprets rejection as acceptance: two no's, he asserts, make a yes. We often read sonnets of self-deprecation, loss, and despair in exactly this way: the speaker's "rudeness" becomes, through the magic of *sprezzatura,* evidence of his mastery.

But, of course, the key to *this* sonnet is that it is totally insincere. Neither grammar rules, nor displays of wit, nor testaments of suffering entitle Astrophil to love. And the genre itself precludes external resolution. The next poem picks up not where the last one left off but just about where it began. Even the *Amoretti,* you will remember, headed towards the beautiful *Epithalamion,* stop short, amidst absence and despair. If variation happens in a sequence, it comes from a slow evolution of perspective, from ringing the changes on a particular idea, or from a slow accumulation of images and metaphors.

For Elizabethan writers, sonnets are failure machines: all the weaponry of rhetoric takes aim and the beloved remains unscathed. The momentary mastery of a closing couplet collapses into contradiction, into a new poem that knows that nothing has been resolved. Many sequences dramatize precisely this effect, likening it to the self-exhausting wit of the sonneteer (Sidney), the self-lacerating attempts to justify the beloved's cruelty (Shakespeare), the repetitive shape of female perfidy (Greville), the shifting humors of the poet (Drayton's revisions), the cruel implacability of the sonnet mistress, or the wastefulness of earthly love. Failure, I think, lends itself to allegory.

But we have another contemporary way to understand failure. The outcast. The loser, the slacker, the misfit, the punk, recently the queer, as in Jack Halberstam's *Queer Art of Failure.* What these approaches have in common is that they opt out of dominant values: failure becomes a site of resistance rather than restoration. Now I want to take up this second model of failure, which I'll call the glitch. In the "Glitch Studies Manifesto," Rosa Menkman writes:

> [T]he spectator is forced to acknowledge that the use of the computer is based on a genealogy of conventions, while in reality the computer is a machine that can be bent or used in many different ways. With the creation of breaks within politics and social and economical conventions, the audience may become aware of the preprogrammed patterns. In this way, a distributed awareness of a new interaction gestalt can take form. (3)[6]

Glitches confound data and code. The procedures that smoothly convert data structures into meaning fail, rendering themselves on screen as new, alien patterns that intersect and combine with the original. (Often this is quite literal: the glitch in the '80s video game *Yar's Revenge,* for instance, is the code of the game itself, processed just beyond recognition.)[7]

So what happens if we read sonnets as glitch? Not as a way of recapturing ugly feelings in service of mastery but a break that calls those conventions to account. Or rather, if we accept that the failure of own procedures—our own proclivity to unite "love" and "style" but to separate "sincerity" and "skill"—is part of what the sonnet renders, at least on our mental screens.

Note the recurring backdrop in the *Sonnets* in which poetic evaluation is imagined as a deeply social activity. In the speaker's self-reproach and his remarks on other poets, we feel the pressure of a newly-forming community of tastes. The 'conventional' tropes of poetic humility, in turn, repeatedly serve to opt out of that community:

> Let them say more that like of hearsay well;
> I will not praise that purpose not to sell.
>
> (21.13–14)

> Why with the time do I not glance aside
> To new-found methods and to compounds strange?
>
> (76.3–4)

> And therefore [thou] art enforced to seek anew
> Some fresher stamp of the time-bettering days.
>
> (82.7–8)

> I think good thoughts whilst other write good words.
>
> (85.5)

Resisting the pressures of the "good," the "fresh," the "new," and the "modern," these poems assert values of "truth" and "love": keywords on which the *Sonnets* ring the changes.

But, I insist, neither of these terms articulates a positive poetic program. As the shifting valences of words like "beauty," "painting," and "ornament" make clear, Shakespeare does not offer a consistent stylistic critique of contemporary practice. Rather, the tropes of badness imagine an escape from one set of values—the public performance of wit and skill—in favor of a quieter, less steady connection between reader and writer. Take, for example, the rival poet series. Far more than they critique stylistic excesses, these poems repeatedly personify the discord between these two value systems, presenting the rival as a full and successful participant in a social world of lyric, writing "dedicated words" that "disperse" (82.3; 78.4) and circulate broadly, while the speaker links his silence, his feebleness, and his truth.

Wrongly or rightly, we cannot take these poems as sincere. Neither love nor truth are categories the sonnets give us access to. Rather, the sequence reflects upon and dramatizes this deep incommensurability between what poems say and what they mean, between craft and desire, skill and love. To read as glitch is to insist that we cannot evade this problem through a more subtle reckoning of skill. It is to imagine the sonnet not—or rather, *not only*—as a parade of ingenious platitudes, but also as a hitch, a failure, in that relentless allegorical process that harnesses ugly feelings for the glib narratives of mastery, of domination, of self.

Glitch teaches us that convention is a procedure rather than a form, a key rather than a lock. And Renaissance artists, I would argue, are fascinated by the *limits* of such procedures—the distortions of modesty, the awkward failures of *sprezzatura*. To understand the prehistory of modern notions of aesthetic independence, we need to attend more carefully to accounts of failure: Shakespeare's imagined faults, Spenser's "rudeness," Sidney's endless "bates." Such moments never quite manage to undo the whole tragic enterprise of comic failure, never quite manage to unravel the conventions within which they are interwoven. But in their frustrations, their ugliness, their distortions, they offer something which cannot be recuperated but can be lived within. An opting out, an escape, a stop.

Notes

1. David West, ed., *Shakespeare's Sonnets* (London: Duckworth, 2007). My thanks to Laura Kolb, Sara Saylor, Emily Vasiliauskas, and Ana Harrison for suggestions on drafts of this talk. Michael Lutz offered an initial provocation. Many thanks as well to the SAA Organizing Committee, Holly Dugan, Bailey Yeager, Mario DiGangi, and to my fellow Next Generation Plenarists. And I owe a great debt to Diana Henderson, James Siemon, and others at *Shakespeare Studies* for their assistance with this edition of this talk.

2. Shakespeare's *Sonnets* are cited from the Folger Digital Text edition. Barbara Mowat and Paul Werstine, eds. 2010. Web. Accessed November 2014. <http://www.folgerdigitaltexts.org/?chapter = 5&play = Son&loc = Son-001>

3. Carl Atkins, ed., *Shakespeare's Sonnets* (Madison, NJ: Farleigh Dickinson University Press, 2007); Helen Vendler, ed., *The Art of Shakespeare's Sonnets* (Cambridge, Mass.: Belknap Press of Harvard University Press, 1997).

4. See Catherine Bates's *Masculinity, Gender, and Identity* (Cambridge: Cambridge University Press, 2007), which describes and critiques the editorial tendency to recuperate accounts of authorial abjection. Matthew Zarnowiecki's *Fair Copies* (Toronto: University of Toronto Press, 2014) came out after I submitted this

talk, but his chapter on Shakespeare's sonnets is similarly interested in taking seriously the rhetoric of "fault" and "error" that surrounds them. But where my overarching metaphor is the "glitch," his is the textual error: he concludes, provocatively: "Poetics *is* reproduction with a difference" (130).

5. My thoughts on "failure" and "play" are very much influenced by the slides for Merritt Kopas and Naomi Clark's keynote, "Queering Human-Game Relations" for the 2014 Queerness and Games conference. <http://deadpixel.co/QGCON-2014.keynote.kopas-clark.pdf> Kopas and Clark offer an account of and a response to contemporary writing on "queering" games and play. To me, at least, their work suggests a critique of our preconceptions about the Green World as a liberating space of play. See, in particular, 41–43.

6. Rosa Menkman, "The *Glitch Studies* Manifesto," *Sunshine in My Throat.* January 2010. Web. Accessed November 2014. <http://rosa-menkman.blogspot.com/2010/02/glitch-studies-manifesto.html>

7. For more on the glitch effect in *Yar's Revenge,* see Scott Stiphen, "Howard Scott Warshaw," *Digit Press Interviews.* Web. Accessed November 2014. <http://www.digitpress.com/library/interviews/interview_howard_scott_warshaw.html>

Part-Believed Shakespeare

Daniel L. Keegan

WHAT IS SHAKESPEAREAN DRAMA UP TO THESE DAYS? What has it been doing in the theater since the advent of performance studies and that discipline's critique of drama's authority over performance? We should begin with the comments of W. B. Worthen, who offers the decisive rearticulation of drama's participation in performance, dissolving fantasies of Shakespearean authority that have for generations, if not for centuries, thrilled and, more recently, dismayed critics. For Worthen, drama is *working:*

> To the extent that [social and theatrical] technologies change, we have only two choices: either to find new affordances in the text that enable us to use it to *do new work,* or to consign the drama to a forlorn heap of plays echoing in the dustbin.[1]

It is being *put to work* through the behaviors of performers, directors, ensembles, productions. With any luck, drama is being put to new, interesting, and engaging work. Far from dominating performance, drama is set in motion by repertoires of performance practice.

Thinking dramatic writing as "writing for use" by these repertoires, as Worthen does, undoes ideologies of dramatic authority and affirms the value of theatrical practice.[2] Our question, then, might be this: What happens after hours? What happens if our metaphors for drama's theatrical participation take us *out* of the office, *out* of the factory, and *to* the party or the protest? In putting drama to work do we risk filtering out dramatic energies that chafe against the work set down for them, that clown around during necessary questions, and that dream uselessly of other, *unnecessary* inquiries (cf. *Hamlet* 3.2.38–43)?[3]

Shakespeare's *Hamlet,* much against its protagonist's neoclassicizing will, presents a protracted encounter with such clowning dramatic agencies, an encounter that discloses more *playful* possibilities for the interaction between drama and performance. In doing so, it conducts us into a zone of the performance event that is to us scholars and critics as the rooster's cry is to Horatio: something that we (as theatregoers and practitioners) have heard and seen, but (as scholars and theorists) only in part believed (cf. 1.1.170).

For our purposes here today, I will focus on the sequence by which *Hamlet* ushers its clowning dramatic agencies into this part-believed zone. This happens in the movement between two of the play's most famous dramatic agencies: between Hamlet's "globe" and his "machine."

Both of these terms chafe against the work set down for them, but the manner of their chafing marks an epochal transformation of drama's theatrical role. The globe chafes famously, even brazenly. It ripples out concentrically from Hamlet's initial enunciation—"Remember thee? / Ay, thou poor ghost, whiles memory holds a seat / In this distracted globe" (1.5.95–97)—to implicate not only the Globe Theatre in which the audience hold their seats, but also the "great globe itself" beyond the theatre. The "machine," by contrast, clowns so discreetly that it has become disproportionately more famous for its modern, industrialized shenanigans than for its early modern ones.

But . . . Hamlet's attempt to use this term to indicate his body and, in turn, to use his body as collateral for constancy—"Thine evermore, most dear lady, *whilst this machine is to him*" (2.2.122–23; emphasis added)—is hobbled by the fact that this sense of machine-as-body is not so consolidated that it can hold at bay the term's earlier meanings. In fact, Hamlet's use of "machine" is the *OED*'s first citation in this sense,[4] and the earlier senses go to work stitching Hamlet's letter—which emerges as part of Polonius's misguided fantasy of Hamlet's love madness—together with the play's revenge plot.

To bullet-point things:

- The "machine" as a "material or immaterial structure, esp. the fabric of the world or of the universe" (*OED* 1a; from 1545) lands on nearby employment in the text of the letter itself which suggests that Ophelia should "Doubt that the stars are fire / Doubt that the sun doth move / Doubt truth to be a liar / But never doubt I love" (2.2.115–18). It also evokes the play's texture of cosmic anxieties, as when we learn that Hamlet's eyes might "start from their spheres" (1.5.17).

- The machine as "scheme or plot" (*OED* 1b; from 1595) finds ample employment with the various scheme-engines of murder, revenge, spying, and detection that have, by this point in the play, come to light.
- The machine as "military engine or siege tower" (*OED* 3; from 1583) tele-commutes to the nervous battlements where we heard of the hectic "mart for implements of war" (1.1.77) and met the Ghost who, in his armor-machine, laid siege to the night watch.

*

Both terms clown their initial enunciation. But the relationship between each clowning term and the necessary questions of its scene is starkly different. The "globe" clowns in a cooperative spirit—yoking the inhabitants, first, of the theatre and, then, of the whole world as co-signatories to the moment's necessary question: Hamlet's promise of remembrance. The "machine," by contrast, achieves escape velocity from the *apparently* necessary questions of its scene—Polonius's oral-interpretation of Hamlet's missive to Ophelia—in order to hook up with the *even more necessary* questions of the play: Ghosts, schemes, cosmic dislocation.

What shall we make of this? At first glance, we are given little guidance as to how we should understand the relationship between the machine's "necessary" efforts and its "unnecessary"—or, rather, even more necessary—ones. We have, we might say, *heard* its puns, but we are only partly sure—or really not at all—how we should *believe* them. The "machine" puns gratuitously, as if to remind us that what had seemed like a promising revenge tragedy has since been derailed by Reynaldo, Voltemand, and Polonius's predilection for a tale of bawdry between Hamlet and Ophelia.

What *has* happened is a redistribution of dramatic agency: a Copernican shift in drama's clowning dynamics. While the "globe," in its concentric puns, evokes a geocentric cosmology with Hamlet's globe, the Globe Theatre, and the great globe itself as the heavenly spheres, the machine, by contrast, draws our attention to the fact that the son—and here we are talking about the s-o-n son, the one who has identified himself with the "globe," the earth—doth move.

This Copernican shift is given an elaborate staging that confirms its dynamics. From the moment of its first enunciation, after the interview with his father, Hamlet admits that his "globe" is "distracted" (1.5.97), perhaps threatening to start from its station. This distraction is realized onstage as the Prince—calling furiously for his tables, excoriating the asymmetry between outward smiles and inward villainy—reels a bit in his stance, paces, looks . . . just like a celestial object about to come unstuck from its long-standing pride of place. Then, when his companions hesitate to swear a second time, they are surprised to hear the command of the Ghost issuing up through the floor: "Swear" (1.5.157). Hamlet decides that it is time to "shift our ground" (1.5.164). His globe is now on the move, he and his companions forming a little, scurrying planetary system wheeling across the stage.

The son, as we have said, doth move.

*

So. What is drama up to here? Where the globe's supplemental senses collaborated neatly with its primary project, the machine's connotations not only jailbreak from the necessary questions of its scene but seem to inflict themselves on the body that the "machine" was supposed to evoke. I mean this quite literally. In the "Swear" sequence, the cosmic machinery of the distracted, dissolving "globe" and the furiously burrowing siege-machine of the father lead Hamlet on a merry chase. By the time he is able to calm this "old mole" (1.5.170) and to say "[r]est, rest, perturbed spirit" (1.5.190), Hamlet is in need of a rest himself. His arms and legs are shaking, his breath heaving. (All the more reason for a break with Reynaldo and Voltemand!) Contrary to his enunciated tastes, things are not "well digested in the scenes" (2.2.435–36): they are *indigested* in the scenes. "It"—theatrical performance, that is—has not been given "smoothness," as Hamlet suggests in his Advice to the Players (3.2.8); instead, through this in(di)gestion of dramatic agency, it has been given *unsmoothness.*

The "machine" is not so much "put to work *by*" the repertoire as it "*goes* to work *on*" the repertoire. In doing so, it clowns Hamlet's Advice. It also, I have wanted to suggest, charts a course through a zone of dramatic performance that our interpretive protocols have only partly believed. If we were once confident that drama authorized performance, more recent critics have tended either to abandon this relationship—giving rise to a "widening gap between literary and performance studies"[5]—or to negotiate between these terms under the sign of technical competence and theatrical "work." The "machine," by contrast, brings text crashing back into performance, using the energy from the collision to kick off a party (or a protest) in the supposedly widening gap between them.

The stakes of attending this party are not only epistemological—what we can see or hear or say about performance—but also ethical—what and who we can care about in performance. If the work of the last generation was to relocate the competence of performance from the author to the performer, the "machine" summons our attention to the (always potentially) *in*competent encounter of player and text.

If the "machine" diagrams this moment on a cosmic scale, the play concludes on a more quotidian one. Refusing Hamlet's injunction to "report . . . [his] cause aright," Horatio replies that he will drink the poison after all because he is "more an antique Roman than a Dane" (5.2.344, 346). Or that is what he says in our modern editions. The word is printed "anticke" in the Second Quarto and "Antike" in the Folio and First Quarto, clowning Horatio's efforts at classical allusion. It is not until Q5 in 1637 that some bold printer "fortifies our ears" (cf. 1.1.34–35) against this clowning term.

Until then, Horatio highlights the unsmooth struggle between actor and text. He also highlights the *potentiality,* the *creativity* of this moment, refusing to refer this rough-hewn encounter to the divinity of textual meaning or theatrical competence. At the moment that Hamlet puts Horatio to work on the imaginary forces of the future and of Fortinbras's regime, the eternal grad student hesitates. In doing so, he opens up a space where we might let part-belief take hold of us, even if the blank verse halts for it.

Notes

1. W. B. Worthen, *Drama: Between Poetry and Performance* (Chichester, UK: Wiley-Blackwell, 2010), 34; emphasis added. This and subsequent citations were presented as Powerpoint slides at the conference.

2. Worthen, *Drama,* xv.

3. William Shakespeare, *Hamlet.* Ed. Harold Jenkins (London: Methuen, 1982). All citations refer to this edition.

4. "A living body, esp. the human body considered in general or individually" (*OED* 2; from 1604).

5. Joseph Roach, "Performance: The Blunders of Orpheus," *PMLA* 125.4 (2010): 1080.

Sounding Spaces: *The Tempest's* Uncanny Near-East Echoes

JENNIFER LINHART WOOD

"WHAT COUNTRY (FRIENDS) IS THIS?" asks the shipwrecked Viola as she comes ashore to Illyria in *Twelfth Night*.[1] That question is neither raised, nor answered, in the play-text of *The Tempest*, although it has been asked by centuries of theatergoers, readers, and scholars determined to identify *The Tempest*'s island. Compounding this geographical challenge is the fact that the music and sounds audible in *The Tempest* offer confusing—if not downright contradictory—clues about the location of its island. Because its sounds ring uncannily familiar and foreign at once, this play calls into question its own geographic location as constructed through sonic phenomena. *The Tempest* layers sounds suggestive of points from around the globe in the performance space of the theater, both by experimenting with the creation of sounds of cultural otherness, and by attempting to "sound," or explore, the depths of otherness.

As a counterpoint to the critical interpretation that *The Tempest* is a play primarily about the New World, I argue for its significant Eastern and classical resonances. Among these are oblique references at several moments in the play to Virgil's *Aeneid,* Prospero's soliloquy in act 5, scene 1, that recapitulates lines spoken by the Eastern witch Medea in Ovid's *Metamorphoses,* and Ariel's music that echoes passages from Christopher Marlowe's epyllion *Hero and Leander.* This paper will describe the Near East resonances of *The Tempest* in the first two examples of what Caliban calls the island's "sweet aires" (TLN 1493). These scored musical pieces, "Come Unto These Yellow Sands" and "Full Fathom Five," loudly echo *Hero and Leander.* Marlowe's poem is set in and around the Hellespont that flows between Sestos, located on the Greco-Turkish shore, and Abydos, on the Asiatic coast. The Hellespont, much like the island in *The Tempest,* marks the intersection of Europe and Asia, West and East.

It is a counterintuitive claim to suggest that the island of *The Tempest* has Eastern characteristics, and the doubtful nature of this statement is compounded by our twenty-first-century sense of definite geography. Logically, the island should be somewhere in the Mediterranean between Tunis and Italy, and near enough to where Prospero and Miranda might have landed after their exile from Milan. While the Italian nobles who are shipwrecked in the opening scene have been travelling across the Mediterranean from Claribel's marriage in Tunis back home to Naples, the tempest reroutes their ship to the remote island on which Prospero and Miranda arrived years earlier. Here, the audience is aligned with Ferdinand when the invisible Ariel's singing begins; like Ferdinand, we are unsure where this tempest has brought us. The music Ariel sings suggests that the Italian ship was blown eastward on its return voyage, especially if the audience members at Blackfriars were familiar with Marlowe's popular *Hero and Leander,* first published in 1598 and later available in several other posthumous editions.[2] Recognition of the Marlovian echoes could have prompted the audience to conclude that the tempest had redirected the characters toward the East, if not to the Hellespont itself.

The lyrics of "Come Unto These Yellow Sands" are imperative, drawing the shipwrecked Ferdinand onto the island:

> Come vnto these yellow sands,
> and then take hands:
> Curtsied when you haue, and kist
> the wilde waues whist:
>
> (TLN 520–23)

The "yellow sands" to which Ferdinand is invited have several connections to the East. They might have subliminally evoked the exotic East Indian setting of Titania's love idyll with her votaress in act 2, scene 1 of *A Midsummer Night's Dream;* she terms this setting—perhaps in another Marlovian resonance—"Neptunes yellow sands" (TLN 502). Elisabetta Tarantino also recognizes echoes of Virgil's *Aeneid* and of Arthur Golding's translation of Ovid's *Metamorphoses* in these "yellow sands," a phrase found twice in Golding's version (4.410, 575).[3] Yet another echo may be heard between these opening lines of the musical air and lines from Marlowe's *Hero and Leander.* Hero describes her seaside tower as "Far from the towne[,] where all is whist and still, / Saue that the sea playing on yellow sand, / Sends foorth a ratling murmure to the land" (C2v).[4] The "sea" Hero describes is the Hellespont, a multivalent and multitemporal space, and one that features in Book 1 of the *Argonautika.* Hero's tower is located at Sestos, an ancient Greek town on the modern Gallipoli peninsula in Turkey, on the European side of the Hellespont. Abydos, on the Asiatic mainland, is across the Hellespont from Sestos and is where Leander resides. A liminal space between Europe and Asia, the Hellespont shares characteristics with the island in *The Tempest,* an island that also occupies an intermediate space among Europe, Asia, the Mediterranean, and perhaps even the New World.

Spatial location becomes even more disoriented in Ariel's next song "Full Fathom Five." The alleged death of Ferdinand's father, Alonso, is described in poetic detail:

> Full fadom fiue thy Father lies,
> Of his bones are Corrall made:
> Those are pearles that were his eies,
> Nothing of him that doth fade,
> But doth suffer a Sea-change
> Into something rich, & strange [.]
>
> (TLN 539–44)

These lyrics offer an image of global metamorphosis through the sea's transformation of Alonso's Italian "bones" into tropical coral. But the Mediterranean seas also touch an Eastern shore, as Alonso's optic pearls indicate. The "rich and strange" transformed pearl is suggestive of the opulent "orient pearl." The *OED* defines this as "a pearl from the seas around India, as distinguished from those of less beauty found in European mussels; (hence, more generally) a brilliant or precious pearl."[5] "Pearles" may have also signaled the New World, for they appear in William Strachey's *A True Reportory,* a well-known source linking the play to Bermuda.[6] However, the pearl is featured most often in Shakespearean representations of eastward spaces; for example, "Her bed is *India,*" Troilus says of Cressida, and "there she lies, a Pearle," in another play set near the convergent Hellespont (TLN 134). The melodic waters create in Alonso's fictionalized body a "Sea-change" that incorporates skeletal coral and multidirectional pearls.

Echoes of Marlowe's *Hero and Leander* are audible in this air as

well: in describing the deep fathoms to which Neptune has pulled
Leander, we find that

> the ground
> Was strewd with pearle, and in low corrall groues,
> Sweet singing Meremaids, sported with their loues
> On heapes of heauie gold, and tooke great pleasure,
> To spurne in carelesse sort, the shipwracke treasure.

(D5v)

Shakespeare utilizes this same combination of "pearle" and "corrall" found at the bottom of Marlowe's Hellespont to create the
fabricated version of Alonso's "shipwracked," drowned, and metamorphosed body submerged five fathoms under the sea.[7] The
echoes of Marlowe's epyllion demonstrate a further uncanny effect
of these airs in *The Tempest:* auditors who recognized Marlowe's
poem through Shakespeare's "yellow sands," "corrall," and
"pearle" would have heard these words sung by Ariel in yet
another reverberating echo of Marlowe's poem. Ariel's singing
refashions Marlowe's written poetry—read silently or aloud—into
music that makes familiar text sound different when the lyrics are
set to musical tones and rhythms. Ariel's water-nymph consort of
"spirits" enacts Marlowe's "Sweet singing Meremaids" when they
vocalize the bell-refrain to conclude "Full Fathom Five." Moreover, the air ostensibly memorializing Alonso more accurately pays
tribute to Christopher Marlowe as the ghost-like presence in this
passage: it is not Alonso, after all, who suffers this sea-change.[8]
Rather Marlowe's writing, which has not "faded," is likewise transformed when Shakespeare echoes his poetry through Ariel's songs.
   Ariel's two airs demonstrate that—like the construction of space
in *The Tempest*—sound is also uncanny through its blending of
familiar and foreign elements. Michel Serres recognizes the implicit connection between sound and space, and theorizes that
sound has "a universal reach" through the vibrating soundwave.
He argues for what he calls "global listening" because "the soundwave has immediate access to totality" through its wide-ranging, or
"global" compass.[9] I would like to propose that Serres's apt phrase
might be expanded to include listening to sounds that resonate
from points around the worldly globe, as well as to soundwaves
washing over audience members in spaces like the Globe Theatre.
While the Globe may or may not have been a venue for *The Tem-*

pest, its nomenclature echoes the fact that the Globe Theatre worked to perform the earthly globe.[10] It did so, not only by presenting global locations (including Denmark, Italy, Illyria, Cyprus) and characters (like African Moors and Egyptian Queens), but also by importing real and imagined sounds of otherness to the domestic theater.

"Come Unto These Yellow Sands" and "Full Fathom Five" offer a "rich and strange" uncanny echo of Marlowe's poem about the intermediary space of the Hellespont. The sung word "strange" further insists on the exotic location of the island. The lutenist Robert Johnson calls attention to the word "strange" by making it the musical climax of the piece in what is an early, if not the original, musical setting of "Full Fathom Five."[11] "Strange" is defined by the *OED* as indicative of foreignness: "Of persons, language, customs, etc.: Of or belonging to another country; foreign, alien" (1a), and "Situated outside one's own land" (1b). *The Tempest* is both "rich," due to its incorporation of passages from other possibly familiar texts, such as Marlowe's *Hero and Leander,* and "strange," as these citations are from texts about various and varied foreign lands. *The Tempest* suggests that each encounter in a contact zone space—whether in a strange land or in the theater itself—is an uncanny experience.

The Globe, like any other theater, is simultaneously a sonic laboratory in which strange and alien cultures are staged, while it is also a completely familiar, domestic playhouse, as when Prospero reminds us "Our Reuels now are ended" (TLN 1819). While this doubleness is uncanny, we move away from sounding otherness to something safer and more familiar in the task of returning home. And yet, the theater takes travelers on sonic journeys. Whether it creates an experience of Calibanesque "delight" (TLN 1493) or the Boatswain's exasperation at hearing a "diuersitie of sounds, all horrible" (TLN 2223), the noise of the theater affects its audience. *The Tempest* uses sonic disorientation as the basis for its pervasive geographic disorientations because sound is at once internal and external to a body. Sound's uncanny vibratory force moves bodies in directions, even directions we still attempt to navigate today. This experience simulates the experience of otherness in foreign locations, while exploring ways otherness might be sounded in the homely space of the London theater. The "noyses, / Sounds, and sweet aires" Caliban describes are orchestrated into "something rich and strange" indeed—both sonically and spatially—in *The Tempest* (TLN 1492–93).

Notes

1. TLN 51. Citations to Shakespeare's plays are from the First Folio, accessed through the Folger LUNA collection. STC 22273 Fo.1 no.05, 5. William Shakespeare, *Mr. William Shakespeares Comedies, Histories, & Tragedies. Published according to the True Originall Copies,* ed. John Heminge and Henry Condell (London, 1623). Through-line numbers (TLN) are given according to *The First Folio of Shakespeare: the Norton Facsimile,* 2nd ed., ed. Charlton Hinman and Peter W. M. Blayney (New York: Norton, 1996).

2. The second edition of the poem, also published in 1598, was completed by George Chapman, who lengthened Marlowe's original considerably. Three subsequent editions of the Marlowe-Chapman version followed (1600, 1606, and 1609) that predated *The Tempest's* performance. The language of Marlowe's poem—and not the Chapman additions—is echoed in Shakespeare's play.

3. Tarantino cites the reference to Virgil's *Aeneid* that comes from Thomas Phaer's 1558 translation (4.577–583). Elisabetta Tarantino, "Morpheus, Leander, and Ariel," *Review of English Studies* 48, no. 192 (1997): 489–98, esp. 491.

4. Citations from Marlowe's *Hero and Leander* are from the 1598 version that does not contain Chapman's additions. Christopher Marlo[w]e, *Hero and Leander* (London: 1598). STC 17413. Accessed through the Folger LUNA collection. It is notable that the word "whist," defined by the *OED* as "Silent, quiet, still, hushed; making no sound; free from noise or disturbance" (*adj.* 1a), appears in conjunction with "yellow sands" in both Marlowe's and Shakespeare's texts. The line from "Come Unto These Yellow Sands" that includes "whist" (TLN 523) is cited in the *OED* entry.

5. This is the definition for "pearl of orient *n,*" listed under "orient, *n.* and *adj.,*" A. 1. b. "Pearl" was also used to refer to the pupil or lens of the eye; see *OED* "pearl," n.1 A.I.1.a. Miriam Jacobson is also interested in the significance of orient pearls to Marlowe's *Hero and Leander;* see *Barbarous Antiquity: Reorienting the Past in the Poetry of Early Modern England* (Philadelphia: University of Pennsylvania Press, 2014), especially 149–87.

6. Even Strachey's pearl is itself multidirectional, for he mentions that some of their men on the island of Bermuda have fished for pearls "(which some say, and I believe well, [are] as good there as in any of their other Indian islands)"; William Strachey, "A True Reportory," in Edward Wright Haile, *Jamestown Narratives: Eyewitness Accounts of the Virginia Colony, the First Decade, 1607–1617* (Champlain, VA: Roundhouse, 1998), 394. For an excellent discussion of the importance of Strachey's writing to *The Tempest,* see Alden T. Vaughan, "William Strachey's 'True Reportory' and Shakespeare: A Closer Look at the Evidence," *Shakespeare Quarterly* 59, no. 3 (2008): 245–73. In the New World, the pearl resounds with Eastern overtones, as "Indian islands" can refer to a variety of east or west locations. See also Karen Raber, "Chains of Pearls: Gender, Property, Identity," in *Ornamentalism: The Art of Renaissance Accessories,* ed. Bella Mirabella (Ann Arbor: University of Michigan Press, 2011), 159–80; and Karen Robertson, "Playing Indian: John Smith, Pocahontas, and a Dialogue about a Chain of Pearl," in *Indography: Writing the 'Indian' in Early Modern England,* ed. Jonathan Gil Harris (New York: Palgrave Macmillan, 2012), 105–16.

7. Given the difference in posthumous publication dates of the two texts—

Marlowe's in 1598 and Shakespeare's in 1623—it is remarkable that the spellings of both "corrall" and "pearle" are identical in these passages. Although Edward Blount published *Hero and Leander* and was one of the publishers of the First Folio, this lexical uniformity between texts is unusual.

8. I am grateful to Diana Henderson for sharing this observation.

9. Michel Serres, *The Five Senses: A Philosophy of Mingled Bodies,* trans. Margaret Sankey and Peter Cowley (New York: Continuum, 2008), 47.

10. In *"The Tempest*'s Tempest at Blackfriars," Andrew Gurr writes *"The Tempest* was the first play Shakespeare unquestionably wrote for the Blackfriars rather than the Globe"; see *Shakespeare Survey Volume 41: Shakespearian Stages and Staging,* ed. Stanley Wells (Cambridge: Cambridge University Press, 1989), 92. It is well known that *The Tempest* was performed at the Blackfriars Theater, for an audience who may have been more familiar with Marlowe's poetry than attendees of the public theater. The audience members experiencing this play likely had something of a similar response as the characters of the play: each perceives different aspects of the island.

11. The extant manuscript copy of "Full Fathom Five" was written by John Wilson, who attributes the tune to the well-known court lutenist Robert Johnson. This manuscript dates from 1660, nearly half a century after the play was initially staged. Folger MS V.a.411, fol. 11r, from the Folger LUNA collection.

Incited Minds: Rethinking
Early Modern Girls

Caroline Bicks

THE HUMORAL MODEL that dominates current understandings of the early modern body has left an uninspiring legacy when it comes to the study of female minds. Women, generally unable to produce enough heat to keep their bodily fluids efficiently in motion, had sub-standard physiologies compared to those of men; as a result, their brains were deficient when it came to the heat-refining process necessary to produce quality animal spirits. Without such spirits, images and ideas could not easily and adeptly move through the brain's three ventricles: the anterior, where imagination and the five senses resided, the middle—site of judgment—and the posterior, the seat of memory.[1]

Adolescent virgin girls were uniquely disadvantaged. Their bodies were not yet broken in by marital intercourse and opened up by regular menstruation, so they were prone to the retention of seed and blood, and to the diseases of the mind that followed. Unlike her colder, older self, this newly mature female was imagined to be excessively hot, and her body and mind reacted to this atypical heat in specific ways. When abundant seed is "over long retained in Bodies prone to lust, and full of heat," wrote Lazarus Riverius, it works like yeast in the seminal vessels, inflaming sexual desire and madness: "Vapors ascend unto the Brain, which disturb the Rational Faculty, and depose it from its throne."[2] This medically-based belief found its fictional expression in characters like the raging, greensick Jailer's Daughter in *Two Noble Kinsmen,* who is cured of her insanity once she has sex—one of the "pushes," perhaps, wenches are "driven to / When fifteen once has found us" (2.4.6–7).[3]

Fourteen and fifteen often do appear as dangerous ages, sexually speaking, for girls in early modern discourses. In her study of teenagers in early modern drama, Ursula Potter notes that "[i]t is rare in early modern drama to find any character given a chronological age, but the exceptions to this general rule are plays that depict teenage girls whose sexual development is central to the plot." Potter considers how such plays often tag these girls' ages early on as a cue for the audience to consider "the risky sexual behaviors commonly associated with the virginal body at puberty."[4] Such a reading does help explain seemingly out-of-character comments like that made by the kind-hearted Antigonus in *The Winter's Tale* about his three pre-pubescent girls, ages 11, 9, and 5. Should Hermione prove false, he swears to her jealous husband Leontes that "I'll geld 'em all. Fourteen they shall not see, / To bring false generations" (2.1.149–50).

The criticism on early modern adolescent girls tends to focus on their newly mature sexual bodies. Given the early modern fixation on controlling daughters, exemplified so gruesomely by Antigonus, this work is critical to understanding the larger gender-based networks of oppression in the period. As Kate Chedgzoy asks, "If . . . we focus on female children as they pass through adolescence into adult femininity, what can we learn of the complex interrelations of the politics of gender, sexuality and age in Shakespeare's texts and in the culture from which they emerged?"[5] I would add to this question, and to the vital emerging field of early modern girlhood studies that informs it, the following: If we focus on the adolescent female, what can we learn about the rich interactions between girls' brains and their early modern environments, and what can this tell us about the specific and unique cultural work early moderns imagined these minds to be doing?

Older scholarship read girls' minds as passively impressionable. In 1845, N. J. Halpin wondered, for example, at Juliet's "familiarity with thoughts and expressions not likely in any other way to have obtained entrance into the mind of an innocent and unsophisticated girl of fourteen," and attributed her remarkable speech to the bridal ceremonies and masques in which she likely had participated: "Thus might she have caught up the topics and language appropriated to this species of poetry."[6] Nearly 135 years later, Marjorie Garber would observe of Juliet's speech that, "[f]or a young woman of her age and her sheltered upbringing, this innocent forwardness is as remarkable as it is appealing."[7] What unifies these otherwise vastly different scholars is the lack of intentional invention that marks the early modern girl's mind in their—and so many other critics'—analyses, for even "innocent forwardness" implies behavior that is unplanned and impulsive.[8] Her middle ventricle, where the brain judged and assessed images and ideas, appears inactive. Her front ventricle may take in sensory experiences, and her brain may even store them in its back ventricle for future imitation, but these are relatively limited and unmastered cognitive operations.

More recent work on adolescent girls generally continues along these lines, focusing almost exclusively on the sexual and/or pathological nature of their bodies and the raging of their minds once they neared and then crossed the pubertal threshold. According to Helen King, the sixteenth century in England was one of the historical periods to "focus on the onset of menstruation as the key point of danger for women, a time when their bodies and their minds are equally in turmoil."[9] Her work on the diseases of virgins suggests that greensickness became a condition in its own right associated with post-pubertal girls at this time. Potter uses work like King's to argue that playwrights used fourteen- and fifteen-year-old girl characters as a way "to pander to a public fascination with contemporary medicine and the mysteries of the womb."[10] The recent surge of studies in popular medicine and uterine illness has leant enormous learned support to this view of what early moderns thought about the female body and brain, and, in turn, to the critics, artists, and consumers who continue to see characters like Ophelia, for example, in terms of her troubled adolescent girl's mind and her lovesick body.[11]

But when we challenge ourselves to look beyond this dominant reading of early modern girls, it becomes clear that they did not always, or even primarily, find sexual risk, shame, and madness when they saw fourteen—or when fifteen once had found them. The dramas are rife with teenage heroines who have yet to experience the "cure" or the dangers of sexual intercourse, yet who display considerable cognitive gifts. Multiple stories feature these girls using their minds in focused and inventive ways—and all three ventricles at that: the fourteen-year-old Marina, who makes herself known to her father, Pericles, "by her own most clear remembrance" (22.32), and who, as Tharsia in Twine's version, describes herself as "skilful in the liberal sciences," and able to "resolve" for the people "any manner of questions";[12] John Marston's "quick, deviceful, strong-brain'd Dulcimel, . . . too full of wit to be a wife," who celebrates her fifteenth birthday at the start of

The Fawn (3.1.436–37);[13] and Miranda, age fourteen, whose memory inspires wonder in her father, and (as I will explore in the latter part of this essay) who has a "beating" mind that takes in, assesses, and transforms Prospero's art (1.2.177). Clearly there was an alternative discourse about female brain function in circulation in the early modern period, but the critical history of reading girls in terms of pathology and wandering minds has obscured it.

So, how do we find these productively brainy girls? This essay offers some possible ways in to this question by pointing to other stories about how early moderns experienced and imagined adolescent girls' minds, stories in which girls—particularly those who are marked in relation to the pubertal threshold of fourteen or fifteen—are seen to absorb, process, store, and invent in ways that, I argue, are unique to this particular stage of female development. The girls I study here are physically mature, but not married. Their minds are not yet absorbed by the demands of a household, a husband, and children, and, as such, they are free to move in unusual ways. I employ the term "girl" here fully aware of its lack of consistency in the period. As Jennifer Higginbotham's research reveals, there was no one dominant word to describe female children at this time, and "girl" could be applied to females of any age.[14] I use it here to mark a specific group of females who were not defined solely in relation to their fathers or husbands. They are neither female children nor "women," positions that each were seen to limit the female mind—in the first case because of her undeveloped brain function and, in the second, because her mental focus was expected to stay fixed on domestic responsibilities and spousal relations.

This alternative interpretive lens, I argue, allows us to rethink some of Shakespeare's girls, among others—even the "mad" Ophelia, who, as Bruce Smith's work on winks and cognitive perceptual moments suggests, certainly deserves a more nuanced consideration: "her winks, and nods, and gestures . . . / . . . Indeed would make one think there might be thought . . ." (4.5.11–12).[15] These thoughtful, often inventive girls appear in medical texts, popular handbooks, histories, letters, plays; they are virtually everywhere once you start looking for them.

The real early modern girls who cluster around this age-specific threshold offer up rich examples of cognitive invention: the fourteen-year-old Rachel Fane who wrote masques for performances at her family's household in Apethorpe; Joan Waste, the blind

Protestant martyr who, from about fourteen years of age, desired
"to understand and have printed in her memory the sayings of the
Holy Scriptures";[16] the fifteen-year-old Princess Elizabeth who, in
a letter she writes to her brother, King Edward, imagines her body
transported to an alternate space: "my inward mind," she writes,
"wisheth that the body itself were oftener in your presence."[17]

When the Jesuitess Mary Ward wrote her autobiography, she figures her fifteen-year-old self as a girl whose mind, body, and spirit
work together toward one future transformative state:

> When I was about fifteen years old, while living in the house of a rela-
> tion of my mother, in great measure because the retirement was more
> to my taste, I had a religious vocation. This grace by the mercy of God
> has been so continuous that not for one moment since then have I had
> the least thought of embracing a contrary state . . . I practiced much
> prayer, some few fasts, and some austerities, and internal and external
> mortifications . . . I delighted in reading spiritual books, and I spent
> much time by day and sometimes by night in this employment. . . . I
> had during these years burning desires to be a martyr and my mind for
> a long time together fixed upon that happy event; the sufferings of the
> martyrs appeared to me delightful for attaining to so great a good, and
> my favourite thoughts were how? And when?[18]

The only desires that burn in Ward's fifteen-year-old girl's self are
the kind that fix her mind upon the future happy event of her
hoped-for martyrdom. Her thoughts, bolstered by her reading,
show no sign of moving to a "contrary state."

Theorists of early modern embodiment have brought important
attention to the kinds of interactive dynamics of mind, body, and
surroundings that Mary Ward articulates here as she seeks retire-
ment in her relative's home, reads day and night, and puts her body
through a series of punishments and constraints, fixing her mind
on her future. Their work is especially important for a study such
as this one, for it offers a way to see beyond the narrative of female
pathology that I am looking to read against in my larger project.[19]
When we consider the embodied interactions between these post-
pubertal girls' brains and their environments, even more possibilities for how early moderns thought about and experienced the
female adolescent mind open up. What could these girls imagine,
remember, and produce in the space of the convent, for example,
or in the pastoral countryside; in the heat of Verona, or the sea air
of a tropical island?

For the remainder of this essay, I will be exploring some of the interpretive spaces that reveal themselves when we consider this creative brain-work and start paying attention to the many girls who are marked (and sometimes mark themselves) in relation to this pubertal threshold. Before they were married, and obligated to think upon one husband and household, in what ways were the minds of these particular early modern girls imagined as free to think, create, and move? What could they inspire and embody? This group clearly captured the imaginations of early modern playwrights, and their teenage heroines are not always or only enacting fantasies about future husbands. They are using all three parts of their brains, often in connected ways, to actively engage and sometimes challenge their audiences. Their imaginations shape the arts in its many forms—drawing, healing, performance; their memories store up their countries' and families' pasts; they assess and judge what others would rather forget: "Where is the beauteous majesty of Denmark?" (*Hamlet* 4.5.21).

In the first part of this essay, I turn primarily to medical descriptions of the female body and mind as girls crossed the pubertal threshold at age fourteen or fifteen. Next, I consider the story of Dibutades's daughter, an ancient myth about the origins of the plastic arts that resurfaced and morphed in the late-sixteenth century to feature a desiring girl as the inventor of painting; finally, I focus on the beating mind of *The Tempest*'s fourteen-year-old Miranda to explore how attention to these stories of girls' artful minds allows for a new reading of Prospero's daughter—one that shows the impact of her brain's operations on her father's mind and art.

Incited Minds

Early modern writers often presented conflicting accounts of how male and female bodies worked. They were atypically unanimous, however, when it came to marking and describing the moment of female puberty: when a girl reached the age of fourteen or fifteen, her body began to heat up, her breasts began to swell, and she began to menstruate. "Now at the second seven yeares," wrote the popular physician Helkiah Crooke,

> the heate begins to gather strength, to burst foorth as the Sunne in his brightness, and to rule in the Horizon of the body; from which heate

doe proceede as necessary consequences, the largeness of the wayes
and vesselles, the motions and commotions of the humours . . . and
finally the strength of the expelling faculty.[20]

This description of a fourteen-year-old girl's body bursting with
heat presents the thermal transformation of puberty as ordered and
entirely non-pathological. Crooke connects these females, not to
the cold and changeable moon, but to the sun in his brightness. The
heat "gather[s] strength," "rules" and produces the "strength of the
expelling faulty." This model offers a significant exception, then,
to the gendered rules of early modern humoral theory in which the
female body and mind wallow in their cold and wet inadequacies.
The expansion of the vessels, movement of the humors, and first
menstrual flow are all "necessary consequences" of this increased
heat. Thomas Willis, in his *Practice of Physick,* gives a similarly
positive description of these vigorous movements of the blood girls
experience "about the time of ripe age":

> for as the Blood pours forth something before destinated for the brain
> through the spermatic Arteries to the genitals, so also it receives as a
> recompence, a certain ferment from those parts through the Veins, to
> wit, certain Particles imbued with a seminal tincture, are carried back
> into the bloody mass, which makes it vigorous, and inspire into it a new
> and lively virtue; wherefore at that time the gifts both of the Body and
> Mind chiefly shew themselves. [21]

Inspiration, liveliness, gifts of the body and mind: this vision of
pubertal transformation decidedly challenges the conventional
scholarly narrative of pathological and raging adolescence.

This increase in heat was not always viewed in positive terms,
of course. Helen King argues that "the humoral model presented
puberty in both sexes as a time of excess heat, and therefore of
lust."[22] Lust is certainly a problem that early moderns grapple with
in their discussions of the hot, post-pubertal female, and many
writers (medical and otherwise) connected these bodily changes to
the incitement of lustful thoughts. In his *Anatomy of Melancholy,*
for example, Robert Burton describes how, "Generally women
begin Pubescere as they call it, at 14 yeeres old, and then they begin
to offer themselves, and some to rage. Leo Afer saith that in Africke
a man shall scarce finde a maide at 14 yeeres old, they are so forward, and many amongst us after they come into the teenes, do not
live but linger."[23] The anonymous author(s) of *Aristotle's Master-*

Piece similarly describe how, "when they arrive to Puberty (which is usually about the Fourteenth or Fifteenth Year of their Age, according to their respective Habits and Constitutions) then their *Menses,* or Natural Purgations begin to flow: And the Blood, which is no longer taken to augment their Bodies, abounding, incites their Minds and Imaginations to Venery."[24]

At first blush, this heat-incited, venerous mind does not appear to be a positive development for the female. But what these writers do offer us in their depictions of these pubertal girls is a female imagination that is newly activated. And when we turn back to Crooke's section on puberty, we can see that this mind is not always imagined as unruly in its newfound movements. After describing the heat of the female body bursting like the sun, Crooke turns to the effects of the body's pubertal transformations on both male and female minds. At age fourteen, he writes, "men begin to grow hairy, to have lustfull imaginations and to change their voice; womens Pappes begin to swell and they to think upon husbands."[25] The male imagination is prone to lust over which young men appear to have little control. Fourteen-year-old females, on the other hand, are "thinking upon husbands." While we could write this description off as just one more example of the dominance of the marital narrative in determining the stages of female development, Crooke's description of the thinking female suggests that the process of puberty has incited the female mind in new and potentially inventive ways. In essence, Crooke is making a medical argument for the connection between female puberty, an increase in heat, and the female ability to project herself into as-yet-unknown future scenarios.

In her study of early modern humors, Gail Kern Paster argues that "the onset of maturity in girls and their passage to wifehood are understood to involve a significant increase of bodily heat and of the aggressive agency such heat entails." She describes these increases as "thermal transformations wrought by desire" and demonstrates how love will have heat in a variety of textual representations of adolescent girls.[26] But Crooke and the other writers I have touched on here offer up another way of imagining this post-pubertal heat. It does not always come from the spark of erotic sensation; rather, it bursts forth from the natural development of the female body at puberty. And, from there, the mind and imagination are incited—sometimes to venery, but sometimes to other forms of expanded female agency as well (or instead).

By describing this transition into a stretch of time during which sexually mature females remained unattached while their minds were enabled to consider multiple future possibilities, Crooke shows us a stage of girlhood that has enormous potential for rethinking how early moderns imagined the workings of the adolescent female mind. Depending upon one's social class, the time between thinking of husbands and having one might be a matter of a year, or more than a decade.[27] "The vehemency of Adolescence," as one early modern put it, lasted "betwixt the age of 14 and 28."[28] This extended adolescence may have been affected by what Helen King has coined the sixteenth-century "puberty gap" that developed as people waited to marry until their mid to late 20's.[29] But this prolonged puberty, or vehement adolescence, can be seen as a space of creative potential and interpretive possibilities in the period—not just one of physical illness and venerous madness. While these latter notions are undeniably there in the oral and written discourses of the time, they have overshadowed the other possibilities for female creativity and activity that this temporal space, into which girls were initiated at the moment of puberty, makes possible.

Crooke's distinction between male and female minds at puberty appears to be an early modern invention, for when we turn to the Aristotelian text from which Crooke and his predecessors were working, we get a more egalitarian picture. The *History of Animals* notes many similarities in the pubertal transformation between boys and girls: When they are "twice seven years old," both males' and females' "breasts swell," and just as the boy's voice changes, "[i]n girls, too, about this time the voice changes to a deeper note." Boys and girls also experience similar sexual longings:

> Girls of this age have much need of surveillance. For then in particular they feel a natural impulse to make usage of the sexual faculties that are developing in them. For girls who give way to wantonness grow more and more wanton; and the same is true of boys, unless they be safeguarded from one temptation and another; for the passages become dilated and set up a local flux or running, and besides this the recollection of pleasure associated with former indulgence creates a longing for its repetition.[30]

Although Aristotle's girls are initially singled out for "surveillance," and their dilated passages contribute to their sexual feelings, their minds operate in indistinguishable ways from those of their male counterparts. Both genders are prone to the "recollection of pleasure" once they have indulged in wanton behavior.[31] But it is only Crooke's fourteen-year-old males who are held captive by their lustful imaginings, thoughts that eventually and inevitably will be tied to past pleasures. His girls are busy inventing their futures.

Dibutades's Daughter

In his *Historia naturalis,* Pliny the Elder tells a story about art that brings an adolescent girl's thoughts on a husband front and center. In describing the origins of clay bas-relief he describes how

> modelling portraits from clay was first invented by Butades, a potter of Sicyon, at Corinth. He did this owing to his daughter [*filiae opera*], who was in love with a young man; and she, when he was going abroad, drew in outline [*lineis circumscripsit*] on the wall the shadow of his face thrown by a lamp. Her father pressed clay on this and made a relief, which he hardened by exposure to fire with the rest of his pottery.[32]

In Pliny's tale, the father devises his creation by means of both his daughter's desire and her act of tracing a shadow.[33] There is no invention involved on her part. The power relations here are clearly defined. The father discovers the art; the daughter is the instrument through which he does so.

This story of Dibutades (Butades' later incarnation) and his daughter would become enormously popular in the second half of the eighteenth century, especially in France. Scholars have fastened on to the myth of the "Corinthian Maid" (as she came to be known) in their analyses of the aesthetic, political, and philosophical developments of this period.[34] She was the subject of many paintings, ballads, and poems. Shelley King argues that "the iconography of the myth . . . had by the eighteenth century developed two competing visions of the maid of Corinth as an artist, one a creative human figure possessed of unusual aesthetic power, and the other a mere instrument guided by Cupid in her invention."[35] This latter vision undergirds Derrida's reading of the pictorial tradition, which focuses on paintings of the Maid looking away from her lover and toward his shadow—a pose that he uses to found his idea of the blindness at the origins of representation.[36]

These aesthetic theories, however, do not necessarily apply to earlier, non-visual depictions of Dibutades's daughter. How was she appearing in England's early modern period? What kinds of cultural work were she and her myth doing? On this topic, the scholarship is largely silent. There are many fewer written, and no visual references to her at this time; however, it was during the early seventeenth century that the original myth began to morph into a story, not about a father creating a new art through his daughter's essentially passive act of imitation, but rather building on something she has invented.[37]

A 1601 English translation of Pliny is instructive, for it begins to embellish some details of its source in small but significant ways:

> *Dibutades,* a Sicyonian born, and a Potter, [who] was the first that devised at Corinth to form an image in the same clay whereof he made his pots, by the occasion and meanes of a daughter which hee had: who being in love with a certaine young man, whensoever hee was to take a long journey far from home, used ordinarily to mark upon the wall the shaddow of her lovers face by candle light and to pourfill the same afterwards deeper, that so shee might injoy his visage yet in his absence. This her father perceiving, followed those tracks, and by clapping clay thereupon, perceived that it tooke a print, and made a sensible forme of a face: which when hee saw, hee put it into the furnace to bake among other vessels, & when it was hardened, shewed it abroad.[38]

Here, the potter's daughter does more than trace her lover's shadow, she "pourfill[s] the same afterwards deeper." "Pourfill" is an obscure term rarely used in English, but it does appear in a 1610 tract on heraldry to describe "the outward Tract, Purfle, or shadow of a thing."[39] Although such adumbration is associated in that text with "expressing to the view a vacant forme," it evokes in Pliny's text a girl's desire to "injoy" her lover "in his absence" (a phrase that recalls the originating emotion from which so many art forms spring). She retraces the lines, creating "tracks" that form a blueprint of her lover's face that her father's clay then picks up. The father is still the deviser of the art, and the daughter still appears as the "meanes" through which he comes to form images in clay; but her desire translates here into a drawing that does not just capture an initial act of tracing, but figures a repeated and deepening act of inking that continues after the beloved is gone.[40] Given the rarity of the term "pourfill," it is remarkable that Pliny's translator uses it again, two chapters earlier, to praise the contributions of Pausias to the art of painting, singling him out for his superior skill: "to pourfill well, that is to say, to make the extremities of any parts, to marke duly the divisions of parcels, and to give every one their just compasse and measure, is exceeding difficult."[41] This coincidence in terms connects a great painter to the artful acts of a desiring girl and lends even more evidence to my argument here that early moderns were seeing these mature, yet unmarried females as potential inventors.

When Robert Burton tells her story in his 1624 edition of *The Anatomy of Melancholy,* he takes this suggestion of artfulness to a new level. She appears in his section on Love-Melancholy, and he leads up to the anecdote with a story of "young men and maids" interrupting a Christmas mass with their love songs. The priest, in anger, prays that they will continue singing for twelve months as a punishment. They do, without food or drink, and are then forgiven. "They will in all places be doing thus," Burton writes, "young folks reading love stories, singing, telling or hearing lascivious tales, tunes, such objects are their sole delight, their continual meditation, they can thinke, discourse willingly, or speake almost of no other subject." Unlike some writers who saw this fixation as purely negative, however, Burton writes that such love is at the root of all literary and visual art forms: "maskques, mummings, banquets, merry meetings, weddings, pleasing songs, fine tunes, Poems, Love-stories, . . . Elegies, Odes &c. Symbols, Emblems, Impreses, devises . . . may be ascribed to it."[42]

It is in this context of love and the art forms it spawns that he introduces the daughter of Dibutades (whose name appears incorrectly as Deburiades):

> Most of our arts and sciences, painting amongst the rest, was first invented, saith *Patritius, ex amoris beneficio.* For when the daughter of Deburiades the Sicyonian, was to take leave of her sweet heart now going to warres . . . to comfort her selfe in his absence shee tooke his picture with a cole upon the wall, as the candle gave the shadowe which her father admiring perfected afterwards and *it was the first picture that ever was made.*[43]

Burton's tale of Dibutades's daughter is remarkable for its reshaping of Pliny's origin story: the potter's craft disappears entirely here, subsumed by a new art form altogether—picture-making, or possibly painting itself given the way Burton introduces the story.[44] This art originates with a girl's thoughts, desires, and actions, and has no connection to the materials of her father's trade. He does not create something new from what she has done; rather, he perfects a form that she herself has invented.

This departure from the myth is suggestive, I believe, of a larger early modern shift in the perception of girls' minds and their capacities, for here the adolescent girl is imagined to be a foundational agent of a new art form's creation. The myth also connects girls' desires to methodical acts of the imagination. In this story, the daughter of Dibutades does not act on her longings by offering her body, nor does she rage with greensickness. Rather, she comforts herself by drawing a figure of her beloved.

In the next two editions, Burton adds to the story and its run-up in ways that showcase the relationship between adolescent desire and the foundations of art forms. In 1628, he expands the list of creative productions that are indebted to love to include "plays, Comoedies, Attelans [Roman farces]." And he adds that that first picture, one that originated with a girl's desire both for her lover and her comfort, had helped make her city famous: "ever after Sycion for painting, carving, statuary, musicke and philosophy was preferred before all cities in Greece" (493).

Not all early modern writers gave the potter's daughter such credit. By 1638 she had become a controversial figure whom certain writers sought to put back in her passive place. She appears in Franciscus Junius's *The Ancient Art of Painting* as

> A Corinthian Maid . . . taught by Love, [who] ventured to put her unskillful hand to the first beginnings of art, drawing lines about the shadow of her Lover that was to go a great journey. Whereupon (as it is the custome of men to prosecute small beginnings with a stedfast study), her father Dibutades, a Potter by his trade, cut the space comprised within the lines, and filling it with clay, he made a pattern and hardened it in the fire, proferring to Greece the first rudiments of picture & Statuary.[45]

Junius's version is markedly more skeptical toward the girl's role. She is "unskillful," and her drawing is a "small beginning" to what her father will produce with his "stedfast study." Earlier in his work, Junius had described the "first beginnings of Art" as "very poore and imperfect" because they were rooted in "bare Imitation": "We will never rise above servile Imitation, without raising our thoughts to a more free and generous confidence," he writes, and using "our own natural wit" (29, 31). Junius imagines the truly inventive mind as male, and "natural wit" as a solitary genius far removed from the small unskillful attempts of Dibutades's daughter. But she already had emerged from the shadow of her father's story, shifting the relation of his art's creation to hers, and making it dependent on her foundational designs.

'Tis Beating in my Mind

And now, I pray you, sir—
For still 'tis beating in my mind—your reason
For raising this sea-storm.

(*The Tempest,* 1.2.176–78)

Just as Dibutades's daughter was beginning her transformation from passive means for her father's art to active inventor of her own, Shakespeare was imagining Miranda, a heroine whose father's art is arguably the most famous in Shakespeare's canon. What makes Miranda especially relevant to the set of questions I am asking here is that she is one of the girls whom Shakespeare specifically keys to the age of fourteen. "Twelve year since, Miranda, twelve year since," Prospero repeats, "Thy father was the Duke of Milan"; and she was "not / Out three years old" when they arrived on the island (1.2.53–54, 40–41). Fifteen, to recall the words of the Jailer's Daughter, has not yet found her (although Prospero's desire to marry her off suggests that he fears the pushes she may be driven to when it does). Shakespeare also, notably, gives Miranda a beating mind in her opening scene. This image appears three times in *The Tempest,* in fact, which is half the total number of such references in all of Shakespeare's plays combined. Clearly he found in it a guiding motif for his play. And it begins inside the head of an adolescent girl.[46]

Yet it is Miranda's bleeding heart—not her beating mind—to which critics are drawn. Arthur Kirsch, for example, argues that Shakespeare called upon Montaigne's essay "On Cruelty" to dramatize Prospero's struggle for virtue: "The ordeals to which Prospero subjects others on the island are at once recapitulations of his beating memories and images of his effort to overcome them."[47] This internal struggle for virtue differentiates his labors from the natural, innocent expression of virtuous compassion and co-suffering that "is revealed throughout the play in the 'piteous heart' of Miranda."

This polarizing division between Prospero's "beating memories" and Miranda's piteous heart is symptomatic of a larger bias, not only in the critical tradition around *The Tempest,* but around adolescent girlhood more broadly—one that treats men and their creative struggles as a story of isolated genius and ambition, with girls like Miranda acting as artlessly emotional subsidiaries and sometime helpers. Rather than read Miranda as a "dependent, innocent, feminine extension of Prospero,"[48] I propose to look more closely at how her "beating" mind—which, true to the discourse of early modern psycho-physiognomy, is reciprocally connected to her body and environment—works to incorporate, assess, and ultimately shape the operations of Prospero's mind, and ultimately the future of his art.

Miranda has provided the only human counterpoint to Prospero's behaviors and perspectives for the past twelve years. As such, her reactions to the tempest he produces at the start of the play matter, and they are all filtered through the language of her cognitive activities. The witnessing and evaluation of Prospero's art, in other words, depend on Miranda's mind—a point that complements Heather James's reading of Prospero's dependence on Miranda's compassionate ear throughout this scene.[49] The cries of the mariners, Miranda exclaims, "did knock / Against my very heart!" (1.2.8–9), and the image of the sea storm is "still beating in [her] mind" pages later. Here, the mind-body connection is not one of madness or distraction, but of potentially positive empathy. As one religious text from 1600 describes it, a beating mind that thinks upon Christ's suffering, for example, was considered to have an immensely healing effect on one's body: "the minde beating upon a remembraunce of Christes passion, shall mitigate in part the bodies paynes."[50]

Thomas Wright described this productive conjunction of the mind and heart in *The Passions of the Minde*:

> First, then, to our imagination cometh by sense or memorie some object to be knowne, convenient or disconvenient to Nature, the which being knowne . . . presently the purer spirits flock from the braine by certain secret channels to the heart, where they pitch at the doore. . . . The heart immediately bendeth either to prosecute it or to eschew it, and the better to effect that affection draweth other humours to help him.[51]

There are two ways, however, to read Miranda's reference to her beating mind, which suggests that something else may beat there besides the image and sounds of the shipwrecked mariners that have entered her brain through her senses and knocked at her heart for assessment. She also has a question for her father that beats in her mind: What is your reason for raising this sea storm—for using your art in this way? In this alternative reading, she takes in his art, but also evaluates it, which signals the work of the brain's middle ventricle. Prospero (and famously the play itself) ultimately will abandon his magic, but it is vital to recognize that the process starts with Miranda's adolescent perception and judgment—both of which circulate and refine themselves through the channels of her mind and body.

Miranda's cognitive operations, as many critics have noted, become more prominent and challenging for her father as the scene goes on. Prospero wants her to "ope thine ear" to hear his story—and by association hers (1.2.37)—but at fourteen, Miranda's memory is ready to recall its own stories of the past. When she tells her father, "Certainly, sir, I can" recall some moments from her life before the island, Prospero is surprised, and asks her to tell him the "image . . . kept with thy remembrance" (1.2.41, 43–44). When she does share her memories, they have nothing to do with Prospero's myopic story of one man wronged by other men; rather, they feature the four or five women whom she now remembers as tending on her in Milan.

Evelyn Tribble reads this scene as a kind of mnemonic competition, and notes how Prospero responds to her memories of tending women by attempting to train her "in a memory discipline" by imposing his fantasy of parthenogenesis upon her shadowy memories.[52] And in many ways Prospero's need to control her senses and her memory here do reflect what Stephen Orgel describes as the play's "fantasy about controlling other people's minds."[53] Although Prospero is clearly threatened in this scene by his adolescent daughter's memory, however, he does also wonder at it. Yes, it is shadowy, and he ultimately will put her to sleep rather than engage it further, but her mind also has a kind of endurance—and even authority. Before he attempts to discipline her memory, he asks Miranda what else she sees in "the dark backward and abyss of time" (1.2.50). What is he hoping that she will produce for him?

The fact that Miranda displays her memory here (and to her father's awe and surprise) suggests that she has recently crossed the pubertal threshold, for memory was not seen to be strong in the minds of children. A seventeenth-century handbook poses the question: "Wherefore is it that neither young children, nor old folkes, have any hold in their memories?" and then gives the Answer:

> Because that both the one and the other, are in perpetuall mooving, the one in increasing, and the other in declining, which is the cause that the Images of the objects are not so deeply ingraven in their memories, or else it may bee for this cause, that young children have the Organ of the memorie too moyst, and old folkes to dry, so that the one cannot imprint and strongly engrave the Images of the objects deepe enough in their memory, and the other perceive the object too lightly.[54]

Prospero's surprise at Miranda's powers of memory indicates that he is not used to seeing her as anything but a child. Perhaps this is the first time he perceives her as an adolescent. We know that he wants to marry her off to Ferdinand, and that this drive is likely tied to her newly ripened body; but this moment in which her memory makes itself known is just as embedded in early modern discourses about the post-pubertal female mind.[55]

Miranda's beating mind and newly sharpened memory together mark the adolescent girl's increased mental capacities. It is telling, then, that it is Prospero's declining memory (appropriate to the old, dry brain described above) that sets off the other beating mind in the play—his own.[56] The moment puts his and his daughter's brains in stark contrast and places hers in the more cognitively active and productive position. Prospero grapples with this beating at a key dramatic moment in act four, when he interrupts the "vanity of mine art" (4.1.41)—the wedding masque—because he has forgotten about the actual people plotting against him. His "old brain is troubled" by this recognition, and he is overwhelmed with "passion" (4.1.159, 143): "A turn or two I'll take to still my beating mind" (4.1.162–63).

Prospero's disturbed reaction to his beating mind counteracts his previous claim to be in control of his "Spirits, which by mine art / I have from their confines called to enact / My present fancies" (4.1.120–22). Mary Crane's cognitive readings of Shakespeare, and of this moment from *The Tempest* especially, are instructive here: "Prospero repeatedly conceives of the internal psychological disturbances of others as involving confinement and constraint, perhaps as a projection of his own feeling that he has powerful emotions trapped within a small and fragile space."[57] His earlier, vain reliance on his art to control the movement of his "Spirits" and enact his fantasies takes on a richer meaning when placed in this psycho-physiological context. His suggestion that Ferdinand and Miranda "retire into my cell," while he walks outside, bespeaks a kind of lingering, cognitive control he hopes to conjure. He dissolves the "solemn temples, the great globe itself" (4.1.161, 153) and so ends his artful revels; but the resonances here with the temples of the head/globe suggest that he seeks to escape the all-too-human and embodied confines of his brain.

Miranda does not control those spirits that early moderns believed circulated through all bodies and brains; nor does she control the sights, sounds and heart-felt passions that her father's art initially moves her beating mind to express. Yet Shakespeare represents her responses to the natural fluidity of these cognitive operations as thoughtfully grounded, not disordered. Upon witnessing the tempest, Miranda cries, "O, I have sufferèd / With those that I saw suffer!" (1.2.5–6). Her beating mind registers this event as an inter-subjective sensory experience involving heart, brain and environment; but her beating mind also assesses her father's actions and asks him to do the same. In the last scene, Prospero releases his enemies and comes to his more inter-dependent and embodied end via a similarly "beating mind" and an expression of fluid compassion for Gonzalo: "Mine eyes, ev'n sociable to the show of thine, / Fall fellowly drops. / [*Aside*] The charm dissolves apace" (5.1.63–65).

From its first staged workings to its final dispersal, then, Prospero's art depends on his daughter's beating mind. And this relationship does not presume that she holds a passive or secondary role to his starring genius. Rather, Shakespeare imagines Miranda's brain-work, like that of Dibutades's daughter, as a kind of blueprint for her father's future productions. Prospero's mind must, in a sense, copy what originated with Miranda's if he is to progress from being a man living in a cell, trying vainly to control the movement of his spirits, to a human who accepts his embodied relationship to the world and others. To do so, he must reject his single-minded art and imitate what started with a girl's incited mind.

Notes

1. For a contemporary description of these ventricles and the movement of the spirits through the brain, see Thomas Vicary, *The Englishemans treasure* (London, 1586), 17.

2. Lazarus Riverius, *The practice of physick* (London, 1655), 417–18.

3. All references to Shakespeare's plays come from *The Norton Shakespeare* (based on the Oxford edition), gen. ed. Stephen Greenblatt (New York: W.W. Norton & Co., 1997).

4. Ursula Potter, "Navigating the Dangers of Female Puberty in Renaissance Drama," *Studies in English Literature* 53, no. 2 (2013): 421–39, quotation on 424.

5. Kate Chedgzoy, "Playing With Cupid: Gender, Sexuality and Adolescence," in *Alternative Shakespeares 3,* ed. Diana Henderson (New York: Routledge, 2008), 138–51, quotation on 139.

6. *A New Variorum Edition of Shakespeare,* ed. Horace Howard Furness, vol. 1 (Philadelphia: J.B. Lipincott & Co., 1873), 374.

7. Marjorie Garber, *"Romeo and Juliet:* Patterns and Paradigms," in *Romeo and Juliet: Critical Essays,* ed. John F. Andrews (New York: Garland, 1993), 119–31, quotation on 124.

8. In her book-in-progress, *Diva Envy: Italian Actresses and the Shakespearean Stage,* Pamela Allan Brown notably departs from this reading of early modern girls by focusing on their adept performative skills. In her chapter, "The Arte of Juliet," she argues that Shakespeare's thirteen-year-old heroine is "such an icon of young love that we no longer notice how artful and theatrical she is" (unpublished ms, 1). See, as well, Deanne Williams's argument that girlhood itself is "defined by performance," put forth in her book, *Shakespeare and the Performance of Girlhood* (New York: Palgrave, 2014), 6. Williams's work offers many examples of actual early modern girls who created and performed. Mary Bly comments on the long line of critics who have found Juliet's use of the erotic epithalamium distressing. She reads Juliet's speech as "elaborately rhetorical and self-consciously erotic." See her "Bawdy Puns and Lustful Virgins: The Legacy of Juliet's Desire in Comedies of the Early 1600s," *Shakespeare Survey* 49 (2007): 97–109, quotation on 99.

9. Helen King, *The Disease of Virgins: Green Sickness, Chlorosis and the Problems of Puberty* (New York: Routledge, 2004), 88.

10. Potter, "Navigating the Dangers of Female Puberty in Renaissance Drama," 424.

11. See, for example Kaara Peterson's *Popular Medicine, Hysterical Disease, and Social Controversy in Shakespeare's England* (Aldershot: Ashgate, 2010); and Sara Read, *Menstruation and the Female Body in Early Modern England* (New York: Palgrave, 2013). I share Lesel Dawson's interest in pushing back against this model of gender and illness. In the chapter "Beyond Ophelia," in her *Lovesickness and Gender in Early Modern English Literature* (Oxford: Oxford University Press, 2008), she argues for the potential creativity of the melancholic female mind.

12. Thomas Twyne, *The patterne of painfull adventures* (London, 1594), chapter XIV.

13. John Marston, *The Fawn,* ed. Gerald A. Smith (Lincoln: University of Nebraska Press, 1965).

14. Jennifer Higginbotham, *The Girlhood of Shakespeare's Sisters: Gender, Transgression, Adolescence* (Edinburgh: Edinburgh University Press, 2013).

15. See Bruce R. Smith "Cut and Run: Perceptual Cuts in Hearing, Seeing, and Remembering," in his *Shakespeare / Cut: Forms and Effects across Four Centuries* (Oxford: Oxford University Press, 2016). In a previous essay, I offer an extended reading of Ophelia as an insightful performer of Denmark's (and Protestant

England's) lost histories. See my "Instructional Performances: Ophelia and the Staging of History," in *Performing Pedagogy in Early Modern England,* ed. Kathryn Moncrief and Kathryn McPherson (Surrey: Ashgate, 2011): 205–16.

16. John Foxe, *The Unabridged Acts and Monuments Online* (1570 edition) (HRI Online Publications, Sheffield, 2011). Available from: http//www.johnfoxe .org [Accessed: 10.23.15], p. 2176.

17. Leah S. Marcus, Janel Mueller, and Mary Beth Rose, eds. *Elizabeth I: Collected Works* (Chicago: University of Chicago Press, 2002), 35.

18. *Till God Will: Mary Ward Through Her Writings*, ed. M. Emmanuel Orchard (London: Darton, Longman and Todd, 1985), 9–10.

19. See, for example, the pioneering essays in *Environment and Embodiment in Early Modern England,* Mary Floyd-Wilson and Garrett A. Sullivan, Jr., eds. (New York: Palgrave, 2007); and those in *Embodied Cognition and Shakespeare's Theatre: The Early Modern Body-Mind,* Lawrence Johnson, John Sutton, and Evelyn Tribble, eds. (New York: Routledge, 2014).

20. Helkiah Crooke, *Mikrokosmographia* (London, 1615), 261. While most medical texts point to age fourteen or fifteen as the age of puberty for girls, some writers did locate this change at age twelve. Jean Bodin writes that "as men begin to feele the heat of youth at fourteene yeares; women wax ripe at twelue, and so holding on from six to six, still so find in themselues some notable chaunge in the disposition either of their bodies, or of their mindes" (*The six bookes of a common-weale* [London, 1606], 460).

21. *Dr. Willis's practice of physick* (London, 1684), Treatise VIII, 16. Helen King suggests that this theory of fermentation, based on the idea that all processes in the body were due to chemical changes, was developing earlier in the seventeenth century as an alternative to the plethora theory of menstruation. This competing model allows for a healthy and hot female body (King, *Disease,* 71–72).

22. King, *Disease,* 86.

23. Robert Burton, *The Anatomy of Melancholy* (London, 1621), 541.

24. *Aristotle's Master-Piece* (London, 1694), 2. Levinus Lemnius similarly writes of girls "in the 14 or 15 years of their age," whose blood, "no longer taken to augment their bodies, abounding, makes their minds fasten upon venerous imaginations." See *The secret miracles of nature* (London, 1658), 308. Jane Sharp emphasizes this venerous imagination in her 1671 rewriting of Crooke: "Men about the same age begin to change their faces and to grow downy with hair, and to change their notes and voices; Maids breasts swell; lustful thoughts draw away their minds, and some fall into Consumptions. Others rage and grow almost mad with love" (*The Midwives Book,* ed. Elaine Hobby [Oxford: Oxford University Press, 1999], 69).

25. Crooke, *Mikrokosmographia,* 261.

26. Gail Kern Paster, *Humoring the Body: Emotions and the Shakespearean Stage* (Chicago: University of Chicago Press, 2004), 87 and 109.

27. Ilana Krausman Ben-Amos's work on early modern youth is especially helpful to consider here. She considers the period of time when many teenage daughters left their families to serve in formal or informal apprenticeships or to work as domestics in large towns. This phase, she argues, "left considerable scope for independence and initiative during their adolescent and youthful years." See her *Adolescence and Youth in Early Modern England* (New Haven: Yale University Press, 1994), quote on 135.

28. Will Greenwood, *Description of the Passion of Love* (London, 1657), 82.

29. King, *Disease,* 86.

30. Aristotle, *Historia animalium,* trans. D'Arcy Wentworth Thompson (Oxford: Clarendon Press, 1910), Book 7, part 1 (581 a-b). In his note to this section, Thompson states that this book "is of doubtful authenticity. Nearly one half of its contents may be closely paralleled with passages in the third and fourth books of the *de Gen.*; and much also appears to be drawn directly from the writings of the Hippocratic School."

31. Aristotle also offers a male parallel to the girls' titillating "dilated passages" when he writes of the 14-year-old boy that "the breasts swell and likewise the private parts, altering in size and shape. (And by the way, at this time of life those who try by friction to provoke emission of seed are apt to experience pain as well as voluptuous sensations.)" (*Historia animalium,* trans. Thompson, Book 7, part 1).

32. Pliny the Elder, *Natural History,* trans. H. Rackham (Cambridge, MA: Harvard University Press, 1938), 371–72 (35.43).

33. "The personal agent, when considered as instrument or means, is often expressed . . . by *operā* with a genitive or possessive." *Allen and Greenough's New Latin Grammar for Schools and Colleges,* eds. J. B. Greenough, G. L. Kitteredge, A. A. Howard, and Benjamin L. D'Ooge (Boston: Ginn & Co., 1903), 253–54. Thank you to Brendon Reay for helping me with this point of Latin grammar.

34. Robert Rosenblum was the first to argue that, "For an age which was to venerate the outline engravings of Flaxman and which sought out the linear simplicity of presumably primitive and uncorrupted phases of an artistic evolution . . . the legend of the origin of painting must have offered still another confirmation of the historical priority and essentiality of pure outline." See his "The Origin of Painting: A Problem in the Iconography of Romantic Classicism," *The Art Bulletin,* 39, no. 4 (Dec., 1957): 279–90, quote on 285. Ann Bermingham reads the myth's depiction in the late eighteenth century as being informed by an intertwining set of interests: the "cultural hegemony of the fine arts" and the place of women "vis-à-vis artistic production and consumption." See her "The Origin of Painting and the Ends of Art: Wright of Derby's Corinthian Maid," in *Painting and the Politics of Culture: New Essays on British Art, 1700–1850,* ed. John Barrell (Oxford: Oxford University Press, 1992), 135–65, quotation on 141.

35. Shelley King, "Amelia Opie's 'Maid of Corinth' and the Origins of Art," *Eighteenth-Century Studies* 37, no. 4 (2004): 629–51, quote on 630.

36. See Jacques Derrida, *Memoirs of the Blind: The Self-Portrait and Other Ruins,* Pascale-Anne Brault and Michael Naas, trans. (Chicago: University of Chicago Press, 1993), 49–51.

37. The myth of Butades and his daughter was often cited by Italian Renaissance artists in their treatises on painting, most notably Leon Battista Alberti, who refers to the myth, but ultimately attributes the origins of picture making to Narcissus. Cristelle L. Baskins's analysis suggests that Alberti's rewriting of the myth significantly downgrades the daughter's role: "Whereas Pliny overdetermines the invention of art, noting both the 'shadow theory' and the collaborative conception of Butades and Dibutades [his daughter], Alberti's text limits pictorial invention to male parthenogenesis." See her "Echoing Narcissus in Alberti's *Della Pittura,*" *Oxford Art Journal* 16.1(1993): 25–33, quotation on 27.

38. Pliny the Elder, *The historie of the world* (London, 1601), 551–52 (book 35, chapter 12).

39. John Guillim, *A Display of Heraldrie* (London, 1610), 42.

40. I suspect that Shakespeare had Dibutades's daughter in mind when he wrote *All's Well That Ends Well's* Helen, a desiring adolescent who claims that her "imagination / Carries no favour in't but Bertram's," and describes how she did "sit and draw / His archèd brows, his hawking eye, his curls, / In our heart's table" (1.1.77–78, 88–90). The fact that Bertram's face has led her to forget her father's is especially provocative given the early modern revision of Pliny's story with its emphasis on the daughter's art.

41. *Historie of the world,* 535. The story of Parrhasius (his name in the original Pliny) appears in Book 35, chapter 36, and does not include any such terms to connect the actions of Butades's daughter to the artistry of this ancient painter.

42. Robert Burton, *Anatomy of Melancholy* (London, 1624), 423.

43. Burton, *Anatomy of Melancholy,* 423–24, second emphasis mine. In an earlier sixteenth-century translation of Polydore Vergil, the story of Dibutades is included in the chapter "Painting, and the potters crafte," but is used to describe the origins of pottery (following Pliny), not painting. See, *An Abridgement of the notable works of Polidore Vergil* (London, 1546), fol. 45. Vergil presents different classical views on Painting's origins, citing the names of men from Egypt, Athens and Corinth, but not naming Dibutades. His discussion is informed by Pliny the Elder's and Quintillian's in *Institutio oratoria* x, ii, 7. Richard Whitlock, clearly working from Burton's version (evidenced by his use of "Deburiades"), repeats it in 1654, writing that "the Daughter of Deburiades" traced her lover's shadow with coal "which her father perfected, and it was the first Picture that ever was made, according to Pliny." See his, *Zootomia, or Observations of the present manners of the English* (London, 1654), 488.

44. King explains that "[b]y the eighteenth century, the myth was variously described as the origin of drawing, or of painting, or of art" ("Amelia Opie's 'Maid of Corinth,' " 629).

45. Franciscus Junius, *The Painting of the Ancients* (London, 1638), 140–41. Frances Muecke traces the European literary and visual sources of the story, which (in prints and painting especially) came to show Cupid guiding the girl's hand: "the detail of Love's inspiration or guidance is not found in the Pliny version, nor, to my knowledge, in any other version before Junius. Junius has introduced the personification of Love by rewriting Pliny's 'capta amore iuvenis,' in love with a youth, as 'amore suadente,' taught by Love." I would argue that Burton's use of the story, presented in the context of Love's inspirational powers, provides an earlier example of this later iconographic and literary tradition. See Muecke, " 'Taught By Love': The Origin of Painting Again," *The Art Bulletin* 81, no. 2 (1999): 297–302, quotation on 299.

46. The eighteen-year-old Jailer's Daughter is described by the Doctor as having a mind that "beats" upon Palamon (4.3.67); King Lear describes how "the tempest in my mind / Doth from my senses take all feeling else / Save what beats there: Filial ingratitude" (3.4.12–14); and Claudius complains of Hamlet that "This something-settled matter in his heart / Whereon his brains still beating puts him thus / From fashion of himself" (3.1.172–74).

47. Arthur Kirsch, "Virtue, Vice and Compassion in Montaigne and *The Tempest*," *SEL* 37, no. 2 (1997): 337–52, quote on 343. Jessica Slights gives a helpful

overview of this critical tradition, noting that Miranda is typically read as an agent-less pawn in Prospero's colonialist mission. She reads Miranda as "strong-willed and independent minded," but considers those mental acts primarily in terms of her "domestic defiance" of her father and future husband. See her "Rape and the Romanticization of Shakespeare's Miranda," *SEL* 41, no. 2 (2001): 357–79, quote on 365. Elizabeth Spiller does read Miranda as an enabler of her father's art, although she does not read her as an active or inventive agent: "Shakespeare makes clear that Prospero's art depends on the presence of Miranda as an audience who is in some way necessary to the creation of that art." See her "Shakespeare and the making of early modern science: resituating Prospero's art," *South Central Review* 26, no. 1 (2009): 24–41, quotation on 30.

48. Lorrie Jerrell Leininger, "The Miranda Trap: Sexism and Racism in Shake-speare's *Tempest*," in *The Woman's Part,* Ruth Swift Lenz, Gayle Greene, and Carol Thomas Neely, eds. (Urbana: University of Illinois Press, 1983), 285–94, quote on 289.

49. Heather James, "Dido's Ear: Tragedy and the Politics of Response," *Shake-speare Quarterly* 52, no. 3 (2001): 360–82.

50. Christopher Sutton, *Disce mori. A religious discourse, moouing euery Chris-tian man to enter into a serious remembrance of his ende.* (London, 1600), 241.

51. Thomas Wright, *The Passions of the Minde* (London, 1601), 82–83.

52. Evelyn B. Tribble, " 'The Dark Backward and Abysm of Time': *The Tempest* and Memory," *College Literature* 33, no.1 (2006): 151–68, quotation on 159. Trib-ble reads the play's persistent figuring of beating minds primarily in terms of Pros-pero's, not Miranda's: "beating within the skull, on the edge of escaping or imploding, [it] reveals the limitations of imagining the bounded subject and the fear of the loss of control should memory be lost" (155).

53. Stephen Orgel, "Prospero's Wife," *Representations* 8 (1984): 1–13, quota-tion on 9.

54. Scipion, Dupleix, The resoluer; or Curiosities of nature written in French by Scipio Du Plesis counseller and historiographer to the French King. Vsefull & pleasant for all (London, 1635), 280–81.

55. Kathryn Moncrief considers how this scene echoes early modern domestic guides on how to educate daughters in obedience and feminine virtue. Although she reads Miranda as a devoted student at first, her analysis of Miranda's final speech in the play leaves room for a much more active female mind: "Does this staged moment of delight and inquisitiveness show her as . . . cripplingly hindered by . . . a gendered educational system that seeks only to keep her obedient? Or, does it show a keen and hungry mind and allow for the possibility of growth?" " 'Obey and Be Attentive': Gender and Household Instruction in Shakespeare's *The Tempest*," in *Gender and Early Modern Constructions of Childhood,* ed. Naomi J. Miller and Naomi Yavneh (Surry: Ashgate, 2011), 127–38, quotation on 137.

56. The third reference to a beating mind in the play comes in the form of an admonition from Prospero to Alonso: "Do not infest your mind with beating on / The strangeness of this business" (5.1.249–50).

57. Mary Crane, *Shakespeare's Brain: Reading with Cognitive Theory* (Princeton, NJ: Princeton University Press, 2001), 200. See, as well, Tribble's argu-ment that the play "examines the cognitive and emotive costs of misrecognizing the intersubjective nature of memory and relying upon a monadic model of mem-ory and cognition" (155).

Shakespeare and the Girl Masquer

Deanne Williams

FROM THE MEDIEVAL RELIGIOUS DRAMA to the Stuart court masque, girls can be found on early English stages: in pageants and masques, entries, processions, and other dramatic entertainments.[1] They appeared, in fact, almost everywhere except on the professional stage. In the Middle Ages, girls performed in religious drama, and they danced, sang, and played music in religious festivals and folk celebrations. In Tudor England, girls appeared in civic pageants and processions, as well as in royal entries, triumphs, and other entertainments. And in Stuart England, girls were an important part of the evolving genre of the court masque. Until very recently, however, historical accounts of children's performance in early modern England have focused on the more visible boy actor, who famously played on the public stage and in the children's companies.[2] The ongoing scholarly process of recovering evidence of women's performance, moreover, focuses largely on adult performers, subsuming girls within the larger category of "women."[3]

This essay charts the history of the girl masquer—little girls as well as unmarried teenagers—on early English stages, defining her as a distinctive category of female performer, and locating her in a variety of contexts and venues. Meriting her own chapter in the histories of the child actor as well as women's performance, the girl masquer also makes a contribution to the professional stage. Besides providing evidence of girls as speakers in medieval religious drama, Tudor civic pageantry, Elizabethan entertainments, and Stuart court masques, what also matters about the girl masquer is her creation of an arresting spectacle through dance, music, and costume.[4] This, I argue, is the legacy of the girl masquer: a distinct physical and visual code that was adopted, or translated, by the boy actors on Shakespeare's stage as they performed girl characters such as Juliet, Perdita, the "airy spirit" Ariel, and others. These

Shakespearean girl characters provide an archive of, as well as a glimpse into, performances that were occasional and ephemeral, and seldom recorded for posterity. In different ways, they draw upon and preserve the tradition of the girl masquer that was enshrined in private, domestic, and courtly spaces, as well as in more public ceremonial contexts. The performance of these Shakespearean roles by boy actors developed from the lived experience of girls' performance, and the process of adapting the legacy of the girl masquer to the contexts of the professional stage produced complex and polyvalent engagements with girlhood and with the tradition of the girl masquer.

The history of the girl performer begins with the singers and actresses of the ancient world: the *partheneia* of Ancient Greece, for example, were maiden performers of sacred wedding songs, while ancient Roman actresses learned their trade performing in traveling family troupes.[5] In medieval Europe, the dramatic writings of the learned tenth-century abbess, Hrosvitha of Gandersheim, are filled with interesting parts for medieval convent girls that depict the "laudable chastity of Christian virgins."[6] In medieval France, girls performed in Passion Plays and plays of the Presentation of the Virgin at the Temple, and took parts ranging from the Virgin Mary and Saint Catherine of Alexandria, to Mary Magdalen and Herodias's daughter, to the maidens of the Temple and the daughters of Jerusalem.[7] In Metz, France, in 1468, the teenaged daughter of a glazier performed the meaty role of Saint Catherine, speaking "so spiritedly and piteously that she prompted many people to weep."[8] A masque of youth also produced in Metz, in 1471, included a cart filled with children, including "une jonne fillette acoustree comme une deesse et se nommoit la deesse de jonesse" [a young girl dressed as a goddess and who was called the goddess of youth].[9] This was the nine-year-old daughter of Philippe de Vigneulles, who organized the entertainment and recorded it in his journal. Philippe de Mézière's "Presentation of Mary in the Temple" at Avignon in 1372 contains very precise details concerning the "young and most beautiful girl, about three or four years old" who would play the young Virgin Mary, and the "two other most beautiful girls of the same age" who served as her attendants: Mary wore a "white tunic of sendal [fine silk]" to show her "innocence and virginality," and the other girls wore "green and blue, with circlets of silver," holding candles as they walk in procession.[10]

"Girls," as John Marshall puts it, "should not be entirely

excluded from the pleasures of medieval theatre."[11] And Meg Twy-cross observes that "it seems to have been permissible for the girls to appear (both here and on the continent)."[12] In England, the *N-Town Play* records a substantial girl's part in its play of "The Girlhood of the Virgin Mary," which focuses on her prodigious learning and entrance into the Temple.[13] And the now-canonical Digby *Play of Mary Magdalene,* which depicts the spiritual struggle and reformation of its girl protagonist, illustrates a strong dramatic interest in the challenges of girlhood, and in the tension between the sacred and profane, the spiritual and the worldly.[14] The Digby play registers, as well, the intense interest in dramatizing saints' lives as illustrated by the extensive evidence of plays about virgin martyrs, including Saint Catherine of Alexandria (London, 1393 and Coventry, 1491), Saint Susanna and Saint Clara (Lincoln, 1447–48 and 1455–56), Saints Feliciana and Sabina (Shrewsbury, 1516), and Saint Christina (Kent, 1522): all of which would require, along with the dramatic depiction of horrific tortures and awe-inducing miracles, significant acting ability.[15]

This fascination with virgin martyrs extends to civic and royal pageantry. The young Catherine of Aragon was greeted, upon her arrival in England, by "a faire yong lady w^t a whele in hir hand, in liknes of Seint Kathryn, w^t right many virgins on eu(e)ry side of her; and . . . another lady in likenes of Seint Ursula, w^t her great multitude of virgyns right goodly dressed and arrayed."[16] Saint Catherine was an appropriate choice not only because the fifteen-year-old Spanish princess was named for her, but because, with the saint's heyday between her conversion at fourteen and martyrdom at eighteen, she was also her peer. With her reputation for learning and debate, she constituted, as well, a nice compliment to the future queen. The betrothal of Saint Ursula to a pagan governor drew an obvious and rather witty parallel to Catherine's own betrothal to the foreign prince King Arthur, while her 11,000 virgin companions provided an opportunity for multitudes of girl per-formers. Records of payment to "Gleyns daughter for thassump-cion & Child(es) eldest daughter for Saynt Ursula and VJ virgens" for the London Lord Mayor's Pageant in 1523 indicate the ongoing popularity of pageants that involved the theatrical display of girl-hood: like Saint Ursula and her virgins, the Assumption involves numerous angels.[17] Anne Boleyn's coronation, similarly, featured various girls, including the Virgin Mary and the daughters of Saint Anne, who supplied images of innocent and virtuous girlhood

intended to symbolize (with painful retrospective irony) the pregnant Anne's chaste and fruitful union with Henry.[18]

In Reformation England, the opportunity for girls to play the rich
dramatic roles represented by the saints, virgin martyrs, and the
Virgin Mary evaporated with the suppression of religious drama.
Whereas Catherine of Aragon had been welcomed by a pair of virgin martyrs in 1501, her daughter Mary I was greeted by just "a
girl" on her royal entry in 1553; in James I's Royal Entry into London in 1604, by contrast, "seventeen damsels" met the monarch.[19]
During this time, girls' parts in royal masques and civic pageantry
shifted from the saints and virgins to mythological figures such as
nymphs, naiads, and the classical virtues, opening up a different
set of roles. Thus, only a few years after pageants and royal entries
featuring Saint Catherine, Saint Ursula, and Virgin Mary, Edward
VI's 1537 birth was celebrated by a "Masque of Nymphs" (1537) at
Hampton Court, in which naiads wore "garlands of poplar leaves,"
dryads displayed "unbound hair decorated with oak leaves," and
oreads (i.e., nymphs of mountains, valleys, and ravines) sported
deerskin, identifying the girl masquer with exuberant figures tied
to the natural world.[20] In the 1585 London Lord Mayor's Pageant,
four nymphs "gorgeously appareled" deliver speeches along with
the River Thames, a "sweete and dainty nymph" who asserts both
her beauty and her utility with lines that also offer implicit stage
directions to run, glide, leap, and play: "with silver glide my pleasant streames doo runne,/ where leaping fishes play betwixt the
shores."[21] Religious figures were also replaced by personifications
of abstract values and virtues. In the 1556 Norwich Mayor's Pageant, "four young maids" addressed their listeners as the four
cardinal virtues, Prudence, Justice, Temperance, and Fortitude. The
maids emphasize their power and centrality to good government:
as Prudence puts it, "all things work by my advice."[22]

Meg Twycross contends that girls enjoyed a freedom to perform
that was not extended to grown women: "in general . . . the rule
seems to be that young girls were allowed to play, but older women
were not." [23] While much important current scholarship questions
this claim about adult women, there is no question as to the rich
tradition of performing girls.[24] If, as James Stokes puts it, "the
records show that women participated everywhere" (32) this is also
true for girls, perhaps even moreso.[25] However, the evidence of
girls' ongoing presence and acceptance on early English stages
complicates any attempt to locate a watershed moment of "first-

ness" in relation to the history of female performance, disrupting prevailing assumptions about female public and dramatic speech. In this context, the 1592 *Entertainment for Queen Elizabeth at Bisham,* described by modern scholars as "the first occasion on which English noblewomen took speaking roles in a quasi-dramatic performance," looks less revolutionary, and more like an especially rich and accomplished example of a longstanding tradition that includes the 1585 London Lord Mayor's Pageant and, before that, the 1556 Norwich Mayor's Pageant.[26] *The Bisham Entertainment* casts two teenaged girl performers, the sisters Lady Elizabeth and Lady Anne Russell, aged 18 and 16, respectively, as Virgin shepherdesses, Isabella and Sybilla: "keeping sheep, and sowing in their samplers." Composed or "devised" by their mother, Lady Elizabeth Russell, the *Entertainment* engages the girls in witty dialogue with Pan, their would-be, and swiftly converted, seducer.[27]

While girls were known to address various audiences, from those of the religious drama to those of the civic pageant or the country entertainment, they also made an impact through dance. In medieval drama, the story of Salome provided an opportunity for seductive dancing and striking costumes. Together, the girls of the guild of Saint John the Baptist at Baston, in Lincolnshire, danced Salome's seductive dance before King Herod, performed in exchange for the head of John the Baptist, in the parish's annual festivities.[28] At Mons, France, in 1501 one versatile "Wandru, daughter of Jorge de Nerle" played both the Virgin Mary and Salome.[29] The Computus rolls, college accounts for Peterhouse, Cambridge, admit repeatedly to the payment of dancing girls, latter-day Salomes entertaining powerful men.[30] Girls were also paid for dancing at the court of Henry VII: £30 for the "young damoysell that daunceth" in 1493 and, in 1497, £12 for the "litell mayden that daunceth."[31] The Digby Candlemas play of *The Killing of the Children* included *virgines,* "as many as a man will," who sang and danced, going "rounde aboute the tempille" holding "tapers in ther hands."[32] The virgins of the Candlemas play convey and enact what Theresa Coletti calls the "sexuality and sacred power" of chastity and generation associated with Saint Anne, to whom the play is dedicated.[33]

Eye-witness accounts of girls' dance performances dwell on their visual impact, drawing inspiration from a tradition that puts virginal girlhood at the forefront of religious devotion. In Tudor England, the eleven-year-old Princess Mary dazzled all in the

Greenwich triumphs of May, 1527, celebrating the conclusion of a two-month-long French embassy.[34] According to Gasparo Spinelli, the secretary to the Italian ambassador who gave an account of the events to the Venetian court, Mary and her entourage danced as "beautiful nymphs:"

> Dancing thus they presented themselves to the King, their dance being very delightful by reason of its variety, as they formed certain groups and figures most pleasing to the sight. Their dance being finished, they ranged themselves on one side, and in like order the eight youths, leaving their torches, came down from the cave, and after performing their dance, each of them took by the hand one of those beautiful nymphs, and having led a courant together for a while, returned to their places.[35]

This is the account in Hall's *Chronicle:*

> then out of a caue issued out the ladie Mary doughter to the kyng & with her seuen ladies, all appareled after the romayne fashion in rich clothe of gold of tissue & Crimosin tinsel bendy & their heres wrapped in calles of golde with bonetes of Crimosin veluet on their heddes, set full of pearle and stone: these eight Ladies daunced with the eight Lordes of the mount.[36]

Spinelli tries to recreate the dance steps for his reader, while Hall provides a careful account of the costumes: both attempt to convey the experience of watching Mary's performance. Spinelli was particularly impressed by all the jewels:

> On her person were so many precious stones that their splendor and radiance dazzled the sight, in such wise as to make one believe that she was decked with all the gems of the eighth sphere.

The masquing over, Henry VIII let down his daughter's long hair:

> in the presence of the French ambassadors [he] took off her cap, and the net being displaced, a profusion of silver tresses as beautiful as ever seen on human head fell over her shoulders, forming a most agreeable sight.

As a symbol of virginity, Princess Mary's long locks signal not only her youth but also her potential value to the French as a future consort: as Janette Dillon points out, this concluding spectacle may also highlight "the time that must elapse before the marriage could

be carried through to completion."[37] But for Spinelli, Mary's trans-
fixing beauty also makes an affective impact that transcends politics:

> Her beauty in this array produced such effect on everybody that all the
> other marvelous sights previously witnessed were forgotten, and they
> gave themselves up solely to contemplation of so fair an angel.

For Spinelli, then, watching the princess perform is a kind of com-
munion with the divine, just as charged, spiritually, as any encounter with a saint.

The girl masquers that figure in the 1596 memorial portrait of the
Elizabethan diplomat Henry Unton communicate a similar sense of
divinity. Roy Strong describes the girls who are depicted dancing
in a masque at Unton's wedding, carrying garlands of flowers for
presentation to the wedding guests:

> The glittering procession is headed by Diana, Goddess of the moon and
> the chase, wearing a crescent moon in her headdress and clasping a
> bow and arrow. . . . Behind her walks a train of six maidens in pairs
> carrying bows and garlands, their heads crowned with flowers, wearing
> grey-green robes and white skirts patterned with red flowers. (104–5)[38]

Unton's portrait represents the most significant aspects of his life:
his writing of diplomatic letters dominates the portrait, and other
scenes include his birth, studies at Oxford, continental travels,
death in France, and the transportation of his body back to England
for funeral and burial. The girl masquers, representing Diana, goddess of chastity and childbirth, are key to the depiction of Unton's
wedding, just as the image of Oriel College emblematizes his time
at Oxford. Unton himself had a personal history with girl performers: he described his relationship with Lady Elizabeth Russell,
author or "deviser" of the *Entertainment at Bisham,* as "as respective as of my own mother."[39] In the *Entertainment at Bisham,* shepherdesses chatter away wittily, but in the Unton portrait, Diana's
maidens convey stateliness and artistic control through their physical action: from their movements we can just about gauge the beat
of the music played by the broken consort.

Humanist writers theorized dance as "a language of command
and control" (115), as Janette Dillon puts it, enacting political principles of sovereignty and mastery. "Like Oratory," writes Skiles
Howard, "courtly dancing was classically authorized, codified,

Detail from Unton Portrait © National Portrait Gallery, London

rehearsed, and devised to control response." [40] It was a "fully framed political discourse," in which "the expansion of the dancer's control at the centre of the hall" became "a micrometonym of the centralized state." Thus, George Peele's lines, in *Anglorum Feriae* (1595), call upon England's nymphs, the "sacred daughters of King Jove" (1), to spread their "sparkling wings" (2) and celebrate "England's high holiday" (46), Queen Elizabeth's birthday:

> Wear eglantine,
> And wreaths of roses red and white put on
> In honour of that day, you lovely nymphs,
> And paeans sing and sweet melodious songs;
> Along the chalky hills of Albion
> Lead England's lovely shepherds in a dance.
>
> (39–44)

The nymphs' dance here symbolizes the Queen's long, orderly reign: "years that for us beget this golden age,/ Wherein we live in safety under her" (50–51).[41]

In *The Book of the Governor* (1531), Sir Thomas Elyot extends the orderliness of dance to the heavenly spheres, aligning it with Platonic notions of celestial harmony:

> the interpretours of Plato do thinke that the wonderfull and incomprehensible ordre of the celestial bodies, I meane sterres and planettes, and their motions harmonicall, gave to them that intensity, and by the deepe serche of raison beholde their coursis, in the sondrye diversities of nombre and tyme, a fourme of imitation of a semblable motion, whiche they called daunsinge or saltation; wherefore the more nere they approached to that temperance and subtile modulation of the saide superior bodies, the more perfecte and commendable is their daunsinge, which is most like to the trouthe of any opinion that I have hitherto founden.[42]

Here Elyot describes the planets as dancers, holding fast to the rules of number and time, and emphasizing the subtlety and control of their movements. Sir John Davies's *Orchestra, or a Poem of Dancing* (1596) expands upon this idea, as Antinous justifies dancing to Penelope, waiting for the return of Ulysses, by explaining that dancing is "love's proper exercise:" a form of participation in the divinely-ordered structures of nature, with the whole universe viewed as a well-structured dance.[43] Sir Thomas Churchyard reconciles the divine and the political spheres in *A Musical Consort of Heavenly Harmony* (1595) by making it clear that musical and divine harmony equally derive, in fact, from Queen Elizabeth herself.[44]

Along with its symbolic enactment of and engagement with political and divine order, dance was also regarded as a courtly accomplishment, reflecting the carefully cultivated skills of the individual courtier: as Skiles Howard puts it, "an instrument for the acquisition and exercise of social power" (3). In *The Scholemaster* (1570), Roger Ascham includes dancing in a list of aristocratic skills that includes riding, swimming, and playing instruments: "to dance cumlie, to sing and play on instruments cunningly." Here, adjectives such as "cumlie" and "cunningly" convey a sense of personal, individual accomplishment, reflecting a broader sense of the orderly, not to mention clever, self: "nothynge is brought to the moost profytable use" he writes, "which is not handled after the moost cumlye fashion."[45]

Insofar as it draws eyes to the body, however, dance opens itself up to charges of sinful indulgence. Juan Luis Vives writes dismissively, in *The Education of a Christian Woman* (1524), of "such light and trifling pleasures, wherein the light fantasies of maids have delight, as songs, dances, and such other wanton and peevish plays" and complains of "this newe fasshyon of daunsynge of ours, so unreasonable, and full of shakynge and braggying, and unclenely handlynges, gropynges and kyssynges: and a very kendlynge of lechery."[46] In John Northbrooke's *A Treatise Wherein Dicing, Dancing, Vaine plaies or Enterludes with other idle pastimes, etc. commonly used on the Sabboth Day are reproved* (1579) the allegorical figure, Age, turns Youth against dancing through the example of Salome, whose dance for King Herod brought about the death of John the Baptist.[47] Salome is a favorite figure for critics of the dance: John Bromyard's *Summa praedicantium* (1360) complains about miracle plays generally, but he has specific words for dancers: "dancers whose feet are swift to seek out evil . . . dancers are like that dancing daughter of Herodias, through whom John the Baptist lost his head; thus, through dancers, many lose their souls."[48]

What does not come through in these moralizing discussions of dance (pro or con) is a sense of how the dancer was experienced as a lived presence, as a lively experience. Contemporary descriptions of court masques, however, provide insight into what the audience experienced and considered significant enough to record about the girl masquer. In an otherwise dismissive account of Jonson's *Pleasure Reconciled to Virtue,* performed on Twelfth Night, 1618, Jacobean court insider John Chamberlain observes to Dudley Carleton, that the best thing about it was the "Master Controllers daughter":

> There was nothing in yt extraordinarie but rather the invention proved dull. Master Controllers daughter bare away the bell for delicat dauncing, though remarquable for nothing els, but the multitude of jewells wherewith she was hangd as yt were all over.[49]

It is fitting that what was most memorable about *Pleasure Reconciled with Virtue* was the spectacle of the dancing daughter: the masque's depiction of the temptation of Hercules by Comus, the mythological figure for sensuous pleasure, inspired Milton's 1634 *Comus,* or *A Mask Presented at Ludlow Castle,* featuring the 15-year-old Alice Egerton. Like Spinelli, Chamberlain was particularly taken with the sparkling jewelry. For Chamberlain, the girl masquer elevates an otherwise unenjoyable masque, making an impression on even the toughest audience. In fact, her performance would be lost to the historical record, were she not fulfilling a rhetorical purpose for a letter writer intent on conveying just how little he thought of the Jonsonian masque. Here Chamberlain, albeit unintentionally, shifts the terms of our discussion of dance away from abstract concepts of sin or divine harmony, or even the courtier's fetishization of skill, to instead an acknowledgement of the effect of the girl masquer, however haphazard and amateurish, on her audience.

John Finnett, Master of the Ceremonies to James I, records a highly enthusiastic audience response to the girl masquers of Samuel Daniel's *Tethys' Festival* (1610):

> they performed their Dance to the Amazement of all the Beholders, considering the Tenderness of their Years and the many intricate Changes of the Dance, which was so disposed, that which way soever the Changes went the little Duke was still found to be in the midst of these little Dancers.[50]

Performing in a masque that celebrated the investiture of Prince Henry as Prince of Wales in 1610, little girl masquers appeared as Naiads, with the ten-year-old Prince Charles, Duke of York, who played Zephirus, the west wind. According to Samuel Daniel's stage directions:

A Lady as a Naiad (pen & ink on paper). Inigo Jones. Bridgeman Art Library International.

Eight little ladies near of his stature represented the naiads, and were attired in light robes adorned with flowers, their hair hanging down and waving, with garlands of water ornaments on their heads. (57–60)[51]

The masque featured Anne of Denmark, as Tethys, "Queen/ Of nymphs and rivers" (93–94). Her attendant nymphs, representing the rivers of England, included the thirteen year-old Princess Elizabeth as "the lovely nymph of stately Thames/ Darling of the Ocean" (111–12). The Princess had written breathlessly to her brother, Henry, Prince of Wales, about her preparations for "the ballet . . . about to be enacted."[52] With her fellow nymphs she danced "measures, corantos, and galliards" (309) to songs that drew attention to their "glory bright" (261) and "beauteous shapes" (325) until they were magically returned to their own "fair shapes" (349).

Finnett's account of the pleasure that the audience took in the little girls' appearance on stage implies that the experience was charged with the tension between their young age and inexperience, and their mastery of the steps. The child performer rises to the challenge, registering the awkwardness of her intense effort, and the novelty of just-acquired steps, while the audience witnesses the excitement and charm of a fresh accomplishment. There is pleasure, too, in the audience's recognition of the performers, as Horatio Busino, the chaplain of the Venetian Ambassador, suggests in his account of *Pleasure Reconciled to Virtue:*

> they discerned beautiful and most delightful faces, and at every moment they would say, 'Oh look at this one, oh see that one; whose wife is that one in the third row, and whose daughter is that pretty one nearby?'[53]

The naiads of *Tethys' Festival* were not paid professionals: although their identity was not recorded for posterity (unlike those of Princess Elizabeth and her nymphs), they were nevertheless well known to the audience, as John Finnett puts it, "all of them the daughters of earls or Barons."

The girl masquer's appearance as a nymph or naiad in *Tethys' Festival* and other court masques embeds her within the natural cycle of life.[54] Nymphs and naiads bring together the spheres of the human, the natural, and the divine, by animating aspects of nature, personifying the natural outflow of a spring or a river into the form of a young girl. Symbolizing nature's ebbs and flows, the girls are physical embodiments of its ongoing processes: "Breathe out new

flowers" sing the Tritons, "which yet were never known / Unto the
spring, nor blown, / Before this time, to beautify the earth" (77–80).
As the masque concludes, the girl masquers represent the swift passage of time, in all its melancholic beauty: "Glory is most bright
and gay/ In a flash, and so away. / Feed apace then, greedy eyes/ On
the wonder you behold;/ Take it sudden as it flies, / Though you
take it not to hold" (300–305).

In her discussion of Tudor court masques, Howard reflects upon
dance as a unique form of discursive practice:

> the word 'discourse' etymologically derives from *discurrere,* moving
> 'back and forth,' or 'running to and fro,' . . . Inherent in the meaning of
> 'discourse' is the iconicity of transformation, and the paradoxical mate-
> riality and evanescence of dancing. (23)[55]

This "paradoxical materiality and evancescence" underwrites the
discursive power of the girl masquer: in these examples, she
embodies youth and beauty and poignantly invokes the swift passage of time. Dance and youth are both ephemeral: "In a flash, and
so away." Mitigating against the eternal structures of divine harmony or the idealized constructs of political power, the girl
masquer is a poignant reminder of the beauty of temporality, sub-
verting by her very presence and movements the discourse of a
genre invested in permanence and universality.

Shakespeare registers and represents the impact of the girl
masquer, her "paradoxical materiality and evancescence," in
Romeo and Juliet (1594). This may be the Shakespearean play in
which dance is most significant: the lovers meet at a dance, the play
makes frequent references to dance, and it has proven easily adaptable to ballet and musical theater from Sergei Prokofiev to Jerome
Robbins and beyond. [56] Romeo is eventually persuaded against his
better judgment to attend Capulet's "mask," which he learns about
when he reads aloud the invitation's addressees—a catalogue of
daughters—creating a mental image of throngs of young females,
"all the admirèd beauties of Verona" (1.2.87), that recalls Saint
Ursula and her 11, 000 Virgins:

> Signior Martino and his wife and daughters;
> County Anselme and his beauteous sisters; the lady
> widow of Vitravio; Signior Placentio and his lovely
> nieces; Mercutio and his brother Valentine; mine
> uncle Capulet, his wife and daughters; my fair niece

Rosaline; and Livia; Signior Valentio and his cousin
Tybalt, Lucio and the lively Helena.
A fair assembly.[57]

(1.2.65–74)

Romeo's arrival at the Capulet's "mask" brings with it another image of dancing girls: "A torch for me. Let wantons light of heart/ Tickle the senseless rushes with their heels" (1.4.33–44). The play returns repeatedly to the image of the girl's feet, from Capulet's reference to "ladies that have their toes/ Unplagued with corns" (1.4.129–30) to his order "foot it, girls" (139) And the Capulet party provides the opportunity for Romeo to spot the young Juliet, "not fourteen" (1.2.8), in lines that hinge on the theatrically effective interplay between light and dark, and black and white:

O, she doth teach the torches to burn bright!
It seems she hangs upon the cheek of night
Like a rich jewel in an Ethiop's ear,
Beauty too rich for use, for earth too dear.
So shows a snowy dove trooping with crows,
As yonder lady o'er her fellows shows.
The measure done, I'll watch her place of stand,
And, touching hers, make blessèd my rude hand.
Did my heart love till now? Forswear it, sight,
For I ne'er saw true beauty till this night.

(1.4.156–66)

As Romeo's speech narrates the spectacle of the dancing Juliet, comparing her to a "rich jewel," his words continually flicker between light and dark, echoing the binary rhythm of Juliet's feet until she finally reaches stillness, "the measure done." As Romeo consistently figures Juliet as a kind of airborne goddess, he associates her with the kind of roles danced by the girl masquer: "bright angel" (2.1.69) and "wingèd messenger of heaven" (71). While, by contrast, Juliet notices Romeo for his failure to dance, she describes her first feelings of love using the metaphor of a dance: "A rhyme I learn'd even now/ Of one I danced withal" (1.4.255–56). It is this intense liveliness that gives her eventual stillness, first by drug and then by dagger, its extra poignancy: "No warmth, no breath, shall testify thou livest; / The roses in thy lips and cheeks shall fade" (4.1.98–99).

When the lovers arrange to meet at Friar Laurence's cell, Romeo and Friar Laurence are awestruck by the vision of Juliet bounding toward them: *Enter Juliet.* As the Friar puts it, "Here comes the lady. O, so light a foot/ Will ne'er wear out the everlasting flint" (2.5.16–17). The corresponding stage direction in the 1597 first quarto of the play records the boy actor's speed and gestures, just as Friar Laurence observes, "Youth's love is quick, swifter than swiftest speed" (2.5.9): "*Enter Juliet, somewhat fast, and she embraces Romeo.*"[58] John Russell Brown describes this entrance as "as physically alive as it is verbally silent."[59] While "*somewhat*" conveys a sense of hesitation combined with excitement, the stage direction seems, as well, to register a controlled, modulated, movement: the trained steps of a dancer. Friar Laurence's reaction in the first quarto registers the full visual impact of Juliet's arrival: "See where she comes, / So light of foot ne'er hurts the trodden flower. / Of love and joy, see, see, the sovereign power" (2.5.9–11). The Friar's words also serve as gloss to help with the characterization of Juliet, potentially lending support to the work of a less experienced boy actor by telling the audience just what they are supposed to be seeing, here, which is that Juliet moves like a goddess. The trodden flowers, the light feet, the sovereign power: so much is being said here about Juliet's impact, as a lone girl masquer, on her small audience of two. The friar's words convey, as well, the pleasure of watching a girl, well-known to her audience, transfigured by performance: it is as if Juliet, embarking upon a new stage of life, is trying out some new steps.[60]

In the 1599 Second Quarto, Friar Laurence is much gloomier about their prospects, but the traces of this powerful moment remain: "Here comes the Lady/ so light a foot will ne'er wear out the everlasting flint; / A lover may bestride the gossamers/ That idles in the wanton summer air, / And yet not fall" (2.5.16–20). Here, the visual impact of Juliet's swift lightness in Q1 is transformed into a meditation on love itself as the experience of airborne divinity.

Because the visual and physical codes of the girl masquer were dynamic and interactive, they shifted, over time, as Shakespeare's stage opened them to new forms of contestation and complication. Although Ariel in *The Tempest* is gendered as male, at least initially ("Ariel and all *his* quality" 1.2.193), this ostensibly male spirit makes himself into a "nymph o' the sea" (1.2.301), at Prospero's behest.[61] When Ariel appears in a costume typically worn by the girl masquer, he does so, like Juliet, as love's agent. The songs

"Come Unto these Yellow Sands" and "Full Fathom Five" console Ferdinand, "allaying" his "passion," immediately before he encounters Miranda. As "Come Unto these Yellow Sands," narrates a dance, it organizes Ferdinand's emotions:

> And then take hands;
> Curtsied when you have, and kissed
> The wild waves whist,
> Foot it featly here and there,
> And sweet sprites bear
> The burden.
>
> (1.2.374–80)

Similarly, while the "sea nymphs" that "hourly ring his knell" in "Full Fathom Five" (397–405) mourn the ostensible death of Alonzo, they also mark and shepherd Ferdinand's perceived translation, his "sea-change," into an alternative reality of love and courtship: "i'th'air or th'earth?" (388).

The part of Ariel was consistently played by girl actors, often accomplished singers and dancers, from the Restoration to the twentieth century, and the tradition continues sporadically to this day.[62] And Ariel appears in female disguises throughout the play: as a Harpy, a bird with a woman's face, in the banquet scene, and as the Goddess Ceres in Prospero's wedding masque for Miranda and Ferdinand. Stephen Orgel suggests that the goddess Iris's call to "you nymphs called naiads of the windring brooks" (4.1.128) may be a reference to *Tethys' Festival*.[63] The masque suddenly ends, just as the nymphs have joined the reapers, "sunburned sickle-men," in "*a graceful dance*" (138 sd): the natural world dancing with its human controllers. Ariel re-appears again in masquing garb, "*loaden with glistering apparel*" (4.1.193 sd), to set the dogs on the conspirators. And when Ariel anticipates his promised free-dom with the song, "Where the Bee Sucks," the song focuses on the bee's restless movement from lying on the "cowslips's bell" (5.1.89) to flying "on the bat's back . . . Merrily, merrily shall I live now" (91–3). With dance, nymph costumes, and "glistering apparel" so central to the play's conception of Ariel, the legacy of the girl masquer can be charted in this "airy spirit," just as Pros-pero addresses him, throughout, in feminine terms: "delicate," "dainty," "chick." Even "tricksy" (5.1.226), which Orgel glosses as "playful, sportive," reinforces the girl masquer's association with dance and swift physical movement. While Ariel's costumes constitute a memorialization of courtly practice and cultural poetics, they also serve as a reminder of the always dressed-up, performative sense of gender, returning the focus to Shakespeare's own transvestite stage.

Shakespeare's representations of the girl masquer are, thus, acutely conscious of the boy actor beneath the glittering garb. When Perdita in *The Winter's Tale* appears at the sheep-shearing as Flora, "peering in April's front" (4.4.3), she comes in the guise of a courtly girl performer: "poor lowly maid/ Most goddess-like pranked up" (4.4.9–10).[64] Flora, as Orgel explains, was "the nymph Chloris" who, in Ovid's *Fasti*, was "transformed into the goddess of flowers by the love of Zephyrus, the west wind" (168, sd). While Zephyrus was the part that young Prince Charles played in *Tethys' Festival,* Flora is precisely the kind of role that Perdita would have played if she had spent her girlhood at court. And her upbringing as a shepherdess casts her in yet another role for the girl masquer, recalling the Russell sisters in the *Entertainment at Bisham.* Perdita is also reminded of Pentecost, another popular occasion for girls to perform: "Methinks I play as I have seen them do / In Whitsun pastorals" (4.4.133–34). Just as Ariel sings, "Foot it featly here and there" (4.4.179–99), implying neatness and elegance, Polixenes notes, of Perdita, that "she dances featly" (4.4.178–99) in the *"dance of Shepherds and Shepherdesses."* Florizel provides a more detailed sense of how Perdita's dancing modulates effectively between motion and stillness: "When you do dance, I wish you / A wave o'the'sea, that you might ever do/ Nothing but that; move still, still so, / And own no other function" (4.4.140–4). Just as part of the girl masquer's charm comes from knowing her, so, too, does Perdita's audience marvel at how her distinctive personality shines through her costume, as Florizel observes: "Each your doing / So singular in each particular, / Crowns what you are doing in the present deeds, / That all your acts are queens" (4.4.143–46).[65]

Although Perdita plays the goddess Flora in *The Winter's Tale,* Flora was also performed by a professional boy actor in Thomas Campion's 1607 *Lord Hay's Masque.* Shakespeare thus invokes the girl masquer not simply to reinforce the gendered identity of girlhood, but also to complicate it. The girl masquer has no exclusive claim to the part of Flora, and Shakespeare's representations of her call attention to the presence of the boy actor.[66] Boy masquers figure, along with girls, in *The Merry Wives of Windsor.* Mistress Page is disguised, with her little brothers, as "Like urchins, oafs, and

ARIEL - Miss VIOLA TREE.

Viola Tree as Ariel, 1904. By permission of the Folger Shakespeare Library.

fairies, green and white, / With rounds of waxen tapers on their heads,/ And rattles in their hands" (4.4.47–51) as they perform the Masque of Herne the Hunter, designed to humiliate Falstaff: "then let them all encircle him about/ And fairy-like to pinch the unclean knight" (56–57).[66] It is in the guise of a fairy that young Anne is supposed to be shuffled away to marry Doctor Caius or Slender, but, taking "a boy for a girl" (5.5.189), they each get a wrong fairy and end up marrying "lubberly" (182) little boys; "lubberly" here classifies their dancing as the opposite of "featly": clumsy, heavy, dull, cloddish.[67] Fenton, of course, is not bamboozled: he sees Mistress Page as his own "Fairy Queen," and it is in this guise, as "the queen of all the faeries/Finely attired in a robe of white" (4.4.70), that she claims her own freedom, like Ariel, to run away (although in this case it is to join her lover, like the cross-dressed Julia in *Two Gentlemen of Verona,* or Rosalind in *As You Like It*).[69]

As I have shown, little girls are typically nymphs and naiads, while it is more often little *boys* who played the fairies: as in Jonson's *Masque of Oberon the Faery Prince,* or Shakespeare's Good Master Mustardseed and Peaseblossom.[70] The fairy costume, then, may be a kind of cross-dressing for Mistress Anne, but not for her brothers. On the other hand, when Queen Elizabeth visited Norwich in August, 1578, *The Show of the Nymphs* featured boys costumed as nymphs who were so persuasively nymph-like that everyone thought they were actually girls, and it was considered so supremely and dangerously comical that the next day the boys were all given fairy costumes, so that things could return to normal.[71] And while Robert Greene's *James IV* (1590) includes any number of fairies in it, including Oberon, it also calls for a "boy or wench" to play the part of a child who dances a hornpipe.[71] So perhaps girls did make it onto the professional stage after all.[72]

Illustrating the many ways in which a performance can make an impression beyond words, the girl masquer revises our presuppositions about speech as the key indicator of a dramatically significant role. She embodies an alternative to the humanist modes of speech and declamation that underwrote professional performance in the early modern period and that continue to shape our own definitions of dramatic performance. She offers, instead, the experience of the body in motion. While Shakespeare deploys the rich vocabulary of girlhood associated with this tradition, the girl masquer appears to us, in his plays, in boyish guise, leaving her open to dynamic and interactive appropriations, shifts, and contestations.

Girls have a place in a variety of performance spaces throughout early modern England, defying any attempt to exclude them from the pleasures of the stage. And although she may never have found her place on Shakespeare's stage, the girl masquer is evoked by Shakespeare in a way that acknowledges her performative power and communicates, as well, a poignant sense of desire for her theatrical presence.

Notes

This research was first presented in a panel on "Shakespeare's Girls" at the Shakespeare Association of America in Vancouver, 2015. I thank Linda Phyllis Austern, Dympna Callaghan, Terry Goldie, David Goldstein, Jean Howard, Seth Lerer, and Randall Martin for their helpful and supportive comments and feedback, and Bernice Neal for superlative research assistance. I dedicate this essay to my teacher and friend, Stephen Orgel.

1. Throughout this essay, I use the word "girl" to refer to girl children and female teenagers, in accordance with how the term was defined in the early modern period and continues to be used today in the context of the recent emergence of the field of Girls Studies. See my *Shakespeare and the Performance of Girlhood* (Basingstoke: Palgrave, 2014), and Jennifer Higginbotham, *The Girlhood of Shakespeare's Sisters* (Edinburgh: University of Edinburgh Press, 2013).

2. On the boy actor and the children's companies, see Lucy Munro, *Children of the Queen's Revels: A Jacobean Theatre Repertory* (Cambridge: Cambridge University Press, 2005) and Edel Lamb, *Performing Childhood in the Early Modern Theatre: The Children's Playing Companies, 1599–1613* (Basingstoke: Palgrave, 2009). See also Harold Newcomb Hillebrand, *The Child Actors: A Chapter in Elizabethan Stage History* (New York: Russell and Russell, 1964), Katherine Hudson, *The Story of the Elizabethan Boy-Actors* (Oxford: Oxford University Press, 1971), and Michael Shapiro, *Children of the Revels : The Boy Companies of Shakespeare's Time and Their Plays* (New York: Columbia University Press, 1977).

3. On women and the early modern stage, see Clare McManus, *Women on the Renaissance Stage: Anna of Denmark and Female Masquing in the Stuart Court 1590–1619* (Manchester: Manchester University Press, 2002); *Women and Culture at the Courts of the Stuart Queens,* ed. Clare McManus (Basingstoke: Palgrave, 2003); *Women Players in England 1500–1600: Beyond the All-Male Stage,* ed. Pamela Allen Brown and Peter Parolin (Burlington: Ashgate, 2005); Karen Britland, *Drama at the Courts of Queen Henrietta Maria* (Cambridge: Cambridge University Press, 2006); Sophie Tomlinson, *Women on Stage in Stuart Drama* (Cambridge: Cambridge University Press, 2009). See also two recent special journal issues on the subject of women and performance: *Access and Contestation: Women's Performance in Early Modern England, Italy, France And Spain,* ed. Helen Ostovich and Erin E. Kelly, *Early Theatre* 15 (2012) and *Renaissance Women's Performance and the Dramatic Canon: Theatre History, Evidence, and Narratives,* ed. Clare McManus and Lucy Munro, *Shakespeare Bulletin* 33 (2015).

4. On girls' dramatic speech, see my "Chastity, Speech, and the Girl Masquer,"

in *Childhood, Education, and the Stage in Early Modern England,* ed. Deanne Williams and Richard Preiss (Cambridge: Cambridge University Press, forthcoming 2016).

5. Anne Klink, *Women's Songs in Ancient Greece* (Montreal: McGill-Queens University Press, 2008); John H. Starks, Jr., "Actresses in the Roman World," University of North Carolina dissertation, 2004; and Evelyn Fertl, *Von Musen, Miminnen und leichten Mädchen. Die Schauspielerin in der römischen Antike* [Of Muses, mime actresses and prostitutes. The Actress in the Roman theatre] (Vienna: Braumüller, 2005).

6. Hroswit of Gandersheim, *Opera Omnia* ed. Walter Berschin. Bibliotheca scriptorum Graecorum et Romanorum Teubneriana (Munich: K. G. Sauer Verlag, 2001). On female performers in the Middle Ages see Kim M. Phillips, *Medieval Maidens: Young Women and Gender in England 1270–1540* (Manchester: University of Manchester Press, 2003).

7. Lynette R. Muir, "Women on the Medieval Stage: The Evidence from France," *Medieval English Theatre* 7 (1985): 107–19, Meg Twycross, "Transvestism in the Mystery Plays," *Medieval English Theatre* 5 (1983): 123–80.

8. Clifford Davidson, "Women and the Medieval Stage," *Women's Studies* 11 (1984); 99–113 at 104. For discussion see Jody Enders, *Death by Drama and other Medieval Urban Legends* (Chicago: University of Chicago Press, 2002), 17, and Twycross, "Transvestism," 134. For the French account see Louis Petit de Julleville, *Les Mystères,* 2 vols. (Paris: Hachette, 1880), 2: 32.

9. Muir, "Women on the Medieval Stage," 115.

10. William Tydeman, *The Medieval European Stage 500–1550* (Cambridge: Cambridge University Press, 2001), 121–30; Philippe de Mézières, *Philippe de Mézières's Campaign for the Feast of Mary's Presentation,* ed. William Emmett Coleman (Toronto: University of Toronto Press, 1981); and Susan Udry, "'Putting on the Girls': Mary's Girlhood and the Performance of Monarchical Authority in Philippe de Mézières's Dramatic office for the *Presentation of the Virgin in the Temple,*" *European Medieval Drama* 8 (2004): 1–18.

11. John Marshall, "Her virgynes, as many as a man wylle': Dance and Provenance in Three Late Medieval Plays: *Wisdom, The Killing of the Children, The Conversion of St Paul,*" *Leeds Studies in English* 25 (1994): 111–48 at 131.

12. Twycross, "Transvestitism," 132.

13. *The Mary Play from the N-Town Manuscript* ed. Peter Meredith (London: Longman, 1987). See J. A. Tasioulas, "Between doctrine and domesticity: the portrayal of Mary in the N-Town Plays," *Medieval Women in their Communities,* ed. Diane Watt (Toronto: University of Toronto Press, 1997), 222–45 and Katie Normington, *Gender in Medieval* Drama (Cambridge: D.S. Brewer, 2004), 39–44.

14. Theresa Coletti, *Mary Magdalene and the Drama of Saints: Theater, Gender and Religion in Late Medieval England* (Philadelphia: University of Pennsylvania Press, 2004).

15. See Catherine B. C. Thomas, "The Miracle Play at Dunstable," *Modern Language Notes* 32 (1917): 337–44; E. K. Chambers, *The Medieval Stage,* 2 vols. (Oxford: Clarendon Press, 1903), 2: 380; Clifford Davidson, "Women and the Medieval Stage" *Women's Studies* 11 (1984): 99–113 at 104. For a rich discussion of medieval saints' plays see Catherine Sanok, "Performing Sanctity in Late Medieval England: Parish Guilds, Saint's Plays, and the Second Nun's Tale," *Journal of Medieval and Early Modern Studies* 32 (2002): 269–303.

16. Twycross, "Transvestism," 131; Glynne Wickham, *Early English Stages 1300–1660,* 5 vols. (London: Routledge, 1963), 1: 87. See also *The Receyt of Ladie Kateryne,* ed. Gordon Kipling EETS o.s. 296 (Oxford: Oxford University Press, 1990); and, for further discussion, Gordon Kipling, *Triumph of Honor* (The Hague: Leiden University Press, 1977), 75–90, and Sydney Anglo, *Spectacle, Pageantry, and Early Tudor Policy* (Oxford: Clarendon Press, 1969), 56–97.

17. *A Calendar of Dramatic Records in the Books of the Livery Companies of London,* ed. Jean Robertson and D. J. Gordon (Malone Society Collections 3, 1954), 14. See also Wickham, *Early English Stages,* 1: 272; and Twycross, "Transvestism," 130. "2 maidens" were also paid for appearing in the pageant of our Lady and Saint Elizabeth 1519 and the Pageant of the Lady Mary in 1534. Robertson and Gordon, *A Calendar of Dramatic Records,* 4, 14, 24; and Wickham, *Early English Stages,* 1: 272.

18. "The Coronation of Anne Boleyn," *John Nichols's The Progresses and Public Processions of Queen Elizabeth. A New Edition of the Early Modern Sources* ed. Elizabeth Goldring, Faith Eales, Elizabeth Clarke and Jayne Elizabeth Archer (Oxford: Oxford University Press, 2014): Appendix 1; and Tracey Sowerby, "The Coronation of Anne Boleyn," *The Oxford Handbook of Tudor Drama,* ed. Thomas Betteridge and Greg Walker (Oxford: Oxford University Press, 2012), 386–401.

19. See Martin Wiggins and Catherine Richardson, *British Drama 1533–1642: A Catalogue,* 5 vols. (Oxford: Oxford University Press, 2012), 1: 260 and 5: 81. Edward VI's royal entry included a pageant of Saint George, with a girl as the "fair maiden" (1: 158–62).

20. Wiggins and Richardson, *British Drama,* 1: 44–45.

21. George Peele, *The device of the pageant borne before Woolstone Dixi* (London, 1585). See also Wiggins and Richardson, *British Drama,* 2: 343–44. Thames continues: "This gracious good hath God and kinde begun, / for Londons use with help of sailes and ores./ London rejoice and give thy God the praise:/ For her whose highness lengths thy happy daies."

22. Wiggins and Richardson, *British Drama,* 1: 303–4 at 303; and David Galloway, *Records of Early English Drama: Norwich 1540–1642* (Toronto: University of Toronto Press, 1984), 31–42.

23. Twycross, "Transvestitism," 133. Writing about girl performers in the later Stuart courts, Clare McManus makes the point that "it is possible that the youthfulness of Ann Watkins and Alice Egerton granted a degree of impunity similar to that exploited by the earlier children's theatre companies—an impunity less available to those who no longer stood beneath the control of a father, a family or a school." McManus, *Women on the Renaissance Stage,* 186.

24. On women performers in medieval and early modern drama see the work of James Stokes, "Women and Mimesis in Medieval and Renaissance Somerset (and Beyond)," *Comparative Drama* 27 (1993): 176–96; "Women and Performance: Evidence of Universal Cultural Suffrage in Medieval and Early Modern Lincolnshire," *Women Players in England,* ed. Brown and Parolin, 25–44; and "The Ongoing Exploration of Women and Performance in Early Modern England: Evidences, Issues, and Questions," *Shakespeare Bulletin* 33 (2015): 9–31.

25. Stokes, "The Ongoing Exploration of Women and Performance," 32.

26. *Speeches Delivered to her Maiestie this last Progress* (London, 1592) and Wiggins and Richardson, *British Drama,* 3: 190–92; Peter Davidson and Jane Ste-

venson, "Elizabeth I's Reception at Bisham (1592): Elite Women as Writers and Devisers," in *The Progresses, Pageants, and Entertainments of Queen Elizabeth I,* ed. Jayne Archer, Elizabeth Goldring and Sarah Knight (Oxford: Oxford University Press, 2007): 207–26. Davidson and Stevenson point out that Lady Russell had printed a translation from Latin, John Ponet's *A Way of Reconciliation* (1605) and wrote verses in Latin and Greek.

27. On Lady Russell's status as "deviser" of the entertainment see Davidson and Stevenson, "Elizabeth I's Reception." See also, Alexandra F. Johnson, "The 'Lady of the farme': the context of Lady Russell's *Entertainment of Elizabeth at Bisham,*" *Early Theatre* 5 (2002): 71–85; and Elizabeth Zeman Kolkovich, "Lady Russell, Elizabeth I, and Female Political Alliances Through Performance," *ELR* 39 (2009): 290–314.

28. Catherine Sanok, *Her Life Historical. Exemplarity and Female Saints' Lives in Late Medieval England* (Philadelphia: University of Pennsylvania Press, 2007), 163. H. F. Westlake, *The Parish Guilds of Mediaeval England* (London: Macmillan, 1919), 34.

29. William Tydeman, *Theatre in the Middle Ages: Western European Stage Conditions 800–1576* (Cambridge: Cambridge University Press, 1978), 200.

30. "et de xij d datis puellis tripudantibus in festo dedicacionis (Peterhouse Computus Roll 1429–30), " et de viij d puellis tripudiantibus in festo dedicacionis (Peterhouse Computus Roll 1446–47); "et de viij d puellis tripudiantibus in festo dedicacionis (Peterhouse Computus Roll 1450–51). Alan Nelson, *Records of Early English Drama: Cambridge* (Toronto: University of Toronto Press, 1989), 25, 30, 33.

31. *Records of English Court Music,* ed. Andrew Ashbee, 9 vols. (Snodland, Kent, 1991): 7: 152, 158, discussed in Barbara Ravelhofer, "Dancing at the Court of Queen Elizabeth" in *Queen Elizabeth I: Past and Present,* ed. Christa Jansohn (Münster: Münster Verlag, 2004): 101–16.

32. Adolphus William Ward, *A History of English Dramatic Literature to the Death of Queen Anne,* 2 vols. (New York: Octagon, 1966), 1: 92–93.

33. Theresa Coletti, "Genealogy, Sexuality, and Sacred Power: The Saint Anne Dedication of the Digby *Candlemas Play and the Killing of the Children of Israel,*" *Journal of Medieval and Early Modern Studies* 29 (1999): 25–59.

34. Kent Rawlinson, "Hall's Chronicle and the Greenwich Triumphs of 1527," in *The Oxford Handbook of Tudor Drama,* ed. Thomas Betteridge and Greg Walker (Oxford: Oxford University Press, 2012): 402–28.

35. "Venice: May 1527," *Calendar of State Papers Relating to English Affairs in the Archives of Venice, Volume 4: 1527–1533* (London: Her Majesty's Stationery Office, 1871): 56–66.

36. *Hall's Chronicle,* ed. H. Ellis (London: J. Johnson, 1809), 723.

37. Janette Dillon, *The Language of Space in Court Performance* (Cambridge: Cambridge University Press, 2010), 121. For a detailed discussion of the importance of beautiful hair in the early modern period, see Edith Snook, "Beautiful Hair, Health, and Privilege in Early Modern England," *Journal for Early Modern Cultural Studies* 15 (2015): 22–51.

38. Roy C. Strong, "The Ambassador," in *The Cult of Elizabeth: Elizabethan Portraiture and Pageantry* (London: Thames and Hudson, 1977): 84–110 at 104.

39. Lady Russell's son, Edward (by her first marriage to Sir Edward Hoby of Bisham) married Henry Unton's sister Cecily. As a girl, Henry Unton's mother,

Anne Seymour, composed the influential *Hecatodistichon* (1550) on the death of Marguerite de Navarre, with her sisters. Its publication in France moved Ronsard, Du Bellay and others to produce memorial verses about Marguerite de Navarre.

40. Skiles Howard, *The Politics of Courtly Dancing in Early Modern England* (Amherst: University of Massachusetts Press, 1998), 23. On Shakespeare and dance, see Alan Brissenden, *Shakespeare and the Dance* (Atlantic Highlands, NJ: Humanities Press, 1981) and Anne Daye, *A Lively Shape of Dauncing: Dances of Shakespeare's Time* (Salisbury, Wiltshire: Dolmetsch Historical Dance Society, 1994); for European contexts, see *Women's Work: Making Dance in Europe Before 1800*, ed. Lynn Matluck Brooks (Madison: University of Wisconsin Press, 2007) and *Dance, Spectacle, and the Body Politick, 1270–1750*, ed. Jennifer Nevile (Bloomington: Indiana University Press, 2008); on France, see Mark Franko, *Dance as Text: Ideologies of the Baroque Body* (Cambridge: Cambridge University Press, 1993) and Margaret M. McGowan, *Dance in the Renaissance: European Fashion, French Obsession* (New Haven, CT: Yale University Press, 2008); and on England, see Emily F. Winerock, "Reformation and Revelry: The Practices and Politics of Dancing in Early Modern England, c.1550–c.1640," PhD diss., University of Toronto, 2012. On dancing in masques, see Barbara Ravelhofer, *The Early Stuart Masque: Dance, Costume, and Music* (Oxford: Oxford University Press, 2006) and Suzanne Gossett, " 'Man-maid, begone!': Women in Masques," *English Literary Renaissance* 18 (1988): 96–113.

41. George Peele, *Anglorum Feriae* in *The Works of George Peele* ed. A. H. Bullen 2 vols. (London: John C. Nimmo, 1888), 2: 339–56.

42. Sir Thomas Elyot, *The Book of the Governor* (London, 1531), 89.

43. Sir John Davies, *Orchestra, Or a Poem of Dancing* (London, 1596), 126.

44. See Sarah Thesiger, "The *Orchestra* of Sir John Davies and the Image of the Dance" *Journal of the Warburg and Courtauld Institutes* 36 (1973): 277–304, and Katherine Butler, *Music and Elizabethan Court Politics* (Woodbridge: The Boydell Press, 2015).

45. Roger Ascham, *The Scholemaster* in *The Whole Works of Roger Ascham* ed. Rev. Dr. Giles, 3 vols. (London: John Russell Smith, 1864), 3: 139.

46. Juan Luis Vives, *A Very Fruitful and Pleasant Book, Called the Instruction of a Christian Woman*, trans. Richard Hyrde (London, 1585), 27. This passage is discussed in Butler, *Music*, 22–23.

47. John Northbrooke, *A Treatise Wherein Dicing, Dancing, Vaine plaies or Enterludes with other idle pastimes, etc. commonly used on the Sabboth Day* (London: Shakespeare Society, 1953). See also Thesiger, "*Orchestra*," 280.

48. John Bromyard, *Summa praedicantium*, trans. G. G. Coulton, *Five Centuries of Religion* vol. 1, 1000–1200 (Cambridge: Cambridge University Press, 1923), 535–56; quoted in Tydeman, *The Medieval European Stage*, 260. And two lost anti-Catholic plays from the 1530s, John Bale's *Vita divi Joannis Bapistae* (1534) and James Wedderburn's *The Beheading of John the Baptist* (1539), possibly performed at Trinity College, Cambridge, would have included the dance of Herodias's daughter, as did Nicholas Grimald's *Archipropheta* (1546), which gained the author a place at Christ Church, Oxford. *British Drama*, ed. Wiggins and Richardson, 1: 14, 76, 150–53.

49. *The Letters of John Chamberlain*, ed. Norman Egbert McClure, 2 vols. (Philadelphia: The American Philosophical Society, 1939), 2: 128.

50. Winwood, *Memorials of the Affairs of Stage in the Reigns of Queen Eliza-*

beth and King James I, 3 vols. (London, 1725), 3: 179; E. K. Chambers, *The Elizabe-than Stage,* 4 vols. (Oxford: Clarendon Press, 1923), 3: 281–83; Stephen Orgel and Roy Strong, *Inigo Jones, The Theatre of the Stuart Court* , 2 vols. (Berkeley: University of California Press, 1973), 1: 192.

51. Samuel Daniel, *Tethys' Festival,* in Orgel and Strong, *Inigo Jones,* 1: 191–201.

52. Elizabeth Benger, *Memoirs of Elizabeth Stuart, Queen of Bohemia,* 2 vols. (London: Longman, Hurst, 1825), 1: 93.

53. Orgel and Strong, *Inigo Jones,* 1: 282. See also Andrew Gurr, *The Shakespearean Stage 1574–1642* (Cambridge: Cambridge University Press, 1992), 206.

54. Court masques featuring nymphs include George Peele's "The Arraignment of Paris," Robert White's "Cupid's Banishment," Jonson's "Masque of Beauty," "Pan's Anniversary," and "Chloridia: Rites to Chloris and her Nymphs."

55. Howard makes an important point about dance as a form of discourse: "suggesting both the protean nature of dancing as cultural artifact and the means by which it stimulated a social metamorphosis" (23).

56. On *Romeo and Juliet* and dance, see Philip C. McGuire, "On the Dancing in *Romeo and Juliet," Renaissance and Reformation/ Rénaissance et Réforme* 5 (1981): 87–97; Brissenden, *Shakespeare and the Dance,* 63–66.

57. William Shakespeare, *Romeo and Juliet,* ed. Jill L. Levenson, Oxford World's Classics (Oxford: Oxford University Press, 2000).

58. *Romeo and Juliet, First Quarto,* in *Romeo and Juliet,* ed. Levenson, 261–429.

59. John Russell Brown, *Shakespeare and the Theatrical Event* (New York: Palgrave 2002), 57.

60. Juliet is characterized by physical movement elsewhere the play, when she discusses with Friar Laurence the dangers she would happily face in order to marry Romeo: "O, bid me leap, rather than marry Paris, / From off the battlements of yonder tower; / Or walk in thievish ways; or bid me lurk / Where serpents are; chain me with roaring bears" (4.1.77–80).

61. William Shakespeare, *The Tempest,* ed. Stephen Orgel, Oxford World's Classics (Oxford: Oxford University Press, 1987).

62. See my "Prospero's Girls," *Borrowers and Lenders: the Journal of Shakespeare and Appropriation* 9.1 (2014). http://www.borrowers.uga.edu/1382/show ; and the Introduction to *The Tempest,* ed. Orgel, 69–87.

63. *The Tempest,* ed. Orgel, 178n.

64. William Shakespeare, *The Winter's Tale,* ed. Stephen Orgel, Oxford World's Classics (Oxford: Oxford University Press, 1996).

65. Polixenes makes a similar observation: "This is the prettiest low-born lass that ever/ Ran on the greensward. Nothing she does or seems / But smacks of something greater than herself, / Too noble for this place" (4.4.156–59).

66. Orgel and Strong, *Inigo Jones,* 1: 115–20.

67. William Shakespeare, *The Merry Wives of Windsor,* ed. Giorgio Melchiori. The Arden Shakespeare, 3rd Series (Walton-on-Thames: Thomas Nelson and Sons, 2000).

68. Her plan: "let them circle all about / And fairy-like to pinch the unclean knight/ And ask him why, that hour of fairy revel, / In their so sacred paths he dares to tread / In shape profane" (56–59).

69. Whether in white, as her father instructs her (or, in Q1, as she arranges with Fenton), or green, to please her mother.

70. For boys as fairies, see *The Royal Entertainment at Woodstock* (1575); Wiggins and Richardson, *British Drama*, 2: 140; *The Althorp Entertainment* (1603); Wiggins and Richardson, *British Drama*, 5: 46–48.

71. Wiggins and Richardson, *British Drama*, 2: 199–203.

72. Wiggins and Richardson, *British Drama*, 3: 35.

73. Kay Savage suggests that this stage direction, which she classifies as "permissive," was "penned with touring in mind," with the idea that a provincial audience, "accustomed to seasonal festivities, might have been more complacent than their metropolitan counterparts"; see "Stage Directions: Valuable Clues in the Exploration of Elizabethan Performance Practice," *Studies in Theatre and Performance* 28 (2008): 161–82 at 173.

Jewel, Purse, Trash: Reckoning and Reputation in *Othello*

Laura Kolb

IN A MOCKING LIST OF MORAL lessons to be drawn from *Othello,* Thomas Rymer writes, "Thirdly, this may be a lesson to Husbands, that before their Jealousie be Tragical, the proofs may be Mathematical."[1] The double-meaning of "proofs"—both the demonstration of truth and the derivation of a mathematical theorem—underscores what will become Rymer's major critique of Shakespeare's play in *A Short View of Tragedy* (1693).[2] The human calculations on display are, to Rymer, ridiculous: inexact to the point of improbability, based on hints and inferences rather than demonstrations systematically pursued. Despite his tone of ridicule, by contrasting Othello's "Tragical" jealousy to "proofs . . . Mathematical," Rymer makes a serious point: *Othello* is deeply concerned with evaluation, and evaluation, in *Othello,* opens onto the domain of mathematics. Throughout, language of calculation abounds, from Iago's denigration of Cassio as a paltry account-keeper, calling him "debitor and creditor" and "counter-caster" (1.1.30), to Bianca's "weary reckoning" (3.4.171) of her beloved's "absent hours" (3.4.169).[3] More centrally, Iago's scheme to have Desdemona "undo her credit with the Moor" (2.3.344) involves a lesson in reckoning: he teaches Othello to evaluate his wife in a new way, reading her according to a hermeneutic of suspicion more appropriate to commercial credit (which he here invokes) than to marital trust.[4] Following this linguistic and conceptual thread, what might it mean to push back against Rymer's critique—to claim that reckoning in *Othello* is, in a very real sense, mathematical?

Critics from Rymer's day to ours have called attention to the "improbable" suddenness and totality of Othello's turn to jealousy.[5] The most illuminating explanations center on the structures of knowledge Iago instills (or awakens) in Othello: sexual anxiety, philosophical skepticism, a sense of the potentially arbitrary tie between word and thing, a rhetoricized view of sociability and selfhood.[6] Iago teaches Othello to *know* differently, critics argue, and his understanding of his wife, his world, and himself undergoes a swift and utter metamorphosis. Here, in contrast, I argue that the mechanism Iago makes available to Othello is primarily evaluative. That is, the ensign offers his general a new mode not simply of seeing and knowing the world, but of reckoning it, of calculating worth—in particular, his own, and his wife's. In order to make this argument, this essay revisits Othello's turn to jealousy and its corollary, his altered sense of self, in light of a little-remarked aspect of the play: the strain of economically charged language that runs from Iago's sneering epithets for Cassio and plot against Desdemona's "credit" to Othello's comparison of his murdered wife to a discarded "pearl" (5.2.346). The evaluation of others and of the self are linked, in *Othello,* to acts of reckoning drawn from the world of trade. Othello's re-evaluation of his wife and of himself is informed by practices and habits of mind from the domain of early modern commercial calculation.

In attending to Othello's language of valuing, I draw on two recent strands of criticism on the play. Several new studies of *Othello* have characterized the play's Venice as a site exemplifying the multi-cultural Mediterranean, a heterocosm brought into being by expanding networks of trade and cosmopolitanism. Both Emily Bartels and Daniel Vitkus treat *Othello* as a key text for historicist criticism that thinks, in Bartels' words, "In terms of 'worlds,' charted . . . across bodies of waters and boundaries of nation-states, configured dynamically as transnational and international economies, and defined by mixed and ethnically mixed populations."[7] Vitkus argues that contact with strangers sometimes forced the solidifying of identities along oppositional, often binary lines, but at other times facilitated tolerance and cultural exchange.[8] Similarly, Bartels calls attention to "how and where we draw the line on difference."[9] I am interested in that line—not only in how and where we draw it, but what tools we bring to bear on the act of drawing. As Joel Altman writes, by his final lines, Othello has discovered that "The self can harbor an unexpected stranger from a foreign land, who is introjected through the gaze of another."[10] In my account, the destabilizing gaze Iago makes available to Othello is not primarily Christian or European, as has been argued.[11] It is instead a commercial gaze, imported from the world of trade in which the play is set. It is, to borrow Rymer's term, mathematical.

Patricia Parker has recently demonstrated the extent to which *Othello* is in dialogue with sixteenth-century mathematics and, further, the extent to which mathematics itself was a field of wide and varied associations.[12] Arithmetic or "algorism," Parker notes, spread through the heterogeneous trade-world that Vitkus and Bartels describe, entering Europe through "early contacts with the Muslim world" and remaining "identified with Arabs, Saracens, and Moors" even as Arabic numerals overtook Roman, and arithmetical calculation "with the pen" replaced older forms of reckoning "with the counters."[13] Parker's interest lies in the dense web of associations whereby Shakespeare links numeracy to infidels, calculation to enchantment, and account-keeping to secrets, both economic and sexual. Here, I take a narrower focus, attending to Shakespeare's dramatic portrayal of the act of reckoning. In so doing, I draw on recent work on commercial credit, one significant arena in which numerical or economic values come into contact with social value, virtue, public opinion, honor, and other less-quantifiable forms of worth. Historians of credit have suggested that economic credit seamlessly merged with other forms of social value—honor, reputation, opinion—in the sixteenth and seventeenth centuries.[14] *Othello* registers a moment of greater complexity than this body of historical work might suggest, a moment when the terms *honor* and *credit* designated distinct forms of worth even as they at times overlapped. At its start, the play presents a world rife with multiple forms of evaluation, existing as choices within a broad and multiplicitous field. These choices are—tragically—organized into binary oppositions: between intrinsic and extrinsic values, for instance, and between honor and credit. Iago, I argue, promotes these binaries. Over the course of the play, he forces the tools of trade—the cognitive habits and the social practices of determining (and conferring) value in the marketplace—into conflict with other forms of valuation, in particular, military and marital honor.

In what follows, I will first lay out the play's engagement with early modern arithmetics, following Parker's suggestion that the spread of mathematics had important cultural ramifications. I will then turn to the play's economic language and its presentation of reputation, credit, and honor, before concluding with a consideration of *Othello*'s engagement with the genre of Romance. Michael

Murrin has recently argued that expanding trade networks in the early modern period shaped the heterogeneous worlds and episodic structures of Renaissance Romance, a genre that critical tradition links to Shakespeare's tragedy.[15] Here, I suggest that Romance eclecticism offers a counterpoint to the tragic, binarizing logic promoted by Iago.

Othello as partnership problem

An Introduction for to lerne to recken with the pen or with the counters (1536/7), the first printed arithmetic in English, contains a problem titled "The rule and questyon of zarasins for to cast them within the see." It runs:

> There is a galle[y] upon the see wherein be thyrty marchauntes, that is to wit 15 crysten men, and 15 sarazyns, ther falleth great tempest where upon it behoveth them to cast all the marchaundyse in to the see, and yet for all that they be not in surete from perysshynge, for the galle[y] is feble and weke, so that by ordynaunce made by the patrone, it is necessary that there be caste into the see the halfe of the thyrty marchauntes, but the sarazyns wyll not be cast in, nor also the christiens: then by apoyntment made, they shall sette them down upon a rowe & then counte them unto 9 and he that sholde fall upon the 9 to be caste into the see, how wolde ye set them that none of the chrystyens shold be caste into the see[?][16]

Up to a point, the question is not so unusual. *An Introduction* consists largely of word problems that develop skills for calculation, measurement, and conversion. These problems invoke a range of situations from the mundane (calculating the price of everyday goods sold by weight or length) to the specialized (figuring the returns on an investment made by several merchants jointly). The majority deal with rate, proportion, and interest, and the "reckening" involved is rarely abstract. Scenarios involve retailers measuring cloth; women selling apples in a market; a householder sending a servant to buy pepper, sugar and "fine spyces." Grounded in particular goods and situations, the problems in *An Introduction* present arithmetical calculation as a practice embedded in and instrumental to material and social life.[17]

Many of these problems are about merchants, and the book probably would have been used primarily by members of the "business community" of early modern England.[18] As the genre flourished and branched out in later decades, printed arithmetics were touted as practically useful for a variety of disciplines, in addition to trade. These ranged from astronomy and surveying to medicine and warfare. One type of manual, the cheap and handy "ready reckoner," appealed to a particularly broad audience. *The Treasurers Almanacke, or the Money-Master* (1627; an expanded version of the less auspiciously titled *The Money Monger, or the Usurers Almanacke* of 1626) bears on its title page a list of people for whom the pamphlet should prove "most necessary and helpful." The list includes members of specific professions—Merchant, Grocer, Goldsmith, Scrivener, Mercer, Draper, Fishmonger, Usurer—broad social and professional groups—Artificer, Tradesman, Nobleman, Gentleman—situational types—Buyer, Lender, Seller, Borrower— and military men—General, Coronell, Knight, Commander. The list ends by broadening out even more inclusively: "And whosoever else. Also may fitly serve for the Sea."

"The rule and questyon of zarasins" bears the situational and professional specificity of many early math problems, but its function within a program of practical education remains uncertain. What would a real merchant learn from the plight of these fictional ones? How would *this* puzzle "fitly serve for the sea"? It has been classified as "recreational" rather than "practical and real."[19] Indeed, it cannot be solved using the skills taught elsewhere in the book. The author does, however, provide a solution.[20] To "set them that none of the chrystyens shold be caste into the see," the merchants must be arranged as follows: "4 christiens 5 sarazins 2 christyens 1 sarazyn, 3 christyens 1 sarazin 1 christien 2 sarasyns, 2 christiens 3 sarazyns, 1 chrystyen 2 sarazyns, 2 christiens 1 sarazyn." There is no immediately discernible sequence to the numbers (indeed, until the nineteenth century, brute force "counting-out" remained the only way to solve the problem numerically).[21] The visible pattern is, rather, the alternation of "christiens" with "sarazins." The real reckoning involved seems to be social and religious, a stark division of the band into two groups: Saracens and Christians, the drowned and the saved. "The rule and questyon of zarasins" assumes and promotes a system of value not typically expressed in terms of numerical calculation, in which merchandise is worth less than lives and Muslim lives are worth less than Christian ones.

Yet perhaps this problem *is* useful for merchants. A sixteenth-century reader unfamiliar with the puzzle might think at first glance that he was encountering a "partnership problem," a genre that addressed profit-sharing in the age before corporations.[22] Like "The rule and questyon of zarasins," partnership problems open by specifying a number of merchants and continue through a brief narrative that culminates in a question—generally, sketching the merchants' outlays in a venture and asking pupils to calculate the division of profits. A typical example from *An Introduction* runs:

> Thre marchauntes put theyr monye togyther for to have gaynes, the whiche have boughte suche marchaundyse as hath cost 125 francz, whereof the fyrste hath laide 15 francz. The seconde 64 [f]z. and the thyrde 36, fz. And they have goten 54 franc. of clere gaynes.[23]

The text then addresses the reader: "I demaund how shall they devide it, so that eche man have gaines accordynge to the moneye that he hath layd downe." "The rule and questyon of zarasins" asks a very different kind of question—"how wolde ye set them that none of the chrystyens shold be caste into the see[?]"—but the generic elements of partnership and shared enterprise remain in play. In fact, the problem's mercantile setting seems to have been *added* by the book's author. Notably, "The rule and questyon of zarasins" does not appear in any of recognized sources for *An Introduction.* Similar problems do show up in a number of Medieval and early modern texts. Other versions place different groups on board ship: students and "good-for-nothings," Christians and Jews, Christians and Turks, friars and monks. Nowhere else, however, are the thirty travelers identified as merchants and nowhere else do they throw anything besides men overboard.[24] These details alter the puzzle's meaning. Behind the traditional riddle and its us/them logic, a world of commercial fellowship and shared endeavor opens up.

In early modern Europe, commercial relations increasingly brought strangers together "for mutual profit," as another question in *An Introduction* puts it. The bonds that arose from shared ventures might be fragile and contingent, but they might also be lasting and firm. Gerard de Malynes writes of "sinceritie and Candor Animi amongst Merchants of all nations" and Hugh Oldcastle suggests that the "outwarde fayth or promise of a marchaunt" inspires inward trust.[25] Even if the puzzle's Saracens and Christians do not bear each other affection during their voyage, they do form a functional, cooperative group. As "thyrty marchauntes," they travel together, throw away their goods together, and at last line up together. In the end, the Saracens are tricked because they trust. For them, the bonds of shared enterprise trump differences in race and religion. This must also to be the case for the Christians, at least up to a point; it is only when the storm arises that they "recken" differently. And that is also a practical skill: knowing how to value human beings, according to what criteria, and when.

Othello, too, contains a storm at sea with no Christian lives lost. "Our wars are done, the Turks are drowned" (2.1.197), the general declares as he comes ashore at Cyprus. Beyond this surface similarity, *Othello* resembles the puzzle in a deeper sense. It is also a kind of partnership problem, where the boundary between Venetian and other shifts depending on the needs of the state, personal loyalties, and public opinion. "The rule and questyon of the zarasins" offers a schematic version of a problem at the heart of *Othello:* the problem of assigning value to persons in a community at once predicated on and threatened by the absorption of difference. Like the band of merchants on the galley, Shakespeare's Venice is a society in which incorporating strangers is both necessary and risky. The ship in the puzzle and the city in the play are both commercial enterprises that depend on cooperation and trust among members of different racial, national, and religious backgrounds. In both spaces, the boundary separating insider and outsider is fluid and shifting, at times obscure, at others sharply evident.[26]

The center of a trading and military empire, Venice drew people from across the Mediterranean and beyond. Thomas Coryate wrote that Venice facilitated "concourse and meeting of so many distinct and sundry nations," including "Polonians, Slavonians, Persians, Grecians, Turks, Iewes, Christians of all the famousest regions of Christendome" as well as "barbarous Ethnicks," natives of Barbary, or North Africa.[27] English readers of Lewis Lewkenor's translation of Gasparo Contarini's *Commonwealth and government of Venice* (1599) would find mercantile enterprise linked to social heterogeneity on the first page: "so unmeasurable a quantity of all sorts of marchandise to be brought out of all realmes and countries into this Citie" and "wonderful concourse of strange and forraine people" inspire "infinit marvaile" in the city's visitors.[28] Such "concourse" took many forms and entailed varying relations with the state. Especially in the arenas of trade, banking, and the military, aliens imported specific skills necessary to protect and fund Venice's commercial empire. War and commerce offered aliens "a legitimate, valued, and to some degree respected place within the social, economic, and political community."[29]

The figure of Othello embodies the ambiguous, insider-outsider status fostered by Venetian cosmopolitanism. Professionally, his "occupation" (3.3.359) depends both on his loyalty to the Venetian state and his foreignness. Contarini explains that Venetians prefer "forreyn mercenarie souldiers" in their armies; the "Captaine Generall of our Armie," he reports, is "alwaies a straunger."[30] Some Venetians speak of Othello with racist epithets; most, however, esteem him highly. Few of the play's characters seem either consistently concerned or consistently *un*concerned with the question of Othello's difference.[31] No one, including Iago, conceives of him as an outsider all of the time, while even Desdemona acknowledges that his "visage" (1.3.250) sets him apart. Brabantio's broken bond with Othello epitomizes the complexity of his position within Venetian society. Desdemona's father "loved" Othello and "oft invited" (1.3.128) him into their home before accusing him of bewitching Desdemona to run to the "sooty bosom/ Of such a thing as thou—to fear, not to delight" (1.2.70–71).

The links that bind the Moor to Venice complicate his otherness, not only for the Venetians, but for himself. In his final speech, Othello separates himself into two opposed identities before committing suicide:

> Set you down this;
> And say besides that in Aleppo once,
> Where a malignant and a turbaned Turk
> Beat a Venetian and traduced the state,
> I took by th' throat the circumcisèd dog
> And smote him—thus!
>
> (5.2.350–55)

He appears to divide himself into that which is of Venice and that which is opposed to it—foreign, Turkish, Other—and casts the latter out. Othello's stark self-division speaks to the success of Iago's plot, which not only destroys his faith in his wife, but also corrodes his sense of self. But it also reveals something that existed dormant within him before that plot began: a multiple self-hood that reflects Venice's heterogeneity and his own complex status as both insider and outsider. Like the group of merchants in the storm-tossed ship, Othello is both unified and divided. Or rather, he is unified *until* he is divided. The action of the play resembles the storm at sea, revealing fault lines hidden within a symbiotic partnership. Instead of setting Christian against Saracen or even Venetian against Turk, it pits Othello against himself. The play is itself a kind of partnership problem, one in which rating people is always at issue. Through the stormy events of the middle acts, the complex multimodal judgments possible in the Venice of the play's start re-emerge as a tragic binary. In what follows, I lay out the mechanics behind this shift; to do this, I turn to first to the play's symbolic language of value, then to its presentation of good name.

Economic language in *Othello*

Unlike other English dramatic representations of Venice, such as Ben Jonson's *Volpone* or Shakespeare's *Merchant of Venice, Othello*'s plot does not hinge on economic issues.[32] Throughout the text, however, money and property form a leitmotif, locating the play's action in a society structured by the moment of cash, gifts, land, and other bearers of material value.[33] Examples include Brabantio's "bags" (1.1.80); Roderigo's "purse" (1.1.2), the "land" (1.3.370) he incontinently sells; the "gold, and jewels" (5.1.16) he gives Iago to give Desdemona; Desdemona's own "purse full of crusadoes" (3.4.23–24); the metaphorical "purchase" and "profit" between Othello and his bride and his literal "house" (5.2.364) and "fortunes" (5.2.365), which Gratiano inherits. Moreover, the "service" Othello has "done the state" (5.2.338) results from an economic arrangement. Like many historical Venetian officers, he is foreign; like all of them, he is a mercenary, and his mercenary status simultaneously depends on and mitigates his foreignness.[34] At stake in the ongoing conflict against the Turks, and the raison d'être of the Venetian military, is control of a commercial empire within which Cyprus is an important trading post. At the broadest level, the play's sea voyage, its Venetian-Cypriot setting, and the far-flung places to which it alludes (among them Barbary, Rhodes, Aleppo) locate its action within the criss-crossing trade routes of the Mediterranean.

If invocations of possessions and currency inflect the play with a sense of the commercial Mediterranean in which it is set, metaphors of value, exchange, and theft supply a symbolic vocabulary for concerns with human value and social evaluation.[35] Two examples begin to illustrate the point: Desdemona, as we have seen, is likened to a pearl near the play's end. Earlier, Othello compares her to a more hyperbolically precious object, a "world/ Of one entire and perfect chrysolite" (5.2.142–43). She is also figured, twice, as the profits of a mercantile voyage: she is "a land-carrack" (1.2.50) and "the riches of the ship" (2.1.83). On the other end of the play's scale of value, Roderigo is conflated with his own money: "Thus do I ever make my fool my purse" (1.3.372), Iago comments. Later, Iago suggests that his patron-gull has no value at all, demoting him from "my purse" to "this poor trash of Venice" (2.1.294).[36]

Taken individually, the play's metaphors of value might seem to imply a straightforward symbolic logic: pearls and jewels symbolize inherent human value while purses symbolize more unstable, instrumental value, of the kind Roderigo has for Iago. A purse derives its value from the circulating money that fills it and so can be seen as worthless—or rather worth *less*—when compared to a jewel. The coins that fill a purse were sometimes denigrated on the grounds that they drew value less from intrinsic metallic content (which might be debased, clipped, or counterfeited) than from circulation.[37] Bassanio's characterization of silver money as the "pale and common drudge/ 'Tween man and man" (3.2.103–4) in *The Merchant of Venice* follows this logic.[38] Like coins, jewels also had "extrinsical" value, but, being rare and precious, they did symbolic duty as bearers of stable, inherent worth.[39] By this logic, we might say that Roderigo is worth less than Desdemona, a judgment that the play at least to some extent endorses. Yet taken in aggregate, the web of symbolic equations linking objects to persons does more than figure merit or its absence, inherent or exchange value. Instead, the play's rhetoric of value calls attention to varied modes of evaluation. Through the language of rich objects, money, and "trash," *Othello* articulates competing strategies of assigning worth to persons, which represent amplified extremes drawn from a mixed, commercial world.

When we take into account that Othello speaks most of the play's lines about jewels (and pearls) and Iago all of the lines about trash (and purses), the opposition developed through *Othello*'s rhetoric of value appears in a new light: not as symbolic of two forms of human value but rather as indexical of two modes of evaluating. Looked at in this way, the play seems to juxtapose an idealistic and a skeptical view of human value: the former somewhat rigidly essentialist in its ideological content, the other flexible, worldly, and instrumentalizing. Such an opposition maps onto the powerful account of the play recently mounted by Joel Altman. Altman detects two forms of personhood in the play: Othello's, which is, at the play's outset, stable and self-consistent, and Iago's, which is labile, shifting, and situationally constructed. In this account, Othello assumes meaningful correspondence between outward and inner qualities, his own and others'. His declaration that "my parts, my title and my perfect soul/ Shall manifest me rightly" (1.2.31– 32) implies a model of the self in which intrinsic virtue aligns with outward behavior and both, in turn, with reputation, or social esteem. By contrast, Iago holds that only this last category truly counts. He operates from a sense of reputation as a slippery and manipulable signifier, with no definite link to inward worth. Iago assumes—and exploits—a gap between inward *being* and outward *seeming,* as well as a second gap, between seeming and social esti- mation, or "good name" (3.3.159). Altman argues that Iago teaches Othello to see himself as alien by effecting "a weakening in the tis- sue connecting the outer and inner self."[40]

An economic reading of the play that followed this logic might argue that Iago's lesson—the poison he pours in Othello's ears—is that human worth lies in the act of reckoning.[41] What I want to show here, though, is that instead of adopting Iago's own concep- tion of evaluation (imagining all human value as externally con- ferred) Othello enters into what is arguably a *more* nightmarish cognitive space. Iago teaches him to see both ways at once—to understand human value as both inwardly rooted and outwardly conferred—while making him view these two modes of reckoning worth as fundamentally incompatible. In so doing, he amplifies and problematizes a key feature of the play's commercial setting. As Shakespeare presents it, Venice requires that multiple modes of valuation work together. In the trial scene, for example, Othello prevails both because he is needed in the wars against the Turks and because the Duke and assembled nobles appreciate his innate merit. Iago reveals the fault line in this "both"/ "and" position. He re-describes these modes of valuing people as ideologically op- posed extremes, rather than options within a field of choices. In so doing, he organizes an eclectic, continuously negotiated suspen- sion of divergent motives and ideals into a rigid binary: *either* Othello's value is based on his intrinsic merit *or* it is externally constructed. Just as the storm in the puzzle forces a stark us/them logic on the merchants (whose initial partnership depended on the

suppression of such logic), Iago's insinuations produce an opposition between two models of understanding the self hitherto not
brought into conflict for Othello.

Nowhere is Iago's binarizing logic so apparent or so subtly executed as in his speech on "good name" in Act Three:

> Good name in man—and woman—dear my lord,
> Is the immediate jewel of their souls;
> Who steals my purse, steals trash: 'tis something, nothing;
> 'Twas mine, 'tis his, and has been slave to thousands.
> But he that filches from me my good name
> Robs me of that which not enriches him,
> And makes me poor indeed.
>
> (3.3.159–65)

In context, Cassio's is the good name in danger of being filched.
Iago has feigned reluctance to slander the Lieutenant, claiming a
curious kind of self-knowledge: "oft my jealousy/ Shapes faults
that are not" (3.3.151–52). Yet he speaks in such general terms that
he might just as easily be referring to any number of good names:
Desdemona's, for instance, whose reputation he has already begun
to ruin with the first hints of sexual slander, or Othello's honor as a
husband, predicated on his wife's virtue. The speech both justifies
Iago's reticence to slander Cassio, and works to instill anxiety about
reputation in Othello.

The speech's generic quality, its applicability to multiple characters and situations, allows Iago to accomplish competing tasks. On
the one hand, from its opening move, it assigns absolute value to
Cassio's reputation. On the other, as it unfolds, it calls attention to
the constructed nature of good name. In effect, it makes two contradictory claims at once: first, that good name is above the marketplace where value derives from exchange and second that good
name is constructed *in* that marketplace, by processes of social circulation. A skilled rhetorician, Iago can argue *in utramque partem,*
as his commentary on "reputation" (2.3.253) to Cassio, a few
scenes earlier, demonstrates. There, he dismisses it as "an idle and
most false imposition, oft got without merit, and lost without
deserving" (2.3.259–61) on the grounds that it is intangible: "As I
am an honest man, I thought you had received some bodily wound;
there is more of sense in that than in 'reputation'" (2.3.256–59).
Reputation, like Falstaff's "honor," is a "mere scutcheon" (*1 Henry
IV,* 5.1.139). Iago goes on, asserting that reputation cannot be lost

without the individual loser's admission of that loss: "You have lost no reputation at all, unless you repute yourself such a loser" (2.3.261–62). To Othello, by contrast, he argues two apparently contradictory positions at once: first claiming reputation's essential reality, then pointing to its fragile externality. Good name, here, is both grounded in the self and an outward-facing possession that others may easily "filch."

To take the former, simpler argument first. Iago's topic is the proverbial notion that a good name is more precious than money.[42] This line of thinking depends on symbolic contrast between the relatively stable, high value of a jewel and the comparatively variable, low value held by a purse. We might think, here, of Marlowe's Barabas, tired of counting up "paltry silverlings" (1.1.6) and longing instead for "bags of fiery opals/ sapphires, amethysts/ Jacinths, hard topaz, grass-green emeralds" and "Beauteous rubies" (1.1.25–27).[43] Indeed, in Iago's speech, the terms "jewel" and "purse" are opposed, most obviously, on the worldly plane that Barabas, in his counting-house, inhabits. Though both had both exchange and intrinsic value—a point discussed more fully below—jewels could operate as a shorthand for intrinsic value in contrast to purses (and the coins in them), which derive their value primarily from exchange. Iago's sneer, "'Twas mine, 'tis his, and has been slave to thousands" (3.3.162), echoes Bassanio's characterization of silver, the "pale and common drudge/ 'Tween man and man" (3.2.103–4). In these formulations, circulating money derives value from exchange and, because of this, lacks "real" value. In Iago's extreme version of this paradox, true money resembles counterfeit. Seeming to be "something," it is, in essence, "nothing."

Iago's chosen terms thereby invoke a second opposition: between things of the world and things of the soul. In the sixteenth century, the word "trash" often designated specifically temporal worthlessness; it was synonymous with "dross." Countless warnings to worldlings figure money as trash, the epitome of the "frail and transitory things of this world" that tempt the soul from "constant and immortal treasures."[44] The term "jewel," by contrast, often expressed the quality of being invaluable, beyond price. A jewel might represent a beloved child, health, virginity, learning, or piety.[45] Even more than other precious stones, pearls in particular symbolized transcendent spiritual value, following the biblical comparison of the kingdom of heaven to "one pearl of great price," for which a merchant sold all of his worldly possessions (which, beside the transcendent value of this spiritual "pearl" are mere dross).[46] Following this culturally available logic, Iago's speech posits a jewel-like "good name" as not only more valuable than a drossy "purse," but as belonging to a completely different order of value: spiritual rather than material, "of the soul" rather than of the world.[47] Moreover, the good name "jewel" is not just a precious possession but a constitutive one: the jewel that is a good name makes a person who he is. A purse's contents can belong to anyone—" 'twas mine, 'tis his"—but a jewel is immediate, unmediated, and "of the soul." On the surface, then, Iago says the opposite of what he has just said to Cassio. In that exchange, he openly challenged the idea of meaningful correspondence between inner self and "reputation." Here, he pretends to uphold it.

The model of reputation put forward by a surface reading of the speech is fairly clear: good name is the outwardly recognized reflection of the inward qualities that make a person fundamentally himself or herself. Yet the very materiality of Iago's language works against such a reading. As the speech unfolds, it draws together a set of symbolically freighted object-nouns—adding "purse" and "trash" to "jewel"—and verbs that speak to the relationships of people to property: steals, filches, robs, enriches. In this discursive context, "good name" itself almost seems to materialize. It becomes yet another thing: of great worth to its possessor, but frighteningly alienable for a property "of the soul." The simple fact that it can be "filched" brings the stability of good name's value into question. After all, reputations do enter into circulation, as Othello himself knows. They can be devalued or inflated by external factors like slander or praise. The surface logic of the speech is that value that is currency bears a constructed kind of value, which is "nothing" in comparison to "real" or essential value. The problem is that good name—supposedly possessed of such real, essential value—is also closely akin to currency. Good name always in some sense belongs to others. " 'Tis his," as Iago says of the purse.

And what about that purse, and its supposed valuelessness? Even as a modern, commercialized understanding of money began to take shape, a traditional understanding of coins' value as tied to their metal content remained firmly in place.[48] The worth of coins was understood to be tied not only to their instrumental role in exchange but to myriad material factors, including weight, purity, wear, and clipping and the stamps that made them current. A purse is only "trash" if it is called trash. It may have contingent and unstable value, but it only *lacks* value if described in a very specific, limited way. Later in *Othello,* Desdemona says that she would rather have lost her "purse/ Full of crusadoes" (3.4.23) than her handkerchief. Crucially, this moment does not illustrate how little she esteems money. Rather, it shows how highly she values the handkerchief. Her purse has real worth in the world, and this fact allows her to express the even greater worth she places on Othello's gift.

Jewels are even harder to value than purses. Germano Maifreda documents a rising awareness in the Renaissance that precious metals and gemstones had exchange value that fluctuated according to market forces.[49] Even outside of economic thought, their values could be understood as imputed rather than essential, contingent rather than stable, and at times deeply subjective. In common usage, a jewel was a wearable ornament, and the jewel-as-jewelry invited the gaze of others, drawing to itself the surplus value of admiration. Jewels were symbols of status and actual wealth, both cultural and actual capital.[50] At the same time, as small, precious possessions frequently exchanged as gifts, they could be invested with idiosyncratic private value (not unlike Desdemona's handkerchief, in fact). Think of Shylock's turquoise. It is worth about as much as a pet monkey, but Shylock would not have traded it for "a wilderness of monkeys" (or, presumably, their cash value) because "I had it of Leah when I was a bachelor" (3.1.111). Brabantio invokes this model of private value when he addresses his daughter: "For your sake, jewel,/ I am glad at soul I have no other child" (1.3.194–95). She is a jewel *to him,* and he feels her value most when he feels her loss.

All this is to say that, if we pay attention to the vehicles of the metaphors through which Iago describes "good name"—that is, if we think about jewels and purses in themselves as material objects, circulating and owned, rather than purely symbolic placeholders—the stark opposition between value and valuelessness falls apart. On the surface, Iago articulates a point of view close to Othello's own at this point in the play: *some* value is real, essential, innate. Yet his subsidiary claim—that lesser forms of value are unstable, fluctuating, and externally constructed—ultimately undermines the notion of innate worth. Iago's comparison (a good name is like a jewel, unlike a purse) dissolves, since good name actually resembles both. Yet because of the powerful, essentializing surface claim, it is difficult to imagine it as a composite. We are left with a seemingly impossible choice: either to believe that human worth is innate and reputation bound to virtue or to believe that human worth is socially conferred and unrelated to the inmost self.

After he grows jealous, Othello begins viewing himself from a hostile outside perspective. He imagines himself "the fixèd figure for the scorn of time, / To point his slow and moving finger at!" (4.2.54–55). The social gaze that he hitherto felt to recognize his innermost qualities now seems as though it must be fixed on externals alone. It is mocking rather than loving and destructive to his selfhood, rather than constitutive of it. He experiences Desdemona's gaze differently as well. Taking to heart Iago's suggestion that there are "foul disproportions" (3.3.237) in the match, he begins to feel Other in relation to his white, Venetian wife, protesting "she had eyes and chose me" (3.3.192) and later conjecturing that "Haply, for I am black" (267), she has turned from him to Cassio. The realization that the gazes upon him may not value him according to the criteria by which he values himself sets up the internal division between Venetian self and Turkish "other," in the final speech. He once claimed that "my parts, my title, and my perfect soul/ Shall manifest me rightly" (1.2.31–32), and believed Desdemona when she claimed to see no contrast between his "visage" and "mind" (1.2.250). He now perceives a potential split between the way he sees himself, and the way others esteem him. Iago initiates this process by claiming that good name resembles a precious possession: simultaneously integral to its owner's sense of self, and fragile, alienable, indeterminate. Using a rhetoric of value that interrogates the nature of value itself, Iago makes jewels look like purses, and purses look like trash.

Reckoning reputation: credit versus honor

As Iago uses it, the language of value promotes a destructive logic, organizing a plurality of evaluative habits of mind into stark opposition between idealism, on the one hand and skepticism, on the other.[51] In itself, however, each object he names invites multiple modes of evaluation, reflecting in miniature the multifaceted kind of "reckoning" fostered by commercial cosmopolitanism. Good name, the subject of his speech, also invites competing evaluative strategies and is also subject to the kind of binarization Iago promotes. In Shakespeare's day, economic conditions put new

pressures on the fit between outward-facing and inward-rooted
models of good name. Reputation at once represented "society's
judgment of an individual's worth" and referred to "internalized,
personal, integrity."[52] The dominant form of currency in early modern England was credit, and credit, as economic historian Craig
Muldrew tells us, consisted of communal estimation both of a person's financial standing and his or her character.[53] In what follows,
I link the play's concern with reputation, particularly martial and
sexual reputation, with commercial credit. Reputation is Iago's
medium, the stuff of which he spins his plots. Over the course of
the action, in addition to destroying Desdemona's "credit with the
Moor" (2.3.344), he gives Cassio a reputation for drunkenness,
Othello a reputation for violence, and Emilia a reputation for
shrewishness, while cultivating his own reputation as "honest
Iago." What I want to show here is how much this process, too, is
inflected with habits of commercial reckoning.

Before turning back to the play, it is worthwhile to note just how
complex early modern credit was. To "credit" someone was to
reckon up his or her worth, and this worth was moral as well
as monetary. In economic matters, "reputation," "credit," and
"name" referred to what other people thought both about someone's honesty and trustworthiness as much as to his or her access
to resources.[54] Despite its relation to character, though, credit did
not always map cleanly onto other forms of social value. Even as
reputation functioned as kind of "current money in [one's] cash-
chest" it remained possible to claim that a "good name" belonged
to a different order of value from a "purse."[55] Muldrew's work,
which remains the most comprehensive account of early modern
credit as an economic and social phenomenon, overlooks this complexity, suggesting that all forms of reputation—honor, name, public opinion—quietly became indistinguishable from commercial
credit sometime in the mid-sixteenth century. Aaron Kitch offers a
more direct version of Muldrew's claim: "As credit and debt relations expanded in sixteenth-century England, traditional concepts
of 'honor' were translated to the domain of every day transactions."[56] Yet the merging of various types of "name" was not so
straightforward, especially when it came to the forms of reputation
associated with "honor." As recent studies of aristocratic, military,
and gendered forms of social value demonstrate, the metamorphosis of *honor* into *credit* was an uneven and complex process.[57] In a
nutshell: "honor" seems to have remained associated with elite

values of birth, merit, public office, martial prowess, learning and civility—and, for women, with sexual chastity. Nevertheless, "honor" could also refer to the ability to keep faith in economic matters.[58] "Credit" referred most frequently to economized forms of reputation; most broadly, though, it denoted communal belief in a person's worth and word. Thus, commercial and non-commercial forms of reputation co-existed and could be conceived of separately. At the same time, they were described with partially overlapping vocabularies, signaling ideological overlap, as well. *Othello* takes place in the long composite moment when credit was both outward-facing and inwardly rooted, both a matter of money and one of morals, and both separate from honor and closely related to it.

Iago exploits the slipperiness of these terms. When he and Cassio discuss reputation, the two operate from different understandings of the same word. Their exchange captures two positions—one essentially chivalric, the other commercial—in which reputation is an equally central category, but has different ideological content. The same thing happens in a later exchange with Othello, when he calls Desdemona's sexual honor, "an essence that's not seen" (4.1.15), adding, "They have it very oft that have it not" (16). He derides honor as a matter of words and opinions, importing a meaning to the term that is at odds with Othello's apparent sense of female sexual virtue as both real, rooted in the body, and an index of male virtue. Iago's sense of honor-as-construct aligns with a commercial viewpoint, which understood "reputation, in the form of language" to be "produced and communicated for profit."[59] When Iago names Desdemona's "credit with the Moor" (2.3.344) as the object of his attack, the word *credit* obviously does not mean "purchasing power" but rather Othello's faith in her fidelity. Yet the term hints at fungibility and instrumentality, qualities adhering to commercial reputation and antithetical to sexual honor. Over and over, in Othello, "honor" and "credit" are shown to be separable but hard to keep apart. Iago's plot depends on this dynamic. He relies on both honor and credit coming to equal conceptual weight in Othello's mind. For Iago to succeed, his victim has to continue to believe that honor matters to identity (in a way that Iago himself does not believe), while at the same time accepting that it is constructed through language and social interpretation (in a way that Iago does believe).

The tension between these positions differed in different social contexts. While in business matters honor and credit aligned closely, in other spheres they remained at odds. In what follows, I want to pay particular attention to honor and credit within the military troop and within marriage—non-market contexts nevertheless affected by economic modes of reckoning. Traditional, non-monetary concepts of honor seem to have been particularly durable in the spheres of sexual propriety and military life. Even as credit for men became increasingly tied to financial responsibility, women's honor remained linked to sexual purity, and "the association of female honour and reputation with chastity was perhaps the least contested principle of social evaluation in early modern England."[60] Similarly, martial honor became more rather than less important to soldiers as England's military structures developed in the seventeenth century.[61] As a setting for *Othello,* Venice offered Shakespeare a site for exploring the ways in which commercial rhetoric, attitudes, and ideological structures put pressure on the traditional models of soldierly valor and marital virtue. In addition to its reputation for commercial cosmopolitanism, Venice was known for well-developed codes of courtship and marriage, on one hand, and military prowess, on the other.[62]

To take the military first.[63] In early modern Europe, an expanding economy gave rise to larger, more organized and technologically advanced armies. At the same time, the internal organization of military bodies resembled vertical feudal structures more than horizontal market relations. Military units replicated the hierarchical arrangements of "traditional social groupings—the very groupings that were everywhere dissolving or were at least called into question by the spread of impersonal market relations."[64] Within these units, a tiered system of offices replaced "customary hierarchies of prowess and status."[65] These hierarchies were not inflexible, however, and a certain degree of upward mobility operated as a stabilizing force. In his *Theorike and practike of moderne warres* (1598) Robert Barret describes how service is rewarded with rank, in a process "whereby many men of low degree and base linage" may rise to "great dignitie, credit, and fame."[66] In its ideal form, the military unit assigns office and honor to a captain according to "vertue, valour, magnanimitie, resolution, and [. . .] above all, loyalty."[67]

The dominant discourse of soldiership insisted on honor rather than profit as the true reward for military service.[68] In practice, however, service could and did lead to material rewards, from ordinary soldiers' pay to the land, houses and monuments granted to the great Venetian *condottieri*.[69] Thus, though martial honor and monetary rewards were frequently thought of in oppositional terms—in a way that commercial credit and money were not—in fact, the structuring tensions between good name and goods, and between outward estimation and inward worth, existed in the military context as well as in the commercial sphere. This complex situation is apparent in *An arithmeticall warlike treatise named Stratioticos* (1579; repr. 1590), Shakespeare's source for some of *Othello*'s military material.[70] Begun by Tudor mathematician Leonard Digges and completed by his son, Thomas, *Stratioticos* is half primer on practical arithmetic and half conduct book. Books I and II provide lessons in military mathematics, many of which are recognizable descendants of those offered in the mercantile arithmetics of a generation before. Book III lays out the personal qualities and duties of soldiers and officers. Especially in this latter portion, *Stratioticos* stresses that the desire for money ought to be subordinate to the quest for honor. Under "The Office and duetie of a Captaine," we find:

> He ought not to be covetous or niggardly: never to keep backe his souldiers paye, but by al meanes to seeke to get them their pay, & to his abilitie rewarding them over and above, for by that meanes he gaineth honor, and maketh them assured to him in any perilous service. And contrariwise if he be a scraper and a spoiler of his souldiers, & bend his wits rather to pray on them & their pay, then [sic] to traine and teach them their dutie: Such a one ought to be disarmed and rejected as a baseminded mercenarie marchant, that shameth and soileth his profession.[71]

The passage implies a complex internal economy: paying soldiers fairly leads to a captain's increased honor among them and their increased loyalty towards him. Narrow self-interest, associated with "marchants," ill befits a high-ranking officer. Even for common soldiers, honor trumps money: in the expanded 1590 edition of the work, Digges writes "If [a new soldier] be bare in apparell, [old soldiers] furnish him of their owne purses, because he should not be a dishonor to their Nation."[72] The collective outward-facing honor of the troop depends on the voluntary redistribution of private resources.

One of the math problems from *Stratioticos*'s first half, however, suggests a more direct relationship of honor to cash:

> Admit there be a Praye or Bootie taken 300 Pounds sterling to be distrib-
> uted to a Bande of 150 footemen, wherein there is 20 Souldiers wanting
> of a Bande complet: I demaunde how much the Captaine and every sev-
> erall Officer and Souldier of the Bande should have for their part or
> share ratably made according to true auncient Discipline Militare.[73]

This is the traditional partnership problem, recontextualized, with
soldiers replacing merchants. Instead of calculating profit based on
outlay, Digges asks his reader to divide booty based on rank. Solv-
ing the problem requires knowing the rate of pay for persons of
each degree in a complete band, and then calculating the distribution of the booty, taking into account twenty missing soldiers. It
also requires tacit acknowledgement that the highest offices, which
bear the most honor, also deserve the most cash. The problem illustrates a larger cultural dynamic in miniature: martial and monetary
values cannot be kept neatly separate, any more than military and
commercial enterprise could have been.

Iago's methods (and to an extent, his motives) become clearer
when viewed against the backdrop of the early modern discourses
of military honor and profit. In the play's opening scene, he
explains his hatred of Othello in terms of professional displacement. He resents being "his Moorship's ensign" (1.1.32) and envies
Othello's choice of Cassio as his lieutenant. Iago casts his displacement in commercial terms: "I know my price, I am worth no worse
a place" (10), he tells Roderigo. What he will later state to Cassio as
a basic fact about the world, he here expresses as a bitter realization: innate merit and social value do not align. He is not honorable
except insofar as he is honored—or rather, dishonored, held at a
lower rate by Othello than that rate he "setteth on himself."[74]
Worse, Iago feels that his "price" lacks reference to his qualities as
a soldier, which he tells Roderigo have been manifestly proven
in battle. Like the purse, his price comes from outside. It is a
"something-nothing," and so is he: "I am not what I am" (65). It is
possible to paraphrase this statement as "I am not what I seem,"
but it also bears a secondary meaning: "I am not (intrinsically) what
I am (as an externally constructed reputation, a price, a quantity of
honor)."[75]

An analogue to Iago's discovery of the misalignment of self with
world may be found in revenge tragedies. Katharine Maus has
argued that revengers are often motivated by the sense that their
place within a larger social order has been violated.[76] The system

having failed him, the revenger comes to view it as a false construct, whose unreality only he can perceive. It is at this point,
Maus argues, that victims become machiavels. The social roles they
once carried out naturally they now perform self-consciously, con-
cealing secret motives and vengeful plots. *Othello*'s Iago follows a
similar trajectory. His complaint that "Preferment goes by letter
and affection/ And not by old gradation, where each second/ Stood
heir to th' first" (1.1.35–37) speaks to a sense of order violated.
Feeling himself caught in a social structure where service, valor,
and experience go unrewarded, Iago becomes that structure's critic
and manipulator. He acts the part of an "honest" soldier expertly:
deferential to his Captain, hearty and bluff with fellow officers like
Cassio, and cheerfully if crudely insulting towards women. In his
soliloquies, he reveals himself to be a protean, actorly machiavel,
to such an extent that there remains no core *being* left under all the
seeming.

I suggest that Iago's sense of violated worth is a new mode,
roughly coincident with the start of the play, less to pinpoint his
malignity's elusive motive, than to excavate the remnants of
another way of thinking that lodge in his speech. His outrage is particularly apparent in his denigration of Cassio, who has the place
Iago covets. Iago describes Cassio as "a great arithmetician"
(1.1.18), one "That never set a squadron in the field/ Nor the division of a battle knows/ More than a spinster" (1.1.21–23). As Paul
Jorgensen suggests, the "bookish theoric" Iago associates with Cassio is probably not dusty, antiquarian learning (like that possessed
by Captain Fluellen in *Henry* V), but contemporary military science: "Cassio [. . .] was probably an 'arithmetician' in that he was
studying gunnery, fortification, and the scientific marshalling of
troops as presented in Digges's [. . .] *Stratioticos* and Thomas
Smith's *The Art of Gunnery*."[77] Claiming that his own practical
experience is worth more than Cassio's academic background, Iago
terms this kind of learning "mere prattle without practice" (1.1.25).
Digges and other military theorists complained of exactly this line
of attack from "old soldiers," who regarded theoretical approaches
with suspicion.[78]

Iago's epithets for Cassio—"debitor and creditor," "counter-
caster"—seem strange in the context of the debate between martial
"theorike" and "practike." Cassio has, as Jorgensen notes, probably
been reading books similar to *Stratioticos*. Though these descended
from and still bore a family resemblance to early arithmetics like

An introduction for to lerne to recken, they articulated soldierly rather than mercantile values and bore little resemblance to contemporary works on bookkeeping, the activity to which Iago directly alludes with his "debitor and creditor," the English name for double-entry accounting. Iago conflates all mathematical study first with "theorick" ("prattle without practice") and then with the grubby "practick" of money matters. His epithets link the lieutenant to the ledger, and the ledger itself to petty worldliness: getting and spending, borrowing and lending, tracking the ebb and flow of money and debt. The logic behind this strange conflation has to do with the estimation of persons in military and commercial systems. Iago once felt himself within a system where human worth was correctly discerned and evaluated. That system is violated when it fails to reward his virtue and valor, which ought to produce both honor and office. The evaluative gaze of military ideology—which once determined Iago's selfhood and fixed his place in the world—now seems fallible, subjective, determined by contingency and circumstance. It has become a gaze that assigns price without recognizing worth. Iago's commercialized rhetoric and his insistence that reckoning itself is the only source of value in the world originate in this break. A soldier with a trader's eye, Iago straddles martial and commercial understandings of value. He maintains a sense that he is above commerce, even as he draws on it to hollow out the martial order, rendering it useless as a meaning-making system for others.[79]

Iago's martial office affords him a uniquely advantageous position from which to attack military ideology. Digges and Barret express concern with the relationship between inward honor and its external signs in multiple passages on the ensign, or ancient. The title derives from this officer's primary duty, which is to bear the ensign, or standard, belonging to his troop. The standard symbolized the band's collective honor. Digges wrote that "The losse of the Ensigne is not only to the Ensigne bearer, but also to the whole bande a perpetuall shame."[80] The symbolic function of the flag created an aura of equal importance around its bearer. "The value and vertue of the Ensigne," Digges writes, "Setteth forthe the vertue and valour of the Captaine and the whole band."[81] Soldiers should fearlessly protect both the ensign and the flag he bears on the battlefield; the loss of either would court collective dishonor. As Barret put it, "The Ensigne is the verie foundation of the Companie, and therein consisteth the honour, & his, & his souldiers reputation."[82]

To use Iago's own terms, the ensign should be the "jewel" of the company: the external badge of collective, intrinsic worth. But Iago is more like a purse. He has face value—a reputation for honesty—but it bears no reference to his mettle.

The structures of martial honor are, in *Othello,* displaced onto marriage, another form of partnership corroded by Iago's binaries.[83] Within the context of Othello and Desdemona's marriage, we again find the notion that inwardly-rooted virtue could be externalized, embodied in symbolic objects and persons. Desdemona's handkerchief, for instance, functions as the external emblem of her honor. In a very real sense it *is* her honor: a domestic, miniature version of the ensign's flag. Digges and Barret wrote that the loss of the standard brought dishonor not only on the Ensign but the whole company. Similarly, the loss of the handkerchief dishonors both Desdemona and her husband. Her virtue stands for his, just as "The value and vertue of the Ensigne setteth forth the vertue and valour of the Captaine." This is why, when he believes his wife has been unfaithful, Othello feels he has lost his office as well, declaring, "Othello's occupation's gone" (3.3.359). Desdemona resembles the jewel-like form of Othello's reputation: an external badge of honor, an adornment, a prize, but also a property of his deepest self, his soul.

Jewels are not just symbols of alienable and precarious reputations in the play. In a competing strain of rhetoric, they are part of a complex of symbols for that-which-lies-beyond-exchange. While Iago uses the language of precious objects to question the very possibility of 'real' value, both Desdemona and Othello employ metaphors of wealth and precious objects to express subjective perception of inestimable worth. Early in the play, Othello declares:

> But that I love the gentle Desdemona,
> I would not my unhousèd free condition
> Put into circumscription and confine
> For the seas' worth.
>
> (1.2.25–28)

He figures his marriage as an exchange and freedom as the price for Desdemona. What he has lost is greater, to him, than all the treasures in the sea; his wife is worth more even than that. Similarly, Desdemona insists that she would not commit adultery for "the world's mass of vanity" (4.2.164) or "for all the world" (4.3.63), remaining firm in the face of Emilia's very different reckoning: "The world's a huge thing: it is a great price / For a small vice" (4.3.64–65). In the most elaborate of these hypothetical, hyperbolic exchanges, Othello declares:

> Nay, had she been true,
> If heaven would make me such another world
> Of one entire and perfect chrysolite,
> I'd not have sold her for it.
>
> (5.2.141–44)

A green gemstone, chrysolite bore specific associations with female chastity, according to early modern lapidaries and Francis Meres' *Palladis Tamia, Wits Treasury* (1598).[84] Meres notes that, "the Chrysolite being worne on the finger of an Adulteresse, so detesteth the crime, as it cracketh in peeces by meere instinct of nature."[85] By the speech's logic, since she is in fact chaste, Desdemona's worth exceeds the value of a jewel the size of a world, and her chastity surpasses that of a world as pure as the purest gem. Believing his wife false, Othello in fact offers a clear articulation of her true worth. Desdemona was *so* valuable that she lay beyond the realm of exchange.

In this conceit, as in Othello's later image of the discarded pearl, Iago's rhetoric of value asserts itself. To imagine a man or woman entirely outside of exchange is to imagine someone who cannot live *in the world,* structured as it is by shifting and composite partnerships. To imagine that all forms of reckoning and exchange devalue persons is to find worldly life sullying, compromised. In *Othello,* the rhetoric of value works according to a polarizing logic, which associates persons either with the purest gems or the drossiest trash. The rhetoric of value evacuates the middle ground, especially in Othello's mind. Either Desdemona is a whore or she is too good to live. Either he himself is a noble Venetian who deserves to live immortally—"speak of me as I am" he tells the assembled company in his last speech, mindful of his reputation after death—or he is a "dog" who deserves to die nameless.

"For the seas' worth"

Throughout, I have been arguing that *Othello* dramatizes the problems of social and commercial evaluation raised in "The rule

and question of the zarasins." But the puzzle has another set of resonances, which, in closing, I would like to note as an important
countercurrent to Iago's relentless binarizing. "The rule and question of the zarasins" is about one group of merchants tricking
another, but it is also a story of a voyage diverted, and of a tempest-
driven vessel whose journeying passengers have lost their way.
Their "feble galley" is a distant but recognizable relative of what
David Quint identifies as "the boat of Romance," the narrative
trope of an errant vessel that "embodies an adventure principle that
counterbalances an equally constitutive quest principle."[86] Othello's own past is as much meandering Romance as a strongly teleological epic: his experiences prior to the play's start were those of a
storm-tossed wanderer more than those of a self-determining warrior. His course was shaped by "disastrous chances, / Of moving
accidents by flood and field" (1.3.134–35), "hair-breadth scapes"
(136) and being "sold to slavery" (138) and then redeemed. His
story seems to have been recounted to Brabantio and Desdemona
in episodic flashes: "the story of my life/ From year to year: the bat-
tles, sieges, fortunes/ That I have passed" (1.3.129–31). In a way,
the episodes in Venice and Cyprus—where Othello ends up by virtue of his resourcefulness and valor, but also by chance—are simply the last of these narrative "islands."[87] Romance is the field in
which commercial venturing and chivalric adventure meet. Typically, Romance suspends contradictions and enfolds variety; it
resists the kind of binarizing thought—us/them, jewel/trash, white/
black—that Iago promotes. The merchants in the boat of commerce
are not driven by an adventure principle, but their journey becomes
an adventure nonetheless.[88] Othello does not buy and sell, but he
traverses the trade routes of the early modern Mediterranean
world.[89]

The possibility of Romance inflects *Othello* lightly, in Othello's
fantastical past and the off-stage action of the storm. Soon after Desdemona and Othello arrive in Cyprus, in their separate storm-
tossed ships, the possibility of Romance quietly enters and then
swiftly leaves the central story of their marriage. Having given
order for the watch, Othello addresses his new wife, figuring the
pair of them as merchants who ventured and succeeded jointly:
"The purchase made, the fruits are to ensue: / That profit's yet to
come 'tween me and you" (2.3.9–10). In this momentary scenario,
Desdemona is not a pearl, or a jewel, or even "the riches of the
ship." She is not "the purchase made." Nor is she relegated, in this

conceit, to a realm of transcendent value beyond exchange. Othello's conceit is that of a mercantile partnership. Both parties have invested, and both will reap the rewards. Venice's martial, gendered, and commercial systems for "reckoning" human worth reassert themselves soon afterwards and are made destructive by Iago's stark re-organization of their complexity. But for a moment, *Othello* envisions an alternate story.

Two lovers embark on a voyage. I demand of you how they shall share the profits.

Notes

1. Thomas Rymer, *A Short View of Tragedy* (London, 1693), 89. I would like to thank the anonymous reader and the editors of *Shakespeare Studies* for their rigorous engagement with this essay; Bradin Cormack, Josh Scodel, Richard Strier, and Matthew Harrison for insightful commentary on earlier drafts; and Megan Heffernan for generously sharing her bibliographic expertise.

2. See "proof," n. 1 and 3. *OED* Online.

3. Quotations from *Othello* are from the Oxford Shakespeare, ed. Michael Neill (Oxford: Oxford University Press, 2006).

4. On suspicion in the early modern credit-based marketplace, see David J. Baker, "William Shakespeare's *Troilus and Cressida:* Credit Risks," in *On Demand: Writing for the Market in Early Modern England* (Stanford, CA: Stanford University Press, 2010), 62–92, 63. Period writers on credit frequently counseled suspicion as a basic strategy in making decisions about borrowing and lending; see, among others, Thomas Tusser, *Five Hundreth Points of Good Husbandry* (London, 1573), esp. C1r, and Henry Wilkinson, *The Debt Book* (London 1625), esp. 91.

5. Rymer complains that "never was any Play fraught, like this of *Othello,* with improbabilities" (92) and remarks on the "wonderful scene, where Iago by shrugs, half words, and ambiguous reflections, works Othello up to be Jealous" (118). Later, more sympathetic critics have made similar observations. Stanley Cavell calls attention to the swiftness of Othello's change: "One standing issue about the rhythm of Othello's plot is that the progress from the completeness of Othello's love to the perfection of his doubt is too precipitous for the fictional time of the play." "Othello and the Stake of the Other," in *Disowning Knowledge in Seven Plays of Shakespeare* (1987; updated, New York: Cambridge University Press, 2003), 125–42, 128. Stephen Greenblatt notes the disparity between slender cause and totalizing effect: "All of the cheap tricks Iago plays seem somehow inadequate to produce the unshakable conviction of his wife's defilement that seizes Othello's soul and drives him mad." "The Improvisation of Power," *Renaissance Self-Fashioning: From More to Shakespeare* (Chicago, IL: University of Chicago Press, 1980), 222–54, 247. Joel B. Altman locates Rymer's complaint at the heart of the tragedy, arguing that the plot's improbabilities are functions of the characters' immersion in rhetorical forms of knowledge based on supposition, inference, and

implication. *The Improbability of Othello: Rhetorical Anthropology and Shake-spearean Selfhoo*d (Chicago, IL: University of Chicago Press, 2010).

6. The accounts invoked briefly here are, in order: Greenblatt, "The Improvisation of Power"; Cavell, "Othello and the Stake of the Other"; Kenneth Gross, "Slander and Skepticism in *Othello*," *ELH* 56, no. 4 (1989): 819–52; and Altman, *Improbability*.

7. Emily Bartels, *Speaking of the Moor: From* Alcazar *to* Othello (Philadelphia: University of Pennsylvania Press, 2008), 13.

8. Daniel Vitkus, *Turning Turk: English Theater and the Multicultural Mediterranean, 1570–1630* (New York: Palgrave Macmillan, 2003), 8–9, 16–18.

9. Bartels, *Speaking of the Moor*, 7.

10. Altman, *Improbability*, 287. Altman identifies Othello's discovery of his audience with the discovery of his otherness. By contrast, Greenblatt argues that Othello's identity is *always* oriented towards an audience that *always* potentially views him as alien: "His identity depends upon a constant performance, as we have seen, of his 'story,' a loss of his own origins, an embrace and perpetual reiteration of the norms of another culture. It is this dependence that gives Othello, the warrior and alien, a relation to Christian values that is the existential equivalent of a religious vocation; he cannot allow himself the moderately flexible adherence that most ordinary men have toward their own formal beliefs. Christianity is the alienating yet constitutive force in Othello's identity . . . " ("The Improvisation of Power," 254).

11. Vitkus writes, "Othello is not to be identified with a specific, historically accurate racial category; rather he is a hybrid who might be associated, in the minds of Shakespeare's audience, with a whole set of related terms—*Moor, Turk, Ottomite, Saracen, Mahometan, Egyptian, Judean, Indian*—all constructed and positioned in opposition to Christian faith and virtue" (160). The flexible label "Moor" conjures myriad threatening others against which to construct a shared identity, an "us." Altman likewise notes that that the figure of "the Moor had no stable identity" (*Improbability*, 293) in the English imagination, where it bore a "miscellany" of associations. In his account, however, what is at stake in the multiplicity of the Moor is not the construction of a clearly defined "us," but rather the destabilization of identity *tout court*.

12. Patricia Parker, "Cassio, Cash, and the 'Infidel O': Arithmetic, Double-entry Bookkeeping, and Othello's Unfaithful Accounts," in *A Companion to The Global Renaissance: English Literature and Culture in the Era of Expansion*, ed. Jyotsna G. Singh (2009; repr. Malden, MA: Wiley Blackwell, 2013), 223–41.

13. Parker, "Cassio," 223. The phrases "with the pen" and "with the counters" appear in the title of the earliest arithmetic in English, *An introduction for to lerne to recken with the pen or with the counters* (1536/7; repr. London, 1546) and are stock phrases in later textbooks. As Parker notes, English arithmetics usually included "sections on counters" until "well into the seventeenth century," perhaps due to resistance to unfamiliar "Arabyan" numerals (225).

14. In particular, see Craig Muldrew, *The Economy of Obligation: The Culture of Credit and Social Relations in Early Modern England* (New York: Palgrave Macmillan, 1998), esp. 148–72. Muldrew's discussion of honor, money, and credit in the writings of Thomas Wilson and Daniel Defoe (154–55) is particularly problematic. Whereas Wilson posits a near-total opposition between "purse" and "name,"

Defoe assumes their fungibility; Muldrew, however, uses both authors as evidence for the seamless merging of good name with commercial credit.

15. Michael Murrin, *Trade and Romance* (Chicago: University of Chicago Press, 2014). For *Othello* and Romance see in particular Mark Rose, "Othello's Occupation: Shakespeare and the Romance of Chivalry," *ELR* 15, no. 3 (1985): 293–311; Dennis Austin Britton, "Re-'turning' *Othello:* Transformative and Restorative Romance," *ELH* 78, no. 1 (2011): 27–50; Greenblatt, "The Improvisation of Power," 237–39.

16. Anonymous, *An introduction for to lerne to recken,* sigs. I1v-I3r.All quotations from this text are from the British Library's 1546 edition. Citing this and other non-dramatic sixteenth- and seventeenth-century works, I have retained original spelling but modernized *u/v* and *i/j;* expanded *yᵉ* to *the,* and substituted *m* or *n* for superscript ~. On *An introduction for to lerne to recken,* see A.W. Richeson, "The First Printed Arithmetic in English," *Isis* 37, no. 1/2 (May 1947): 47–56 and P. Bockstaele, "Notes on the First Arithmetics Printed in Dutch and English," *Isis* 51, no. 3 (1960): 315–21. On the date of the (extremely rare) first edition, see the "Introduction" to the modern facsimile (2009; repr. Mickleover, UK: TGR Renascent Books, 2013): i.

17. W. W. Rouse Ball, *A Short Account of the History of Mathematics* (London: MacMillan, 1888), 195.

18. Richard Grassby, *The Business Community of Seventeenth Century England* (Cambridge: Cambridge University Press, 1995), 9–11. See also Natalie Zemon Davis, "Sixteenth-Century French Arithmetics on the Business Life," *The Journal of the History of Ideas* 21 no. 1 (1960): 18–48.

19. Richeson, "First Printed Arithmetic," 55.

20. The solution is given in Latin and English with a postscript: "Or for to know it more shortely ye may work by ths verse following by the number of vowels: *Populeam virgam matrem regina tenebat.*" Eliot Oring explains this mnemonic: "Each vowel is accorded a numerical value (a = 1; e = 2; i = 3; o = 4; u = 5) and the thirty passengers are ordered according to the numerical value of the vowels of the verse beginning first with 4 Christians." "On the Tradition and Mathematics of Counting-Out," *Western Folklore* 56, no. 2 (1997): 139–52, 142.

21. See Oring, "Tradition," 145.

22. Smith, *Special Topics,* 554–56. Rhetorically and in terms of its narrative set-up, if not in terms of its mathematical solution, "The rule and questyon of zarasins," resembles this type of problem.

23. These numbers do not add up. The first merchant is probably meant to have put in 25 francs.

24. See for comparison the version from Nicola Tartaglia's 1556 Venetian arithmetic (cited in Ball, *Short Account,* 196) and problem XXIII in Claude-Gaspard Bachet's *Problèmes plaisants & délectables* (1612; repr., Paris: Gauthier-Villars, 1879), 118–21. An overview of this type of problem appears in *Rudi Mathematici* 75 (2003), 21–24; none of the surveyed examples identify the different groups on board ship specifically as merchants.

25. Gerard de Malynes, *Lex Mercatoria* (London, 1622), 101, and Hugh Oldcastle and John Mellis, *A Briefe Instruction and Maner how to Keepe Books of Accompts* (London, 1588), sig. A6v.

26. On this point, see Bartels, *Speaking of the Moor,* esp. 7, 13 and Vitkus, *Turning Turk,* 7–24.

27. Thomas Coryate, *Coryats crudities* (London, 1611), 171.

28. Gasparo Contarini, *The Commonwealth and government of Venice,* trans. Lewis Lewkenor (London, 1599), 1.

29. Graham Holderness, *Shakespeare and Venice* (Burlington, VT: Ashgate, 2010), 193.

30. Contarini, *Commonwealth,* 131–32. Though not all soldiers or commanders were foreign, mercenaries were generally perceived and represented as non-Venetian. See Michael Mallet, *Mercenaries and their Masters: Warfare in Renaissance Italy* (Totowa, NJ: Rowman and Littlefield, 1974), 43–45, 209.

31. Bartels notes that in Shakespeare's Venice "terms of prejudice seem hard to stand by, if not hard to come by." *Speaking of the Moor,* 163.

32. On representations of Venice on the English stage, see Holderness, *Shakespeare and Venice;* David C. McPherson, *Shakespeare, Jonson, and the Myth of Venice* (Newark: University of Delaware Press, 1990); and Laura Tosi and Shaul Bassi, eds., *Visions of Venice in Shakespeare* (Burlington, VT: Ashgate, 2011).

33. Besides Parker, few critics have examined *Othello*'s commercial language. Those who do tend to locate it within a Christian contrast between worldly dross and spiritual treasure, or as evidence of Shakespeare's moralizing stance on profit seeking. See, for example, Lawrence J. Ross, "World and Chrysolite in *Othello,*" *Modern Language Notes* 76, no. 9 (1961): 683–92, 688 and Robert B. Heilman, "The Economics of Iago and Others," *PMLA* 68, no. 3 (1953): 555–71.

34. High-ranking *condottieri* like Othello benefited from a "system of rewards," including offices, houses, and land, "designed . . . to turn fidelity and long service into norms." Michael Mallet and John Hale, *The Military Organization of a Renaissance State: Venice c. 1400–1617* (Cambridge: Cambridge University Press, 1984), 186.

35. On social evaluation in *Othello,* see Altman, *Improbability,* throughout; Madeleine Doran, "Good Name in *Othello,*" *SEL* 7 (1967): 195–217; and Gross, "Slander and Skepticism."

36. The word's association with refuse did not become current until the 20th century. In early modern usage, it denoted "anything of little or no worth or value; worthless stuff; rubbish; dross." "trash, n., 3.a." *OED* online.

37. For the factors effecting coins' intrinsic and extrinsic value, see Stephen Deng, *Coinage and State Formation in Early Modern English Literature* (New York: Palgrave Macmillan, 2011), 9–17, and Deborah Valenze, *The Social Life of Money in the English Past* (Cambridge: Cambridge University Press, 2006). Germano Maifreda offers a strong overview of Classical and Renaissance theories of material value with particular attention to how these theories changed in response to both New World exploration and growing trade networks linking Europe and the East in *From Oikonomia to Political Economy: Constructing Economic Knowledge from the Renaissance to the Scientific Revolution* (Burlington, VT: Ashgate, 2012).

38. All quotations from *The Merchant of Venice* are from the Arden III edition, edited by John Drakakis (London: Bloomsbury, 2010).

39. The term "extrinsical" is from Rice Vaughan, *A discourse of coin and coinage* (London, 1675), 8.

40. Altman, *Improbability,* 72.

41. Cf. Troilus's famous question about Helen, "What's aught but as 'tis valued?" (2.2.52). *Troilus and Cressida,* ed. Anthony B. Dawson (Cambridge: Cambridge University Press, 2003). Criticism of *Troilus and Cressida* has long

recognized the overlap of economic worth and human worth in that play; of particular use to me in writing this essay were C. C. Barfoot, "*Troilus and Cressida:* 'Praise us as we are tasted,' " *Shakespeare Quarterly* 39, no. 1 (1988): 45–57 and Baker, "Credit Risks."

42. Variants of the biblical proverb, "A good name is rather to be chosen than great riches" occur frequently in early modern texts. Morris Palmer Tilley, *A Dictionary of the Proverbs in England in the Sixteenth and Seventeenth Centuries* (Ann Arbor: University of Michigan Press, 1950), 489.

43. Barabas concludes:

> And thus methinks should men of judgment frame
> Their means of traffic from the vulgar trade,
> And as their wealth increaseth, so enclose
> Infinite riches in a little room.
>
> (34–37)

Each imagined gem is itself a compressed bearer of great value, "infinite riches in a little room." And a literal little room filled with such objects would be both a better, richer version of his counting house and a space where the wearying need to reckon-up would be, finally, done away with. Quotations are from Stephen J. Lynch's edition of *The Jew of Malta* (Indianapolis, IN: Hackett, 2009).

44. Ross, "World and Chrysolite," 687.

45. In the English translation to Plutarch's *Table of Cebes* (London, 1545), we find, "My sonne is dead . . . I haue loste a great iewell." In *The precepts of the excellent clerke* (London, 1543), health is a jewel; in Erasmus' *Paraphrases* (London, 1548), virginity is one. Learning is a jewel in Thomas Nashe's *Almond for a Parrat* (London, 1589).

46. Matt. 13:45–46. For an extended contemporary treatment of the passage, see Samuel Gardiner, *A Pearle of Price or, the best Purchase* (London, 1600). Gardiner emphasizes the distinction between goods of the world and goods of the soul in his prefatory letter to the reader: "The Apostle accounted all things but dung to gain Jesus Christ. This is better then the gold of Ophyr or India . . . Buy therefore this Pearl and Treasure of the soule, and lodge it in thy hart: it will be instead of all ritches unto thee" (sig. A7r).

47. On Shakespeare's representations of "spiritual accounting," especially in *The Merchant of Venice,* see Natasha Korda, *Labors Lost: Women's Work and the Early Modern English Stage* (Philadelphia: University of Pennsylvania Press, 2011), 71–92, 91.

48. This history is complex; see among others Deng, *Coinage,* 9–17, and Valenze, *Social Life,* throughout.

49. Maifreda, *Oikonomia,* 20–22.

50. "jewel, n." *OED* Online.

51. Cavell's "Othello and the Stake of the Other" remains the classical account of skepticism in the play; see also Gross, "Slander and Skepticism."

52. The quoted phrases are from Linda Pollock, "Honor, Gender, and Reconciliation in Elite Culture, 1570–1700," *Journal of British Studies* 46, no. 1 (2007), 3–29, 5 and Barbara Donagan, "The Web of Honour: Soldiers, Christians, and Gentlemen in the English Civil War," *The Historical Journal* 44, no. 2 (2001): 365–89, 366.

53. Muldrew, *Economy,* 151.

54. Ibid., 148–51.

55. The quotation is from Daniel Defoe, *The Complete English Tradesman* (London, 1726), 225; cited in Muldrew, *Economy,* 155.

56. Aaron Kitch, *Political Economy and the States of Literature in Early Modern England* (Burlington, VT: Ashgate, 2009), 130.

57. See Pollock, "Honor"; Donagan, "Web"; Alexandra Shepard, "Manhood, Credit and Patriarchy in Early Modern England c. 1580–1640," *Past and Present* 167 (2000): 75–106; and Garthine Walker, "Expanding the Boundaries of Female Honour in Early Modern England," *Transactions of the Royal Historical Society* 6 (1996): 235–45. David Scott Kastan's introduction to the Arden III 1 *Henry IV* (London: Thompson Learning, 2002), 62–73, offers an analysis of that play's complex treatment of martial honor, financial credit, and political power with wider implications for study of the period.

58. See Muldrew, *Economy,* especially 148–57 and Pollock, "Honor," esp. 17–18.

59. Doran, "Good Name," 199.

60. Shepard, "Manhood," 76.

61. Donagan, "Web," 365–89.

62. See McPherson, *Myth of Venice,* 38–45.

63. On military matters in *Othello,* see Paul A. Jorgensen, *Shakespeare's Military World* (1956; repr. Berkeley: University of California Press, 1973), 100–118; Virginia Mason Vaughan, "Military Discourse: Knights and Mercenaries," in *Othello: A Contextual History* (Cambridge: Cambridge University Press, 1997), 35–50; Julia Genster, "Lieutenancy, Standing in, and *Othello,*" *ELH* 57, no.4 (1990): 785–809; and Tom McBride, "Othello's Orotund Occupation," *Texas Studies in Literature and Language* 30 (1988), 412–30.

64. William H. McNeill, *The Pursuit of Power: Technology, Armed Force, and Society since A.D. 1000* (Chicago: The University of Chicago Press 1982), 132.

65. Ibid., 132.

66. Robert Barret, *Theorike and practike of moderne warres* (London 1598), 9.

67. Ibid., 240

68. Donagan, "Web," 366.

69. Michael Mallet and John Hale, *The Military Organization of a Renaissance State: Venice c. 1400–1617* (Cambridge: Cambridge University Press, 1984), 186.

70. For military treatises and *Othello,* see Jorgensen, *Military World,* 113–15, and Genster, "Lieutenancy," 789–97.

71. Leonard and Thomas Digges, *An arithmeticall warlike treatise named Stratioticos* (1579; repr. London, 1590), 96.

72. Digges, *Stratioticos,* 80.

73. Ibid., 72

74. The quoted phrase is from Thomas Hobbes, *Leviathan* (London, 1651), 42; cited in Muldrew, *Economy,* 148.

75. See Greenblatt, "The Improvisation of Power," 238.

76. Katharine Eisaman Maus, "Machiavels and Family Men," in *Inwardness and Theater in the English Renaissance* (Chicago: University of Chicago Press, 1995), 35–72.

77. Jorgensen, *Military World,* 113.

78. Ibid., 114–15.

79. As Neill points out, Iago's dismissal of courtly Cassio as an accountant is ironic. It is Iago, not Cassio, who inhabits "the shadowy borderlands that marked the all-important boundary between the gentry and the great mass of people without 'name or note'" ("Introduction," 150), and it is Iago, not Cassio, who typically employs the language and calculus of accounting.

80. Digges, *Stratioticos,* 82.

81. Ibid., 94.

82. Barret, *Theorike,* 19.

83. On the slide of the martial into the marital, see both McBride, "Orotund," and Genster, "Lieutenancy."

84. See Lynda Boose, "Chrysolite and the Song of Songs Tradition," *PQ* 60 (1981): 427–37; Jessica Cooke, "Othello's 'Entire and Perfect Chrysolite,'" *Notes and Queries* 44, no. 4 (Dec. 1997), 505–6; and Catherine Loomis, "Othello's 'Entire and Perfect Chrysolite': A Reply," *Notes and Queries* 46, no. 2 (June 1999), 238–39

85. Frances Meres, *Palladis Tamia, Wits Treasury* (London: 1598), sig. Rr5v.

86. David Quint, *Epic and Empire: Politics and Generic Form from Vergil to Milton* (Princeton, NJ: Princeton University Press, 1993), 249.

87. Ibid., 249.

88. On mercantile ventures and the literary tradition of *aventure,* see Michael Nerlich, *Ideology of Adventure: Studies in Modern Consciousness, 1100–1750,* trans. Ruth Crowley (1977; Minneapolis: University of Minnesota Press, 1987), 1:51–75.

89. On the relation of trade routes to the form of literary Romance, see Murrin, *Trade and Romance.*

"Bid the players make haste": Speed-Making and Motion Sickness in *Hamlet*

KARA NORTHWAY

> We'll not offend one stomach with our play.
> —*Life of Henry the Fifth*

> *Enter* HAMLET . . . , *swaying as if on ship's bridge. He wipes his eyes, and becomes seasick.*
> —Tom Stoppard, "The Fifteen-Minute Hamlet," *Dogg's Hamlet*

WHILE SHAKESPEARE CRITICS have discussed time, movement, and space—and even the relationship among the three, namely, distance divided by time equals rate—they have given only modest attention to changes in rate, or acceleration.[1] Dympna Callaghan contends that Shakespeare conceives of speed as constant and intellectual, with his sonnets exhibiting a need to combat life's brevity: "their pace, one of 'continual haste' (123.12)."[2] Howard Marchitello notes a similar haste in *Macbeth*. Based on the work of Paul Virilio, Marchitello's study examines Macbeth's desire for absolute speed, as seen in the instantaneous disappearance of the three witches and the trope of the burst bubble.[3] In an article on the early modern representation of footmen, David Carnegie identifies the often-used theatrical convention of fast running, likely used in *Hamlet*. This convention, along with its stage direction, *"in haste,"* expressed energetic and incessant running (in place or around other characters), perspiring, acting out of breath, and wearing particular costuming.[4] He cites as an example the following 1605 *Eastward Ho* stage direction for its humorous allusion to *Hamlet* performances: *"Enter Hamlet, a footman, in haste,"* followed by the dialogue "Hamlet, are you mad? Whither run you now?"[5] Car-

negie consequently wonders, "why is the running footman in such
haste? . . . A more general comment on very active performance by
[Richard] Burbage [in 1.5 or 4.2] may be intended. . . . Or . . . [w]as
Burbage's melancholic Dane generally so slow that showing a running Hamlet was funny in itself? . . . Or is there some other possibility?"[6] Like Callaghan and Marchitello, Carnegie recognizes
Shakespeare's interest in speed, in this case physical and dramaturgical rather than conceptual. Traditionally, of course, scholars have
associated Shakespeare's *Hamlet* not with speed, but with speed's
absence, deferral, or hindrance.[7] Margreta de Grazia calls Hamlet's
delay "*the* question to ask of the play . . . even among today's most
theoretically sophisticated literary critics."[8] Shankar Raman, writing on the kinesis of cognition in *Hamlet,* claims, "It is this movement that Hamlet repeatedly fails to produce within himself."[9]
Constant speed and deceleration, however, form parts of a larger,
more complex pattern of varying speed rates in *Hamlet.*

Building on these studies, I argue that *Hamlet* showcases and
problematizes acceleration, or what early moderns referred to as
"speed-making."[10] The theater industry, which valued speed for
financial profit, addressed an early modern fascination with speed
by setting up vicarious sensations of swiftness for the audience.[11]
Hamlet exploits and heightens this potential of speed in the theater
by juxtaposing a language of haste with representations of irregular
physical speed levels that are punctuated by sudden accelerations
of actors on stage. Consequently, scenes in the play that mismatch
speedy discourse heard and action seen disorient the senses of the
characters—and increasingly aim to confound the audience's,
too—resulting in a type of theatrical motion sickness.[12] *Love's
Labour's Lost, The Winter's Tale, Romeo and Juliet,* and *The Life of
Henry the Fifth* briefly correlate drama and seasickness for either
the characters or the audience.[13] But *Hamlet* pervasively uses character and audience disorientation in concert. In response to cultural validation of decorum in speed, this disorientation highlights
both the futility outside the theater of controlling or judging one's
speed rates and the necessity inside the theater of speed-making for
practical and successful storytelling. Shakespeare, therefore,
employs disorientation in *Hamlet* to interrogate individual agency
over speed-making and speed perception.

During the early modern period, the word "speed" denoted not
only velocity, but also profit and success, while "haste" implied
quick action done without deliberation, a distinction noted in the

proverbial "The more haste the lesse spede"; however, the terms' definitions overlapped significantly in cultural usage.[14] Shakespeare slightly preferred the term "haste" (175 total references) to "speed" (128 references).[15] His plays sometimes distinguish finer meanings, in phrases such as "happy speed" or "cursed haste"; but often Shakespeare, as was common, interchanged the terms to indicate velocity generally: "th' affair cries haste, / And speed must answer it."[16] More important, Shakespeare added modifiers before these terms to intensify them, qualifying "speed" with "dearest," "greatest," "timeless," "a sevennight's," "winged," along with "speedier" and "speediest," and magnifying "haste" with "best," "swift," "sudden," "soonest," and "haste-post-haste," as well as the comparative "more than haste."[17] Shakespeare, therefore, frequently amplified speedy language in his works.

The first instance in the English language of the concept and term "speedemakyng" arose synonymously with the word "haast" in the 1548 dictionary *Bibliotheca Eliotae* in the translation of the Latin *"Properantia."*[18] In 1576, "hast making," from Abraham Flemming's *Panoplie of Epistles,* served as a synonym for "speedinesse" and "festination."[19] Much later, Randle Cotgrave's *Dictionarie of the French and English Tongves* (1611) substantiates that the denotation of speed-making as hastening continued into the early seventeenth century, such as in the entry "Acceleration. *Hast, or speedmaking."*[20]

Many books well known to Shakespeare and his culture circulated these meanings by inverting "speed-making" or "haste-making" to the phrases "to make speed" or "to make haste," such as *The Booke of the Common Prayer,* e.g., the opening prayer of both daily matins and vespers, "O God, make spede to saue me," and the response, "O Lorde, make haste to helpe me"; Raphael Holinshed's *Chronicles of England;* Plutarch's *Lives;* Nicholas Udall's *Floweres or Eloquent Phrases of the Latine Speach,* e.g., "*Hominem propero inuenire,* I make speede, or hast to find hym"; *Seneca His Tenne Tragedies;* John Foxe's *Actes and Monuments;* Philip Sidney's *Countesse of Pembrokes Arcadia; The Romane Historie Written by T. Livius of Padua;* Michel de Montaigne's *Essayes;* as well as several turn-of-the-century plays, such as *The Spanish Tragedie,* e.g., "*Hieronimo* make haste to see thy sonne."[21] Shakespeare liked the phrase "making haste" much better than "making speed," opting for the former and variants six times as often as the latter in his writings (33 references v. 5 references).[22] *Richard III* even combined the terms: "make all the speedy haste you may" (3.1.60). These examples of collocations of the words "speed" or "haste" and "making" demonstrate the early modern assumption that speed was not only experienced but also produced.

How did everyday people in the early modern period practice speed-making? Travel supplied one major source in the cultural conception and mechanized experience of speed, primarily occurring by means of foot, horse, and boat. Most travel still happened by foot.[23] Then, as now, humans walked at rates of 2–4 mph and ran at top speeds well under 25 mph.[24] But the majority of people desired horses as a mode of transportation: "early modern life was saturated with horses and horse culture. The animals themselves were the literal and figurative vehicles for the transmission of goods, people, and ideas. . . . They functioned . . . as a kind of technology."[25] Indeed, this "technology" enabled relatively significant speed. A horse ambulates at 4 mph, trots at 8 mph, and gallops for short periods at top speeds of 55 mph, depending on the breed.[26] Riders yearned for the ability to increase this speed suddenly. In *The Art of Riding* (1584), Claudio Corte taught gentlemen how to accelerate an untrained horse less with spurs than with a "speedie voice": "if you would incourage the horsse to go with more speed, saie, *Via, via,* beating him on the contrarie shoulder with the rod: and if you would yet encrease his speed, then say, *Via, via, via,* & in the same instant strike him on the contrarie shoulder, and likewise with the contrarie heele."[27] While fast riding and horse racing grew in popularity in the seventeenth century, people eventually favored breeds of trotting horses over ambling and galloping horses because of high speeds maintained over the longest distances without fatigue.[28] Nevertheless, Karen Raber and Treva J. Tucker have linked the popular practice of horse racing to a positive new idea of English identity and freedom in the seventeenth century: "liberty represented by fast riding echoed a sense of national identity in which those qualities became a key part of what it meant to be English."[29] Faster speeds signified more freedom of choice as well as national identity.

In the same way, issues of English identity influenced the evolution of faster ships in the late sixteenth century. While the tides and current of the River Thames flowed 1 to 8 mph, water-going Elizabethans could not always take advantage of these potential speeds because of congested boat traffic.[30] The open waters of the ocean provided an opportunity for greater velocity. In the 1570s, to increase speed, John Hawkins radically rebuilt ships to have elongated hulls and shorter structures on the deck for less wind and water resistance.[31] These "race built galleons" became the dominant model for later ships.[32] The highest speed of these galleons has been estimated at eight knots.[33] Names like the *Flight,* the *Mercury,* the *Swiftsure,* the *Speedwell,* and, in fact, from Queen Elizabeth's fleet, the *Make-Speede* reflected the seagoing community's particular appreciation of speed in Hawkins's new design: "The Hawkins galleons represented the peak of Tudor technology. Ordinary ships were the largest movable man-made objects . . . and, as such, were considered to be the embodiment of technology in any age. Hawkins' ships were much faster than the other warships of the period," giving England an international edge.[34] These changes show the desirability of moving over water swiftly.

Even though early modern people could not usually travel across distances at more than ten miles per hour, many craved and valued speed, particularly the speed of information or communication across distances. Advertising on title pages in early modern how-to books promoted such results to readers. For example, recreational fencing books taught how to handle swords and rapiers faster and gain this knowledge swiftly. Joseph Swetnam's *The Schoole of the Noble and Worthy Science of Defence* (1617) promised that "any man may quickly | *come to the true knowledge of their weapons.*"[35] Similarly, William Rastell's frequently republished table to "quickely accomp[t]" the Julian calendar with the regnal year of the king suggests the appetite for acquiring information rapidly.[36] John Blagrave's title page for *The Mathematical Ievvel* (1585) assured that this book "with great and incredible speede" would "lea- | deth any man practicing [on this instrument] the direct pathway . . . | through the whole Artes of Astronomy, Cosmography, Geography, Topography, | Nauigation."[37] A significant market existed to meet the demand for books on communicating faster, such as handwriting guides: Timoth[i]e Bright's *Characterie: An Arte of Shorte, Swifte, and Secret Writing by Character* (1588) and Peter Bales's *The Writing Schoolemaster* (1590), containing the first book, *The Arte of Brachygraphie: that is, to | write as fast as a man speaketh,* and the third book, *The Key of Calygraphie: opening the rea- | die waie to write faire in verie short time.*[38]

The need to attain or share intelligence—or sometimes affect—impelled the need for speed. Books on letter writing, such as I. W.'s *A Speedie Poste* (1625), reflected anxiety about insufficient rates of communication.[39] The excuse of writing "in haste" did not just adhere to epistolary conventions, but also frequently signaled writing under actual hurried conditions.[40] Letter writers therefore sometimes wrote quickly, leaving material traces of speed in their handwriting.[41] These letter writers complained about the lack of speed in the conveyance of their hastily penned mail, despite the fact that delivery time of increasing amounts of mail had doubled since the 1450s.[42] In 1641, one letter writer lamented "how slow the posts are, who by this accompt ride not 3 myles an howre," and he requested that the recipient "quicken ye post-masters."[43] Because of such frustration, letter writers sometimes hoped for immediate, almost email-style communication, such as in this June 1, 1609 letter enclosing a list of Catholic sympathizers: "had I Wings as I have Will, mine Eyes should receive nothing that might either concern your Life or Honour but it should be as soon in yours as Possibility would permit it. Much grieved I am that I have no better nor *speedier* Meanes to convey this enclosed . . . I cannot but wishe it *instantly* in your Hands."[44] In *The Culture of Epistolarity,* Gary Schneider explains, "the desire for instant, even 'telepathic' communication imagined in these letters was symptomatic of the desire for an ideal communicative system that easily and quickly spanned time and distance."[45] This type of expeditious correspondence envisioned by letter writers was desirable because it was what made possible immediate knowledge and affect, as well as political benefits. For instance, in 1603 Robert Carey decided to secure his court status by notifying King James VI of Scotland before anyone else that Queen Elizabeth had died; he traveled from Richmond Palace to Holyrood in Edinburgh in an astounding two and a half days.[46] In reward for communicating news with breakneck speed, Carey received a promotion to Gentleman of the Bedchamber.[47]

Early modern culture, however, did not universally consider speed desirable for travel, communication, or personal conduct. While modern life takes for granted the value of speed—witness the quest for ever faster microprocessors—early modern emblems warned against too much speed and counseled readers to choose appropriate speeds. The emblem "Temeritas [*Rashness*]," found in Geffrey Whitney's *A Choice of Emblemes* (1586), displays a wagoner with wild horses to illustrate unsuitable speed because failure to bridle his "will" and "affections fowle vmtam'de" lead him to "fal[l] . . . to his deface."[48] Other emblems concern control over

speed of communication, such as "Scripta non temerè edenda
[*Writings must not rashly be published*]," containing Quintillius
guiding an immature, "too faste" writer: "euer rashenes, yeeldes
repente, and most dispised liues [*sic*, lines?]."[49] Two emblems
bestow the most specific advice: "Festina lentè [*Hasten slowly*]"
and "Maturandum [*make good speed*]." The first well-known
motto advises princes weighing death sentences to "learne the
truthe": "Then muste they haste, but verie slowe awaie, / Like but-
terflie whome creepinge crabbe dothe staie"; and the second "bides
vs in our actions haste, no more then reason woulde."[50] Likewise,
George Wither's much later *Collection of Emblemes* (1635) differentiates rates of action by their outcomes, drawing familiarly on the
1548 adage "*Haste, Waste may make.*"[51] In another emblem, Wither
links speed to travel, reasoning, "We are all *Travellers*" and giving
the lesson of one traveler who may

> *slip* by walking over-fast;
> Or . . . by his hast:
> And, so (for want of better taking heed)
> Incurre the mischiefes of *Vnwary-speed*.[52]

Elsewhere, Wither cautions those pushing speed limits, namely, in
his example schoolboys, who

> seeke to force
> The *Sands,* to runne more speedily away,
> They interrupt them; and they passe the worse.
>
> . . . .
>
> But, let this *Emblem* teach us to regard
> What *Way of Working,* to each *Worke* pertaines.[53]

Wither believes his readers "seeke" speed, and he argues for decorum in its application at the end of this emblem, moralizing, "much
Haste will marre thy *Speed* [success]."[54] In essence, the Renaissance iconography about the desire for speed in these emblem
books implies that readers individually make choices about their
own appropriate rates of action, and people can learn to judge and
adjust speed with decorum.

As theater historians have established, the speed demons who
ran the London theater industry by which *Hamlet* first came to the
stage ignored such cautions, preferring instead the economic
potential of speed. Early modern theater professionals wrote, pre-

pared, and staged their drama on tour in a frenetic style. According to Neil Carson, playwrights composed plays rapidly, usually completing them in a month or month and a half.[55] He also notes the "exceptional haste" with which companies copied, licensed, and studied their plays, with a usual production time of two weeks and occasionally as few as nine, six, or three days.[56] This pace of writing and production achieved efficiency: "the playing company . . . devoured a new play a fortnight. New plays became old plays overnight."[57] This necessary hasty output made for profits—new plays sold to hungry audiences.[58]

When players took their quickly written and produced plays on tour, they did so rapidly to increase income for the box. Andrew Gurr notes that companies could travel far "at a surprisingly high speed." He gives as an example Queen Anne's Men, who in 1613 toured over 230 miles in two and a half weeks, likely performing at stopping points along the route. Similarly, the Queen's Men in 1594 acted in Norwich on June 25 and in Coventry on July 4, covering 130 miles in eight days. Gurr conjectures that companies may have sometimes stuck to sea routes along the coast in order to speed up their travels, as records reveal especially fast trips between Dover and Norwich or Plymouth.[59]

Those who worked in the London theaters not only required speed to produce drama, but also then rendered this same swift sensation during performances, attempting to fulfill audiences' desires for speed. Audiences participated vicariously in speed-making through the kinetic energy of the characters on stage. We can add to Carnegie's stage direction *in haste* by noting other common stage directions from the period that indicate an actor entering, exiting, and performing action on stage in a hurried manner. In both *The Taming of the Shrew* and *Comedy of Errors,* for example, characters leave the stage "*as fast as may be*" (*Shr.* 5.1.112; *C of E* 4.4.146). Other stage directions include descriptors like *hastily; suddenly; sweating; panting;* and *out of breath;* as well as verbs like to *hurry, rush, post,* and the commonly used imperative to *fly,* which Alan Dessen and Leslie Thomson's *Dictionary of Stage Directions* explains meant to "enter or exit rapidly," usually in battle.[60] Gurr writes that what he calls "Vigorous and rapid staging" indulged the groundlings, who stood for extensive time in front of the stage.[61] According to his inference, then, all of this quick movement would have kept some from perceiving just how long their own feet had been still.

In addition to the movement of the players, the pace of actors delivering lines in the theater allowed the audience to experience speed auditorially. Gurr claims that early modern actors spoke Shakespeare's words much more rapidly than actors today: "Quicker speaking, quicker stage action, no intermissions, and the audience's ability to grasp the language more quickly meant that the plays galloped along."[62] Scholars such as Michael Hirrel estimate the rate of early modern players' speeches at 21–22 lines or 175–200 words a minute.[63] This rate outpaces by up to 25–50 words what we might hear when listening to the radio now.[64] Of course, in practicality, any speed of elocution cannot exceed the rate at which listeners can determine the import of recited sentences.[65] Like the emblem-book authors, some early modern commentators within the theater questioned the value of high speed. Thomas Heywood gave aesthetic reasons for speed limits, writing in his 1612 *Apology for Actors* that a good scholar who puts on plays should not "teare his words *hastily* betwixt his teeth."[66]

Fast stage directions and fast line delivery were two ways the theaters made speed. But built into plays were also theatrical conventions for speeding up plots. How audiences should and did react to these different experiences of speed in the theater was the subject of various comments by playwrights and detractors. On stage, devices for accelerated affect, such as love-at-first-sight, were standard. The sudden appearance of the character Time in act 4 of *The Winter's Tale* calls attention to such conventions and mockingly anticipates critique for the lack of decorum, teasing the audience with a witty and superficial apology:

> Impute it not a crime
> To me, or my swift passage, that I slide
> O'er sixteen years.
>
> (4.1.4–6)

The word "crime" marks a hyperbole here. Time asks the audience to "allo[w]" him "with speed so pace / To speak of Perdita, now grown" (*WT*, 4.1.15, 23–24). Shakespeare anticipated that theatergoers would hear language about hasty movement or see quick actions on stage and take pleasure in such efforts, the opposite of time "spent . . . worse ere now" (*WT*, 4.1.30). *Apology for Actors* delineates the relationship between quick movement on stage and the positive response of audiences: "so bewitching a thing is liuely and well spirited action, that it hath power to new mold the harts of the spectators and fashion them to the shape of any noble and notable attempt."[67] Those critical of the theater associated it with speed and feared a negative or sinful effect on audiences, as did John Northbrooke in his anti-theatrical tract *Spiritus est vicarius Christi in terra* (1577): "I am persuaded that Satan hath not a more speedie way and fitter schoole to work and teach his desire, to bring men and women into his snare of concupiscence and filthie lustes of wicked whoredome, than those places and playes, and theatres are."[68] This speed of influence worked particularly effectively on the emotions. In "E/loco/co/motion," Bruce Smith explains this early modern belief that drama affected the emotions, as emotions accelerated in response to fiction. Imagination generated a "quicknesse" of "thoughts," of "springings and glances of the heart" arising in "sudden" fashion.[69] Early moderns found the heart the "site of our affective sensibilities."[70] Thus, contemporaries saw speed as both a necessity for and an effect of theater.

Hamlet intensifies the potential of speed already inherent in the early modern theatrical experience by providing a discourse of haste, such as Marcellus's "this sweaty haste / Doth make the night joint-labourer with the day" and Horatio's "this post-haste and rummage in the land."[71] In fact, *Hamlet* has more references to the words "speed" and "haste" than any other Shakespearean work except for *Romeo and Juliet,* which has an equal number.[72] Sometimes this discourse in *Hamlet* refers to intellectual or metaphorical perceptions of speed. The Ghost describes the poison in a double figure of mercury and of a horse running through a village, or perhaps, one could say, through a *hamlet:* "swift as quicksilver it courses through / The natural gates and alleys of the body" (1.5.66–67).[73] This poison curdled the Ghost's blood in an accelerated manner, "with a sudden vigour," and caused an "instant" rash (1.5.68, 71).

Most of the references to speed from the opening moments occur in imperatives for characters to move physically over land or water. In other words, characters issue demands for speed-making. These include Barnardo's request to Francisco, "The rivals of my watch, bid them *make haste*"; Hamlet's "To a nunnery go, and quickly too"; Polonius's call for decorously speedy departure: "Yet here, Laertes? Aboard, aboard for shame! / The wind sits in the shoulder of your sail"; and Claudius's insistence that Hamlet must "With fiery quickness" leave for England on a ship: "The bark is ready and the wind at help" (1.1.11, emphasis added; 3.1.139; 1.3.54–55; F1, 3.6.41; 4.3.43). Most of these commands anticipate hurried off-stage action. Peter Holland explains that plays frequently ask spectators to imagine journeys transpiring behind the scenes because "Placing a voyage on stage is, of course, a direct route to dramaturgical difficulty."[74] Instead, through a language of hurried commands, *Hamlet* requires that audiences envision rushed activity and travel about to happen somewhere just off stage.

Characters use imperatives also to hasten speed of communication. Fortinbras rushes to listen to Horatio's story and to acquire new information: "Let us haste to hear it" (5.2.370). Using analogies with thinking and affect, Hamlet sees positively the speed of communicating knowledge that will enable vengeance: "Haste me to know't that I with wings as swift / As meditation or the thoughts of love / May sweep to my revenge" (1.5.29–31). Other commands for the quick travel of communication proliferate. Laertes urges Ophelia to send him letters promptly conveyed by boat: "as the winds give benefit / And convey is assistant" (1.3.2–3). Claudius recognizes the benefits of speed for the ambassadors, who represent royal communication. He commands them: "let your haste commend your duty" (1.2.39). Indeed, at 1.2.41, the ambassadors receive a farewell and then "Are joyfully returned" with their news from Norway at approximately the same point in the next act, 2.2.41.

The play does not emphasize the speed of other characters solely in order to distinguish the delay of Hamlet because he also at times moves with alacrity. For example, his sea voyage and abrupt return outdo in speed the ambassadors' quick expedition to Norway, and characters' depictions of his journey combine references to fast travel and to hurried communication. *Hamlet* describes every character at some point as speedy except for Claudius. While he is quick-thinking, for actions he prefers to employ fleet instruments, namely, Rosencrantz and Guildenstern, those men "hast[il]y" summoned to fulfill swift commands (2.2.4). Claudius demands speed for Hamlet's crossing, such as with the orders, "I have in quick determination / Thus set it down. He shall with speed to England"; "I your commission will forthwith dispatch"; "Arm you, I pray you, to this speedy voyage"; and "Tempt him with speed aboard. / Delay it not" and "make haste" (3.1.167–68; 3.3.3, 3.3.24; 4.3.52–53, 55). Claudius has great power to control the speed of his desired tasks. Rosencrantz obeys Claudius's orders at 4.4.29; Hamlet replies in the next line: "I'll be with you straight" (4.4.30); the audience learns Hamlet finally departed at 4.5.80; and Hamlet comes back by 4.6, two scenes after he left. Hamlet labels his own voyage "my sudden return" (4.7.46). Certainly, Hamlet's trip represents the fastest movement offstage so far in the play.

Moreover, Hamlet's letter to Horatio characterizes the offstage trip not only as fast in and of itself, but also as an acceleration at sea compared to Rosencrantz and Guildenstern's unwavering maritime speed: *"Ere we were two days old at sea, a pirate of very warlike appointment gave us chase. Finding ourselves too slow of sail, we put on a compelled valour and in the grapple I boarded them. On the instant they got clear of our ship. . . . Rosencrantz and Guildenstern* hold their course *for England"* (4.6.15–27, emphasis added to original italics). Hamlet quickly wants to relay face-to-face this story of his own speed and outcome: *"repair thou to me with as much speed as thou wouldst fly death"* (4.6.22–23, original italics). In response, Horatio agrees to help the sailors with their letters, "the speedier" that he can visit Hamlet (4.6.30). Through Hamlet's epistolary handling and order to execute immediately the letter-bearers, Rosencrantz and Guildenstern, "Without debatement further more or less," Hamlet emblematizes the nearly instantaneous travel and letter-transmission that early modern people themselves craved (5.2.45). He also exhibits attempted agency over his own speed of travel and of the communication of his narrative.

As shown in these moments in the play, characters frequently comment on others' or their own rates as relatively fast or slow, as well as on the value, outcome, or decorum of these speeds. Sometimes characters reach agreement about an action's particular pace. The remark Gertrude makes to Claudius about "our hasty marriage" endorses Hamlet's previous negative assessment of her rush to matrimony: "O most wicked speed! To post / With such dexterity to incestuous sheets" (2.2.57, 1.2.156–57). Hamlet perceives her actions as unsuitably fast, and therefore evil or sinful. Horatio further confirms the accuracy of this assessment of speed when he replies that the wedding "followed hard upon" the funeral (1.2.178). Because Gertrude has less power than Claudius, or perhaps because of her gender, her commands do not elicit the same fast response time that Claudius's do. She orders the usually fast Rosencrantz and Guildenstern, "I beseech you instantly to visit" Hamlet (2.2.35), but it takes them 180 lines to do so. Likewise, after summons of Hamlet to Gertrude by Guildenstern and by Polonius, "the Queen would speak with you, and presently," meaning "immediately; instantly, quickly," the play cues the audience to a slow response when Hamlet acknowledges, "My mother stays" (3.2.288; 3.2.365–66; 3.3.95).[75] Among other tip-offs the audience gets to his failure to make haste are when Hamlet resolves, "now to my mother," but then does not go to her (3.2.382), and when he jokes about "com[ing] by and by," but admits " 'by and by' is easily said" (3.2.376–77). When Hamlet has still not arrived, Polonius promises her correctly: "'A will come straight," which Hamlet does (3.4.1). The audience can follow these judgments because its own perceptions of movement, gleaned through visual and auditory cues, correspond with the actors' movement on stage and the characters' comments about the rate of this movement and lack of decorum.

Dramaturgical theorists explain how playwrights can use theatrical conventions, in other words messengers like Polonius, to quicken the pace of the plot or explain in only a few lines events that take place over much more time. For example, Gary Scrimgeour maintains that playwrights accelerate actions in a play in order to create more narrative movement and to manipulate time: "In the theater, the panoramic play requires that the dramatist continually balance speed of movement and compression of events against the necessity of keeping his audience precisely informed and at ease in the midst of swiftly changing material."[76] Similarly, John Russell Brown exhorts critics thinking about onstage performance to "give attention to expectation and anticipation, to delay and speed of fulfillment. . . . Forms of combat and chase should be carefully noted as basic structural devices that quicken attention."[77] However, Brown differs somewhat from Scrimgeour in highlighting how plays do not always completely apprise the audience about events. Not only onstage action, but also language in Shakespeare engages the audience's imagination, according to Brown. Shakespeare's plays always have "verbal images that express lively sensations and rapidly changing thoughts. . . . Their swiftly succeeding verbal impressions set a pace with which actors and audience will often fail to keep up. . . . [W]hen failing to catch individual images and allusions, or even the sense of what is being said, the attention of audience members can be held merely by the energy of speech, its *speed,* weight, rhythms and variations of sound."[78] Brown recognizes importantly that audiences cannot always "keep up." Shakespeare, however, also considered the consequences of such a failure beyond losing audience interest.

For a theater audience, ascertaining speed of movement and of thematic and dramaturgical information occurs through sensory perception: visually and audibly, as well as through proprioceptive sense of time and movement. In other words, even people deprived of visual or auditory sensation can sense their own acceleration and how much time has passed. *Hamlet,* however, actually considerably disrupts traditional theatrical tenets on managing speed. While creating "speed of movement" and "swiftly changing material," the play keeps its characters and the audience in a state of dis-"ease" and im-"balance" in order to effect disorientation, by means of the audience's contrasting sensory perceptions of speed. Fast motion alone does not cause motion sickness. Instead, disorientation happens for someone when a conflict occurs between expectations and new information taken in by the visual and auditory senses.[79] For example, a body unfamiliar with experiencing ship motion at sea sometimes reacts to information taken in by the eyes (which see the horizon) and by the inner ear or vestibular system (which senses a lurching deck) that contradicts the brain's norm of balance.[80] Brown hints at this problem in *Romeo and Juliet,* when visual information from Juliet's quick entrance in act 2 "speak[s] to the [audience's] eyes only and not at all to the ears."[81] Shakespeare appreciated how the theater could create disorientation; furthermore, playwrights require such disorientation in order to relay a time-spanning story over the duration of only a few hours.

The experience of watching *Hamlet* may have occasioned feelings of uneasiness and disorientation among audience members as they witnessed characters repeatedly disputing each other's speed measurements. The play, in effect, pits characters' simultaneous and often varying perceptions of time and speed of events against each other and then positions characters' assessments against the audience's. Hamlet first claims that over a month has passed since Old Hamlet died (1.2.153). But during a later conversation, Ophelia protests that four months have elapsed, and Hamlet radically recasts the interval: "my father died within's two hours" (3.2.121, 3.2.120). The assertion of two hours clashes with early modern audiences' physical experience of the play's duration up to act 3, which may or may not have been perceived accurately. Polonius sees himself as unprofitably slow, regretting that, with regard to Hamlet, "with better speed . . . / I had not quoted him" (F1, 2.1.109–10). Polonius laments not choosing the good type of speed or profit. The initial witnesses to the Ghost cannot agree on its speed when reporting the supernatural encounter. Horatio reckons that the Ghost stayed "While one with moderate haste might tell a hundred" (1.2.236). Barnardo and Marcellus both refute Horatio's calculation of passing time, saying, "Longer, longer," but Horatio rejects the correction: "Not when I saw't" (1.2.236, 237). The audience, which itself witnessed the appearance of the Ghost in act 1, will of course have had a separate perception. These conflicts about degree of speed suggest the play's attempt to unsettle audience perceptions. What, the audience might have begun to ask, constitutes "moderate haste" in *Hamlet*?

Hamlet frustrates onstage and possibly offstage audiences not only by creating intellectual mismatches in information debated by characters, but also by staging dizzyingly abrupt accelerations of movement. Claudius urges Rosencrantz and Guildenstern to hunt for Hamlet and also for Polonius's body: "I pray you haste in this" (4.1.37). Ten lines later, Rosencrantz and Guildenstern locate Hamlet (4.2.2). The next scene echoes and accelerates this exchange: at 4.3.15, Claudius tells Rosencrantz and Guildenstern to "Bring [Hamlet] before us," while Hamlet stands outside the chamber, and they do so in the second half of the line. In four places, this brisk behind-the-scenes action moves on stage, causing sudden visual accelerations for the witnessing characters. In the first example, Hamlet and others struggle to keep up with the rushing Ghost. Horatio reported to Hamlet the Ghost's bursts of movement while on stage in terms of common Elizabethan stage directions: "at the sound [of the cock crowing] it shrunk *in haste* away" (1.2.218, emphasis added). The Ghost later moves "*under the stage,*" according to stage directions in all early versions of the play, more quickly than Hamlet's oath-taking friends on stage can; and Hamlet perceives it in multiple places simultaneously: "*Hic et ubique?* Then we'll shift our ground" (1.5.148.s.d., 156). To understand these scenes, the audience has to follow the auditory and visual tracks cued by the lines and motions of the actors, without encountering any conflict between the physicality of watching the play and the Ghost's below-stage movements. Hamlet's questions expressing amazement indicate to the audience the unexpected nature of these accelerations: "canst work i'th' earth so fast?" (1.5.161). Similarly, in the second example, Hamlet suddenly stabbing Polonius, himself a "rash" intruder, according to Hamlet, catches the onstage audience by surprise (3.4.29).[82] Gertrude calls Hamlet's killing a "rash and bloody deed," emphasizing the murder's unseemly speed (3.4.26). Arguably, Hamlet's snap decision to kill Polonius behind the arras ruins Hamlet's speed/success because this action gets Hamlet banished and brings back Laertes, which offers a third example. When Laertes returns, breaking down the court doors, the messenger reports a tsunami of indecorum:

> The ocean overpeering of his list
> Eats not the flats with more impiteous haste
> Than young Laertes in a riotous head
> O'erbears your officers.
>
> (4.5.99–102)

In my final example of the acceleration of onstage action, Hamlet's immediate stabbing of the King is one of several moments of sudden activity: Gertrude's murder, the swordfight, Claudius's guilt becoming publicly declared knowledge, and Hamlet's own death (5.2). Fortinbras remarks on this incredible speed, "so many princes at a shot / . . . bloodily . . . struck," signaling to the audience the unexpectedly speedy climax and resolution to the revenge plot (5.2.350–51).

Hamlet suggests that characters' differing assessments of and judgments about rates of speed are due to differing individual sensory perceptions. Characters call attention to and rate discrepancies among each other's senses. Marcellus and Horatio privilege visual perception: the former seeks the latter to "approve our eyes," and in the first scene, Horatio judges his own senses and vision as particularly perceptive: "I might not this believe / Without the sensible and true avouch / Of mine own eyes" (1.1.28; 55–57). Brown argues that Hamlet shows a "presentation of a life that is based in sensation and feeling."[83] But Hamlet problematizes "sensation and feeling" as untrustworthy measures of speed.

In Hamlet, not all characters possess the particularly dependable senses that Horatio claims for himself at the beginning. The play foregrounds varying, but also unreliable sensory perceptions. For example, characters' ears do not seem to assimilate information completely, such as in Horatio's failure to hear the clock: "Indeed? I heard it not"; Gertrude's "Alack, what noise is this?"; Laertes's "what noise is that?"; and the English Ambassador's "The ears are senseless that should give us hearing" (1.4.4; 4.1.95 [only in Q1 and F1]; 4.5.152; 5.2.353). These characters marvel at deficient senses.

Horatio highlights other limited senses when he notes Marcellus's and Barnardo's "oppressed . . . eyes" (1.2.202). If the ears' and eyes' senses malfunction or conflict with each other or with expected information from other senses, disorientation can result; these characters' questions convey just such growing sensory confusion.

Hamlet concludes that Gertrude's unreliable and sick senses (recall she does not see or hear the Ghost [3.4.120, 131]) have misled her judgment in electing to wed Claudius so quickly; thus, she violates decorum in speed. He deduces that Gertrude has not become insane, but has developed a damaged or paralyzed "sense," meaning consciousness or sensory perception:

> Sense, sure, you have—
> Else could you not have motion. But sure, that sense
> Is apoplexed, for madness would not err
> Nor sense to ecstasy was ne'er so thralled
> But it reserved some quantity of choice
> To serve in such a difference.
> (3.4.69–74, only in Q2)

Hamlet rationalizes her defective senses as enslaved to "motion," movement or emotion.[84] Then, after venturing that a devil has tricked Gertrude's visual senses in "hoodman-blind," Hamlet realizes that a paralyzed sense results in mismatched, missing, or ailing sensory perception (3.4.78):

> Eyes without feeling, feeling without sight,
> Ears without hands or eyes, smelling sans all,
> Or but a sickly part of one true sense
> Could not so mope.
> (3.4.76–79, only in Q2)

Gertrude's visual organs cannot accurately process information, or affect, "feeling," nor can her visual, auditory, touch, and olfactory perceptions interconnect. Hamlet therefore suspects a "sickly" condition or sense; otherwise, if her senses worked correctly, or if only one part of an effective, "true" sense, perhaps vision, did, the senses would not have misfired. He realizes that individuals cannot choose to override the senses, and lust, given incorrect sensory information. Senses enslaved to emotion cannot properly perceive or regulate speed.

Characters in *Hamlet* point out not only the untrustworthiness

and susceptibility of the senses to sickness or manipulation by others, but also the self-rationalization of sensory experience, which
impairs one's ability to judge speed. While fully functioning olfactory perceptions do not usually aid in directly recognizing speed in
Hamlet, they can detect the passage of time, especially through the
processes of things burning up or rotting (1.5.3; 1.5.58; 3.3.36;
4.3.35; 5.1.190). Time's passage through the nose forms part of
Laertes's counsel to Ophelia, as a way to deny her emotions for
Hamlet. Laertes devises a figure for her of Hamlet's short-lived love:
"The perfume and suppliance of a minute, / No more" (1.3.9–10).
But Ophelia repeats skeptically Laertes's conception of an emotion
as an imagined, transitory, olfactory experience: "No more but so,"
so that Laertes reassures her, "Think it no more," as if the mind
can choose to deny the body's sensory experience (1.3.10). As other
characters do, Laertes and Ophelia here seem to disagree about the
rate at which such an imagined experience might take place. He
suggests the potential for registering emotions through the senses,
transforming them into other imaginary sensory experiences, and
then willfully speeding them up. Hamlet, similarly, tries to regulate
the speed of sensory input. After hearing the Ghost's story and
reacting emotionally, he calls for deceleration, commanding his
"sinews, [to] grow not instant old" (1.5.94). In relation to auditory
and olfactory sensations, Alexander Cowan and Jill Steward
describe early modern "attempts . . . to suppress and control features of the sensory environment perceived as distasteful, disruptive, subversive and oppositional."[85] This endeavored disciplining
of sensation occurs in *Hamlet* as well, as characters struggle to out-
think the senses that might lead to unpleasant emotions and to hasten or slow down these feelings.

The speeds that Hamlet chooses and declares for himself show
that he, too, rationalizes speed, bordering on such self-deception.
Other characters note that the inability and denial of one's own
sensory and emotional reality can lead to delusion, as Barnardo
hopes to "assail your [Horatio's] ears / . . . so fortified against our
story" (1.1.30–31). Laertes's imperative upon seeing Ophelia dead
suggests the desire to block out visual perception of grief: "tears
seven times salt / Burn out the sense and virtue of mine eye!"
(4.5.153–54). Significantly, these manipulated senses influence a
character's ability to measure others' or his or her own speed and
outcomes. Hamlet, on the one hand, praises his own impulsiveness
when he sprang from his sea cabin to substitute one letter for

another, allowing him to gain knowledge to justify revenge. In recalling discovering Claudius's execution orders on the ship, Hamlet breaks off his story about rash action to digress on the value of rashness: "Rashly—/ And praised be rashness for it" (5.2.6–7). He sees his own speed as positive, not only because he could take revenge on Rosencrantz, Guildenstern, and Claudius quickly, but also because he acquired the knowledge needed to enact a successful outcome. On the other hand, Hamlet's praise for acting "Rashly" recalls for the audience Hamlet's declaration to Laertes in the previous scene: "I am not splenative rash" (5.1.250). Hamlet's self-contradictions about speed signal Shakespeare questioning whether it truly produces "liberty"—and any real opportunities to choose rates with decorum—or whether attempts to regulate speed delude and enslave the self.

In *Hamlet,* theater seems to offer the only opportunity for exercising control over speed-making, a necessary element in effective theatrical practice. Hamlet explains that acting can disrupt audiences' sensory processes; he says that a player with Hamlet's cause would "amaze indeed / The very faculty of eyes and ears" (2.2.500–501). The practice of acting requires the player also to accelerate his own emotion, in other words, "in a fiction . . . / . . . [to] force his soul so to his own conceit" in order to generate "Tears" (2.2.487–88, 490). The scheme to perform the *Murder of Gonzago* appeals to Hamlet not only because of its testing, to "catch the conscience of the King," but also because of its promise of immediate revelation of the truth (2.2.540). The Players' performance will evoke information and emotional reaction instantly:

> Hum, I have heard
> That guilty creatures sitting at a play
> Have by the very cunning of the scene
> Been struck so to the soul that *presently*
> They have proclaimed their malefactions.
> (2.2.523–27, emphasis added)

Hamlet expects that theater distorts the senses and accelerates knowledge and affect for the observing audience—play making becomes speed-making.

Surprisingly, the Players in *Hamlet* do not move particularly fast when they first arrive at Elsinore, but they do have control and agency; and with Hamlet's prompting, they at times both decelerate and accelerate. As they travel to court, the Players move slowly enough that Rosencrantz and Guildenstern report overtaking them: "we coted them on the way" (2.2.283). The audience learns further from Rosencrantz that before their tour, the Players operated at a habitual speed. Despite having an "inhibition," the Players' "endeavour keeps in the wonted pace" (2.2.295, 336–37 [a line found only in F1]). The Players' speech that Hamlet remembers, however, hints that this early slowness or habitually maintained rate prefaces a quick and successful follow-through that will speed up the emotional reactions of observers. The content of this remembered speech deals with the success of sudden accelerations that follow a pause, specifically Pyrrhus's: *"after Pyrrhus' pause / A roused vengeance sets him new a-work,"* resulting in a death by sword-blow and Hecuba's emotional *"instant burst of clamour"* (2.2.425; 453, original italics). Productions of *Hamlet* have often cut the Player's speech and additional lines from this scene, as well as omitted material from the other play-within-the-play, *The Murder of Gonzago,* because of slow pacing.[86] In the words of Polonius, they are "too long" (2.2.436). But Hamlet wants the actors to perform even more lines. When he asks the Players to learn a new speech of "some dozen lines, or sixteen lines," he makes the play longer, but the actors memorize the lines overnight, showing, indeed, an acceleration (2.2.477). Hamlet's enjoyment of these slower plays-within-the-play and his simultaneous demands for quick responsiveness from the players highlight the play's concern with speeds of performance.

Still, Hamlet worries that the Players will not move fast enough once they hit the stage, and he demands excessive speed-making, ultimately making himself sick. In his directions to them, he tells them to avoid a poor performance by overacting or underacting, that is, by "com[ing] tardy off," with "tardy" meaning to move slowly and therefore fall short (3.2.25).[87] He then asks Rosencrantz and Guildenstern to serve as speed-makers and expedite the Players' preparation for performance using the popular cultural idiom to make haste: "Bid the players make haste," followed redundantly by the question "Will you two help to hasten them?" (3.2.46, 47). As we well know, the successive performances by the Players rouse the King, but the Players' motions unsettle Hamlet's equanimity as well. During the Players' second skit, Hamlet reacts by calling out in the First Folio (F1) version, published in 1623, "Wormwood! Wormwood!" (3.2.175) (in Q1 "O, wormwood! Wormwood!"

[9.115]), a common early modern remedy for nausea from traveling at sea.[88] The 1582 diary of Richard Madox explains: " 'I was taught many medcynes to avoyd the sycknes of the sea as namely, . . . to drink the juse of wormwood.' "[89] According to the 1597 *Garden of Health,* wormwood "comforteth the stomacke" and "preuent[s]" "Vomiting on the Sea."[90] Early modern travelers believed unfamiliar sea air primarily caused seasickness, but they conceded "it be true that the motion of the Ship helpes much," and "the motion and agitation may cause this sicknesse" not only in boats, but also "in like sort going in Coaches and Caroaches"; those bodies and stomachs "not acoustomed thereunto . . . are wonderfully moued and changed."[91] Symptoms included loss of "legs, stomach, and courage."[92] In the Second Quarto (Q2), published in 1604–5, the printing of Hamlet's verdict "That's wormwood!" occurs in the right-hand margin next to *"None wed the second but who killed the first"* (3.2.175, 174, original italics). While the Arden 3 editors see in this an "aside" by Hamlet on the bitter play-within-the-play, the placement of the remedy also functions more broadly, as a reader's marginal comment or a metatheatrical onstage assessment of the entire queasy play.[93]

As the Players and onstage audiences' reactions in *Hamlet* show, Shakespeare understood the necessity and difficulty of speed for powerful theater. Given recent textual conversations about *Hamlet,*[94] it is worth noting that in all basic versions of the *Hamlet* texts, Shakespeare and his fellow actors attended to the language of haste. Each of the three early texts reveals, though in different ways, a marked concern with speed. The longer texts, Q2 and F1, talk more about it, but even the shortest, the First Quarto (Q1), printed in 1603, seems to have speed in mind. For example, in the quotes cited in my essay, Q1 has "To a nunnery, go!" (7.185), and Q2/F1 also has "and quickly, too"; Q2/F1 has "sweaty haste" while Q1 has "sweaty march" (1.70.66); Q2/F1 has "moderate haste" while Q1 has "moderate pace" (2.150). F1, while shorter than Q2, makes additions and changes to Q2 in order to exaggerate speed:

> The bark is ready] *With fiery quickness* [new phrase added]
> Haste me to know't] Haste, *haste* me to know it
> our hasty marriage] our *o'er*hasty marriage
> *repair thou to me with as much speed*] *repair thou to me*
>   *with as much* haste
> splenative rash] splenative *and* rash
>   (F1, 3.6.40; 1.5.29; 2.2.56; 4.2.23; 5.1.258)

Other textual differences throughout the three major texts of *Hamlet* reveal similar editorial consciousness about the theme of acceleration in the play, such as Polonius's apology: Polonius's line in Q2 is "I am sorry that with better heed" (2.1.108) and, in F1, "I am sorry that with better speed" (2.1.109) while Corambis's line in Q1 is "I am sorry / That I was so rash" (6.61–62). Such attention to expressions involving haste evidences interest in speed-making and acceleration as tools of successful theatrical production.

Hamlet attests to Shakespeare's fascination with the processes of manipulating and perceiving speed, especially for artistic, emotional, and visceral effects in the theater. The play exploits the potential of performed drama to disorient by producing many concurrent types of speed that often conflict with the onstage and offstage sense of physical time and stage-time, a condition a "little more than kin" to motion sickness (1.2.65). But Shakespeare's attitude toward speed appears to have been conflicted. *Hamlet* expresses doubts about the possibility of agency over the application of speed with decorum or precision, the desirability of speed to produce profitable outcomes, and accurate perception of others' or one's own speed. Critics have long debated which of Shakespeare's works is the fastest.[95] It might be more productive to recognize speed as a hallmark of Shakespeare's works and to examine their varying perspectives on it.

Notes

1. For discussions of time, see Matthew Wagner, *Shakespeare, Theatre, and Time* (New York: Routledge, 2014) and David Houston Wood, *Time, Narrative, and Emotion in Early Modern England* (Farnham, UK: Ashgate, 2009); for movement, see P. A. Skantze, *Stillness in Motion in the Seventeenth-Century Theatre* (London: Routledge, 2003); for space, see Tim Fitzpatrick, *Playwright, Space and Place in Early Modern Performance: Shakespeare and Company* (Farnham, UK: Ashgate, 2011); for the relationship among these three concepts, see Angus Fletcher, *Time, Space, and Motion in the Age of Shakespeare* (Cambridge, MA: Harvard University Press, 2007).

2. Dympna Callaghan, "Confounded by Winter: Speeding Time in Shakespeare's Sonnets," in *A Companion to Shakespeare's Sonnets,* ed. Michael Schoenfeldt (Oxford: Blackwell, 2007), 106.

3. In his passing references to *Hamlet,* Howard Marchitello sees Hamlet as similar to Macbeth, although in lesser intensity: "they wish to accelerate their movement through time and have the future in the instant." "Speed and the Problem of Real Time in *Macbeth,*" *Shakespeare Quarterly* 64, no. 4 (2013): 425–48, 434–35, doi:10.1353/shq.2013.0059. While, like Marchitello, I focus on the desire

for speed, my paper questions the early modern acceptance of the inevitable "drive" toward acceleration; I uncover early modern culture's ambivalent attitudes toward speed and argue that in *Hamlet,* Shakespeare was more interested in the possibility of controlling and perceiving physical speed.

4. David Carnegie, "Running over the Stage: Webster and the Running Footman," *Early Theatre* 3, no. 1 (2010): 121–36, 122 and 133, Academic OneFile.

5. Quoted in ibid., 132.

6. Ibid., 132–33.

7. Robert Hapgood found that many Shakespearean heroes operate at varying rhythms from the "norm" that the audience predicts, with the exception of Hamlet: "In *Hamlet* . . . such slowness is a general malaise verging on paralysis. Virtually everyone in Elsinore is prone to delay in much the same way that Hamlet is." "Shakespeare's Choreography: Pace and Rhythm," in *Shakespeare's More Than Words Can Witness: Essays on Visual and Nonverbal Enactment in the Plays,* ed. Sidney Homan (Lewisburg, PA: Bucknell University Press, 1980), 131 and 136.

8. Margreta de Grazia, *Hamlet Without Hamlet* (Cambridge: Cambridge University Press, 2007), 158, original italics.

9. Shankar Raman, "Hamlet in Motion," in *Knowing Shakespeare: Senses, Embodiment and Cognition,* ed. Lowell Gallagher and Shankar Raman (New York: Palgrave, 2010), 135.

10. *Oxford English Dictionary* (hereafter cited *OED*), 2nd ed., s.v. "speedmaking, speed, *n.,*" C5 and "speed, *v.,*" 11a; see also *OED,* 3rd ed., s.v. "make, *v.,*" IV50.

11. For a discussion of the effect of theatrical motion on early modern audiences' bodies in non-Shakespearean plays, see Skantze, *Stillness in Motion,* 3, 22–23, and 25.

12. In this paper, I focus on theatrical performance, but similar effects occurred for readers; for the relationships among reading and the stomach, body, and emotion, see Katharine A. Craik and Tanya Pollard, *Reading Sensations in Early Modern England* (New York: Palgrave, 2007). For a discussion of the relationships among contagious sickness in the theater, actors, and audiences, see Darryl Chalk, "'A nature but infected': Plague and Embodied Transformation in *Timon of Athens,*" in "Embodying Shakespeare," ed. David McInnis and Brett D. Hirsch, special issue, *Early Modern Literary Studies* 19 (2009): n.p., http://purl.oclc.org/emls/si-19/chalplag.html.

13. *Hamlet* may have been performed on a ship in 1607. For ongoing debates about whether the record for this performance is real or a forgery by J. P. Collier, see Gary Taylor, "Hamlet in Africa, 1607," in *Travel Knowledge: European "Discoveries" in the Early Modern Period,* ed. Ivo Kamps and G. Singh (New York: Palgrave, 2001); Richmond Barbour, *The Third Voyage Journals: Writing and Performance in the London East India Company* (Basingstoke: Palgrave, 2009); and Bernice W. Kliman, "At Sea about *Hamlet* at Sea: A Detective Story," *Shakespeare Quarterly* 62, no. 2 (2011): 180–204, doi:10.1353/shq.2011.0025.

14. *OED,* 2nd ed., s.v. "speed, *n.*" 3a, 5a, 6a, and 10a; and "haste, *n.,*" 1, 2, 5a, 6, and 7.

15. Marvin Spevack, *Complete and Systematic Concordance to the Works of Shakespeare,* 9 vols. (Hildesheim, Germany: Georg Olms, 1968–80), s.v. "haste"; "speed."

16. *Oth.,* 1.3.276–77. References are to act, scene, and line. All further Shake-

speare references, with the exception of those from *Hamlet* (see note 71), come from the Riverside edition and appear in the text. William Shakespeare, *Riverside Shakespeare: The Complete Works,* gen. ed. G. Blakemore Evans, with the assistance of J. J. M. Tobin, 2nd ed. (Boston: Houghton Mifflin, 1997).

17. Spevack, *Concordance,* s.v. "speed"; "haste."

18. Thomas Cooper, comp. *Bibliotheca Eliotae,* 2nd ed. (London, 1548), s.v. "properantia." When citing early texts, I have preserved spelling but normalized long "s" and expanded contractions.

19. Abraham Flemming, trans., *A Panoplie of Epistles,* 2nd ed. (London, 1576), sig. R3v.

20. Randle Cotgrave, comp., *A Dictionarie of the French and English Tongves* (London, 1611), s.v. "acceleration."

21. Church of England, *The Booke of the Common Prayer* (London, 1549), sig. A1r (the prayers are based on *Psalms* 40:13 and 70:1); "the king had great regard of expedition and making speed for the safetie of his owne person," Raphael Holinshed, *The Chronicles of England, from William the Conquerour . . . vntill the Yeare 1577,* rev. ed. ([London?], 1585), sig. 3E1v; "we must make speede by our diligent and continuall reading of histories," Plutarch, *Lives of the Noble Grecians and Romanes,* trans. Thomas North (London, 1579), sig. *5r; Terence, *Floweres or Eloquent Phrases of the Latine Speach,* comp. Nicholas Udall (London, 1581), sig. 2D1v; "make speede apace if from our land thou get thee not away," *Seneca His Tenne Tragedies, Translated into Englysh,* trans. Thomas Newton (London, 1581), sig. R2r; "the king being required to make speede," John Foxe, *Actes and Monuments* (London, 1583), sig. N1r; "The messenger made speede," Philip Sidney, *Countesse of Pembrokes Arcadia* (London, 1590), sig. 2P2v; "they make speed unto the campe," *The Romane Historie Written by T. Livius of Padua* (London, 1600), sig. 2B1v; "in haste, and to makespeede [*sic*], he [a Souldier] would ordinarily swimme over al the Rivers hee met," Michel de Montaigne, *Essayes* (London, 1613), sig. 2P4r; Thomas Kyd, *The Spanish Tragedie,* 2nd ed. (London, 1592), sig. K2r, original italics. For books Shakespeare knew, see Stuart Gillespie's entries for *The Book of Common Prayer,* Holinshed, Plutarch, Terence, Foxe, and Montaigne in *Shakespeare's Books: A Dictionary of Shakespeare Sources* (London: Athlone, 2001); for *Hamlet* allusions to Seneca, Sidney, Livy, and Kyd, see Geoffrey Bullough, ed., "Hamlet," in *Major Tragedies: Hamlet, Othello, Lear, Macbeth,* vol. 7 of *Narrative and Dramatic Sources of Shakespeare* (London: Routledge, 1973): 3–189. Some plays that refer to "making speed" or "making haste" include Christopher Marlowe, *Tamburlaine,* 2nd ed. (London, 1590); Robert Wilson, *Three Ladies of London* (London, 1592); *The Lamentable and Trve Tragedie of M. Arden of Feuersham in Kent,* 2nd ed. (London, 1592); Thomas Lodge, *Looking Glasse of London and England* (London, 1594); Thomas Dekker, *Shoemakers Holiday* (London, 1600); Ben Jonson, *Cynthias Revels* (London, 1601); and Michael Drayton and George Chapman, *The True Chronicle History of King Leir* (London, 1605).

22. Spevack, *Concordance,* s.v. "haste"; "speed."

23. Joseph A. Amato, *On Foot: A History of Walking* (New York: New York University Press, 2004), 73; see also 75, 85–86, and 100.

24. R. McNeill Alexander, "Walking, Running, and Hopping," chap. 7 in *Principles of Animal Locomotion* (Princeton, NJ: Princeton University Press, 2003), 103 and 129; see especially his section "Speed," 103–9.

25. Karen Raber and Treva J. Tucker, introduction to *Culture of the Horse: Status, Discipline, and Identity in the Early Modern World,* ed. Karen Raber and Treva J. Tucker (New York: Palgrave, 2005), 1; for the preference of speedier horse riding to walking, see Amato, *On Foot,* 69 and 60–61.

26. Alexander, "Walking, Running, and Hopping," 103 and 128–129.

27. Claudio Corte, *The Art of Riding* (London, 1584), sigs. H1v and D4r. For the eighteenth-century love of "expedition" leading to "a truly British invention: rising to the trot," see Donna Landry, "Learning to Ride in Early Modern Britain," in *Culture of the Horse: Status, Discipline, and Identity in the Early Modern World,* ed. Karen Raber and Treva J. Tucker (New York: Palgrave, 2005), 341–42.

28. Raber and Tucker, introduction, 26 and 32; Richard Nash, "The Thoroughbred as Cultural Metaphor," in *Culture of the Horse: Status, Discipline, and Identity in the Early Modern World,* ed. Karen Raber and Treva J. Tucker (New York: Palgrave, 2005), 265. Amato calls horse racing the "quintessence of land speed until the advent of the train" (*On Foot,* 95); sixteenth-century carriages also became faster (*On Foot,* 77).

29. Raber and Tucker, introduction, 28; see also Barbara D. Palmer, "Early Modern Mobility: Players, Payments, and Patrons," *Shakespeare Quarterly* 56, no. 3 (2005): 259–305, 287, doi:10.1353/shq.2006.0010.

30. Peter Ackroyd, *Thames: The Biography* (New York: Doubleday, 2007), 4–5; for traffic jams, see 103; for claims that the river has not altered over centuries, see 14.

31. Arthur Nelson, *The Tudor Navy: The Ships, Men and Organisation, 1485–1603* (London: Conway Maritime, 2001), 88 and 101.

32. Ibid., 100.

33. Peter Kemp, ed., *Encyclopedia of Ships and Seafaring* (London: Stanford Maritime, 1980), 209; see also Pierre Barjot and Jean Savant, *History of the World's Shipping,* trans. Carol Tomkins (London: Allan, 1965), 65.

34. Nelson, *Tudor Navy,* 101; for ship names, see 102–3; for the ship-name the *Make-Speede,* see Richard Hakluyt, *Principal Navigations* (London, 1599), sig. 3F2v.

35. Joseph Swetnam, *The Schoole of the Noble and Worthy Science of Defence* (London, 1617), original italics.

36. William Rastell, *A Table Collected of the Yeres of our Lorde God, and of the Yeres of the Kynges of Englande,* 2nd ed. (London, 1558).

37. John Blagrave, *The Mathematical Ievvel* (London, 1585).

38. Timoth[i]e Bright, *Characterie: An Arte of Shorte, Swifte, and Secret Writing by Character* (London, 1588); Peter Bales, *The Writing Schoolemaster* (London, 1590).

39. I. W., *A Speedie Post* (London, 1625).

40. James Daybell, *The Material Letter in Early Modern England* (New York: Palgrave, 2012), 47.

41. Sara Jayne Steen, "Reading Beyond the Words: Material Letters and the Process of Interpretation." *QUIDDITAS* 22 (2001): 55–69, 59, http://humanities.byu.edu/rmmra/pdfs/22.pdf.

42. Mark Brayshay, Philip Harrison, and Brian Chalkley, "Knowledge, Nationhood, and Governance: The Speed of the Royal Post in Early-Modern England," *Journal of Historical Geography* 24, no. 3 (1998): 265–88, 275.

43. Edward Nicholas to Henry Vane, 18 August 1641, in *Nicholas Papers,* ed. George F. Warner (Westminster: Camden Society, 1886), 1:17.

44. Charles Cornwallis to Robert Cecil, 1 June 1609, in *Memorials of Affairs of State in the Reigns of Q. Elizabeth and K. James I,* ed. Edmund Sawyer (London, 1727), 3:48, Eighteenth Century Collections Online (CB130089784).

45. Gary Schneider, *Culture of Epistolarity* (Wilmington: University of Delaware, 2005), 36; see also Daybell, *Material Letter,* 134.

46. A. J. Loomie, "Carey, Robert, first earl of Monmouth (1560–1639)," in *Oxford Dictionary of National Biography* (Oxford: Oxford University Press, 2004–14), n. p., doi:10.1093/ref:odnb/4656.

47. Ibid.

48. Geffrey Whitney, *A Choice of Emblems,* ed. Henry Green, facsimile of the first edition, with an introduction by Frank Fieler (1586; New York: Benjamin Blom, 1967), 6; I use Green's English translations for all emblem titles (lxxxv–lxxxix).

49. Ibid., 185.

50. Ibid., 121, 121, and 188.

51. George Wither, *A Collection of Emblemes,* facsimile of the first edition (1635; Menston, UK: Scolar Press, 1968), sig. C2r, original italics.

52. Ibid., sig. Y2r, original italics. A contemporary translation of Cicero counsels in a similar vein on literal walking rates for young men: "We must take heede also, we use neither to nyce a slownesse in our pase, like pageauntes in triumphes: neither tomuch haste in spede making, like wyldebraines" because one's distorted face and shortness of breath will lead to "a great presump-tion, that they haue no stayednesse." *Marcus Tullius Ciceroes Thre Bokes of Duties to Marcus His Sonne,* trans. Nicholas Grimalde (London, 1556), sig. G1v.

53. Wither, *Choice of Emblemes,* sig. H1r, original italics.

54. Ibid., original italics.

55. Neil Carson, *A Companion to Henslowe's Diary* (Cambridge: Cambridge University Press, 1988), 59.

56. Ibid., 74; see also Andrew Gurr, *Shakespearian Playing Companies* (Oxford: Oxford University Press, 1996), 84 and 101.

57. Carol Chillington Rutter, ed., *Documents of the Rose Playhouse* (Manchester: Manchester University Press, 1999), 28.

58. Ibid. Marchitello also makes an aside about the "enterprise of early modern theater and its machinery" as a rationale for Shakespeare's interest in speed ("*Macbeth,*" 429).

59. Gurr, *Shakespearian Playing Companies,* 46.

60. Alan C. Dessen and Leslie Thomson, *Dictionary of Stage Directions* (Cambridge: Cambridge University Press, 1999), s.v., "hastily," "suddenly," "sweating," "panting," "out of breath," "hurry," "rush," "post," and "fly."

61. Andrew Gurr, "The Shakespearean Stage," in *The Norton Shakespeare: Essential Plays,* gen. ed. Stephen Greenblatt (New York: Norton, 2009), 93. Evidence from an Evesham murder trial shows that some audiences directly took part in speed-making: "'a play . . . cryed about the Towne, whereto both old and young did hasteley repaire.'" Quoted in Alan Somerset, "The Blackfriars on Tour: Provincial Analogies," in *Inside Shakespeare: Essays on the Blackfriars Stage,* ed. Paul Menzer (Selinsgrove, PA: Susquehanna University Press, 2006), 82. Philip Stubbes observed similar behavior in 1583 in London, remarking on "'the flocking

and running to Theaters & curtens.'" Quoted in Michael J. Hirrel, "Duration of Performances and Lengths of Plays: How Shall We Beguile the Lazy Time?" *Shakespeare Quarterly* 61, no. 2 (2010): 159–82, 161, doi:10.1353/shq.0.0140.

62. Gurr, "Shakespearean Stage," 92.

63. Hirrel, "Duration of Performances," 160–61; Bruce R. Smith, "E/loco/com/motion," in *From Script to Stage in Early Modern England,* ed. Peter Holland and Stephen Orgel (Basingstroke, UK: Palgrave, 2004), 131.

64. Althea Smith Mattingly, "The Playing Time and Manner of Delivery of Shakespeare's Plays in the Elizabethan Theatre," *Speech Monographs* 21 (1954): 29–38, 37.

65. Renee Haynes, "Literary Speed Regulations," *English: The Journal of the English Association* 1, no. 4 (1936): 330–32, 330.

66. Thomas Heywood, *An Apology for Actors,* ed. Richard H. Perkinson, facsimile (1612; New York: Scholars' Facsimiles and Reprints, 1941), sig. C4r, emphasis added.

67. Ibid., sig. B4r.

68. John Northbrooke, *Spiritus est vicarius Christi in terra,* 2nd ed. (London, 1577), sigs. I2r–I2v.

69. Edward Reynolds, *A Treatise of the Passions* (London, 1640), 22, as quoted in Smith, "E/loco/com/motion," 145.

70. Scott Manning Stevens, "Sacred Heart and Secular Brain," in *The Body in Parts: Fantasies of Corporeality in Early Modern Europe,* ed. Carla Mazzio and David Hillman (New York: Routledge, 1997), 271.

71. 1.1.76–77; 1.1.106. Unless otherwise noted, all quotes from *Hamlet* derive from Quarto 2 (Q2) (1604), from the Arden 3 edition, vol. 1. William Shakespeare, *Hamlet,* ed. Ann Thompson and Neil Taylor, 2 vols., Arden Shakespeare, 3rd ser. (London: Arden, 2006). Hereafter citations appear parenthetically in-text with any differences noted from the 1623 First Folio (F1) and, occasionally, from the 1603 Quarto 1 (Q1), the latter considered by Paul Menzer a separate *Hamlet* project not for performance. *The* Hamlets*: Cues, Qs, and Remembered Texts* (Newark: University of Delaware Press, 2008), 21. All F1 and Q1 citations come from the Arden 3 edition, vol. 2. On the importance of attention to early modern language describing felt experience, see Bruce R. Smith, *Phenomenal Shakespeare* (Oxford: Wiley-Blackwell, 2010), 34; Laurie Johnson, John Sutton, and Evelyn Tribble, "Introduction: Re-cognising the Body-Mind in Shakespeare's Theatre," in *Embodied Cognition and Shakespeare's Theatre: The Early Modern Body-Mind,* ed. Laurie Johnson, John Sutton, and Evelyn Tribble (New York: Routledge, 2014), 5.

72. Spevack, *Concordance,* s.v. "speed"; "haste." For a discussion of the tragic ironies of untimely speed in *Romeo and Juliet,* see Brents Stirling, "They stumble that run fast," in *Unity in Shakespearian Tragedy: The Interplay of Theme and Character* (New York: Gordian, 1966), chap. 2.

73. *OED,* 2nd ed., s.v. "course, v.," 5a.

74. Peter Holland, " 'Travelling hopefully': The Dramatic Form of Journeys in English Renaissance Drama," in *Travel and Drama in Shakespeare's Time,* ed. Jean-Pierre Maquerlot and Michele Willems (Cambridge: Cambridge University Press, 1996), 160–61.

75. *OED,* 2nd ed., s.v. "presently."

76. Gary Scrimgeour, "The Messenger as a Dramatic Device in Shakespeare," *Shakespeare Quarterly* 19, no. 1 (1968): 41–54, 46, doi:10.2307/2867841.

77. John Russell Brown, *Shakespeare and the Theatrical Event* (New York: Palgrave, 2002), 27.

78. Ibid., 39, emphasis added.

79. Charles Mazel, *Heave-Ho* (New York: Routledge, 1995), i.

80. Ibid.

81. Brown, *Theatrical Event,* 58; see also Hapgood, "Shakespeare's Choreography," 140.

82. Raman asserts that abrupt action like this is not "the norm for most of the play" ("Hamlet in Motion," 136); but, in fact, there are several moments, noteworthy for their accelerations and for onstage audiences' reactions.

83. Brown, *Theatrical Event,* 115.

84. For further discussion of the failure of Gertrude's senses in this speech, see Raman, "Hamlet in Motion," 132.

85. Alexander Cowan and Jill Steward, introduction to *The City and the Senses: Urban Culture Since 1500,* ed. Alexander Cowan and Jill Steward (Aldershot, UK: Ashgate, 2007), 9.

86. Robert Hapgood, introduction to *Hamlet, Prince of Denmark* (Cambridge: Cambridge University Press, 1999), 6–7; Claris Glick, "*Hamlet* in the English Theater: Acting Texts from Betterton (1676) to Olivier (1963)," *Shakespeare Quarterly* 20, no. 1 (1969): 17–35, 26 and 21, doi:10.2307/2868970.

87. *OED,* 2nd ed., s.v. "tardy."

88. Swapan Chakravorty, "A Note on 'Women Beware Women' II.iii.469–477," *Notes and Queries* 41, no. 4 (December 1994): 514, 514, Gale Expanded Academic ASAP (A16452749).

89. Quoted in Chakravorty, "A Note."

90. William Langham, *The Garden of Health* (London, 1597), s.v. "Wormewood."

91. Joseph Acosta from 1588, quoted in Samuel Purchas, *Pvrchas His Pilgrimes in Five Bookes: The Third Part* (London, 1625), sigs. 4G4v–4G5r.

92. *The Naval Tracts of Sir William Monson,* ed. M. Oppenheim (Colchester, UK: Navy Records Society, 1913), 3:434.

93. Thompson and Taylor, *Hamlet,* 1:310n175.

94. Thompson and Taylor, *Hamlet;* Menzer, *The* Hamlets; Zachary Lesser, *Hamlet After Q1* (Philadelphia: University of Pennsylvania Press, 2015). For an excellent comparison of all three basic *Hamlet* texts, see Paul Bertram and Bernice W. Kliman, eds., *The Three-Text Hamlet: Parallel Texts of the First and Second Quartos and First Folio* (New York: AMS, 1991).

95. See, for example, Marchitello, "*Macbeth,*" 430 and 435; and Stirling, "They stumble."

"Ne'er was dream so like a waking": The Temporality of Dreaming and the Depiction of Doubt in *The Winter's Tale*

Lauren Robertson

WHEN LEONTES EXAMINES the mysterious statue of Hermione in the final scene of *The Winter's Tale,* he comments out loud on what he thinks he sees. His statements are notable not only for their attention to detail—"Would you not deem . . . that those veins / Did verily bear blood?" (5.3.64–65)—but for their tendency to resist making certain judgments about the statue: "The figure of her eye has motion in't / As we are mocked with art" (5.3.67–68).[1] What would these comments have meant for the early modern spectator watching the play in what Tiffany Stern has described as the "visually charged" environment of the theater?[2] And what effect would Leontes's words have had on the visual experience of the spectator, who, standing or sitting as much as forty feet from the stage, most likely would not have been able to see the statue with as much detail as Leontes could?[3] In *The Winter's Tale,* Shakespeare dramatizes for spectators the gradual adoption of a set of skeptical ethics, culminating in the final scene that demonstrates Leontes's refusal to make judgments based on his sense impressions and his resolution, instead, to rest in uncertainty.

Like many others, I have been deeply influenced by Stanley Cavell's brilliant readings of Shakespeare, not least his account of Leontes's turn to faith about Hermione by the end of *The Winter's Tale.* But in this essay, I want to question his claim that "If *The Winter's Tale* is understandable as a study of skepticism—that is, as a response to what skepticism is a response to—then its second half must be understandable as a study of its search for recovery," an assertion that characterizes not only the play's engagement with doubt, but much of the ongoing criticism focusing on faith and the final scene of *The Winter's Tale*.[4] Many critics have pointed to the final scene's seeming embrace of the Catholic reverence for the visual image: Gary Waller, for example, identifies Hermione with the Virgin Mary "renewed and transformed" in post-Reformation England, and Michael O'Connell argues that the scene appropriates faith in miracles for a secular setting, confirming fears of antitheatricalists and iconoclasts alike by "press[ing] an audience into idolatry."[5] Others have focused instead on the play's connection to a Reformed Pauline faith, embodied, of course, in the character of Paulina, who famously commands Leontes to "awake" his "faith" just before the statue of Hermione appears to come to life (5.3.95); Huston Diehl, for example, argues that Shakespeare deliberately appropriates the Pauline rhetoric often used by antitheatricalists to create a reformed aesthetic of the theater, maintaining that by making his Pauline figure a woman, the playwright both "arouses and counters the antitheatricalists' fears that theatre bewitches."[6] Richard McCoy draws on a Reformed understanding of the sacrament, in which change occurred "in the heart and soul of the recipient" rather than the bread and wine of the Eucharist, to argue that the play demands not religious, but poetic faith, which "requires the active and energetic participation of every onlooker, on stage and in the audience."[7] Still others have highlighted instead the seeming tension between the conflicting Protestant, Catholic, and pagan forces at the end of the play: Julia Reinhard Lupton argues that the final scene reanimates Catholic idolatry within the secular theater, its "language and visual staging at once mark[ing] and distanc[ing] the 'Christianity' of the scene as Catholic," while Walter S. H. Lim explains the play's use of countervailing religious doctrines as the staging of "early modern England's encounter with the boundaries of the (un)knowable."[8] Many of these readings link the awakening of faith in this final scene to the sense of wonder it creates for Perdita, whose profession to kneel before the statue appears dangerously close to Catholic devotional practice, and for Leontes; as Paulina comments, "I like your silence; it the more shows off / Your wonder" (5.3.21–22).[9] But to focus solely on the final scene of the play as it inspires leaps of faith, whether idolatrous or not, is to ignore, alongside his silence, Leontes's own registered skepticism about the statue, which acts as a kind of check on his sense of wonder. In his refusal to make any judgments about the statue's life-likeness, he keeps himself at a willed distance from it even as he wishes to pronounce it alive. In a play that stages a mixture of Protestant aesthetic, Catholic idolatry and worship, and classical myth, the culminating scene finally pushes past the boundary of the knowable, staging, in the statue of Hermione, a visual spectacle that can be seen, though not understood. In his reaction to the statue and the questionably miraculous and ultimately unresolved return of his wife, Leontes embraces not the faith to which Paulina urges him, but skepticism itself as an ethical code; his ability to resist making certain judgments about the statue of Hermione offers an education for the play's spectators in the process of living with, and resting in, uncertainty.

On what, then, would the early modern spectators of this play have been able to draw in order to understand and perhaps even identify with Leontes's disciplined experience of skepticism? The watershed moment for the emergence of classical skepticism in the early modern period is often said to be 1562, the year Henri Estienne translated Sextus Empiricus's second-century AD work *Outlines of Pyrrhonism* from Greek into Latin, making the principles of Pyrrhonean skepticism widely available to Europe's intellectuals.[10] By means of several examples, Sextus evokes the central tenet in the skeptical discipline of the Greek philosopher Pyrrho (c. 360–270 BC): contradictory sense impressions must lead one to uncertainty about the actual nature of anything in the external world. Sextus highlights, too, that Pyrrhonism resists the dogmatic assertion of Academic skepticism that nothing at all can be known and instead strives for the tranquility, or *ataraxia,* that comes as a result of resting in one's own uncertainty.[11] While Pyrrhonism as Sextus described it and as it was reconsidered and reimagined in the early modern era is crucial to *The Winter's Tale,* I wish in this essay to consider alongside the skepticism of the intellectual elite the less erudite uncertainties that early modern English theatergoers would have brought with them into the playhouse, and in return, how Shakespeare engages, displays, and questions those associations in this play. Early modern drama actively engaged spectators' beliefs about the uncertainties of vision by shaping their experiences of sight. Since, as Erika T. Lin argues, "[Drama] both represents material reality and constructs the interpretive principles through which that reality is to be understood," early modern drama makes the conditions for a skeptical viewing experience possible by drawing on and reinterpreting the doubts and anxieties about vision familiar to its spectators.[12] Rather than the recovery from the doubt Leontes feels about Hermione, which all too quickly

turns into his certainty that she has been unfaithful, I will argue
that the point of entry into uncertainty as a skeptical problem in
The Winter's Tale is Antigonus's dream in 3.3. As Stuart Clark
points out, dreams were thought of as "primarily visual in character" from the classical era onward; in the early modern era, especially in the writing of Michel de Montaigne and René Descartes,
dreams became an epistemological problem because they were
understood as a "visual paradox—the paradox of not being able to
tell the difference between true and false visual experiences."[13]
But, we might ask, were dreams understood and experienced as
visual problems, or even paradoxes, by early modern theatergoers,
and if so, how? As Carole Levin and others have demonstrated, the
explanations for the causes of dreams were manifold and competing in the late-sixteenth and early-seventeenth centuries.[14] By
dramatizing Antigonus's uncertainty about his dream, Shakespeare
stages cultural doubts about the origin and meanings of dreams in
early modern England.

At the time Simon Forman described seeing *The Winter's Tale*
performed at the Globe Theater, in May of 1611, uncertainty about
the origin and meanings of dreams—caused by the multiple and
competing explanations for them—swirled through early modern
England. The belief that dreams could be divine in origin had certainly not yet disappeared from post-Reformation England; as Keith
Thomas notes, "vivid and repetitive dreams" were thought to be
supernatural in origin, as well as to hold prognosticatory power.[15]
As such, guides to dream interpretation were extremely popular
throughout the sixteenth and seventeenth centuries: a Latin edition
of Artemidorus' third-century CE work, *Oneirocritica,* was available in England by 1546; it was translated into English in 1606 and
went through twenty-four editions by 1740. Thomas Hill's *The
Moste Pleasaunte Arte of the Interpretacion of Dreames,* based on
Oneirocritica, was published possibly in 1558, though the earliest
extant edition was published in 1576; it went through seven editions in 50 years.[16] In the work's dedication, Hill foregrounds the
importance of distinguishing between "vain" and "true" dreams:
while true dreams forecast events to come, vain dreams simply
reflect the dreamer's state during the previous day.[17] And English
physicians had inherited a history from Aristotle onward of providing explanations for the natural causes of dreams, though in 1562,
physician William Bullein pointed to a variety of causes for dreams
in his explanation of how humoral compositions could affect their
content:

Now whether it be dreame, illusion, vision. &c. as some do say, or the effects, or works, of the fower complexions, as the cholerike man, to dreame of Fyre, fighting &c. The flegmatike, to dreame of water. &c. And so in the other two complexions, or as *Artemidorus* in hys booke of dreames sayeth, they do presage, diuine, or shew before, what thynges do follow, or come after, good or bad.[18]

An ambivalence about the cause of dreams overlays Bullein's apparent focus on the humours, typifying sixteenth-century England's cultural skepticism regarding dreams and their origins.

Thomas Nashe makes even more strongly skeptical statements about dreams in *Terrors of the Night, or a Discourse of Apparitions,* published in 1594.[19] He initially appears to take an Aristotelian position on dreaming, arguing that dreams are merely the product of thoughts remaining from the previous day, rather than apparitions of divine or demonic origin: "A dreame is nothing els but a bubling scum or froath of the fancie, which the day hath left vndigested; or an after feast made of the fragments of idle imaginations."[20] But Nashe closes his pamphlet on dreaming with an anecdote about a man who reported having "miraculous waking visions" when he lay down for the night; rather than dismissing the visions as dreams, Nashe qualifies the claims he makes earlier in his work, admitting, "whether of true melancholy or true apparition, I will not take vpon me to determine."[21] With this reservation, Nashe adopts a Pyrrhonian dispositional conclusion, ultimately refusing to offer his judgment about what the experience actually was.[22]

Though Hill, Bullein, and Nashe approach the problem of properly crediting dreams from different perspectives, all of these writers exhibit a studied ambivalence about whether dreams are produced simply by natural causes and therefore can tell the dreamer nothing meaningful, or whether they might be able to forecast future events. Clark identifies these kinds of concerns about dreams as part of an Artemidorian, or moral, tradition, while he denominates the other form of dream commentary, typified in the writing of Descartes and Montaigne (which I will examine below), as epistemological.[23] The epistemological tradition was skeptical; it was concerned with whether it was possible to distinguish dreaming from waking with certainty. Clark contends that though the Artemidorian tradition of dream commentary was much more popular than the epistemological one, "the two traditions were never entirely separate"; he further argues that in the intellectual debates of the early modern era, one finds "the possibility of their convergence."[24] While I agree wholeheartedly with Clark that the moral and epistemological concerns of early modern dream commentary converged in intellectual debates of the period, I want to stress their coexistence in popular texts about dreaming, as well. While most of these texts do not explicitly point to the problem of distinguishing dreaming from waking (though Nashe's *Terrors* is an important exception), they do seek to assign with certainty the origin of one's dreams from a range of several competing possibilities. The process, as Richard Saunders admitted in 1653, was often fraught, as "many dreams are ambiguous, double sensed, incertain, and doubtful."[25] The desire to determine the origins of one's dreams thus shares the epistemological concerns of distinguishing dreaming from waking: is it possible to discern the source of a dream—whether divine or natural, true or false—and if so, how does one do it? These are epistemological questions, and in order to answer them, as Levin explains, early modern writers on dreams "tried to develop criteria by which someone could tell if the dream came from the devil, from God and the angels, or simply from severe indigestion."[26] In other words, the popular uncertainties of the Artemidorian tradition of dream commentary were not distinct from the intellectual skepticisms of Montaigne or Descartes; they occupied the same epistemological register.

In the years before Descartes conducted the famous thought experiment recorded in his First Meditation, a skeptical exercise that took as one of its starting points his inability to distinguish between his dreaming and waking states, it was Montaigne who treated dreaming most seriously as a skeptical problem.[27] Though Montaigne's writing on dreams is less likely to have been part of the early seventeenth-century theatergoer's constellation of associations with dreams than the medical, divine, and prognosticatory explanations for them, even after the publication of John Florio's English translation of the *Essayes* in 1603, the French philosopher's writing did directly influence Shakespeare. It has been well established that the playwright was a reader of Montaigne; his nearly direct borrowings from Florio's translation in *The Tempest* demonstrate this relationship most clearly. Shakespeare does not appear to borrow directly from Montaigne's writing on dreams, yet his dramatization of an ambiguous dream vision in *The Winter's Tale* is given special resonance when placed next to Montaigne's writing because both authors treat carefully the specific complexity of incorporating one's dreams into waking life while at once attempting to maintain a clear distinction between the two states.[28] Before turning to Shakespeare's dramatization of dreaming in *The Winter's Tale,* I will first consider how, for Montaigne, dreams blur the border that divides them from waking life.

As he does elsewhere in his work, Montaigne treats the muddled difference between dreaming and waking explicitly in "Of the Lame or Cripple" (an essay which considers more generally the influence of the mind on unreliable sense impressions), where he relates a story about a man who dreamed he was a packhorse, and as a result, became one.[29] The story causes Montaigne to allow for the possibility that dreams can have material consequences for the dreamer, so that "dreames may sometimes be thus incorporated into effects."[30] Even so, Montaigne resists simply equating the material effect of dreams—in other words, their continuation into waking life—with the willed actions of waking reality: "I cannot possibly believe," he maintains, "that our wil should [during dreams made real] therefore be bound to the lawes and justice."[31] His relation of this story is a concise representation of his interest in dreams throughout the *Essayes:* over and over again, he focuses on dreams as they appear in one's waking life; they are relics of past experience, distinctive in kind from waking life, yet curiously mingled with it.

Though Montaigne refuses to simply *equate* dreaming with waking, he does take a position more skeptical than that held by conventional early modern natural philosophy when he contends that the commixture of dreams with waking life blurs the distinction between the two states.[32] In "An Apologie of Raymond Sebond," Montaigne claims, "When we dreame, our soule liveth, worketh and exerciseth all hir faculties even, and as much, as when it waketh; and if more softly, and obscurely; yet verely not so, as that it may admitte so great a difference, as there is betweene a darke night and a cleare day: Yea as betweene a night and a shadow."[33] In this formulation, the soul's operation while one is dreaming is not clearly distinguishable from its operation while one is awake. The result, however, is not that dreaming approximates waking life, but instead, that waking life starts to seem more like dreaming: the clearness of waking life becomes obscured by shadow. Here, the dream invades waking life as it does in "Of the Lame or Cripple"; it muddles the distinction between waking life and dreaming by making the activity of the soul while one is awake resemble that of a dream. But even though dreaming may parallel waking experience as it happens, the process of *recollecting* that experience after one is awake is extremely fraught, as Montaigne describes in "Vpon Some Verses of Virgill": "The next morning, I can well call to minde what colour they [the dreams] were of, whether blyth, sad, or strange; but what in substance, the more I labour to finde out, the more I ouerwhelme them in obliuion."[34] Although Montaigne attempts to make his dreams a part of waking life through recollection, he cannot do so clearly and completely; he recollects the atmosphere of his dreams rather than their content. Enough of his dreams remain in his memory that he continues to try to recall them, but to no avail. As they are faintly remembered in waking life, dreams continue to exist with a paradoxically ambiguous autonomy even while they are reconciled with waking experience.

Shakespeare's depiction of dreaming in *The Winter's Tale* is built upon the complex circulation of information, associations, and uncertainty about dreams—as well as the ambiguity of the passage from dreaming to waking, a familiar experience whether or not one had read Montaigne—that would have followed early modern spectators into the playhouse.[35] Shakespeare devotes the most extended attention to dreaming in the play in 3.3, in which Antigonus describes a dream vision: the ghost of Hermione appeared to him, he reports, and commanded him to leave the infant Perdita in Bohemia. Antigonus's recounted dream resembles the many prognosticatory dreams that, as Marjorie Garber notes, forecast future events in Shakespeare's early works.[36] At the same time, however, the dream appears to be simply a repetition of Leontes's earlier command that Perdita be abandoned in "some remote and desert place" (2.2.174), and in this sense, coheres with the natural philosophical theory that dreams were composed out of the material of the previous day. Is the dream prognosticatory, then, or merely repetitive? From the very beginning of Antigonus's report there is tension about what function his dream vision fulfills, which, by the end of it, is only intensified. For though Antigonus's report *feels* repetitive, it does reveal one new piece of information, in addition to giving Perdita her name: by bringing Leontes's already-stated command into the present moment of the play, Antigonus's dream specifies its location—Bohemia. The play's shift to the pastoral setting of Bohemia thus occurs within this ambivalent middle ground of dreaming, in which the origins of waking action become curiously unclear: had Antigonus already planned to leave Perdita in Bohemia, or did he make the trip in order to obey his dream vision? Would the carrying out of such orders even be possible, given that Antigonus says his dream occurred only the night before? How long is the journey from Sicilia to Bohemia's nonexistent shores? As it does with many others, *The Winter's Tale* leaves these questions resolutely unanswered, rendering what initially appears to be either a prognosticatory dream vision or the mere repetition of past events something else entirely unclear: *what* Antigonus's experience was, though he remembers it so vividly, is uncertain.

Antigonus's dream description illuminates neither past nor future events of the play, then, but his present uncertainty about his sleeping or waking state when he saw the figure of Hermione.[37] At stake at this moment of the play is Antigonus's doubt about the nature of what he has seen, not the content of the command uttered by (the real or false) queen. By overlaying Antigonus's uncertainty about his waking state onto the tests of determining Perdita's origin, as well as whether or not to save her (both of which Antigonus conspicuously fails), Shakespeare translates the morally uncertain moment into one of radical epistemological doubt.[38] In describing his dream, Antigonus quickly qualifies his assertion that he does not believe in ghosts by acknowledging that what he saw was nearly undeniably real: "ne'er was dream / So like a waking" (3.3.17–18). Here, Antigonus registers his two opposing thoughts about his experience: either it was real, and the product of waking life, or false, and the product of a dream. As his speech goes on, he continues to entertain both possibilities.

After describing that he saw a ghost-like Hermione enter his cabin, Antigonus emphasizes that the experience not only *seemed* real, but was: "I did in time collect myself, and thought / This was so and no slumber" (3.3.37–38). But as he goes on, Antigonus complicates this assertion: "Dreams are toys, / Yet for this once, yea superstitiously, / I will be squared by this" (3.3.38–40). Antigonus's statement, "dreams are toys," coheres with his earlier assessments about what he thinks he saw, as well as his dismissal of the power and reality of dream visions. But the use of the pronoun "this" twice in lines 37–40, first in reference to what he saw as part of a waking vision, or "no slumber," and then as part of his conciliation that he will believe in dreams this once, captures Antigonus's uncertainty about the nature of his experience: was the "this" a dream or (more unlikely) a waking vision? The ambiguity of the pronoun enacts Antigonus's epistemological confusion by grammatically muddling the distinction between dreaming and waking, casting the two states in the same light even as Antigonus tries to maintain their separation. Though it lacks the circumstantial consideration of Sextus Empiricus or the systematic inquiry of Descartes, Antigonus's delay in coming to the reluctant conclusion that Hermione's appearance was a true experience to be obeyed is a skeptical performance of its own, a willed consideration of opposed possibilities in relation to each other that exposes the difficulty of discerning the difference between dreaming and waking.

But Antigonus's uncertainty does not emerge immediately; his doubt becomes clear to him only after he pauses to analyze what he has seen. He indicates that his first, immediate reaction to what he saw was fear, and that it took some time for him to be able to question the validity of his dream: "Affrighted much, / I did in time collect myself" (3.3.36–37). His seemingly straightforward explanation deserves further examination. What does it mean to "collect oneself" after a dream, and what are the constituent parts collected? To gather together the pieces of one's own experience in this context suggests a process of recollection similar to Montaigne's attempt to bring his dreams into his waking life. The "vaine image[s]" Montaigne recalls from his dreams, I want to argue, express the same kind of doubt Antigonus feels regarding his own dream; he knows he has seen *something*, but he cannot collect, with his waking mind, enough information about the nature of what he has seen to rid himself completely of his uncertainty about whether he was awake or asleep when he saw Hermione. Is it possible, then, that what Antigonus calls the collection of the self is really a gradual collection of doubt, the gathering of uncertainty into the waking mind?

It is a strange notion, but one that I think is further supported by Montaigne's description of a self that is collected, but not single or coherent: "My selfe, who professe nothing else, finde therein so bottomlesse a depth, and infinit a varietie, that my apprentisage hath no other fruit, than to make me perceive how much more there remaineth for me to learne."[39] This formulation of the self as variously composite is striking when placed next to Antigonus's description of a self composed through collection. This collection process, the composition of the self to which Antigonus alludes, is very much analogous to the process of waking up: it is the storage of the pieces of a dream one can still recall in the memory—the collection of those pieces to become a part of one's waking life—while it is, at the same time, the recognition that a complete collection of the dream into one's waking life is not possible. In this sense, the self is composed *both* by parts of one's waking life and dreaming life, and the necessarily incomplete collection that results cannot but engender doubt about the nature of one's own existence.

What are the consequences of this kind of unsettling waking experience, one that is figured as a collection of doubt, rather than certainty? The main plot of *The Winter's Tale,* of course, is overtly concerned with doubt, specifically, as Cavell has famously put it, Cartesian skepticism about one's own existence transformed into moral doubt about others: "The matter for drama . . . is to investigate the finding of a wife *not* in empirical fact lost, but, let me say, transcendentally lost, lost just because one is blind to her—as it were conceptually unprepared for her—because one is blind to himself, lost to himself."[40] In this case, we might ask: how does Leontes's doubt about Hermione fit into his waking life? Is there a clear distinction between Leontes's waking and dreaming states, or is the line between them blurred? Leontes does not explicitly describe his dreams anywhere in the play, as Antigonus does; however, during her trial, Hermione describes her own waking existence as Leontes's dream:

> Hermione
>   You speak a language that I understand not.
>   My life stands in the level of your dreams,
>   Which I'll lay down.
> Leontes   Your actions are my dreams.
>   You had a bastard by Polixenes,
>   And I but dreamed it.
>
>   (3.2.78–82)

Hermione's allusion to archery—"level" refers to the target at which the archer aims—calls to mind Leontes's lines in 2.3, when he admits he cannot punish Polixenes: "The harlot king / Is quite beyond mine arm, out of the blank / And level of my brain; plot-proof" (2.3.4–6). But Hermione, Leontes asserts, "I can hook to me" (2.3.6), and his sneering retort in 3.2 is a demonstration of his arrow aimed and shot at his wife. Standing in the level of Leontes's dreams, as Hermione acknowledges, makes her a spectacle for Leontes to observe and judge, her language in the midst of her powerful defense anticipating her appearance as a statue in the final scene of the play. Leontes's rhetorical emphasis on dreaming at this moment of the play becomes a glimpse into his own inward state; as Jennifer Lewin argues, "he [Leontes] suggests that he cannot imagine her [Hermione's] actions or Hermione herself as literally existing anywhere else but inside his own delirious mind. Her existence turns him inward because she frighteningly embodies what is uncontrollable and unknowable about other people; that is all he can know about her."[41]

Leontes insists over and over again in these early scenes on the veracity of his senses, as if to imply that his certainty about Hermione's infidelity is firmly part of waking reality and *not* the product of a dream. His derisive denial of any existence for Hermione beyond the level of his brain, however, is a crucial lynchpin in his transition from moral doubt about her to certainty that she has been unfaithful. What is it about Hermione's actions as his dreams that affords Leontes this confidence? In "Dreaming, Motion, and Meaning: Oneiric Transport in Seventeenth-century Europe," Mary Baine Campbell describes the kind of knowledge dreams, and especially prophetic dreams, were thought to offer. She centers her investigation on descriptions of dreams given by Jerome Cardano, the Italian mathematician and astrologer, and Descartes, whose series of prophetic dreams in 1619 are now described as the catalyst that set him down the road to developing his new science. According to Campbell, Cardano's dreams "invoke a form of the interpretive sublime,"[42] not unlike Descartes's formulation of "clear and distinct perception" in his Third Meditation.[43] In her estimation, these dreams created the tantalizing possibility of direct and immediate knowledge that did not require the passage of time to become apparent and certain: "It is an epistemological desire [. . .] to know instantly and without mediation, the desire of the mind to move at the speed of light."[44] For Leontes, the dream seems to offer the possibility of knowledge that does not require time to pass and unfold, to make clear gradually the information necessary to make sound judgments, or even to rest in the recognition of one's own uncertainty.[45] Dreams allow one instantaneous knowledge, and more importantly, they allow the dreamer complete certainty; as Lewin argues, Leontes's "former self becomes the dreaming self, the self dreaming of omniscience because it deeply fears its own shortcomings."[46] While Antigonus' recognition of doubt is concomitant with the process of waking, in describing

Hermione's existence as his dream, Leontes remains firmly within a world where the possibility of unmediated, instantaneous knowledge still seems attainable. His error in judgment about Hermione's infidelity, then, happens in a kind of dream state; Leontes does not allow enough time to pass for him to recognize the essential uncertainty surrounding the question he asks about his wife.

The experience of time and the doubt that results is, from the play's opening scenes, folded into the very mechanisms of theatrical representation in *The Winter's Tale.* Though the first scene of the play refers to Polixenes's stay in Sicilia in terms that evoke a timeless, continuous present—"they have seemed to be together, though absent; shook hands as over a vast; and embraced as it were from the ends of opposed winds" (1.1.28–31)—Polixenes's statement at the opening of the second scene that "Nine changes of the watery star hath been / The shepherd's note since we have left our throne" (1.2.1–2) abruptly reveals that nine months have passed between his arrival in Sicilia and the present moment of the play. In a play where much fuss will later be made over a gap in time, one feels as if this first gap has been deliberately passed over without mention. The visual spectacle of the scene, however, invites spectators to fill it in. For Hermione is also onstage in 1.2, conspicuously nine months pregnant; the effect of Polixenes's words at this moment is to raise, in the minds of the audience watching and listening to the play, the uncomfortable thought that perhaps Hermione *is* pregnant by Polixenes, that she has been unfaithful to her husband. And this, of course, is exactly the same thought that Leontes has about her, which he makes clear as he comments on her interactions with Polixenes to Camillo:

> Is whispering nothing?
> Is leaning cheek to cheek? Is meeting noses?
> Kissing with inside lip? Stopping the career
> Of laughter with a sigh?—A note infallible
> Of breaking honesty.

> (1.2.282–86)

The emphasis on Hermione's advanced pregnancy, combined with Leontes's own registered judgment that her interactions with Polixenes are sinister rather than innocent, demonstrates for audience members what Hermione looks like *to Leontes:* an unfaithful wife, about to give birth to a bastard. The layering of Leontes's perspective over the one afforded the spectators from their positions in the theater invites them, with Leontes's guidance, to view Hermione as a spectacle, though in this moment, what he purports to see goes beyond the external and visual to make a judgment about her inward state. His perspective, in other words, finds in the visual spectacle of Hermione the ocular proof of her infidelity.[47]

The perspective from which Leontes and the play's spectators view Hermione does not remain shared for long, however; spectators quickly become obliged to rethink and reject Leontes's visual interpretation of Hermione's behavior and pregnant body. The spectators of the play are left, then, with two distinct perceptions of—and judgments about—Hermione that cannot be reconciled with each other. In this visual and interpretive irreconcilability, Shakespeare dramatizes how the same thing can look different to two different sets of eyes; the moment stages, in other words, skeptical spectatorship. The author of a short essay called *The Sceptick,* first published in 1651 though likely circulated at the close of the sixteenth century, makes the case for exactly this kind of uncertain seeing; using a skeptical topos drawn from Sextus' *Outlines,* he argues that objective knowledge cannot be guaranteed by sight because the eyes, as instruments of vision, vary from viewer to viewer: "As these instruments [of sense] are affected as disposed, so doth the imagination conceit that which by them is connexed unto it. That very object which seemeth unto us white, unto them which have the jaundice seemeth pale, and red unto those whose eyes are bloodshot."[48] Different eyes necessarily offer different sense impressions to the imagination. The opening of the second scene of *The Winter's Tale* is a dramatization of exactly this problem; for the skeptical spectators of this play, as they first doubt Hermione's faithfulness then come to believe it, the force of this argument is that the eyes are not guarantors of certain knowledge. Leontes's error, then, is his belief that what he imagines to be true about Hermione is objective, certain, and not dependent on subjective and variable sight.

What happens to Leontes, then, after he allows himself to consider the possibility that his wife has been unfaithful to him? Shakespeare dramatizes the speed at which Leontes's mind moves after his doubt about Hermione is realized in lines that are often cited as some of the most notoriously difficult to parse in his work. After looking at his son, he addresses the possibility that his doubt may be the product of his own mind:

> May't be
> Affection?—Thy intention stabs the centre,
> Thou dost make possible things not so held,
> *Communicat'st with dreams*—how can this be?—
> With what's unreal thou coactive art,
> And fellow'st nothing. Then 'tis very credent
> Thou mayst co-join with something, and thou dost,
> And that beyond commission, and I find it,
> And that to the infection of my brains
> And hard'ning of my brows.
>
> (1.2.137–46, emphasis mine)

Leontes suggests that though jealousy may join with something unreal, and thereby make it believable, it can also hook itself to something real (as Leontes later vows to do to Hermione), confirming the truth of the jealous experience. The veiled meaning and difficult syntax of these lines, combined with the abruptly jarring shift to the direct address to Affection, dramatize a condition of the mind that Montaigne argues is common to everyone: "Men misacknowledge the naturall infirmitie of their minde. She doth but quest and firret, and vncessantly goeth turning, winding, building and entangling her selfe in hir owne worke; as doe our silkewormes, and therein stiffleth hirselfe."[49] In Montaigne's argument, the incessant, and inherent, turning of the mind prevents one from coming to certainty. Leontes's doubt is dramatically registered in this scene, but he does not recognize it as a natural infirmity of his mind, or, in other words, a necessary part of his waking life. While Antigonus recognizes the necessity of his doubt in the time that passes as he wakes up, Leontes asserts his immediate certainty lies in his mind's communication with dreams. Leontes's doubt and jealousy are not simply represented as an increase in the speed of the working of his mind, then, but as an abrupt leap forward into a dream. Campbell makes this point clear: "The dream is seen as having leapt years of earthly time and experience, fast-forwarding to a time the still-inexperienced reason may *know* but not yet *understand*."[50] Leontes's leap forward in time, an attempt to know with certainty a fact about Hermione that he cannot, is a break with his waking existence and an entry into a dream. And because her life remains at the level of his dreams during and after her trial, even after the presentation of the oracle that pronounces her innocent, he does not go through a process of awakening to recognize the irresolvable uncertainty surrounding the question he asks. For Leontes, the dream's promise of immediate access to knowledge obfuscates the doubt that, as it moves through time, waking life necessarily creates.

The Winter's Tale, of course, covers the passage of an extraordinarily large amount of time, though its spectators are only allowed to glimpse the beginning and end of the sixteen years the plot encompasses. As Cavell points out, the personified figure of Time who emerges in the play's fourth act "may present itself as a good-humored old man, but what he speaks about in his appearance as Chorus in this play is his lapse, his being spent, as if behind our backs."[51] How, then, might Time's own assertions cohere with the play's earlier dramatizations of the desire for instantaneous certainty in dreams and the counteracting collection of doubt through waking life? Time asserts that a wide gap of time in the play will be passed over, and also that the errors made in the first half of the play will be unfolded—in other words, revealed or made clear, or in a moral sense, made right—in the second half. But the unfolding of error, along with the promise of wrongs made right, carries with it a visual connotation of extension and increase, one that implies not a *solution* to error, but instead, its very opposite: the display of error increased in its enormity and left unresolved. As I shall argue, the end of *The Winter's Tale* confronts the sixteen years folded up by Time's gap, unfolding the very errors of the first half of the play by transforming them into the visual spectacle of the statue of Hermione, which Leontes admits, in his reluctance to claim that it is alive, is unknowable. Rather than providing, finally, a sense of certainty, the last scene of the play instead exposes not just the failure of the dream to provide immediate knowledge, but the inevitability of doubt in the waking passage of time.[52]

In act 5 of the play, the status of Hermione's existence, much like that of her fidelity as it is located in her visible pregnancy in 1.2, is uncertain, though on this occasion the question seems like it should not inspire any doubt at all: has she remained in hiding during her sixteen-year absence from the world of the play, or has she died and come back to life? As Leonard Barkan argues, the question seems like one that could have been easily resolved, and the answer to why Shakespeare instead "run[s] such risks with dramatic verisimilitude" lies in "the significance of a statue that comes to life."[53] For my purposes, however, the importance of Shakespeare's risk lies in exactly its ability to make possible an impossibility, and as a result, to call into question the most basic assumptions about one's ability to be certain about anything, both on the part of the characters in the play, as well as the spectators watching it. As I mentioned at the opening of this essay, Leontes comments on his perception of the statue of Hermione with astonishing clarity—he famously remarks that "Hermione was not so much wrinkled, nothing / So aged as this seems" (5.3.28–29) and asks "Would you not deem it breathed, and that those veins / Did verily bear blood?" (5.3.64–65)—but more noteworthy is his resistance to making any final judgment about whether the statue is alive or not. He frames all of his comments about the statue as questions or statements of seeming, drawing attention to the liveliness of the statue while at once retreating from such a possibility. But these comments do more than simply register Leontes's own skepticism; they direct and shape the viewing experience of spectators as they look at the statue, as well. Just as 1.2 put Hermione on display as she appeared to Leontes, the final scene of the play once again allows spectators to see the statue as he does, though at this moment, his descriptive language encourages spectators to view the seeming liveliness of the statue with a concurrent and unrelenting awareness of the deceptive quality of appearances. Leontes's vision registers the spectacular ambiguity of the statue—which seems at once actually alive and merely art's mocking version of liveliness—and allows spectators themselves to look, to borrow language from another one of Shakespeare's plays, "with parted eye, when everything seems double" (4.1.188–89).[54] This mode of seeing, "with parted eye," is strikingly similar to sight as it is described in *The Sceptick:* from one perspective, the statue looks alive; from another, it does not. It is also exactly the kind of seeing Leontes himself denigrated as he observed Hermione in 1.2, calling Camillo a "hovering temporizer" as a response to Camillo's unwillingness to confirm Hermione's infidelity and instead "with thine eyes at once see good and evil, / Inclining them to both" (1.2.300–303). The doubled seeing that produces uncertainty occurs, as Leontes indicates in his insult, through time. The dramatization of Leontes's uncertainty about the nature of the statue, his own drawn-out hovering over whether or not it is alive, is thus a final instruction in the play's education in the ethics of skeptical vision: the intricacy of his description, combined with his unwillingness to make any perceptual judgments about the statue, enacts the experience of uncertainty for spectators through Leontes's eyes. To see doubly, as the result of doubt accumulated over time, is to see skeptically.

What, then, does Leontes's uncertain perspective, shared by the spectators of the play through his commentary on what he sees, mean for the onstage spectacle of the statue of Hermione? Barkan points to Hermione's necessary fragmentation in his argument about the rediscovery of and fascination with antique sculpture in the Renaissance. He defines the fragment as that which "has been robbed of its completeness by time"; even complete works, he argues, "become fragments if they brandish an identity without fully revealing it."[55] Even after she is re-presented to the world of the play as alive after sixteen years of absence, the nature of Hermione's absence and return is not fully revealed. The only indication Hermione gives of where she has been for the past sixteen years is to tell Perdita that she has "preserved" herself, but it is unclear what that word means in this context (5.3.127); Hermione certainly does not clearly answer the question of whether or not she has died or remained alive while absent from the world of the play.[56] Her reticence contributes to an identity that is not, and cannot be, known completely, although it has been presented—even brandished—on the stage in the form of a statue. In this sense, the last scene of the play is the visual presentation, and analysis, of the fragmentation of one's existence by time as a necessary condition of living in and through it. Hermione's continuity has been fractured as a result of living in time, and when she returns to the world of the play, she must come back as a fragment—essentially unknowable, even as she is displayed onstage as a spectacle.

The final scene of the play dramatizes Leontes's recognition of his own uncertainty about Hermione in the form of his self-conscious statements of doubt regarding the nature of the statue. His awakening, then, coincides with Hermione's; the process by which Antigonus describes collecting himself in time in act 3 is exactly what Leontes does regarding Hermione in this scene, and this is exactly what he could not do sixteen years earlier.[57] And it is no accident that Hermione's "awakening" is a spectacular occurrence that, in itself, reveals nothing about the nature of her disappearance: the awakening registers this gap in knowledge and makes no effort to close it. Though Leontes sees it happen, it remains unclear what the awakening means. This, of course, is not the only perspective given to the presentation and awakening of Hermione's statue: for Paulina, the occasion is an opportunity to "awake [one's] faith" (5.3.95).[58] But as Kathryn Lynch argues, Shakespeare's radical skepticism finds "finally an opening for the possibility of belief, and belief that finds its grounds within, rather than outside, itself."[59] This possibility of belief within the confines of skepticism, as dramatically represented in *The Winter's Tale,* is the recognition and collection of doubt throughout one's waking existence. So while Paulina's words are an ethical prescription, they are not a description of what is visually presented onstage in the figure of Hermione. Her very presence announces an existence that cannot be fully known by others, an uncertainty that is a necessary consequence of an existence lived through time. Indeed, even the focus on Hermione's wrinkles seems to highlight this fact; when Leontes observes that "Hermione was not so much wrinkled, nothing / So aged as this seems" (5.3.28–29), he draws attention not only to the amount of time that has passed in the world of the play, but to the folding-in and recession of Hermione's own outward and visually discernable appearance.[60] Her wrinkles are the visual version of the sixteen-year gap in the play, but they are also a reminder that, though the dream holds the desirable promise of transcendent, immediate knowledge, in its movement through time, waking life is pervaded by essential and irreparable uncertainty.

Notes

1. Citations from William Shakespeare, *The Winter's Tale,* ed. John Pitcher (London: Arden Shakespeare, 2010).

2. Tiffany Stern, " 'This Wide and Universal Theatre': The Theatre as Prop in Shakespeare's Metadrama," in *Shakespeare's Theatres and the Effects of Performance,* ed. Farrah Karim-Cooper and Tiffany Stern (London: Arden Shakespeare, 2013), 13.

3. For more on the dimensions of early modern theaters, see Mariko Ichikawa, *The Shakespearean Stage Space* (Cambridge: Cambridge University Press, 2013), 1–17.

4. Stanley Cavell, *Disowning Knowledge in Seven Plays of Shakespeare* (Cambridge: Cambridge University Press, 2003), 198. Both David Hillman and Anita Gilman Sherman include Cavell's reading of *The Winter's Tale,* for example, in their recent studies of the play's encounters with skepticism. Hillman's work on embodiment relies heavily on Cavell's understanding of the play's ending as a return from skepticism to the social world; Hillman argues that *The Winter's Tale* "portrays the imagined recovery of a world in which language is accepted as emerging from the interior of the body and in which mutual corporeal inhabitation is a newfound possibility." See Hillman, *Shakespeare's Entrails: Belief, Scepticism and the Interior of the Body* (New York: Palgrave Macmillan, 2007), 52. Sherman, by contrast, argues that Shakespeare dramatizes in Paulina the vindictiveness of memory, which is displaced only by the "therapeutic forgetting" of skeptical wonder—what Sherman calls the "intimations of empiricism." Sher-

man, *Skepticism and Memory in Shakespeare and Donne* (New York: Palgrave
Macmillan, 2007), 65, 85. And though he does not invoke Cavell explicitly, James
A. Knapp shares his understanding of the ending of *The Winter's Tale* as a rejection of skeptical solitude: Knapp argues that the final scene of *The Winter's Tale*
stages interpretive engagement as the ethical response to the demand from another
person, maintaining that though Leontes's early judgment about Hermione is
wrong, "the fact that he makes a choice constitutes the ethical nature of his character *contra* indeterminacy, against endless deferral." While I agree that the final
scene of the play encourages interpretive judgment on the part of both Leontes
and the play's spectators, I argue that Leontes's choice ultimately to resist any
judgment about the statue is itself an ethics, not of stasis or endless deferral, but
of the acceptance of living with uncertainty. See Knapp, "Visual and Ethical Truth
in *The Winter's Tale*," *Shakespeare Quarterly* 55, no. 3 (2004): 253.

    5. Gary Waller, *The Virgin Mary in Late Medieval and Early Modern English
Literature and Popular Culture* (Cambridge: Cambridge University Press, 2011),
171; Michael O'Connell, *The Idolatrous Eye: Iconoclasm and Theater in Early-
Modern England* (New York: Oxford University Press, 2000), 141. See also David
N. Beauregard, who argues that Shakespeare "reflects a Catholic theological per-
spective" in the structure of *The Winter's Tale,* which is organized around the
"Roman Catholic sacrament of penance, following the movements of contrition,
confession, and satisfaction." Beauregard, *Catholic Theology in Shakespeare's
Plays* (Cranbury, NJ: Associated University Presses, 2008), 109.

    6. Huston Diehl, " 'Does not the stone rebuke me?': The Pauline Rebuke and
Paulina's Lawful Magic in *The Winter's Tale*," *Shakespeare and the Cultures of
Performance,* ed. Paul Yachnin and Patricia Badir (Burlington, VT: Ashgate, 2008),
76. See also Roy Battenhouse, who characterizes Paulina's embodiment of Paul as
gradual over the course of the play, arguing that "once Paulina's sense of mission
shifts from denunciation to an aiding of Leontes . . . she manifests arts characteristic of a mature pastor." Battenhouse, "Theme and Structure in *The Winter's Tale*,"
Shakespeare Survey 33 (1981): 137. By contrast, James Kuzner considers Montaig-
nian skepticism in his study of *The Winter's Tale* to argue that the version of Pauline faith that emerges in the play is "thoroughly nonconfessional," consisting
instead in the acceptance of one's own "epistemological weakness." Kuzner's
reading of the final scene focuses on Leontes's wonder regarding the statue of Hermione, a state of enrapture to which he is passively transported, and an event
"that he cannot evaluate properly but to which he means to remain faithful."
While I agree that Leontes recognizes he cannot make a judgment about the statue
and avoids doing so, I will stress that that recognition, as an ethics, continues for
Leontes past the point of wonder, registering instead as the skeptical ability both
to collect one's doubts and live with them. See Kuzner, "*The Winter's Tale*: Faith
in Law and the Law of Faith," *Exemplaria* 24, no. 3 (2012): 266, 274, 273.

    7. Richard McCoy, "Awakening Faith in *The Winter's Tale*," in *Shakespeare
and Early Modern Religion,* ed. David Loewenstein and Michael Witmore (Oxford:
Oxford University Press, 2015), 221, 227.

    8. Lupton, *Afterlives of the Saints: Hagiography, Typology, and Renaissance
Literature* (Stanford: Stanford University Press, 1996), 207; Walter S. H. Lim,
"Knowledge and Belief in *The Winter's Tale*," *Studies in English Literature* 41, no.
2 (2001): 327. While this essay does not explicitly focus on doubt in the early modern era brought on by confessional clashes, religious uncertainty was a crucial fea-

ture of the period's skepticism in both intellectual and popular cultures; indeed, Richard Popkin characterizes the Protestant Reformation as a skeptical crisis in response to the breakdown of "a criterion for true and certain religious knowledge." Popkin, *The History of Scepticism from Savonarola to Bayle* (Oxford: Oxford University Press, 2003), 3.

9. See, for example, Waller, *The Virgin Mary,* 176; Kuzner, "Faith in Law and the Law of Faith," 272; and Sherman, *Skepticism and Memory in Shakespeare and Donne,* 85. T.G. Bishop treats the subject of wonder in *The Winter's Tale* at length in *Shakespeare and the Theatre of Wonder* (Cambridge: Cambridge University Press, 1996).

10. For more on the recovery and transmission of Pyrrhonism in Renaissance Europe, see Popkin, *The History of Scepticism from Savonarola to Bayle,* 17–43; Charles Schmitt, *Cicero Scepticus: The Influence of the Academica in the Renaissance* (The Hague: Martinus Nijhoff, 1972), 18–77; and Lucio Floridi, "The Diffusion of Sextus Empiricus' Works in the Renaissance," *Journal of the History of Ideas* 56, no.1 (1995): 63–85.

11. For more on the philosophy of Pyrrhonism, see Julia Annas and Jonathan Barnes, *The Modes of Scepticism: Ancient Texts and Modern Interpretations* (Cambridge: Cambridge University Press, 1985),10–30; and Alan Bailey, *Sextus Empiricus and Pyrrhonean Scepticism* (Oxford: Clarendon Press, 2002), 119–46.

12. Erika T. Lin, "Popular Worship and Visual Paradigms in *Love's Labors Lost,*" in *Religion and Drama in Early Modern England: The Performance of Religion on the Renaissance Stage,* ed. Jane Hwang Degenhardt and Elizabeth Williamson (Aldershot: Ashgate, 2011), 92.

13. Stuart Clark, *Vanities of the Eye: Vision in Early Modern European Culture* (Oxford: Oxford University Press, 2007), 302, 303.

14. See Carole Levin, *Dreaming the English Renaissance: Politics and Desire and Court and Culture* (New York: Palgrave Macmillan, 2008), esp. 33–60. See also Peter Holland, " 'The Interpretation of Dreams' in the Renaissance," in *Reading Dreams: The Interpretation of Dreams from Chaucer to Shakespeare,* ed. Peter Brown (Oxford: Oxford University Press, 1999), 125–46; and Per Sivefors, " 'All this tractate is but a dream': The Ethics of Dream Narration in Thomas Nashe's *The Terrors of the Night,*" in *Textual Ethos Studies, or Locating Ethics,* ed. Anna Fahraeus and Ann Katrin Jonsson (Amsterdam: Rodopi, 2005), 161–74. Janine Rivière documents the growing skepticism regarding the prognosticatory power of dreams in the seventeenth century in " 'Visions of the Night': The Reform of Popular Dream Beliefs in Early Modern England," *Parergon: Journal of the Australian and New Zealand Association for Medieval and Early Modern Studies* 20, no.1 (2003): 109–38. In a similar vein, Mary Baine Campbell points to the shift in regarding dreams as experiences belonging to the realm of thought rather than embodied sight; Enlightenment philosophy's focus on mechanism, she argues, relegated the status of dreams as sources of certain knowledge merely "to that of individual physiological delusion rising from digestive vapors." Campbell, "The Inner Eye: Early Modern Dreaming and Disembodied Sight," in *Dreams, Dreamers, and Visions: The Early Modern Atlantic World,* ed. Ann Marie Plane and Leslie Tuttle (Philadelphia: University of Pennsylvania Press, 2013), 34.

15. Keith Thomas, *Religion and the Decline of Magic* (New York: Charles Scribner's Sons, 1971), 128.

16. For more on the reception of Artemidorus in the Renaissance, see S. R. F.

Price, "The Future of Dreams: From Freud to Artemidorus," *Past and Present* 113 (1986): 3–37. For an outline of the difficulties of dating Hill's work, see Holland, " 'The Interpretation of Dreams' in the Renaissance," 129 n10.

17. Thomas Hill, *The Moste Pleasaunte Arte of the Interpretacion of Dreames* (London, 1576), A2r-A2v.

18. William Bullein, *Bullein's Bulwarke of Defense against all Sicknesse, Soarenesse, and Woundes that doe Dayly Assaulte Mankinde* (London, 1562), J6v. For more on medical explanations for dreams in sixteenth- and seventeenth-century England, see Karl H. Dannenfeldt, "Sleep: Theory and Practice in the Late Renaissance," *The Journal of the History of Medicine and Allied Sciences* 41, no. 4 (1986): 414–41; and Levin, *Dreaming the English Renaissance,* 33–60.

19. Nashe, it is worth noting, was familiar with classical skepticism, and Pyrrhonism specifically. In his 1591 introduction to Philip Sidney's *Astrophel and Stella,* he mentions a recent English translation of Sextus's *Outlines.* See Thomas Nashe, Introduction to *Astrophel and Stella,* by Philip Sidney (London: Thomas Newman, 1591), A4v.

20. Thomas Nashe, *Terrors of the Night, or a Discourse of Apparitions* (London: William Jones, 1594), C3v.

21. Ibid., G1v.

22. See also Holland's account of *Terrors of the Night,* in which he points out that Nashe registers a wide range of possible origins of dreams while making "no substantial attempt to discriminate among the competing theories." Holland, " 'The Interpretation of Dreams' in the Renaissance," 130. Levin historicizes Nashe's ambivalence regarding dreams to similar effect, arguing that he "has his foot in both worlds, medieval as well as modern," by at once dismissing the prognosticatory power of dreams and assenting to the possibility that the devil used dreams to torment sinners while they slept. See Levin, *Dreaming the English Renaissance,* 45.

23. As Clark outlines it, the Artemidorian tradition was concerned with the dream *world,* which was "either morally true or morally false; according to the universally adopted early modern categories, dreams were either sent by God for a good purpose or sent by the devil for an evil one, or produced by morally neutral (or at least ambivalent) natural causes." By contrast, the dream *state,* with which Clark explains philosophers such as Descartes and Montaigne were concerned, "was epistemologically paradoxical; it consisted of experiences, predominantly visual, which seemed to be true (in the sense of being real) but were objectively false." Clark, *Vanities of the Eye,* 308–9.

24. Ibid., 308.

25. Richard Saunders, *Physiognomie* (London: Nathaniel Brooke, 1653), 235.

26. Levin, *Dreaming the English Renaissance,* 62.

27. As Descartes initially contends, "When I think about this [the similarity of dreaming and waking experiences] more carefully, I see so clearly that I can never distinguish, by reliable signs, being awake from being asleep, that I am confused and this feeling of confusion almost confirms me in believing that I am asleep." See René Descartes, *Meditations and Other Metaphysical Writings,* trans. Desmond M. Clarke (New York: Penguin Books, 2000), 19.

28. For more on the specific connection between Shakespeare, Montaigne, and Renaissance skepticism, see Terence Cave, "Ancients and Moderns," in *The Cambridge History of Literary Criticism Volume III: The Renaissance,* ed. Glyn P. Nor-

ton (Cambridge: Cambridge University Press, 1999), 417–25; and William Hamlin, "What Did Montaigne's Skepticism Mean to Shakespeare and His Contemporaries?," *Montaigne Studies: An Interdisciplinary Forum* 17, no. 1 (2005): 195–210.

29. Michel de Montaigne, *The Essayes or Morall, Politike and Millitarie Discourses of Lo: Michaell de Montaigne,* trans. John Florio (London: Edward Blount, 1603), 616. Though Montaigne does not acknowledge it, his source for this story is almost certainly Book 18, Chapter 18 of Augustine's *City of God.* While Augustine describes a discrepancy between the sleeper's interpretation of events—that he was dreaming when he imagined himself to be a packhorse—and *others* who describe those same events as if they had actually occurred, Montaigne conflates the two distinct, contradictory interpretations of dreamer and others into a singular paradox for the dreamer. For Montaigne, dreaming as a skeptical problem is centered solely on the attempt (and failure) of the self to maintain coherence in the face of inconsistent experience. See Augustine, *The City of God, Books XVII-XXII,* trans. Gerald G. Walsh and Daniel J. Honan (Washington, DC: The Catholic University of America Press, 1954), 108.

30. Montaigne, *Essayes,* 616.

31. Ibid., 616.

32. The more conventional view held, as Ann Marie Plane and Leslie Tuttle explain it, that "the sleeping human soul lacked its full capacity to exercise reason," while the imagination proceeded uninhibited, reworking in fantastic combinations the material of the previous day. See Plane and Tuttle, *Dreams, Dreamers, and Visions: The Early Modern Atlantic World* (Philadelphia: University of Pennsylvania Press, 2013), 12. As Robert Burton explained in *The Anatomy of Melancholy* (1621), "In time of sleep this faculty [the imagination] is free, and many times conceive strange, stupend, absurd shapes, as in sick men we commonly observe." *The Anatomy of Melancholy,* ed. Holbrook Jackson (New York: New York Review of Books, 2001), 159. See also, for example, *The Atheist's Tragedy,* in which Charlemont expresses a similar view of the imagination's role in the production of dreams when he at first tries to explain the appearance of his father's ghost by means of natural causes: "Our boiling fantasies / Like troubled waters falsify the shapes / Of things retained in them, and make 'em seem / Confounded when they are distinguished. So / My actions daily conversant with war, / The argument of blood and death, had left,/ Perhaps, th'imaginary presence of / Some bloody accident upon my mind, / Which, mixed confusedly with other thoughts, / Whereof th'remembrance of my father might / Be one, all together seem / Incorporate, as if his body were / The owner of that blood, the subject of / That death, when he's at Paris and that blood / Shed here." Cyril Tourneur, *The Atheist's Tragedy,* in *Four Revenge Tragedies,* ed. Katharine Eisaman Maus (Oxford: Oxford University Press, 1995), 2.6.46–60.

33. Montaigne, *Essayes,* 347.

34. Ibid., 492.

35. Indeed, Roger Ekirch argues that the segmentation of a night's sleep into two major periods, common in pre-industrial Western European societies, allowed sleepers to reflect on dreams and visions much more immediately and vividly than they would have been able to had they slept through the night until morning. See Robert Ekirch, *At Day's Close: Night in Times Past* (New York: W. W. Norton, 2005), 300.

36. Marjorie Garber, *Dream in Shakespeare: From Metaphor to Metamorphosis* (New Haven: Yale University Press, 1974), 16.

37. As Stephen Orgel says of this moment, "Roman Catholic thinking admitted the existence of ghosts, but Protestantism was sceptical and in the official view, ghosts were delusions produced by the devil. To the drama of the period, however, they were indispensable, and Antigonus keeps all options open." Orgel, *The Winter's Tale* (Oxford: Oxford University Press, 1996), 153.

38. The location—Bohemia—in which he is to leave Perdita, Antigonus explains, convinces him that she is a bastard: "I do believe / Hermione hath suffered death, and that / Apollo would—this being indeed the issue / Of King Polixenes—it should here be laid / Either for life or death, upon the earth / Of its right father" (3.3.40–45).

39. Montaigne, *Essayes,* 640.

40. Cavell, *Disowning Knowledge in Seven Plays of Shakespeare,* 204 (emphasis his).

41. Jennifer Lewin, " 'Your Actions Are My Dreams': Sleepy Minds in Shakespeare's Last Plays," *Shakespeare Studies* 31 (2003): 188.

42. Mary Baine Campbell, "Dreaming, Motion, and Meaning: Oneiric Transport in Seventeenth-century Europe," in *Reading the Early Modern Dream: The Terrors of the Night,* ed. Katharine Hodgkin, Michelle O'Callaghan and Susan Wiseman (London: Routledge, 2008), 17.

43. Descartes, *Meditations,* 31.

44. Campbell, "Dreaming, Motion, and Meaning," 17.

45. Theresa Krier argues that time in *The Winter's Tale* speeds up from Leontes's perspective after he acknowledges his doubt about Hermione in "The Triumph of Time: Paradox in *The Winter's Tale*," *Centennial Review* 26 (1982): 341–53, esp. 348. Though I agree with her point that time does increase in speed at this point of the play, Leontes's entry into a dream state represents, to my mind, a crucial break from continuous, speeding time to *instantaneous* knowledge.

46. Lewin, "Sleepy Minds," 187.

47. Leontes himself explicitly makes the interpretive leap beyond what he can see as he describes watching Hermione and Polixenes interact to Camillo. After first commenting on behavior that he can see, he then moves beyond those appearances to what he thinks they mean, though he presents this evidence as if it is ocular: "Skulking in corners? Wishing clocks more swift? / Hours, minutes? Noon, midnight? And all eyes / Blind with the pin and web but theirs, theirs only, / That would unseen be wicked? Is this nothing?" (1.2.287–90).

48. "The Sceptick," in *The Works of Sir Walter Ralegh* (Oxford: Oxford University Press, 1829), 2: 548–49. *The Sceptick* is often attributed to Walter Ralegh, though no evidence of his authorship exists before the essay's posthumous publication in 1651. The essay is essentially a loose translation of Book I, Chapter 14 of Sextus's *Outlines of Pyrrhonism;* for the argument that the essay may come from the same lost English translation of *Outlines of Pyrrhonism* to which Thomas Nashe alludes in 1591, see William Hamlin, *Tragedy and Scepticism in Shakespeare's England* (New York: Palgrave Macmillan, 2005), 48–54.

49. Montaigne, *Essayes,* 625.

50. Campbell, "Dreaming, Motion, Meaning," 23 (emphases hers).

51. Cavell, *Disowning Knowledge in Seven Plays of Shakespeare,* 193.

52. This reading of Time's instrumentality in the production and increase of

error diverges from more traditional interpretations of Time's function in the play, which often emphasize the personified figure's resemblance to the iconographic and emblematic Time of Shakespeare's sonnets. For more on the resemblance of Time in *The Winter's Tale* and the sonnets, see Stanton B. Garner, "Time and Presence in *The Winter's Tale*," *Modern Language Quarterly* 46, no. 4 (1985): 347–67; Inga-Stina Ewbank, "The Triumph of Time in *The Winter's Tale*," in The Winter's Tale*: Critical Essays,* ed. Maurice Hunt (New York: Garland Publishing, Inc., 1995), 139–55; and John Pitcher, introduction to *The Winter's Tale* (London: Arden Shakespeare, 2010), 79–81. For more on the representation of time in the sonnets themselves, see Jonathan Hart, "Conflicting Monuments: Time, Beyond Time, and the Poetics of Shakespeare's Dramatic and Nondramatic Sonnets," in *In the Company of Shakespeare: Essays on English Renaissance Literature in Honor of G. Blakemore Evans,* ed. Thomas Moison and Douglas Bruster (Madison, NJ: Fairleigh Dickinson University Press, 2002), 177–205.

53. Leonard Barkan, " 'Living Sculptures': Ovid, Michelangelo, and *The Winter's Tale*," *English Literary History* 48, no. 4 (1981): 639–67; 641.

54. William Shakespeare, *A Midsummer Night's Dream,* ed. Harold F. Brooks (London: Arden Shakespeare, 2007).

55. Barkan, *Unearthing the Past: Archaeology and Aesthetics in the Making of Renaissance Culture* (New Haven, CT: Yale University Press, 1999), 119, 124.

56. Of course, Rogero's earlier comment that Paulina has visited the "removed house" where the statue is located "privately twice or thrice a day, ever since the death of Hermione," is a broader hint about where Hermione has been for the past sixteen years (5.2.103–5). To recall these lines after Hermione's seemingly miraculous appearance in 5.3, I would argue, adds to, rather than resolves, the mystery surrounding her disappearance from and return to the world of the play.

57. See also Diehl's argument regarding Leontes's awakening that "although the scene appears to present a miraculous resurrection—the dead Hermione comes to life—it marks that miracle as a fiction and uses it to dramatize a different kind of rebirth, one that is internal to Leontes (who, from a theological perspective, could be said to undergo a kind of Pauline spiritual regeneration, the mortifying of the 'old man' and the 'quickening' of the 'new man')." "The Pauline Rebuke and Paulina's Lawful Magic in *The Winter's Tale*," 82.

58. As Sherman argues, "Paulina is a confident knower—passionate, headstrong, and full of conviction, never shown internally debating or pondering a choice. Her grasp on the truth of past events defeats the doubts of Leontes." See *Skepticism and Memory in Shakespeare and Donne,* 72.

59. Kathryn Lynch, "Baring Bottom: Shakespeare and the Chaucerian Dream Vision," in *Reading Dreams: The Interpretation of Dreams from Chaucer to Shakespeare,* ed. Peter Brown (Oxford: Oxford University Press, 1999), 123.

60. As Kenneth Gross argues of Leontes's focus on Hermione's wrinkles, "the scene registers . . . not just the loss of a young bride but the loss of an older woman, that is to say, the loss of a space of time in which a husband and wife could grow old together." Kenneth Gross, *The Dream of the Moving Statue* (Ithaca, NY: Cornell University Press, 1992), 101.

REVIEWS

Taking Exception to the Law: Materializing Injustice in Early Modern Literature
Edited by Donald Beecher, Travis DeCook, Andrew Wallace, and Grant Williams
Toronto: University of Toronto Press, 2015

Reviewer: Jessica Winston

Over the past twenty years, English Renaissance law and literature has come into its own as a distinct subfield of early modern studies with major conferences, influential critics, and foundational monographs. Soon the field will also have its own guide in the form of an Oxford Handbook, another sign of the discipline's rise. As this subfield has developed, edited collections have served an important function—as they often do in emerging areas of inquiry—orienting readers to the evolving subject by providing a sense of new questions and methodologies and marking where more work needs to be done. Yet, if law and literature exists now as a distinct research area, it is reasonable to ask what purpose another, general law and literature collection might serve. One answer is that it can register how established the field is. In his introduction to *Taking Exception to the Law,* Grant Williams opens with just this point, admitting that the collection is not a "contribution." Rather, it is "bellwether of the degree to which the entire field of English Renaissance literary studies is absorbing and profiting from the findings, insights, and issues raised by" the interdisciplinary study of law and literature (1). The editors of the volume take the bellwether aim seriously and meet it in nuanced ways. Together they have curated an impressive set of articles demonstrating that issues in law, jurisdiction, and justice are key to making sense of early modern texts and their cultural dynamics, particularly the ways that texts explore and question legal institutions and procedures.

While the individual chapters are all very strong, the highlight is Williams's essay on "Law and the Production of Literature: An Introductory Perspective." Williams surveys ways that law and literature shaped each other in early modern England, and he takes stock of the current state of law and literature as a field, providing a lucid, cogent sense of the historical circumstances that tie law and literature together in the period and a clear overview of major critical concerns. Describing law as "intimately and inescapably implicated" in literary production (5), he points to the origins of early modern rhetoric in classical legal treatises, the legal infrastructure surrounding literary and dramatic production, and the position of readers and viewers as juridical audiences, who, like lawyers and jurors, seek to "intelligibly reconstruct" (13) motives and intentions from particular deeds and words. Williams also outlines and complicates a major emphasis in the criticism devoted to law and literature—the idea that literary texts take a critical stance toward law, legal procedures, and legal officials. He takes seriously literature's place as a separate domain from the law, one that serves to "take exception"—that is, to disapprove of or find fault with—the law. At the same time, explicitly building on the work of Bradin Cormack, he challenges the notion that literature is morally superior to law. Indeed, he points out that in "taking exception" literature also reifies law as a distinct domain. Because of its combination of clarity, conciseness, and command, the chapter is a must read for anyone seeking a foothold in the field.

The rest of the chapters take up range of subjects: legal documents in Shakespeare (Bradin Cormack), the trial of Archbishop Laud (Deborah Shuger), Artegall as ward in *The Faerie Queene* (Judith Owens), discourses of civil religion (Elliott Visconsi), and tyranny and grace in Milton (Paul Stevens), among others. In one sense, this diversity is a limitation, since it opens up the book to classic criticisms of law and literature: the field has no clear boundaries and lacks a central theory, organizing set of questions, or methodology. In another way, however, this diversity advances the volume's central aim—that is, to be an index of current practice. In its variety, then, the volume demonstrates that scholars across early modern literary studies, especially those engaged in historicist work, find their analyses enriched by an engagement with the technicalities of the law—its documents, procedures, jurisdictions, and foundational principles. Moreover, even in their diversity, the chapters are unified by a persistent theme: Whether implicitly or explicitly, literary texts often "take exception to" and render visible various kinds of legal injustice.

As Williams describes it, the editors have grouped the essays in clusters, those dealing with legal instruments (writs, statutes, and bonds), juridical administration (problematic trials), educational institutions (which train men to execute the justice system), and tyranny. While the groupings are reasonable and draw attention to subthemes in the volume, it is not clear that the clusters are necessary to meet the larger "bellwether" aim or to illustrate the subject of injustice, and at times the categories feel strained. David Stymeist's chapter is one example. The chapter appears with others on "trials gone awry" (26), but it does not seem to be about trials, unless "trials" means "hardships." Stymeist argues that criminal biographies, popular reports of compelling criminal cases that circulated as pamphlets, deal with the economic and social factors that contributed to the criminal's life of crime, and in this way, such texts belie the idea that pamphlets always advanced "dominant beliefs and norms surrounding criminality" (142). Regardless of the chapter's categorization, Stymeist writes with verve and commitment, and makes a very compelling case that early modern criminal pamphlets present the causes of criminality in a range of ways.

Alongside the explicit theme of the volume, "taking exception to the law," is another, implicit one: defamiliarlization. Studies in law and literature often denaturalize early modern writings, making their historical specificity more palpable and more exciting. Although any good essay will help readers to see something anew, this defamiliarizing effect is a signal characteristic of criticism in law and literature. Indeed, some readers feel that work in law and literature is very dense and difficult to read. I think that this feeling stems from the technical nature of the law, but it also grows out of something else: once we understand these technicalities and how they influence and shape literature, well-known early modern texts can suddenly seem peculiar and very strange, and this strangeness can be exciting and refreshing, but also puzzling and even a little unsettling. In this volume, the essays defamiliarize well-known texts and subjects, for instance reconfiguring our sense of Milton's ideas of grace and neo-Roman concepts of justice (as Paul Stevens does in his chapter). Still, for readers with some background in early modern studies, the essays themselves are not difficult to read. While some of the chapters are denser than others, just in terms of the ideas and histories they present (Cormack and Visconsi, for example), all of the chapters are clearly and often elegantly argued. For this reason, the volume is accessible to range of early modernists, from Renaissance graduate students and scholars with interests other than law and literature to more advanced readers in the field.

Rather than discuss each chapter in turn, I would like to highlight four essays that illustrate the major themes of the volume mentioned above: first, that early modern literature exposes and criticizes the workings of the law, and second that criticism in law and literature can make texts and issues in early modern studies newly strange and freshly exciting. Perhaps the best example is Tim Stretton's chapter on *Merchant of Venice,* which draws attention to the counterintuitive logic of early modern legal documents. He describes *Merchant* as a response to a particular cultural crisis, the growing sense that Englishmen and women were reluctant to keep their promises, and he discusses the bond as a version of the legal instrument that emerged to deal with this cultural crisis, the conditional bond. As Stretton convincingly tells it, conditional bonds are odd in multiple ways. For one, they suppress original contexts and emphasize penalties. Thus, in the most instructive moment in the chapter, Stretton rewrites Antonio's bond according to the form of early modern conditional bonds:

> Know all men that I, Antonio, am firmly bound to Shylock to have him cut off an equal pound of my fair flesh taken from nearest my heart three months from today. [. . .] The condition of this obligation is that if Antonio pays Shylock three thousand ducats on or before the due date then this obligation shall become void. (78)

In this form, the bond eliminates the original reason for its creation (the loan) and results in a situation where Antonio makes a promise to Shylock that he does not intend to keep—to give him a pound of flesh. For Stretton, the inverted logic of the bond extends to the ring plot. He explains, "Portia and Nerissa pervert the logic of the marriage contract by turning their promises to remain faithful into conditions attaching to the keeping of the rings, a move just as bizarre as making the payment of a debt a condition to prevent a promised sacrifice of a pound of flesh" (83). In essence, according to the strange rationale of the conditional bond, Portia and Nerissa promise to remain *unfaithful,* unless Bassanio and Gratiano keep their "bands" (with a pun on "bonds"). For Stretton, however, the main point is that Antonio's situation is, in form at least, similar to the perplexing one in which Englishmen and women increasingly found themselves—amidst the breakdown in a culture of trust, they were making progressively more and more promises that they did not intend to keep. In the end, Stretton reinterprets Portia's defeat of Shylock as something that Shakespeare's initial audience might have appreciated: a triumph over "the disintegration of neighbour- liness" manifested in the countless lawsuits of the time (88).

In her chapter on "The 'Snared Subject' and the General Pardon State in Late Elizabethan Coterie Literature," Virginia Lee Strain likewise explains unexpected logics in Elizabethan law, in this case, the Elizabethan general pardon statute. Strain demonstrates that the general pardon was a response to the proliferation of stat- utes in the late sixteenth century. This increase created a situation where well-meaning subjects could wind up ensnared in a legal mess, simply because there was no way for them to keep track of so many laws. Lord Keeper Bacon made efforts to correct the situa- tion, seeking to condense and amend statutes, but the general par- don statute offered another remedy. With it, Queen Elizabeth sought to mitigate the effects of snaring statutes by forgiving her subjects' accidental transgressions before they committed them. The general pardon also included list of pardonable and unpardon- able offenses, which guided legal officers to pursue some crimes but not others. In the Gray's Inn Christmas revels of 1594, the Christmas prince parodied this practice when he offered a mock general pardon, which forgave real and imagined crimes, "frauds," as well as "fictions, factions, and fractions" (109). As Strain argues, the mock pardon reveals something about the logic of the real par- don: it seems to promote a culture of permissiveness, under the protection of the leader's clemency, yet it also imagines a legal sys- tem that extends to all subjects and *all* of their activities whether they know it or not. The general pardon, in other words, is built on the premise that the law could know and regulate everything about English subjects, their "conspiracies" and "suppositions," but also their "concavities" and "suppositories" (109). In this sense, the parody illuminates the general pardon's unsettling paradox: it seems merciful, but in fact brings every action within the bounds of the law and in this way is "heavily restrictive" (112).

Moving from documents to procedures, Deborah Shuger finds that Archbishop Laud's diary of his common law trial provides a unique, critical perspective on common law legal processes. Laud had sat on the Star Chamber and High Commission, courts whose workings, Shuger explains, were more akin to canon and civil law that common law. But Laud was tried in a common law court. In his diary, he as an outsider to common law often registers glaring surprise at and trenchant criticism of its procedures, for instance the admission of hearsay as evidence, which was not allowed in the Star Chamber. For Shuger, Laud's criticisms help to correct a legacy of "patriotic-populist celebration" of the superiority of the common law over continental legal processes (132). Shuger then makes a fascinating turn, as she moves to compare common and other legal jurisdictions. She asks why religious dissidents might have preferred common law trials. Comparing Laud's criticisms of his trial to those of men tried in the Star Chamber, she then draws in legal historians who argue that modern criminal courts based in common law are "truth averse" (131). Laud disliked common law procedures because he could not prove his innocence. Religious dissidents, on the other hand, may have preferred common law, since it was designed, like the QWERTY keyboard, she suggests, to be "suboptimal" (131). In common law, trials "were meant to hamper somewhat the detecting and punishments of lawbreaker," giving those who believed that the laws themselves were unjust a chance to escape legal consequences (131).

Finally, in his essay on "Torture and the Tyrant's Injustice from Foxe to *King Lear*," John Staines also discusses legal procedures, in this case eliciting confessions through torture. Staines asks a historical question, why did torture decline in Tudor and Stuart England, but he answers it by turning to rhetoric and literature. He argues that one reason for torture's disappearance was its rhetorical connection to tyranny, a connection established in the mid-Tudor period in books such as Foxe's *Actes and Monuments,* which associated torture with cruel Catholic tyrants. Drawing on the now classic work of Elaine Scarry in *The Body in Pain,* Staines argues that torture is "a sign of the failure of political authority" (243). He then turns to the torture of Gloucester in *King Lear,* an event that indicates Cornwall's tyranny. Yet Staines's more important point concerns Cornwall's servant, who rebels by commanding Cornwall to cease. These various representations of torture from the mid-Tudor to early Stuart period presented torture as an invitation to question authority, and such associations contributed to the decline of the practice itself, making it "an unsuitable option for the English monarchy" (247). While at times Staines's argument seems too causal, the chapter is also exciting because it identifies one way that literature may really have impacted cultural attitudes and cultural practices, in this case monarchic procedures for eliciting confessions and evidence.

As in any volume, it is possible to object to individual points or to the development of particular arguments. In general, in *Taking Exception to the Law,* such moments are rare and do not undercut the power of individual chapters or the collection as a whole. It should be noted however that in terms of theme, the essay on education and distributive justice is the odd one out, since it does not deal with technicalities in law or legal procedure, or even with legal theory (such as neo-Roman concepts of justice). Instead, Elizabeth Hanson's powerfully argued and illuminating essay explores sixteenth-century pedagogical treatises to offer a genealogy for the modern-day association of formal education and distributive justice—that is, that education can remedy the injustices of social inequality. Focusing on Erasmus's *De Pueris Instituendis* (1529) and Richard Mulcaster's *Positions on the Training Up of Children* (1581), Hanson argues, in her evocative phrasing, that "humanist pedagogical thought was haunted by a question of justice that it could not fully articulate, let alone resolve" (184). Hanson expertly unpacks the dense logic of these treatises, uncovering assumptions that (she argues) the authors themselves only vaguely sensed. For instance, in her discussion of Mulcaster, she observes that the author is unable "to embrace the conclusion to which his own observations compel him" and this "derives from the fundamental contradiction between his drive to think economically and the conviction, which he shares with Erasmus, that humanist learning not only is, but ought to be, universally desired" (196). While the chapter does not deal specifically with law, it deserves attention from anyone interested in early modern education or historical relationships between economic justice and theories of educational access.

For me, Hanson's discussion of education also cast the volume in another light, since it points up something that scholars of early modern law and literature have yet to do—collectively take up issues about teaching law and literature, for instance in edited collections, at stand-alone conferences, or in panels at major conferences. *Taking Exception to the Law* does not aim to address pedagogy, and it does not need to, but its absence points to another way that the volume registers current practice. If law and literature has truly permeated early modern literary research, then a future development should involve scholars coming together to explore how the field can now reshape approaches to early modern studies with our graduate and undergraduate students. For now, for anyone already teaching or developing a course in English Renaissance law and literature, this volume will be a useful aid. Williams's essay will help to orient students to the field, and the volume as a whole, or selected essays from it, can guide students to think about ways that literary texts render evident injustices in the early modern legal system, even as they affirm the law's importance.

Sex Before Sex: Figuring the Act in Early Modern England
James Bromley and Will Stockton, eds. Minneapolis: University of Minnesota Press, 2013

Reviewer: *Julie Crawford*

Since the publication of Alan Bray's *Homosexuality in Renaissance England* (1982), the field of early modern literary and cultural studies has been having a robust conversation about the history of sexuality. Yet as Valerie Traub points out in her "Afterword" to James Bromley and Will Stockton's *Sex Before Sex: Figuring the Act in Early Modern England* (Minneapolis: University of Minnesota Press, 2013), "the *content* of sex has been strangely presumable, apparently interpretable through . . . ready-to-hand transhistorical rubrics" (3, emphasis mine). Bromley and Stockton's volume subjects this supposed "content" to close scrutiny, arguing that despite the presumptive *sine qua non* of (penile-vaginal) intercourse, there is no single, transhistorical definition of sex, and no clear taxonomy or hierarchy of sexual acts. ("Sodomy," scholars fluent in the conversation know, "is an utterly confused category"; *Sex Before Sex* suggests that this may be the case for the whole field of sex itself). Bromley and Stockton argue that "the epistemological recalcitrance of sex," and the complexities of its representation make it a singularly exciting, if challenging, area of inquiry: one that asks us to question what we think we know not only about the past, but about the present as well. Fully aware that the authors in the volume are working with both modern and early modern epistemologies of sexuality—or more accurately, that both are working fictions of our own creation—the volume endeavors to theorize and historicize sex through a series of essays based not (only) on particular acts, but on questions about how sexual acts might signify. While the editors take account of legal definitions and injunctions (for example, Edward Coke's precedent-setting legal claim that the "emission of semen without penetration maketh no Rape" [5]), they suggest that the licit is only one way of reading (for) sex; acts that are "unremarkable within [legal] discourses' criteria" may be harder to see, but they are just as worthy of our attention.

Bromley and Stockton are also refreshingly interested not only in new archives and methodologies, but also in refusing to police "the boundary between 'reading' and 'reading into'" (6). (They cite Stanley Wells's prudish and proprietary indictment of the "dirty minds" of certain interpreters, but I always think of Alan Sinfield's amazing line in "How to Read *The Merchant of Venice* Without Being Heterosexist" (1996) when such considerations come up: "If gay men say 'OK, this is how [Antonio] speaks to us'—that, surely, is our business.") If sex is not really 'there' apart from specific discursive "deployments of sexuality," the editors ask, then are not literary texts—and, indeed, our readings *of* those texts—particularly rich sources of knowledge? If we suspend the idea that there is 'knowledge' to be had, then how does attention to acts that have "no immediate connection to the most prevalent, politicized, identitarian discourses of sexuality in the present" help us to "expose the limits of, and challenge the dominance of current discourses of sexuality" (8, 9)? If the earlier project of "queering" the Renaissance meant to "expose the ways that heterosexuality and heteronormativity shape critical perspectives on the Renaissance past as well as to recover expression of homoerotic desire and evidence of homoerotic relationships before the advent of homosexual identity," then is it not time to look at the sexual past not in terms of difference, development, or supersession, but rather in all its hitherto unremarked upon variety? Refusing an approach that defaults "sex to penile-vaginal intercourse" and relegates "all other acts to the category of the queer" (10), the erotic imagination that *Sex Before Sex* brings to the fore is one that is bracingly plural—not only in its variety, but also in its relationship to gender, intimacy, intersubjectivity, and, refreshingly, the presumptively dyadic nature of sexual behavior.

Some essays in the volume focus on specific sexual practices. Will Fisher's essay takes "chin chucking," or the erotic stroke or pinch of another person's chin (as when Hamlet tells Gertrude not to let Claudius "Pinch wanton on your cheek" [3.4.167]), as his subject, and James Bromley focuses on rimming, or oral-anal contact (as when Petruccio jokes: "What, with my tongue in your tail? / Nay, come again, Good Kate, I am a gentleman" [2.1.216–17]). Both chin chucking and anilingus are interesting for their indeterminate status: they can be done by and to both sexes; they are difficult to harness to a sexual orientation or telos; they are not genitally-focused. Sometimes Fisher undersells, and thus underarticulates, his argument ("I simply want to call attention to the existence of this gesture"), and sometimes Bromley oversells his. To call out an essay called "Rimming the Renaissance" for overstatement solicits charges of prudish resistance to queer flamboyance, but the claim that rimming "interrupts the taxonomizing of individuals and the march toward modernity that the proliferation of such taxonomies supposedly implies," is more an assertion than a convincing claim (186). Leo Bersani and Guy Hocquenghem, both of whom Bromley references, have already shown how libidinal investment in the anus avoids the type of indexing to dominant culture's terms, institutions, and goals that goes along with transgression; this central insight, both convincing, and extant in the literature, is thus not the grounds of my resistance. Rather I find the claim in the middle of the essay that rimming conflicts with the "hierarchies of bodies and pleasures that official early modern culture spun anything out of missionary-position heterosexual congress" (189) simply bewildering in the context of a volume keenly aware that there is no "official" early modern culture, let alone one that knew anything called either "heterosexual congress" or something like a "missionary position."

Some essays are perhaps too faithful to earlier ways of queering the Renaissance. Nicholas F. Radel's "'Unmanly Passion,'" for example, which argues that status-based prohibitions on expressions of desire between men help to distinguish between authorized and unauthorized forms, is familiar to readers of earlier work on the subject (notably books by Alan Bray, Alan Stewart, and Mario DiGangi). Others infuse familiar feminist and queer questions with new life. Kathryn Schwarz's essay returns to a familiar concern of feminist Shakespeare critics—the ways in which the (uncertain) project of patrilineal succession relies on virgins and chaste wives as "figures that signify fixed sexual states"—to ask new questions about the "conceptual plurality" of sexual knowledge. Starting with the famous, and almost pathologically reiterated, example of Lucretia, Schwarz argues that as "a social requisite that impersonates a physical fact," chastity "raises the question of whether sexual virtue can either derive from or refer to an embodied condition." In her reading, chastity is only confirmed by the "evocative corpse" of a dead virgin, and reminds us that there is no fixed referent for a given term or concept in the history of sexuality. Will Stockton's essay on *Comus* happily deploys psychoanalysis, for some years a critical red-flag in the field of early modern sexuality studies. Returning, with feminist hindsight, to a 1990s debate between the critics John Leonard and William Kerrigan (Kerrigan argued that Milton's Lady's "virtue is bound to a repressed wish for sex," and Leonard that her resistance is real), Stockton argues that the masque operates in the space of fantasy, staging "an imaginary scene, or a sequence of them, in which the Lady defends herself against the very assault for which she wishes" (235). Stockton is particularly interested in Jean Laplanche's "theory that sexuality originates in [. . .] moments of intrusion on newly constituting and vulnerable egos" as an explanation for "why experiences of desire and violation are so frequently inextricable within fantasy." Seduction experiences "are always undergoing translation, a repeated rendering-into-sense, as the subject matures in his or her desire" (246). In Stockton's reading, this is precisely the trajectory of Milton's masque: the story of a young Lady (with a "newly constituting ego") who experiences an early scene of seduction in which she follows Comus ("Shepherd, I take thy word") into the woods, and later retranslates that experience into a "betra[yal of her] credulous innocence" as she undergoes a series of further temptations (248). Stockton offers new insight into the Lady's "sharp distinction between her infantilized body and her discerning intellect," and of the ways in which sex attaches itself to the alimentary. (Both the cup she refuses to drink from, and the singularly resistant-to-interpretation "gumms of glutenous heat" that paralyze her, look different, and fresh, in his reading.)

Other essays in the volume are more clearly in dialogue with new critical trends, particularly the surge of recent (queer) interest in ecology. Stephen Guy-Bray's "Animal. Vegetable, Sexual," for example, which offers readings of Donne's "Sappho to Philaenis" and Marvell's "The Garden" in light of Sir Thomas Browne's remarkable wish in *Religio Medici* "that we might procreate like trees, without conjunction" (196), resonates nicely with Marjorie Swan's recent, and very good, essay on "Vegetable Love" in *The Indistinct Human in Renaissance Literature* (Jean E. Feerick and Vin Nardizzi, eds. [New York: Palgrave, 2012]). Others evoke contemporary sexual practices and modes of consumption as ways of understanding representations of sexual acts in the past. Melissa J. Jones's "Spectacular Impotence," for example, reminds us that 30% of contemporary porn viewers are women (including on sites like "My Tiny Dick") in her reading of the titillating effects of impotence in poems like Nashe's "Choise of Valentines."

The best essay in *Sex Before Sex,* Christine Varnado's "Invisible Sex!," serves as a kind of headnote for the volume as a whole. Varnado argues that present assumptions about what sex "looks like" condition a critical (non) recognition of sex in literary representations, particularly in plays that gesture toward but do not stage sex acts. She points out that the most famous sex act in *Romeo and Juliet* (commemorated by Juliet's "Wilt thou be done? It is not yet near day" [3.5.1]), which is presumed to be (and often filmed as) heterosexual intercourse, is not actually staged at all. Moreover, it actively—even necessarily—solicits "acts of imagination, recognition, and affective hailing" on the part of the audience. Audiences (and readers) must see what is not there—and this, for Varnado, is a hermeneutic constitutive of playgoing (and of reader-response more broadly) rather than a historical problem. For Varnado eroticism is what "leaps out and hails our libidinal participation in a text." It is not an object of analysis but a way of reading, and we ought to "harness and use the power of erotically and affectively invested critical identification as a new, queer form of knowledge production that can uncover new sites, new forms, and new valences of 'sex' within the vastly different social and discursive contexts of the early modern world" (30). Stockton's insight in his essay that *all* sex is the object of ongoing translation, and, as such, resistant to decisive and singular translation, resonates nicely with Varnado's insight about the ways in which offstage 'sex' hails audiences to translate it into operative meaning in the present. Along with others in the volume, these essays offer exciting bridges between what are sometimes, and falsely, called "historicizing" and "presentist" approaches to early modern texts.

The English Martyr from Reformation to Revolution
By Alice Dailey
Notre Dame: University of Notre Dame Press, 2012

Reviewer: Elizabeth Williamson

Dailey's is the most recent contribution to a rich body of work on martyrdom and early modern literature. Building on Susannah Monta's cross-confessional approach to martyrology as a literary genre, Dailey extends some of her claims forward and backward in time by analyzing medieval hagiographies as well as texts produced later in the seventeenth century. This diachronic approach is reflected in Dailey's invitation to consider what happens "when an old genre encounters the new challenges of radical historical change" (6). Anchoring herself within the field of historical formalism, Dailey examines not only the plot elements and character types contained within martyrological narratives, but also the "organizing behavioral attributes" they valorize and deplore (10). The book is characterized by uncluttered prose and efficient chapters with helpful subheadings. Though Dailey is perhaps overly fond of words such as "rupture" and "fissure," the repetition of key terms makes related arguments visible as the reader traverses the broad range of texts she addresses. For all these reasons, and for its excellent summary of crucial theological concepts, this is the first book I recommend to undergraduates interested in learning about early modern English martyrdom.

Just as she is transparent in articulating her debts to Monta and others, Dailey is deliberate about distinguishing her work from that of scholars less interested in martyrological narratives as literary constructions. For instance, she concisely delineates the limitations of Brad Gregory's otherwise important book, noting that it tends to treat "martyrology as a transparent record of early modern Christian belief" (5).[1] If Gregory's enthusiastic study of popular faith systems represents one potential extreme, Elaine Scarry's influential work on "the body in pain" represents the opposite end of the spectrum.[2] Her thoroughly secular insights, grounded in the experiences of Latin American dissidents, have at times been imported into discussions of early modern martyrdom. As Dailey points out, however, the forms of suffering Scarry describes as world-destroying are entirely antithetical to the martyr's experience, which uses transcendent stories to lend meaning and even beauty to horrifying violence (36). Dailey strikes an elegant balance between these two poles, retaining a healthy skepticism about the literal veracity of martyrological accounts without denigrating the power of the texts themselves.

The English Martyr also clarifies what is at stake in the existing scholarly discourse by focusing on questions of legibility. Specifically, Dailey zeroes in on what Miri Rubin calls "martyr-making," reminding us that martyrdom is co-constituted "by victim and viewer, by historiographer and reader," and that the martyr's experience is only recognized as such if there is some correlation between the viewpoints of these various agents (94). Citing a famous phrase of Augustine's, she suggests that martyrdom "is neither merely cause nor death; it is a set of retrospective, narrative operations that depend on the legible rehearsal of martyr models" (100). In other words, early modern martyrologists used narrative tropes imported from medieval anthologies such as *The Golden Legend* in order to authenticate their own accounts. Equally important, these models were a part of every individual martyr's imagination, and so it is not accurate to say that they were simply imposed upon the events of the martyr's torture and execution after the fact. It is here that the book, which otherwise relies on careful historical research and close readings rather than on critical theory, reaches for some additional vocabulary to buttress its claims. Referencing Pierre Bourdieu's concept of the *habitus,* Dailey clarifies that the martyr paradigm is more than a set of formal narrative structures; it reflects an embodied knowledge that, for early modern Christians, was a thoroughly naturalized part of their worldview.

Though its historical range—which stretches from medieval passion drama to Milton's *Eikonoklastes*—is what most clearly distinguishes *The English Martyr* from other monographs on the subject, Dailey also has thoughtful things to say about the early modern period's central martyrology, John Foxe's *Actes and Monuments*. Her chapter on this text stresses its continuities with medieval hagiography, arguing that its "interplay of traditional martryological formulations and local moments of persecution comprises one of its most important contributions to the developing structure of the martyrological genre" (55). It may seem counterintuitive to claim that Foxe's re-use of Catholic models made his sixteenth-century Protestant martyr stories successful, and in fact some scholars have argued that the combination of visceral documentary accounts and typological structures produces a kind of a "strain on the narrative" (59). Dailey makes a strong case, however, that the elements of the work that appear to signal a departure from Catholic models—tensions between the authentic and the transcendent, the documentary and the typological—can be found within the genre's most emblematic forms. Here, too, Bourdieu is helpful, especially his argument that the limitation of choice produced by a given *habitus* does not in any way preclude "authentic expression" (62).

The book's most compelling chapter deals with the experience of Catholics executed under Elizabeth I—one of whom, John Gerard, Dailey also uses as the subject of the book's opening anecdote. In Chapter 3 she argues that priests like Gerard, who were arrested and tried under the new treason statutes passed in the 1580s, were prevented from making a viable claim to martyrdom. Unlike the heresy trial, in which the martyr was justified in resisting an oppressive religious authority, the treason trial limited the martyr's capacity to testify boldly to her faith. One example of the bind the defendants found themselves in was that in seeking to avoid the charge of acting outside the Queen's secular authority, they often failed to affirm the legitimacy of the Pope's role as head of the Catholic Church, a cornerstone of their belief system. As a result, their trials were marked by a set of "representational glitches" that carried over into accounts of the priests' deaths (115). Thomas Alfield, for instance, devoted most of his defense of Edmund Campion to a rebuttal of the treason charge, and consequently did not fully incorporate the narrative elements of the medieval martyrology that Foxe used so successfully in the *Actes and Monuments.* In other words, Campion, Gerard, and others occupy "a transitional moment in which martyrological discourse had not yet developed viable adaptive strategies or alternative modes of construction" (219). Because of its focus on this "transitional moment," the Campion chapter most clearly demonstrates the merits of Dailey's diachronic approach. And because it deals with some of history's losers, its nuanced argument about the "representational fracture" at the heart of Counter-Reformation martyrology is enlivened by the pathos of the situation these individuals found themselves in (117). This is not the end of the story, however; Dailey's final chapters address some of the "adaptive strategies" that emerged later in the seventeenth century, most notably Charles I's "inward-looking, tenuously metaphorized martyrdom" (245).

Because her most original arguments deal with martyrs whose stories cannot be readily accommodated within conventional hagiographical models, Dailey devotes several paragraphs in her coda to rebutting the idea that she is adding fuel to the "well-worn liberal humanist teleology" that describes western history as a secularizing progression from persecution to toleration (249). What distinguishes Dailey's method from such teleologies—whose proponents she discretely leaves unnamed—is her attention to the cultural work of narrative. Thus, it was not simply Elizabeth's push for uniformity or the English Civil War that re-shaped traditional conceptions of martyrdom. Rather, Dailey suggests, this series of political revolutions was accompanied by a set of literary ones, in which a more rigid set of typological models were rejected in favor of more flexible, metaphorical ones. Dailey also uses her postscript to discuss the veneration of Father Mychal Judge, a chaplain employed by the New York City Fire Department who died on September 11, 2001. She aptly points out that those who hold Father Mychal up as a martyr do so by drawing a contrast between him and the "extremists" who perpetrated the attack, ignoring the fact that suffering for one's faith has for centuries been a key element of Christian extremism (248). In this sense the appropriation of Father Mychal as a martyr demonstrates the effects of the "gradual dehistoricization" of martyrdom that Dailey locates in the seventeenth century (250).

Though her short reading of this modern Franciscan martyr is entirely plausible, and thoroughly in keeping with the nature of the postscript, the reader is left feeling tantalized by it. Specifically, I found myself wanting to hear more about what is lost through the process of turning martyrdom into a comparatively meaningless abstraction and what happens when such an abstraction is pitted against an Islamicist conception of martyrdom through what Dailey calls a series of "contemporary representational contests" (9). Not that martyrdom within anti-western movements is in any sense typologically stable; when the Egyptian intellectual Sayyid Al-Qutb devised a justification for killing Muslims who were allied with American and European imperialists, he fundamentally transformed traditional understandings of what it means to carry out holy war. It would require a longer book, and perhaps one struc-

tured around a series of synchronic case studies, to tackle the transformation of the martyrological paradigm across cultural contexts,
but, to Dailey's credit, this is the kind of expansive thinking her
book invites by contributing in such a lucid way to our developing
understanding of these influential historical—and literary—
upheavals.

Notes

1. Brad S. Gregory, *Salvation at Stake: Christian Martyrdom in Early Modern Europe* (Cambridge, MA: Harvard University Press, 1999).
2. Elaine Scarry, *The Body in Pain: The Making and Unmaking of the World* (Oxford: Oxford University Press, 1985).

Emotional Excess on the Shakespearean Stage: Passion's Slaves
By Bridget Escolme
London; New York: Bloomsbury, 2014

Reviewer: Allison P. Hobgood

Bridget Escolme's *Emotional Excess on the Shakespearean Stage: Passion's Slaves* explores the force of emotions in Renaissance theater, especially feeling's incitement to political and ethical movement, even subversion. Her insistence upon "emotion as movement"[1]—passion in and as action—drives the book's parallel goal of re-politicizing *now* the power of Shakespearean emotions *then*. Escolme is less interested in how feeling happens and more in when feeling is "too much." What, she wonders, does the motion of emotion precipitate, and how does the Shakespearean stage both represent and enact that potential? Further, the book probes the boundaries between reason and excess to posit that extreme emotions were—and still are—pleasurable to watch: turns out, it is often fun to get really carried away.

Through what she describes as a "comparative, transhistorical

336   REVIEWS

project, a project that is always historically contentious,"[2] Escolme
aims to link theater and cultural history to the now of stageplaying.
In other words, the book is definitively comparative as it purposes
"to consider how actors and audiences deal with ideas about emotional excess in early modern drama today."[3] This comparative
methodology opens a broad study of the conception, regulation,
and celebration of emotion as it is represented theatrically. In a
kind of transhistorical navigation of feeling and its historical similarities and differences, she investigates "the ways in which we
receive and remake the cultural artefacts of the past" and ponders
how "we might attempt to perform Then in a range of more exciting
and challenging ways Now."[4]

The book is organized in four main chapters on anger, laughter,
love, and grief. It opens with some historicizing of the term "emotion" that emphasizes feeling's powerful animation and inherent
motion. Every chapter then contains select background in the contours of each emotion, calling most heavily upon early modern
humoral theory, as well as philosophical, religious, and medical
tracts from the period. Chapter 1 explores anger in *Coriolanus* (via a
range of recent stage versions) to ask the question: how does violent
emotion get used, both on stage and more politically out in the
world? Escolme argues that *Coriolanus* fundamentally is a play
about anger and, further, that an audience's positionality in watching *Coriolanus* is contingent upon the anger of the play's characters
in their social and theatrical spaces. Playing with the question of
whether anger can be restorative—it is both valued and eschewed
in early modernity—she focuses most on two productions: first,
Coriolanus at the Globe in 2006; and Ralph Fiennes's *Coriolanus*
on film. Escolme reads the Globe production via a post-Freudian
lens as she examines the psychological underpinnings of Jonathan
Cake's Martius and a modern audience's empathy towards highly
legible anger. Of the Fiennes film, she suggests that " 'extreme rage'
is hardly in excess of what is needed in warfare"[5] and toys with the
notion that angry motion and destruction are political necessities.
The chapter closes with a noteworthy reading of Mike Pearson and
Mike Brookes's National Theatre Wales 2012 production of the
play, the site-specific *Coriolanus: Coriolan / Us,* as "interested in
anger as a political force, as that which makes and destroys communities of needs and interests, rather than as a means or effect of
personal expression."[6]

Chapter 2 uses textual traces to probe the assumption that "a more violent culture laughs at subjects that its more sheltered descendants might consider cruel."[7] Here, Escolme wants to trouble a too easy binary of "cruel laughter" versus "compassionate seriousness."[8] She posits that while early modern audiences indeed might have laughed more freely, "laughter in the early modern theatre is ambivalent and multi-directional rather than simply excessive and cruel."[9] The chapter reads *The Changeling, The Duchess of Malfi, The Honest Whore, Twelfth Night,* (and Tim Crouch's *I, Malvolio*) to argue for madness as producing an always excessive, although sometimes agential, subjectivity. These complexities, Escolme contends, ask spectators to examine the community of people with whom they laugh in challenging ways—laughter functions as a social force that does not necessarily "need to point to a group of outsiders as the objects of laughter" but rather can prompt spectators to laugh at themselves.[10]

Chapters 3 and 4 both loosely explore the ways that feeling—in these instances, love and grief—drive characters to excessive action or inaction and have intense political ramifications: for example, stagings of grief expressly "dramatize the politics and the policing of emotion."[11] Among other things, Chapter 3 focuses on *All's Well That Ends Well* and *Antony and Cleopatra* to parse out how (political and politicized) love has "its anxiety and pleasure-producing excesses,"[12] and this section of the book spends time excavating the nuances of explicitly gendered love as well as the tensions between early modern love and love now. Chapter 4 examines "political grief" in *Richard III, Hamlet,* and the *Henry VI* plays. It contends that early modern theater used representations of extreme grief to provoke audience pleasure, in spite of the cultural belief that expressions of grief required moderation and timeliness. Readings in this chapter remind us of, and support, anti-theatrical logics that saw Renaissance theatre as a "dangerous place of bodied-forth imaginings and imaginary bodies" that prompted audiences to "feel more."[13] Gender as a point of analysis resurfaces in this chapter as Escolme offers a thought-provoking reading of *Richard III* at the Swan in 2012 that, in her estimation, gave modern spectators access to the complex politics of early modern women's grief. Chapter 4 closes with further discussion of grief as it was staged in a production of *Hamlet* at the National Theatre in 2010. Here, grief functions as provocation towards passive arrest, as the possibility of an "insightful grief" that is crucial to subjectivity but appears to bring with it a kind of "stillness or directionless movement rather than clear trajectory."[14]

While there is much to glean in each of these chapters, Escolme's early modern play readings are less convincing than her forays into modern productions. In other words, she posits claims upon which she does not fully elaborate and occasionally devolves into a kind of character analysis that loses sight of the book's historicist aims in the face of a psychology of emotion. Some of the nuanced arguments about the complexities of Escolme's four key feelings fall short of being fully convincing—perhaps because the book takes up too many texts/productions such that the deep tissue of its readings and analyses get lost in that shuffle. In Chapter 3, on love, it was difficult to discern the evident links between then and now as she sets them out theoretically in the book's introduction. Further, the book suffers in spots from what might be called transhistorical slippages. For example, she argues for the consistency of laughter across 400 years while simultaneously espousing that historical dissonance is crucial to remember, particularly in reading and rethinking modern productions. Put differently, Escolme often wants it both ways: then as now; now nothing like then. The book would have benefited throughout from even more explicit excavation of this tension.

Emotional Excess's straightforward structure as outlined above complements its accessible style. In many moments, Escolme's unique voice and illuminating anecdotes—albeit occasionally lost in too much deference to other scholarship—come together to powerfully enliven the stage even as it is being recalled and recovered, both historically and contemporarily, in a narrative form (the monograph) that so frequently seems to do injustice to theatrical "liveness." Too, readers will appreciate both her comparative impulse and willingness to be overtly speculative as she crafts conversation about how emotions work on stage over/in time. The book will be most useful, I would venture, to readers interested in Shakespeare in contemporary performance. For this reader, Escolme's informative, detailed descriptions and analysis of modern plays were the most compelling aspects of the book in ways that will especially appeal to scholars and practitioners invested in modern Shakespeare, materialism, theater, and performance studies.

Notes

1. Bridget Escolme, *Emotional Excess on the Shakespearean Stage: Passion's Slaves* (London; New York: Bloomsbury, 2014), xxiv.

2. Ibid., 220.
3. Ibid., xviii.
4. Ibid., xix, xxx.
5. Ibid., 37.
6. Ibid., 52.
7. Ibid., 57.
8. Ibid., 75.
9. Ibid., 57.
10. Ibid., 63.
11. Ibid., 172.
12. Ibid., 111.
13. Ibid., 181.
14. Ibid., 206.

Dramatic Extracts in Seventeenth-Century English Manuscripts: Watching, Reading, Changing Plays
By Laura Estill
Newark: University of Delaware Press, 2015

Reviewer: Tiffany Stern

As *Dramatic Extracts in Seventeenth-Century English Manuscripts* shows, readers—and spectators—in early modern England often responded textually to the plays they encountered. Sections they "noted" might range from short sententious, lyrical, telling or charming moments, to long segments of masques or entire songs. Giving the history of dramatic excerpting from its beginning in the 1590s to the end of the Restoration, Estill's important book provides the fullest account of dramatic extracting yet told, details several unknown commonplace books, miscellanies and separates (single sheets containing commonplaces), and illustrates the rich and varied literate responses there might be to early modern drama.

The strength of the book is the startling insight it has into reception history. It depicts a world in which authors neglected today, like Peter Hausted, William Peaps and Jaspar Mayne, and seldom-studied plays like *Gorboduc,* were key, and in which play title and play authorship were often less important than the content of the extracted scrap. Indeed, Estill shows that an extract's popularity was often determined by the way it could be reused in another context: so, perversely, the less tied to a particular play a fragment was, the more lasting it might prove. In chapter 6, Estill traces "Fat paunches have lean pates, and dainty bits / Make rich the ribs, but bankrupt quite the wits," for instance, from Shakespeare's *Love's Labour's Lost* (published in 1598), as it is taken up in Robert Allott's *Englands Parnassus* (1600), Thomas Walkington's *Optick Glass* (1607), and W. B.'s *A Helpe to Discourse* (1623); she then shows it in a number of manuscript books that may have sources in Shakespeare's play, any of the intermediary printed texts, or other works no longer extant. Extracted to a new context, free-floating passages were often repurposed to make localized political or social points. Passages from Ben Jonson's masque *The Gypsies Metamorphosed,* Estill demonstrates, were used after production to reflect on a scandal about Frances Coke, Viscountess Purbeck, so that the masque acquired a contentiousness it had not originally had.

Written in chronological order, *Dramatic Extracts in Seventeenth-Century English Manuscripts* is of necessity made up of micro-histories, each of a different commonplace book or compiler. Estill has avoided the temptation to find a "pattern" to what a series of separate people took from plays, explaining that "there is no one-size-fits-all approach to dramatic extracts" (43). Though admirable, this does result in a book that does not have a "through" argument, and works better on a section-by-section basis than as a whole. The chronological approach beautifully illustrates a growth in the nature and complexity of commonplacing drama over time (matching the fact that more plays were published over time), but results in rangy chapters; it is not always easy to say what each chapter is "about." Chapter 1, for instance, which covers the late sixteenth/early seventeenth century, usefully explains the origins of the habit of commonplacing drama, looks at the *Titus Andronicus* passage in the Longleat manuscript, considers William Briton of Kelstone's extracts from Thomas Sackville and Thomas Norton's *Gorboduc,* turns to Edward Pudsey's Shakespeare extracts and the more wide-ranging extracts of William Drummond of Hawthornden, and addresses a series of other commonplace books while also discussing the appearance of dramatic extracts in plays and the nature of erasable tables. It is valuable, then, for someone who wants to know "everything about commonplacing drama in the late sixteenth/ early seventeenth century" but not so helpful for someone who wants to know how many commonplace books survive from the period, what specific extracts from plays were regularly chosen for commonplacing, what other literature is interspersed with commonplaced dramatic passages, and to what extent dramatic commonplace books resemble one another.

In many respects, however, the book's problems are also its strengths. For instance, *Dramatic Extracts in Seventeenth-Century English Manuscripts* is generous in its definition of what commonplacing is—anything from a snippet of dialogue to a section of a masque to a song; and generous too about what a commonplace is— anything from a passage in a dedicated commonplace book to a segment of masque in the State Papers. This helpfully illustrates how diffuse commonplacing might be in conception and location; at the same time, it does not differentiate between a commonplace and an extract, and elides the disparity between a record for oneself and a quotation for someone else—though perhaps the point is that these distinctions were, in the early modern period, not always made.

That the book treats differently the compilers of commonplaces whose names are known and those whose names are not is a necessity arising from the form in which commonplace books survive. When compilers are known, Estill analyzes their choice of passages against their lives: William Sancroft, a principled Archbishop of Canterbury, may have shaped some of his ideas around the literature he read (or, of course, read the literature that would best suit his ideas); Abraham Wright, a devout royalist clergyman, picked extracts that illustrated his loyalties, claims Estill, though the fact that he was a royalist may have affected *her* readings—none of his quotations as presented seemed unambiguously royalist in nature. It was intriguing to consider how the practice of extracting might reflect upon a person's life or *vice versa,* though in such instances, the reason for addressing only play segments—rather than all extracted segments irrespective of genre—was unclear. When commonplace books are anonymous the reasoning behind their choice of dramatic extracts is, of course, considerably harder to determine. Such anonymous works, claims Estill, teach us about "early modern" attitudes in general to plays, but that notion fits uncomfortably with her demonstration that commonplacing is highly individual. In fact it prompts the question how much we can conclude from books by unknown compilers.

Alert to the way new context and historical circumstance changed dramatic extracts, the book was least strong when considering the extracts themselves. For instance, chapter 2 provides a fascinating example of self-commonplacing, when Milton accompanied his signature in an *Album Amicorum* with lines from his own *Comus,* "if Vertue feeble were / Heaven its selfe would stoope to her." But the chapter did not address the meaning of this highly-contested passage, or ask why Milton chose to represent himself by a segment less clear outside context than in it: does this conditional clause suggest that virtue *is* feeble or that it *is not?* Likewise, the chapter did not consider or translate the Horace quotation with which Milton flanked his extract, presumably because that Latin passage is not from a play. *Dramatic Extracts in Seventeenth-Century English Manuscripts* is, then, excellent at addressing the "big picture" and exploring the role of commonplaces in new historic contexts; it does not, however, always consider in equal depth the commonplaces in themselves.

Some of these quibbles will also be solved by Estill. She is currently creating *DEx: A Database of Dramatic Extracts,* a digital tool that will contain transcriptions of dramatic extracts from surviving commonplace books and will be searchable. It will enable the user to see commonplaces in and out of context and between commonplace books; it will thus provide solutions to the questions that have only come about because of the publication of Estill's valuable book.

Dramatic Extracts in Seventeenth-Century English Manuscripts is a major resource for anyone interested in the commonplacing of drama. It suggests new ways of assessing and analyzing audience responses to drama, showing which plays, authors, ideas, or themes in early modern plays captivated audiences, and how commonplaces were used and reused. It points several new directions for further research in this under-studied topic. A detailed account of the amount and variety of noting that plays caused over 150 years, it is a book of range and depth that will reshape the way we consider and interpret historical reception.

Shakespeare's Demonology: A Dictionary
By Marion Gibson and Jo Ann Esra
London: Bloomsbury, 2014.

Reviewer: Deborah Willis

Marion Gibson and Jo Ann Esra's dictionary of Shakespeare's demonological language is part of the topic-centered Arden Shakespeare Dictionaries series, edited by Sandra Clark, which also includes such works as *Shakespeare's Medical Language, Shakespeare and the Language of Food,* and *Music in Shakespeare,* among others. Though called a dictionary in its subtitle, *Shakespeare's Demonology* is in some respects more like an encyclopedia, with many longer entries that include not only definitions and examples from the plays but also extensive analytic commentary and selected references to scholarly work on each topic. A lengthy and useful bibliography is provided at the end. The dictionary covers a field with porous boundaries; as the authors point out in their introduction, demonologists of Shakespeare's time were interested in a variety of phenomena in addition to demons and devils, including ghosts, spirits, angels, astrology, witchcraft, magic, divination and prophecy. Indeed, the boundaries between the "demonic" and the "natural" or "divine"—and hence between demons and other types of beings—were exactly what was in dispute and required investigation. Gibson and Esra rightly take an inclusive approach in their dictionary, with richly satisfying results.

There is, of course, no particular reason to think that Shakespeare's works were grounded in a distinct and internally consistent demonology, given the range of genres he worked in and the varying cultural and historical settings of his plays. Shakespeare does not offer us one cosmology or a single ideological stance; the *Macbeth* world is very different from the world of *The Merry Wives of Windsor* or of *Henry IV, Part I,* or for that matter, of most of the other tragedies. Nevertheless, this dictionary helps us identify some of Shakespeare's characteristic themes and tendencies and see more clearly the cross-currents of early modern thought that engaged his imagination. In so doing, it very successfully fulfills the authors' wish to provide "both a useful reference point and a stimulus to further scholarly work on key terms and ideas" (6).

What, then, are some characteristics of the Shakespearean supernatural that can be teased out from this book? One thing stands out clearly: Shakespeare embraces diversity in his conceptualization of the spirit world, in contrast to the more polarized views of Calvinist contemporaries and indeed, most demonologists, whatever their doctrinal affiliation. As the authors put it in their introduction, the "oversimplifying binary structure" of demonological thought "may perhaps be seen as going against the grain of most of his work" (5). Hence, this dictionary calls our attention not only to demons and angels but to a range of intermediate or indeterminate beings, from the relatively familiar (the fairies of *Midsummer Night's Dream*, Ariel, the ghost of Hamlet's father) to more obscure—ouphs, bugs, urchins, hedge-pigs, goblins, sibyls, mermaids, nymphs, and spirits of many sorts. Such beings could not be easily classified as either good or evil. The highly inclusive term "spirit," very common in Shakespeare, embraced a wide variety of beings across the moral spectrum, making it "a term fizzing with dangerous, anxious energy" (175). Often, a spirit's exact nature was hard to pin down. Puck, for example, is variously called fairy, spirit, and goblin; though not as benign as Ariel and a trickster like many devils, he stops short of being truly cruel or destructive, instead retaining what the authors aptly call an "indefinable edginess" (158). Other beings straddled boundaries of natural and supernatural. Mermaids, as half-human sea-creatures were natural if monstrous, but also sometimes interchangeable with sea-nymphs or water spirits and seductively dangerous like female demons. Shakespeare sometimes associates mermaids with benevolence and harmony, the authors note, but other times with a predatory, siren-like power that makes them resemble witches (134). Even the term "demon" had an element of indeterminacy. Shakespeare uses the word only twice, and one of those times is in the Platonic sense of "daemon," when the soothsayer in *Antony and Cleopatra* refers to Antony's "daemon" as a spirit that protects him. The dictionary also shows that Shakespeare alludes to a range of occult practices associated with astrology, divination, and prophecy without explicitly classifying them as either demonic or angelic. Sigils, charms, auspicious stars, auguries, periapts, oracles—all get their own useful entries.

But Shakespeare had uses for unequivocally evil spirits too, usually referring to them as "devils" or "fiends." Not surprisingly, Satan is the most commonly named devil, followed by Beelzebub and Lucifer. In the early *Henry VI* plays, actual devils appear alongside the witch Joan La Pucelle in *Part I;* and, in *Part II,* a demon named Asmath is conjured by Margery Jourdain at the behest of Eleanor, Duchess of Gloucester. Other named demons are no more than passing references, such as "Amaimon" and "Barbason" in *Merry Wives of Windsor*—names that Master Ford finds less terrifying than "cuckold" (11). More than half of the named demons with entries in this dictionary are those that Edgar pretends are plaguing him while he is disguised as Poor Tom in *King Lear.*

Does Shakespeare, then, view the demonic primarily through a skeptical lens? Shakespeare gives significant attention to demonic possession in *Comedy of Errors, Twelfth Night,* and *King Lear,* but as Gibson and Esra (along with earlier scholars) point out, these examples all turn out to be mistakes or make-believe. As a demonologist, Shakespeare is closer to Reginald Scot and Samuel Harsnett than to James I, Jean Bodin, Nicholas Remy, or most other authors of demonologies in his lifetime. Examples of explicit skepticism about the supernatural are noted in many of the dictionary's entries, such as Hotspur's dismissal of Glendower's conjuring power as "skimble-skamble" stuff (*1 Henry IV* 3.1.152).[1] Hotspur's portrait of Glendower as a "pompous fantasist is funny, and thus hard to dismiss, particularly as we never see Glendower perform any magic," the authors conclude (105). Divination, they note, "is a concept mostly metaphorical in Shakespeare's works, deployed as a joke, political necessity, or self-mockery" (67). References to "fiends" and "devils" are often little more than name-calling, revealing more about the speaker than the thing named, such as when they are used as racial epithets to insult Othello, Shylock, or Caliban (63). Some characters call into question the reality of devils altogether, as when Aaron in *Titus Andronicus* says "if there be devils, would I were a devil" (5.1.147). This "disruptive reflection," according to the authors, could indicate Aaron's non-Christian origin, his location in a pagan classical world, or a radical Sadducism—"either way, it stands out boldly" (64). Elsewhere devils are human vices: "the devil luxury," "the devil wrath" (63). On the other hand, the idea that powers attributed to devils are sometimes all-too-human deceptions, passions, or misunderstandings does not mean they always are, and some devils in Shakespeare's plays even when portrayed as fictions convey a darkly menacing sense that the demonic may be indistinguishable from extreme forms of human villainy. Indeed, Edgar's fictional fiends are a good example; his play-acting is so effective that it is not too great a stretch to think that Mohu or the foul fiend Flibbertigibbet might in fact be tormenting some actual Tom O'Bedlam beggar, even if not Edgar. More indirectly, they are resonantly interconnected with the human "fiends" active elsewhere in of this play. Gibson and Esra also note Othello's speculation that Iago might be a devil—"If thou be'st a devil, I cannot kill thee" (5.2.287)—seemingly confirmed when Iago does not die after Othello stabs him (63).

Perhaps what is most characteristically Shakespearean lies neither in examples of skepticism nor in appearances of actual demons but in instances of uncertainty and blurred boundaries. As the authors point out, "preternatural" might be a better word than "supernatural" for many events outside the usual course of nature that Shakespeare does not allow us to clearly identify (181). Obvious examples are the appearance of the dagger in *Macbeth* and the ghost in *Hamlet.* But the dictionary helps us see more subtle examples, such as in Shakespeare's use of the word "blast," which could refer not only to a purely natural explosion or gust of wind but also to a magical power to blight and destroy with words and looks, sometimes attributed to witches and devils and other supernatural beings (28). Is the "blasted heath" (1.3.77) in *Macbeth* merely windswept or is it afflicted by a magical malevolence? Even more subtly, the innocent word "take" could suggest the possibility of magical malevolence in some contexts; witches were said to "take" the cattle when they caused them harm, usually through illness. The power to "take" in this sense is attributed to Herne the Hunter in *Merry Wives of Windsor* (186) and could also be possessed by fairies. In these and many other examples, Shakespeare keeps alive the sense of ambiguous dark forces that certain individuals could tap into but that could not be fully understood or contained.

Commendably, this dictionary gives considerable attention to Shakespeare's figurative uses of the supernatural, allowing us to see how its terminology provided Shakespeare with tools to think about other types of phenomena. Not surprisingly, sexual passion, love, and the power of physical beauty are especially likely to be described through metaphors of bewitchment, spell-casting, and related terms. Even when used playfully or as compliments, such metaphors hint that something coercive informs experiences of love and desire even in the best of circumstances, something that the person experiencing them may at least partly resist. "Overlooking," for example—the power sometimes attributed to witches to cause harm by the 'evil eye'—is figuratively attributed to Bassanio by Portia in *Merchant of Venice* (3.2.14–16) when she chides, "Beshrew your eyes, / They have o'erlooked me and divided me / One half of me is yours" (146). Love and desire can be alien to the self, and become even more so when associated with deception and betrayal, as is amply demonstrated in the dictionary's entries on "charm," "enchantment," "fiend," "witch," and "witchcraft." While this figurative language is commonly used by Shakespeare's male characters to lash out at or express ambivalence about women's sexual powers, Shakespeare's female characters not infrequently apply it to men (as Portia does above) and occasionally men apply it to other men (as Antonio does when complaining that Sebastian's "witchcraft drew me hither" [5. 1.76] at the end of *Twelfth Night,* or, more playfully, when Falstaff says of Poins that he has been "bewitch'd by the rogue's company" [2.2.17]). Not all such usage is clearly figurative; maybe there is some real witchcraft in women's sexual powers, as in the case of Cleopatra (203). Fathers, moreover, often make quite literal accusations of witchcraft when speaking of unwanted suitors of their daughters, as does Brabantio in *Othello,* Egeus in *A Midsummer Night's Dream,* and King Simonides in *Pericles* (27).

Shakespeare's figurative language also commonly associates magic and witchcraft with the power of words, story-telling, and the arts, especially music and trompe-l'oeil effects in painting and sculpture. Othello's "witchcraft" lies in the stories he tells Desdemona; Iago uses "wit" not "witchcraft" to poison Othello's mind but his exercise of wit strongly resembles witchcraft in the seductively destructive use of words (205). Music charms by being hypnotic and sleep-inducing, while sculpture, painting, and theatre can bewitch by powerfully simulating reality like devils can. A subset of this type of usage occurs in political contexts. Cardinal Wolsey's influence through the power of rhetoric is called "a witchcraft/Over the king" (3.2.18) in *Henry VIII* (204); Cardinal Beaufort warns against a bewitching power in the "smoothing words" (1.1.156) of the future Richard III in *2 Henry VI* (27). The names of famous political figures such as Julius Caesar, Brutus, and Antony are names to conjure with (47), while what the authors call Coriolanus's "charismatic leadership" seems a form of witchcraft to his enemy Aufidius (204).

Finally, the language of magic and witchcraft provided Shakespeare with a way of thinking about inwardness. In the view of many demonologists, dreams, hallucinations, madness, and forbidden desires could be supernaturally caused or aroused and it can often be difficult to distinguish between metaphorical and literal references in Shakespeare's own works. The power of suggestion is a kind of "supernatural soliciting" (*Macbeth,* 1.3.130) resembling witchcraft when it conjures up horrid images in Macbeth's mind, arousing "black and deep desires" (1.4.51) or perhaps it actually is a form of witchcraft (27). In a more comic vein, Master Page asks "What spirit, what devil suggests this imagination" (3. 3.215) when commenting on Master Ford's delusions in *The Merry Wives of Windsor* (177). "Spirit" could refer to natural, vital, or animal spirits within the body according to early modern humoral theory, but, rather confusingly, spirits could also be "ambient evil creatures wreaking havoc independently in the world" (in other words demons or devils), capable of passing into bodily cavities and organs, upsetting humoral balances, and producing disordered mental states (175). As Gibson and Esra note, the spirits invoked by Lady Macbeth hover in "an unspecified place and state awaiting evil thoughts" and then seem to be invited inside her body to "corrupt . . . natural substances such as milk and blood" and "transform humoral spirits" (177)—perhaps contributing to the perturbations of mind later apparent in Lady Macbeth's sleepwalking scene. Shakespeare also refers to certain mental impulses as "devilish spirits," "worser spirits," "ill angels," and to other, better impulses by their more positive counterparts (12–13, 179). The dictionary's entries on "conjuration," "dream," "possession" "spirit," "angel," and "devil" all provide insightful commentary on the porous boundaries between supernatural and psychological phenomena throughout Shakespeare's works.

Indeed, throughout the dictionary the authors are admirably sensitive to ambiguities and resist the temptation to force decisions on the undecidable. They have also done a wonderful job of calling attention to unusual and obscure references, with particularly illuminating entries on "bug," "ducdame," "ecstasy," "elf," "Flibbertigibbet," "mummy," and "ouph." As in most first editions of reference works, there are omissions and small errors,[2] and one could quarrel with some decisions affecting coverage. More about Shakespeare's sources would be very valuable. The demonic pact is discussed briefly in the entry on the term "devil" but could benefit from fuller treatment in an entry of its own. A separate entry on witchcraft accusations would also be helpful. Perhaps most disappointingly, despite the detailed discussion of figurative uses of demonological language, most of the characters we associate with demonic extremes of villainy (Iago, Richard III, Goneril, Macbeth) are discussed only in passing. Yet each and every one of the ghosts that appear in Richard's dream at the end of *Richard III* gets its own entry. Do they really need such extensive attention? Gibson and Esra have restricted their entries on Shakespeare's characters to magical practitioners, persons formally accused of witchcraft, and literal ghosts, fiends or fairies. While this is a sensible principle of selection, it comes with a cost. Lady Macbeth gets her own entry, presumably because she invokes spirits and can therefore be considered a "magical practitioner," but Macbeth, who merely consults with witches, does not. Goneril is mentioned only once in the whole dictionary, Iago six times, but Roger Bolingbroke, a minor character in *2 Henry VI*, is mentioned fifteen times and gets his own entry. An entry on the term "evil" as it relates to the supernatural is brief and superficial. The dictionary thus makes it hard to see how Shakespeare, through his major villains, "foretells demonic modernity," as Ewan Fernie has recently suggested. For Fernie, impressed by "the sheer vitality of the demonic," the demonic is the subjective possibility of evil, "evil not in the abstract but as *a form of life*."[3]

But decisions about what to exclude are always judgment calls, unlikely to please everyone. Ultimately, what is included is far more important. Grounded in impressive scholarship, *Shakespeare's Demonology* is a rich, stimulating, wide-ranging dictionary that makes a major contribution to the study of Shakespeare's use of magic and witchcraft and his place in demonological tradition.

Notes

1. All quotations are from G. Blakemore Evans, ed., *The Riverside Shakespeare* (Boston: Houghton Mifflan, 1974), following the practice of Gibson and Esra. They base their analysis on Marvin Spevack's *Complete and Systematic Concordance to the Works of Shakespeare*, which is keyed to *The Riverside Shakespeare;* hence its use here.

2. For example, Egeon from *Comedy of Errors* is mistakenly substituted for Egeus from *A Midsummer's Night's Dream* on page 27 and in the index. The key

term "bewitched" offers only minimal coverage of scholarship or criticism. The entry on Caliban has none, though there is a vast critical literature on this character. The bibliography at the end, though extensive, leaves out some important works, such as John S. Mebane, *Renaissance Magic and the Return of the Golden Age: The Occult Tradition and Marlowe, Jonson, and Shakespeare;* Linda Woodbridge, *The Scythe of Saturn: Magical Thinking in Shakespeare;* Barbara Traister, *Heavenly Necromancers: The Magician in Renaissance Drama;* and Kristin Poole, *Supernatural Environments in Shakespeare's England.*

    3. In *The Demonic: Literature and Experience* (London and New York: Routledge, 2013), 6, 21.

Shakespeare on the University Stage.
Edited by Andrew James Hartley.
Cambridge: Cambridge University Press, 2015

Reviewer: James N. Loehlin

Andrew James Hartley's collection *Shakespeare on the University Stage* brings together sixteen essays that examine the phenomenon of campus Shakespeare from a range of historical, cultural, aesthetic and theoretical perspectives. As Hartley points out in his introduction, such performances provide the primary experience of live Shakespeare for many people around the world (and especially in the United States), yet they are remarkably evanescent and understudied. This impressive book helps to fill what Hartley has elsewhere called "one of Shakespeare criticism's singular blind spots" (*Shakespeare Survey* 65 [2012], 194). *Shakespeare on the University Stage* asks a range of searching questions in an attempt to understand the complex variety of university Shakespeare: "How does it uniquely manifest larger cultural concerns, assumptions, and prejudices, and how is it shaped by the pedagogical dimension of its academic context? How do such productions subvert or confirm ideas about theatre in general and Shakespeare in particular that are disseminated through the larger culture in complex and unexamined ways, and what is the relationship of those ideas to their equivalents on the professional stage?" (8–9). The diverse essays in *Shakespeare on the University Stage* provide an array of answers to these and other questions, and they certainly encourage sustained future scholarship on this neglected topic.

The book begins and ends with two leaders in the Shakespeare performance field, Peter Holland and W. B. Worthen, who provide, respectively, a historical context for campus Shakespeare and a theoretical interrogation of it. In between, essays explore the development of Shakespeare performance in a range of international educational traditions. Many consider the cultural status of Shakespeare and the politics implicit in his role in education; several note how campus Shakespeare performances provide a laboratory for current concerns about ideology and identity (especially gender identity). Hartley's concern is not with how performance is used in classroom teaching, a topic much discussed elsewhere, but with actual productions: both those formally mounted by university departments as part of their teaching mission and cultural calendar, and those put on by ad hoc student groups for creative expression, intellectual enrichment, or simply fun.

The essays in *Shakespeare on the University Stage* are not subdivided into labeled sections, but there is a meaningful arc to their organization. The book begins with the history of university Shakespeare in the Anglo-American world, then branches out into a consideration of different global traditions, and ends with a consideration of some of the challenges, and new potentialities, for educational Shakespeare performance today. Holland begins the historical section with a series of snapshots of early campus Shakespeare: from Polonius' memories of having "played once i' th' university," to the 1610 Oxford performance at which Desdemona moved the spectators to pity, to the jesting about Shakespeare, Burbage and Kemp in the Cambridge *Parnassus* plays. Surprisingly, there seems to have been no regular performance of Shakespeare at the English universities until well into the nineteenth century. When it came, it was amateur and unofficial, performed by student dramatic societies, and neither connected to the university curriculum nor to the professional theater. Eventually, it became associated with both (at least in the United States), as English and then Drama/Theatre emerged as academic disciplines, each with its own investment in Shakespeare. This brief but complicated history has made campus Shakespeare "a paradoxical cultural and pedagogical event," according to Holland: "It works in the complex interstices of competing and irreconcilable demands between college and community, between pedagogy and pleasure" (26).

Mark C. Pilkinton's essay on Shakespeare at Notre Dame gives a representative history of campus Shakespeare in America. Pilkinton points out that while departments and curricula in United States universities did not become regularized until the twentieth century, theatrical production, including Shakespeare, began much earlier. Pilkinton cites fifty-three performances of thirteen plays at Notre Dame between 1847 and 1941. At this all-male university, female roles were initially played by men, but that began changing by the 1920s. Notre Dame's theater became coeducational nearly fifty years before the university itself did.

Michael Cordner's essay on George Rylands, Cambridge don and theater director, reveals how Shakespearean performance, in the English university at least, could be oddly disconnected from both academic scholarship and professional practice, and yet have a substantial impact on both. Rylands is often given credit, through his influence on Peter Hall, John Barton, Trevor Nunn, and other Cambridge students who went on to the RSC, with infusing the British theater with a new sensitivity to the performance of Shakespeare's language. Cordner is at pains to qualify this claim, and casts Rylands in an unflattering light as a "fundamentalist" unwilling to engage with new developments in either the academy or the theater: "The result was that Shakespeare production under his aegis became locked in a time capsule of his designing" (55). Cordner's account is compelling; especially interesting is a conflict that arose between Rylands and Michael Redgrave, one of his former actors, who came to believe that Shakespearean performance should draw its life from the interpretive contributions of the actor as much as from the impersonal score of the text. Yet Cordner's essay never quite negates Rylands' achievement and influence. Interestingly, it is the only piece in the collection that focuses on the impact of an individual teacher or director, although, in the history of university Shakespeare, such figures have undoubtedly loomed large.

Several of the essays in the book look at different national traditions of Shakespeare in education, each with its own distinctive history and political complexity. In former British colonies, Shakespeare is part of an imperial discourse that has been both contested and co-opted. Angelie Multani argues that for students in India today, the English language itself "has changed in status from being primarily a carrier and symbol of colonial/postcolonial values and elitism to being more Indian than English" (75). Accordingly,

"Shakespeare's plays become important vehicles not for the cultural snobbery they may have represented in the past but as texts that help us explore our own notions of identity" (89). Multani discusses examples in the annual performance competition of the Shakespeare Society of India. While some of the collegiate groups performed in English "competently and effectively in a straightforward elocutionary style," more of them chose to do inventive adaptations that incorporated Indian languages and contemporary political perspectives on issues like gender discrimination and censorship (83–84). Another article, by Nurul Farhana Low bt Abdullah, reveals how similar postcolonial concerns emerge in Malaysian productions of Shakespeare, though here the issues are not so much linguistic as theatrical, with universities finding ways to incorporate traditional forms such as *wayang kulit* puppetry. Interestingly, in the case study on which the article focuses, a production of *A Midsummer Night's Dream* became over-complicated through an attempt to assimilate too many competing cultural forms and practices, in part because of the way it was funded: "in trying to appease various funding bodies the adaptation exhibited some signs of 'schizophrenia' where certain directorial decisions contradicted the spirit of the form that was being promoted" (184).

The articles on various national educational traditions have a certain sameness, usually beginning with a history of university Shakespeare performance in the country in question, then moving to a discussion of the major producing entities, lists of plays produced, some dates and statistics, and finally a discussion of one or two notable performances. Often they are most engaging in addressing specific productions, as in Christa Jansohn's consideration of contrasting *Merchant of Venice* performances in Germany, where the play's difficulties are especially fraught. In a chapter on China, Lee Chee Keng and Yong Li Lan draw an interesting comparison between a celebrated 1980 Beijing *Macbeth,* still weighted with the principles of Soviet socialist realism (and performed in Western-style makeup), and a 2011 Shanghai adaptation called *Love, Desire, Power* in which a collage of thematically linked scenes was performed by an energetic young ensemble in contemporary colloquial idiom. The contrast is made vivid by production photographs, which are a valuable addition to the volume throughout.

Issues that repeatedly come up in the discussion of university Shakespeare performances, especially in the United States, are gender, sexuality, and identity. Yu Jin Ko discusses the performance of gender in the all-female productions of the Wellesley College Shakespeare Society. In a production of *The Taming of the Shrew,* for instance, the female actors of Kate and Petruchio both subverted conventional gender identities, so that "the play became not so much a battle of the sexes that the male definitively wins, but more an internal battle figured in gendered terms in which balance was the issue" (74). Andrea Stevens's essay on the University of Illinois at Urbana-Champaign relates how both the institutional Theatre Department and the independent student troupe What You Will used non-traditional casting and provocative staging to explore *A Midsummer Night's Dream* "as a site for the positive exploration of queer identities" (123). Chad Allen Thomas writes about "Queering Shakespeare in the American South" with a cross-dressed production of *The Comedy of Errors* in Alabama (216). And in Australia, Rob Conkie finds university productions of Shakespeare characterized by "contemporized settings; conceptual interpretations; political critique, most often in the realm of gender; and, often as a result or culmination of these features, radical reinvention of the play and production's ending" (160).

Two essays from the UK take different approaches to Shakespeare performance as research. Jacquelyn Bessell reports on the Performance Research Group's two-person *Antony and Cleopatra,* undertaken (at the Shakespeare Institute in Stratford) as an experiment in "how little is required to make an act of theatre" (185). Her account illuminates the rehearsal process of what must have been a fascinating production. Yet Bessell reveals that the PRG has now moved, perhaps unsurprisingly, "from the research-driven environment of the Shakespeare Institute" to "the industry-facing edge of the Guildford School of Acting" (199). A contrasting approach to performance research is that described by Jonathan Heron at the University of Warwick, in which Shakespeare served as material for quasi-scientific experiments in theatrical "laboratories," also incorporating other disciplines such as medicine and psychiatry. This work had concrete practical results in the Young Vic production of *Hamlet* directed by Ian Rickson, who was a participant in 2011; otherwise I confess I found it a bit difficult, from the essay, to tell exactly what they were up to.

The uncertain status of Shakespeare performance in the academy—is it research, training, liberal arts education, social diversion, or commercial enterprise?—is a nagging question in some rather somber essays in the final section of the book. Paul Menzer, in a funny, bracingly astringent, and finally dispiriting analysis, assesses the economics of what he calls "the Shakespeare-industrial-complex" (203). Menzer calls attention to the "performance of institutional identity sponsored by collegiate Shakespeare," in which the university's rich resources and technical expertise are deployed in elaborate productions built on the labor of students who are not only unpaid, but are paying for the privilege of working on them (204). With wit and cynicism, Menzer contends that "Shakespeare, like American college football, helps produce an idea of university life timeless in its values and comfortingly lavish—an unembarrassment of riches" (205). These "official" productions, moreover, generate their opposite, the bare-bones performances of campus Shakespeare clubs, in a cycle that for Menzer replicates the history of twentieth-century performance, oscillating between lavishness and austerity, Beerbohm Tree and William Poel, the RSC and Original Practices. "Poor Shakespeare and Rich Shakespeare," for Menzer, "collude to produce the same idea: Shakespeare *ad nauseum,* a perpetual performance machine fueled by an unequal distribution of resources that never perfectly aligns" (214). Menzer is not, in the end, wholly cynical, crediting the enthusiasm and energy with which students approach their work; but his critique is sobering. Douglas E. Green's subsequent article on Shakespeare at small colleges, ironically, suggests that the situation may be worse than Menzer suggests. With decreasing arts education, a culture-wide decline in the humanities, and an increasing emphasis on STEM and job training, some colleges and universities may decide they can no longer afford Shakespeare at all.

The book concludes with a rigorous and thoughtful essay by W. B. Worthen that synthesizes many of the recurring themes of the various contributions, especially the question of how campus Shakespeare performance can truly generate knowledge. For Worthen, the key is to conceptualize performance not merely as a set of professional skills nor as a strategy for interpreting literary texts, but as an intellectual practice, a means of inquiry into ourselves and our world. Worthen wants to move performance "away from the dual subordination either to exploitative industry goals or to interpretive service to the literary text, and toward a more self-reflexive sense of performance as inquiry" (282). Worthen's reflections make an appropriate end to a rich and varied book. Yet I worry

that he may be asking for a little too much self-reflection—that the
severity of "performance as inquiry" may compromise some of the
joy and creative energy that student Shakespeare can produce. One
of the lessons of this excellent collection must be that there are
many ways for Shakespearean performance to contribute to the
learning of university students, and that such work is "uniquely
positioned to play a formative role in the lives of those who build
and experience it" (8).

The Future of Illusion
By Victoria Kahn
Chicago: University of Chicago Press, 2014

Reviewer: Paul A. Kottman

Victoria Kahn's *The Future of Illusion* has already received
deserved praise from many reviewers in various venues. I want to
echo much of that praise here, and also to raise a few questions.

Kahn is surely one of the most careful scholars of the early modern period today, and in this new book she moves with finesse
between discussions of Shakespeare, Hobbes, Machiavelli, Spinoza
and Vico, and later modern thinkers of "political theology" (Freud,
Schmitt, Strauss, Arendt, Kantorowicz, Cassirer) for whom these
earlier figures form an essential canon. Given this framing, *The
Future of Illusion* has been rightly perceived as a timely riposte to
trends in two broad quarters of inquiry.

On the one hand, Kahn responds to a resurgent interest in political theology (in the wake of 9/11, the Arab Spring, and ISIS) by
reminding us of the centrality of the early modern canon for any
genealogy of "political theology"—by which she means, "not the
theological legitimation or theological essence of political authority, but rather . . . the *problem* of the relationship between politics
and religion once this theological legitimation is no longer convincing."

On the other hand, Kahn is concerned to correct a somewhat

ironic tendency, on the part of many early modern scholars, to take (too) seriously certain implications of the notion that we are now living in a "postsecular world, in which the Whiggish narrative of increasing secularization in the West has come up against the fact that religion has not withered away." Against critics who affirm the permanence of a "theological imaginary" in politics—and who, somewhat tellingly, rely on Carl Schmitt, Leo Strauss or Lacan to make their case—Kahn insists (with Hans Blumenberg, Erich Auerbach, and Hannah Arendt as her guides) that "a decisive break between modernity and theological modes of explanation" means that, so far as we can know, political authority cannot be explained by revealed religion, or the ahistorical power of the theological "symbolic." When political authority and legitimacy become the *explanandum,* Kahn suggest, then the *explanans* can only be what human beings have believed, done and made—the self-transforming history of human values, works and practices. She thus links "the possibility of a purely secular politics" to "a purely secular conception of poiesis"—and she sees the latter as "central" to the work of Hobbes, Vico, Shakespeare and Spinoza, all of whom (she avers) suggest that human beings "can know only what we have made ourselves." (I will return to Kahn's discussion of *poiesis* in a moment.)

With respect to early modern studies, at least, Kahn has left those who advocate a "return" to the explanatory power of revealed religion with a lot of explaining to do. Odes to the enduring power of the "religious symbolic," in analyses of early modern social history or of so-called "sacramental poetics," might yield something of interest to historians of ideas or antiquarians; but the contribution made by such work to contemporary debates about modernity's secular legitimacy is, Kahn thinks, limited and questionable. She thus calls upon critics of the early modern period to better explain their views with respect to the "neglected dialogue" between contemporary discussions (across the human sciences) about the legitimacy of modern values and institutions, and the early modern figures in whose writings the terms of this dialogue first took shape. After all, if there is one thing on which Schmitt, Benjamin, Strauss, Cassirer, Blumenberg, Arendt, Löwith, Freud, Auerbach, and the rest agree—their stark differences notwithstanding—it is that we are not 'done' with Renaissance or early modern writers and artists when it comes to thinking about what it means to be "modern," or about what, if anything, distinguishes forms of life that have

emerged over the course of the past four or five centuries in the
'West' and elsewhere. In this sense, Kahn encourages critics of the
early modern period to consider whether they have anything "more
alive, more current, more relevant" (as she puts it) to contribute to
debates about the "legitimacy of the modern age," beyond a return
to the theological symbolic. Can those who study Machiavelli,
Shakespeare, Hobbes, Vico or Spinoza for a living read them as
'live' figures and thinkers for discussion today, and not just as
mouthpieces for what human beings once practiced or believed in
a past era?

So far, so good. The provocations Kahn offers to early modern
scholars will certainly find an appreciative audience, this reviewer
included. (It should be noted that Kahn is hardly alone in this
effort—as other recent contributions to the critical literature attest:
for instance, *Political Theology and Early Modernity* [Chicago: University of Chicago Press, 2012], edited by Julia Reinhard Lupton
and Graham Hammill; and Rocco Rubini's *The Other Renaissance*
[Chicago: University of Chicago Press, 2014]). Anyway, who among
us would want to resist the exhortation to take up present debates
through more attentive reading to early modern texts and their
interpreters?

In the space left to me, then, I want to take up Kahn's exhortation,
in order to raise three questions about her approach in *The Future
of Illusion.*

My first question concerns the static terms of "debate" and "side-
taking," which Kahn uses to frame her discussion—as if the central
issue were a quarrel over a kind of perennial question: Does political authority (or poetic activity) have a transcendent-theological
source, or is it immanently 'human' through-and-through? The
'good' moderns, Kahn seems to suggest, are those who take the latter position—and who hit upon new ways of "defending" their
stance. The "reactionary" moderns (Schmitt, Strauss) by contrast,
did not get with the right program—a mistake that, Kahn more than
hints, led one of them to take a disastrous political position in the
twentieth century. In Kahn's telling, the 'good' modernisms of
Machiavelli, Hobbes, Shakespeare, Spinoza, Blumenberg, Arendt,
and Benjamin—"which seem more attuned to the capacity of
human beings to create the values that bind them and give their
lives meaning"—is juxtaposed to what she calls the "reactionary
stance" of Schmitt and Strauss, who suffered from a kind of "ethical nostalgia" (to borrow Bernard Williams's felicitous phrase) for

the 'old gods,' for metaphysical or theological principles as the ground for political life. (Kahn does not mention this, but her perennial-debate-approach invites comparisons to analogous 'debates' in other historical eras. In classical Athens, for example, the struggle between 'old religious' and 'new secular-poetic' models of political legitimacy took shape in Greek tragedy. Was this debate 'modern,' too?)

Now, one need not defend Strauss or Schmitt (Kahn is more than generous to both), in order to ask: Must the 'legitimacy' of the modern age really rest on a defense of modern intellectual revolutions (of Machiavelli, Shakespeare, Hobbes, Spinoza) against other attempts (Strauss's reliance on classical reason; Schmitt's "Catholic paradigm of political representation") to answer the 'great question' of the source of political authority?

At the very least, two of Kahn's own heroes—Blumenberg and Arendt—did not think so. Blumenberg went so far as to say that "we are going to have to free ourselves from the idea that there is a firm canon of 'the great questions' that . . . have occupied human curiosity and motivated the pretension to world and self-interpretation" (65). Indeed, for Blumenberg, the prospect of freeing ourselves from the view that there are right or wrong answers to great questions is one of the modern age's promises—since we can now ask (Blumenberg thinks), why *certain* issues became pressing when they did? Likewise, for Arendt, the 'legitimacy' of secular politics does not rest on any correction of the 'wrong-headed' theological-symbolic model, but on actual, lived failures of recourse to extra-political sources of political authority (violence, God, truth). For Blumenberg and Arendt, put differently, there is no "*problem* of the relationship between politics and religion once theological legitimation is no longer convincing." Theological explanations for political authority are replaced by secular political philosophies because of prior catastrophes (Arendt), or because the modern age and the scientific revolution amounted to "the second overcoming of Gnosticism" (Blumenberg). Now, there are all manner of questions that one could raise—and that *have* been raised (by Bernard Williams, Karl Löwith, Robert Pippin, Richard Rorty and many others)—about the virtues and shortcomings of Blumenberg's 'legitimation' story, or Arendt's "revolutionary" politics. But, at the very least—when it comes to Kahn's book—it would have been helpful to consider the issue of modernity's "legitimacy" as something more than a rejection of the "theological symbolic." Indeed, by making *that* rejection the basis of modernity's legitimacy, Kahn inadvertently keeps "theological symbolism" 'alive' as modernity's "other" (as the chief alternative to secular politics). That is, Kahn risks reifying an epistemological critique of 'the theological' as the sole basis for secularization's legitimacy. But there are many other possible stories to tell about 'how we got to be us' (Hegel's, Marx's, Nietzsche's, Foucault's) that are neither Schmitt's nor Strauss's, nor exactly Blumenberg's or Arendt's—and which do not rely on epistemological critiques of theology, but rather on different narratives of epochal change (whether 'Hegelian' or 'genealogical' or whatever).

Indeed—to get to my second question—there are many stories about modernity, many "secularization theses," that hardly fit within the frame Kahn uses (the 'two-sided' debate model just mentioned). For instance, it is true that Blumenberg (like Kahn) is keen to show how modern notions of "progress" are not merely 'secularized' notions of Christian eschatology. But Blumenberg's thesis arose directly from his confrontation with Löwith, who never meant to suggest that "the notion of progress is just Christian eschatology secularized." Löwith suggested only that it would be difficult to account for *why* "progress" became such an important notion to the modern natural sciences, for instance, unless Christian views about the redemptive character of history had at least something to do with that. And then there is Hegel, who was intensely interested in the 'problem of modernity,' and who has no truck with the kind of transcendent sources of political authority to which Schmitt refers, but who also spoke of "God," the "divine" and so forth (albeit in highly idiosyncratic ways). So, too, Hegel's "modernity" emerges in dialogue with the notion of modernity as "loss" (as in Hölderlin or Schiller)—and all of them, by the way, obsessively 'engaged with' Shakespeare and Spinoza and so forth. And if Hegel came to see "gain" and not just "loss" in modernity, it was also in large measure because of his encounter with the Scottish Enlightenment as filtered through his own Protestant education (see Laurence Dickey's helpful *Hegel: Religion, Economics and the Politics of Spirit: 1770–1807* [Cambridge: Cambridge University Press, 1987]).

Throwing all this onto the table may seem unfair, since Kahn's book expressly avoids the eighteenth century—calling us, instead, to focus on that "neglected dialogue" between the late moderns and early moderns. But much gets muffled in the focus on that neglected dialogue, I think, without a more nuanced appreciation of the whole 'secularization' problem in modern thought and social practice (economics, politics, imperialism, globalization). So, without at least *some* of this material on the table, the "neglected dialogue" that Kahn wants us to hear sounds—I am suggesting—too narrowly 'two sided.' Indeed, part of the woodenness of contemporary debates about 'political theology'—which Kahn rightly wants to criticize—is also attributable, at least in part, to an insufficient reckoning with the various 'secularization theses' that have circulated over the past several centuries.

Lastly, let me turn to Kahn's invocation of "poiesis"—or, to what she calls the "new anthropology" (which she attributes to Hobbes and Vico) according to which human beings can know only what we make: "the entirely human capacity to make least part of the world we live in." Here my questions are straightforward. Kahn seems to see this conception of *poiesis* as something these thinkers simply hit on, a kind of 'great idea' or 'insight' or 'discovery' with which she agrees, and which makes obsolete any reliance on older religious notions of poetic authority, political authority or historical progress. But this conclusion avoids the basic question of 'legitimacy' with which her whole book is concerned. After all, what gives this broad notion of *poiesis* itself its legitimacy? Does Kahn mean to appeal to some ahistorical standard according to which Hobbes and Vico are 'correct,' and if so, on what basis? Is there not a different narrative—more internal, more historical—that one could tell about this "insight" into what Vico called "poetic wisdom"? Indeed, were not Vico and Hobbes themselves both at pains to present precisely this kind of immanent narrative (about the origins of political institutions, in Hobbes; or, about the origins of religious thought, in Vico)—rather than a 'theory' of 'the way things are'?

And this matters, too, when one turns to *poiesis* (as Kahn does) to explain historical developments in the realm of politics. Kahn speaks—in her concluding summary—of the "capacity of human beings to create the values that bind them and give their lives meaning." But is an *ex nihil* 'poetic' creation really a good *explanation* for our values and political commitments? Did we poetically 'create' secularized forms of life, feminism, human rights, the dignity of the individual, the capitalist market, the abolition of the Atlantic slave trade and so forth? Is *that* the strongest, most "secular" account of the "legitimacy" of these world-historical develop-

ments that we can muster, after a careful reading of Shakespeare or
Hobbes or Machiavelli or Spinoza? One hopes not.

Ink, Stink Bait, Revenge, and Queen Elizabeth: A Yorkshire Yeoman's Household Book
Steven W. May and Arthur F. Marotti
Ithaca: Cornell University Press, 2014

Reviewer: Robert Tittler

Several years ago the British Library received a large collection of
papers of the Spencer and Stanhope extended family of Cannon
Hall, Yorkshire, which they considered valuable chiefly for the correspondence of Lord Nelson's second in command at the Battle of
Trafalgar. Upon arrival, a thorough examination of the full contents
of the collection turned up a household book compiled by John
Hanson of Rastrick, Yorkshire, a tenant of the Elizabethan-era family patriarch John Stanhope. Hanson (1517–99), a scrivener and
apparently self-taught legal advisor, proved a man of broad interests. The diverse contents of his book speak to many of them.
Hanson recorded a lengthy prose narrative plus a later ballad concerning a bitter fourteenth-century inter-family feud (Chapter 1);
two long-lost broadside ballads describing Queen Elizabeth's post-
Armada celebratory procession through London (Chapter 2); several texts copied from printed sources (Chapter 3); and other,
unpublished, texts including two poems attributed to Elizabeth
herself (Chapter 4). These are all bound together with lists of
English monarchs, manorial tenants, and English counties, and
instructions and recipes on such diverse subjects as making inks
and pigments and catching fish and fowl.
    This intriguing and hitherto unknown source inspired Steven W.
May and Arthur F. Marotti to undertake their summary and analysis of Hanson's work, to transcribe much of its contents, and more
generally to emphasize the importance of an early modern scribal

culture which has often been overlooked in assessing the intellectual tenor of the times. (Their inventive and certainly distinctive title derives from some of Hanson's own terms and themes: it remains to be seen if it will be easily remembered or readily forgotten in its full extent.)

Hanson proves an apt subject for a discussion of scribal culture. May and Marotti make much of the importance of such a collection emanating from the pen of someone whom they describe as a mere yeoman. One may quibble with that social description, as Hanson appears to have derived his income and reputation from his work as a professional scrivener and legal advisor as well as from the collection of rents. But even this modest status at the lowest rung of the legal profession illustrates the sub-elite social level at which such a culture thrived by the mid-Elizabethan era, whilst his rural west Yorkshire base illustrates its geographic range. Those are important attributes. Modern scholarship has tended to observe pre-modern English scribal culture amongst the elevated social ranks operating from the country houses of the day or in proximity to London and the universities.

Hanson's book may be unusual in emanating from someone of his social status, but it is not unique. May and Marotti very usefully place it in the context of other such efforts carried out, for example, by Thomas Brampton of Kempton, Suffolk; Henry Gurney of Great Ellingham, Norfolk; and, most interestingly, Hanson's fellow west Yorkshireman and contemporary John Kaye of Woodsome.[1] Given the undeniable fact that the material remains of sub-gentry or minor gentry families are far less likely to survive than those of the more affluent and generationally stable status groups, we are fortunate to have such works. As May and Marotti note, the preservation of most surviving household or commonplace books of this era result from the family's subsequent rise to long-term stability and affluence.[2] John Kaye's literary remains, for example, survived as the family became more affluent, influential and affluent in successive generations. John Kaye himself established his 'house' by shrewd investments in agricultural lands and coal mines. His direct descendants included a baronet in the early seventeenth century and a leading inventor of industrial machinery in the eighteenth, whilst the family seat at Woodsome survived into the twentieth.[3] The Hanson clan climbed nowhere near as far, but his book nevertheless survived as part of the Spencer/Stanhope family muniments.

Given the diversity of Hanson's own interests, aptly reflected in the title, it would have been very difficult for May and Marotti to produce a conventionally structured, tightly focused monograph on a single theme. Instead they have produced a series of chapters on disparate subjects held together by the threads of Hanson's initiative and the general subject of scribal culture at work.

The lengthiest part of Hanson's book, and thus the lengthiest chapter in the work before us, concerns a bitter mid-fourteenth-century feud between the Yorkshire families of Elland and Beaumont. The feud, part of the legendary history of that shire, fascinated Hanson, and he took the unique step of recording both prose and ballad narratives of that saga. May and Marotti explore the historicity of these texts at length, comparing the ballads with each other and against the independent evidence of the historical record. This allows them to examine how the prose and ballad versions of this particular story were put to polemical use by later generations, and then to reconsider the definition and utility of the ballad genre itself.

May and Marotti perform similar detective work on the two unique surviving copies of a ballad describing Elizabeth's post-Armada procession to St. Paul's in order to give thanks for the English victory. All copies of these two printed ballads had long been lost before resurfacing in Hanson's collection. They provide an intriguing, detailed, and unique account of the processions, adding substantial detail to what John Stow and others recorded independently. In contrast to Stow's account, they reflect the tensions between the corporate rights of London citizens and the authority of the crown, those between Protestants and Catholics, and those between the theme of regal splendour in the procession and the Queen's show of humility in the St. Paul's service itself. Finally, Hanson's account shows Elizabeth herself playing a much more substantial part in designing the event, and it reveals, for the first time, the names of some of the others involved.

While the provenance of the *manuscript* material which Hanson recorded remains obscure, he also copied—not always very accurately—from *published* sources. These he seems to have borrowed or in some cases came to own. Most, including excerpts from Foxe's *Actes and Monuments* and an epitaph for the earl of Pembroke, will have been printed in London. The first of these enjoyed a virtually mass circulation in every corner of the realm and will not have been difficult to obtain. But Hanson's ready access to the latter shows the extent to which cultural integration of the realm had proceeded by his time. His inclusion of two poems thought to be written by the Queen allow May and Marotti to compare Hanson's copies with others, and to undertake a lengthy and fine-grained "micro reconstruction of the scribal network" in their regard. They conclude that Elizabeth cannot have been the author of the poem "Leave and Let me Rest," which has conventionally been attributed to her.

The penultimate chapter discusses the more conventional contents of a contemporary household book as they appear in Hanson's collection. This consists of practical information on how to make and do things which were integral to the domestic life of that time. Here we find instructions copied from diverse sources or passed on orally through the generations on such subjects as how to catch fish and fowl. But more intriguingly, we also find recipes for making black and colored inks, and for making paint itself. In addition, May and Marotti transcribe Hanson's instructions "*To make an Instrument to portray whythe upon a wall parchement paper/or wheare ye lyke with the blake color.*"[4] The "instrument" in question is not, as one would expect, a conventional brush, but a "good bigge Reede" fashioned for that purpose.

May and Marotti not only provoke further thought on their main concern, which is the literary culture of Hanson's world, but also on subjects lurking at the periphery of that subject. In presenting these household recipes and instructions they suggest Hanson's interest in painting, calligraphy, and perhaps even the pursuit of heraldry as well as in writing, poetry, and history. They open the possibility that Hanson himself may have painted, perhaps for himself and more likely for his clients. Such painterly activities as the illumination of legal documents or the production of heraldic imagery made a close and potentially lucrative fit with his work as a scrivener and legal advisor. His recipe for making black ink seems a common enough necessity for a scrivener at a time when ink was not yet commercially produced. His recipe for *colored* inks suggests use in illuminations and heraldic representation on parchment or paper. But his instructions for shaping reeds into applicators for paint, a very rare reference indeed, suggests the application of broader and less nuanced strokes such as one might apply to wall painting on plaster rather than on paper, parchment, or wood panel.

In recording such practical information along with the more literary contents of his book, Hanson reflected a stage not only in the transition from an oral to a scribal culture, but also in the formation of a burgeoning "public" for painting (especially portraiture and wall painting), and for the associated genres of heraldry and calligraphy. The close imbrication of writing and painting in these years was noted by some of Hanson's contemporaries like the orthographer John Hart,[5] as well as by sundry modern scholars.[6] Both the compilation of written commonplace or household books on the one hand and the often lengthy autobiographical inscriptions and heraldic displays one finds on vernacular portraiture and wall painting of this era served as quasi-experimental media.[7] They offered forms of autobiographical expression and self-presentation operating outside the mainstream of contemporary "high culture," before evolving in the following century to the more enduring genres of, e.g., conventional autobiography or memoire and formal, polite portraiture which required neither inscription nor heraldic imagery.

The confluence of such communicative genres is particularly well exemplified by Hanson's regional neighbour John Kaye, who dwelt for most of his life in Woodsome, perhaps a dozen miles from Hanson's base at Rastrick.[8] (The families may even have known each other as Hanson held and then left to his third son, Nicholas, property in Woodsome.)[9] Kaye not only left the literary remains to which May and Marotti allude,[10] and shared Hanson's familiarity with the writings of Thomas Tusser,[11] but he also left four autobiographical paintings, done on each side of two joined wood panels, which survive to the present day in the Tolson Museum in Huddersfield.[12] These panels display crude painted portrait images of John on one panel and his wife Dorothy on the other. They also squeeze into the picture plane and on the reverse of each panel numerous inscribed moral platitudes, autobiographical poems, and extensive lists and coats of arms of Kaye's friends and family.[13]

May and Marotti view the commonplace book as a new means of personal expression, and as "belonging to a world in transition from orality to script."[14] But perhaps it is also part of an even broader transition in forms of self-expression in which script is but one part . . . and the emerging visual genres of non-elite portraiture and heraldic display are yet others. In sum, they have made a valuable and thought-provoking contribution to what we know of Elizabethan scribal culture, rendered even more important because so very much of that activity can no longer be recalled or interpreted.

Their work is equally valuable for recognizing the potential of that culture in a more balanced view of Early Modern English society in general, and for encouraging the further exploration of contemporary cultural themes and variations.

Notes

1. The editors confusingly use the variant spellings of "Kay" and both "Woodsum" and "Woodsun" in the index entry for Kaye (the conventional modern spelling), and "Woodson" on p. 22 and "Woodsome" in indexing the place.

2. May and Marotti, *Ink, Stink Bait, Revenge, and Queen Elizabeth: A Yorkshire Yeoman's Household Book* (2014), 7.

3. Robert Tittler, "John Kaye," *Oxford Dictionary of National* Biography, doi:10.1093/ref:odnb/107187.

4. May and Marotti, *Ink, Stink Bait, Revenge,* 220.

5. John Hart, *An Orthographie, conteyning the due order and reason, howe to write or paint thimage of mannes voice,* (2nd ed., London, 1569, *STC* 12890), 1–2, 9, and 27–28.

6. See, for example, Juliet Fleming, *Graffiti and the Writing Arts in Early Modern England,* (London: Reaktion Books, 2001), 9–13, *et passim.*

7. On alternative means of personal expression, see Adam Smyth, *Autobiography in Early Modern England* (Cambridge: Cambridge University Press, 2010), especially Chapter 4. For portrait inscriptions, see Robert Tittler, *Portraits, Painters and Publics in Provincial England, 1540–1640,* (Oxford: Oxford University Press, 2012, 2013), 142–43. The literature on wall painting is vast, but a succinct and able summary may be found in Kathryn Davies, *Artisan Art; Vernacular Wall paintings in the Welsh Marches, 1550–1650* (Almeley, Herefordshire: Logaston Press, 2008). For the burgeoning popularity of heraldry in this same era, see especially Nigel Ramsay, ed., *Heralds and Heraldry in Shakespeare's England* (Donington: Shaun Tyas, 2014).

8. Tittler, 'John Kaye', *ODNB.*

9. May and Marotti, *Ink, Stink Bait, Revenge,* 22.

10. Ibid., 8.

11. Ibid., 9.

12. Tolson Memorial Museum, Huddersfield, nos. KLMUS 1990/399 and 399A, and KLMUS 1990/398 and 398A.

13. Robert Tittler, "Social Aspiration and the Malleability of Portraiture in Post-Reformation England: the Kaye Panels of Woodsome, Yorkshire, c. 1567 c. 1567," *Northern History,* 52:2 (2015): 182–99.

14. May and Marotti, *Ink, Stink Bait, Revenge,* 6.

Reading Class through Shakespeare, Donne, and Milton
By Christopher Warley
Cambridge: Cambridge University Press, 2014

Reviewer: Crystal Bartolovich

Christopher Warley's *Reading Class* claims a dual mission; first, it seeks to rehabilitate "class" as a category of literary criticism. For decades, Warley argues, critics have rendered class invisible through a focus on other categories ("sodomy", "domesticity", "refashioning," etc.). This much is probably obvious to most readers whether or not they think of it as a problem. More intriguingly, Warley suggests that, even while displacing class, such critics have continued to rely on an "essentialized" understanding of it, as is evident in their scattered casual references to "middle class" authors or the like. Warley proposes to bring class back to the forefront of criticism in a more useful way by de-reifying it. Second (but not secondarily) Warley affirms the centrality of "literature" to his book.

How do I love this project? Let me count the ways. First of all, Warley's emphasis on class—and his astute observation that even critics who ostensibly ignore it have continued to rely upon it—is timely and salient. Second, Warley's answer to the question "why write literary criticism?"—namely, to explore class—is provocative and refreshing. I also appreciate Warley's clear writing, his wide range of reference, and his provision of a definite case; he takes the risk of identifying the sort of reading from which he wishes to differentiate his own and offers a distinct alternative. Because of his strong argumentative line, Warley has produced an important book, one well worth thinking about whatever your theoretical or critical investments. Furthermore, since Warley focuses on texts that many early modern professors are likely to be teaching, his book offers an excellent resource for the classroom. I enjoyed reading it.

This does not mean that I agree with Warley's approach or with the book's fundamental premise ("if you don't read literature, you can't read class"), but class is such an important topic that I am thrilled to see it extensively and prominently addressed (27). So: why, then, do I disagree? First, "history" is not a threat to literature in the way this book proposes. With his twin concerns—for class and the literary—Warley seeks to shift away, he emphasizes, from habits of criticism that rely on identity politics, especially from readings that ostensibly relegate literature to the status of mere historical document, an excuse to discuss social identities or other "political" concerns while nullifying the specifically literary aspects of texts. This charge has cropped up a lot recently under various banners ("surface reading," "new aestheticism," "new formalism" and so on). The ongoing importance of "close reading" to our field, however, suggests that the marginalization of "aesthetics" by "history" is overstated. More important, though, the presumption that "literature" is primarily under threat *from critics* seems to me to be a serious misrecognition—and a worrisome displacement—of the actual threats faced by English departments—a point to which I will return.

Leaving aside for the moment the question of what forces most threaten the "literary" these days, my other important disagreement with Warley stems from his ultimately *deconstructive* perspective. For Warley, as we and our cultural treasures hurtle through time, there is no making them, or us—or class—stay put. He calls this perspective "dialectical," but his refusal to situate class historically actually positions him closer to what Fredric Jameson calls the "more absolute skepticism of deconstruction" in *The Hegel Variations.* Any dialectical approach, to be sure, has to emphasize process, but, when we are dealing with *class* exploitation and other oppressions, we must also look below capitalism's relentless pace of technological and productive innovation ("all that is solid melts into air") to reveal the enduring unequal *social relations* that underwrite it. Since Warley's project is to de-reify "class" *as a word,* to disconnect it not only from any referent but also any signified, he examines neither the relative fixity of class relations in any given historical moment, nor actual class struggles. Furthermore, even as Warley eschews what he calls "essentialism" with respect to class, he oddly embraces the literary *as such* (he never questions the primacy of the literary, or even defines it). I would have liked to see Warley *situate* "literature" with more historical rigor—and class as well.

To make its case, Warley's book moves through seven chapters that, following a theoretical introduction, offer readings of works by the eponymous authors, taking up, in turn, "A Lover's Complaint," *Hamlet,* "The Flea," "A Valediction: forbidding Mourning," "Lycidas" and, finally, *Paradise Lost.* Although the routes vary, Warley's destination is always the same: "class" cannot be pinned down because it has no determinate content. Thus, he avers, it can only be approached *negatively.* Negative dialectic is, of course, associated with the Frankfurt School—especially Adorno—as well as later critics who work in this tradition, such as Jameson. For the latter, the labor of the negative exposes the insufficiency of all "concepts," since they are *non-identical* with objects. However—and this is where Warley parts ways with them—for Adorno (and Jameson) the specific contradictions that emerge between concept and object are *always* concretely historical. Concepts produced under conditions of slavery or capitalism (in its pre-industrial, industrial, postmodern, neoliberal, informational, etc. moments) betray misidentifications *characteristic of that moment.* Literature internalizes these social contradictions in its form—that is, indirectly, mediated through the demands of aesthetic production under particular historical conditions. This is why we must be historically specific when we talk about "literature," "class," or "society" and their inter-relations.

While Warley identifies examples of "tensions" in early modern texts, he does not consider the specific social conditions that give rise to them. Instead, he rewrites the tensions that he discovers as allegories of Derrida, Bourdieu, Ranciere or other current theorists. For example, in his reading of "Lycidas," Warley, recodes the poem in terms of Ranciere's *Dissensus* to observe:

> The uncouth swain both wraps the poem in a total fiction and undermines the fiction that had been operating. It is a declaration of the poem's nobility and an embrace of the unknown in the world to come. You could try to resolve this tension—by insisting on the finality of either anonymity or Miltonic fame. Or you could dwell on the inescapable melancholy attached to a deferred promise of equality that the poem cannot make arrive (Adorno's characteristic maneuver). . . . But it seems to me a more attentive, and more egalitarian, procedure to try to maintain the tension itself. (139)

First of all, this is a misleading characterization of Adorno, since he too, "maintain[s]" the tension in the contradictions he identifies—though he characterizes it as a historical (not an inevitable, much less desirable) condition. "Melancholy" does not *resolve* "tension" because it is Adorno's response to a world in which, devastatingly, *remediable* suffering persisted despite technological "progress," which was deployed to build bombs and death camps rather than to end hunger. A critic must locate the "tension" in art *historically* to help readers recognize their responsibility for "resolving" concrete social contradictions *in their world.*

Conversely, for Warley, literature is a worthwhile site in which to "read" class because deconstructive undecidability is where it will inevitably bring us: "class has to be read [in literature] because it does not sit still" (12). His rationale for this move is that assigning a "class position" to either an author or a text is an affront to its literariness as well as our understanding of class. On its own terms, the book's "hesitation"—the critical attribute that Warley claims to most admire (27)—responds forcefully and compellingly to the habit of reification Warley associates with historical criticism (albeit too sweepingly in my view), but in his zeal to undermine class "essentialism," Warley refuses to *historicize* it at all, even provisionally or strategically. To keep the concept from settling for his readers, Warley claims class to be permanently *empty;* this is possible because he attaches none of the texts he reads (or his own reading practice) to *actual* historical struggles, sufferings or social relations. Though the blurb claims that the book "offers a detailed historical argument about what class means in the seventeenth century," it actually does nothing of the kind. At the level of abstraction in which Warley's readings and his reading practice move, such materialist muck as "actual" history appears to inhabit a galaxy far, far away. Literature floats above all that crudity so it can continue to tell readers that class "does not sit still" *ad infinitum.* Warley thus promotes his own version of "slow" reading of literature as "a powerful way—perhaps the only way—to study class" (23). The price to be paid is that "class" has—and can have—no meaning at all.

To approach it, then, Warley conjures up a number of alternative linguistic sites in which to stage "readings" that address class but do not arrest it (eg. "fickle," "virtue," "uncouth")—terms whose early modern meanings he takes up in detail—while *class* as a concept remains equivocal. These displacements are historically necessary of course (though Warley does not say so) because—while what a Marxist would call *class struggle* was already underway—the *word* "class" had not yet emerged in its modern form; "Rank," "degree," and the like were the preferred terms for social hierarchy, as Raymond Williams—and a host of historians—have established. Warley can sidestep this problem since his investment is in what reading early modern texts can say about "class" to readers *now*—an investment that emerges in the introductory chapter as well as in little anachronistic stylistic flourishes in ensuing chapters (i.e., "Eden ends up seeming a lot like high school," 152). These temporally marked asides jarred me—though not in a good *ostranenie* way; they do not defamiliarize, nor does Warley follow through on them to situate the reader in relation to specific class struggles now. I would have preferred a more sustained indication of where we are historically at any given moment in the argument—especially, what *trends and forces* here and now demand a return to class, and how the contradictions Warley identifies—mediated aesthetically—relate to these historical conditions (beyond alerting us to the perils of reification).

Such historical situating matters because the *last* thing that I would want to tell my students about class right now is that its content is utterly indeterminate given how nicely that view folds into widespread beliefs that: 1) class relations do not exist; 2) if they did exist they would indicate nothing more than lifestyle choices (i.e. preferring Cartier to Timex); 3) nothing can be done about class relations anyway, whether they exist or not. As we have seen, the lesson Warley imparts about class—"don't reify it"—never slows *class* down long enough to "read" it as invested with particular meanings (and actual struggles!) that emerge in specific historical circumstances. He rejects (albeit equivocally) the "in the last instance" gesture that Marxist critics typically use to slow it down; for Warley, pinning class to "divided labor, as does Marx, or naming it society as does Adorno, or naming it collectivity as does Jameson, always risks making the name into the end-point of a teleological narrative"—a risk that Warley is, ultimately, not willing to take (148).

The one exception to this inexorable process of hesitation in *Reading Class* comes in the introduction when Warley discusses Raymond Williams's brilliant reading of country house poems. Williams points to the fantasy of laborless production on which such poems rely while reminding us of the "actual" laborers who were supplying the bounty that "To Penshurst" attributes to the hospitable beneficence of the Sidney family alone. Warley *affirms* the power of Williams's approach, which he defends from charges of "economism" and crudity. He insightfully suggests that Williams's readings are *immanent* (though, curiously, Warley does not use the term here). That is, Williams, whatever he may say about his method, stays *with* the text when he points out the absences on which it relies (which are therefore part of it). Warley is so enthusiastic in his praise of Williams on this score, in fact, that I was settling in to enjoy a succession of readings in which class is situated historically in Williamsesque fashion but they never arrive.

What we get instead is a displacement of Williams's nuanced *historicized* approach to class with a Derridean "haunting" and abstracting of it. We are told that the "Lover's Complaint" is "a spectral expression of class in and as historical transition" (31). It is "spectral" because it is as "fickle" (changeable) as the Maid who relates her tale of woe in the poem—which is to say that she, time and the poem "continually deconstructs" (36). In the next chapter, *Hamlet,* via Horatio (and Bourdieu), teaches us the impossibility of "disinterestedness"—a position that would seem to demand an accounting of interests (71). Warley concludes instead, however, that "class struggle is as equivocal as anything said by the fickle maid" (50). Next, Donne's poetry (first, "The Flea") displays for us "a hard core of uncertainty" (95), which we find again in "The Valediction" in the next chapter, where Warley, Derrideanly, refuses to "choose" between the poem as "structure" and "event" (119). Finally, the "uncouth" in Milton shows us that "class" is a "certain spirit that haunts a world all before it and makes a future out of its continued transformation" (178). As if this claim were not "uncertain" and vague enough, it is followed by: "Maybe. After all, you really don't know what is going to happen next." The end. Maybe.

Saving me the trouble, Richard Halpern already pointed out long ago the problem with such a deconstructive approach from a Marxist perspective in his excellent review essay on Derrida's *Specters.* There, Halpern demonstrates that emptying out class in an endless chain of undecidabilities empties out politics as well. He further suggests that this depoliticization occurs because Derrida is invested in challenging Marxism with Deconstruction, but not Deconstruction with Marxism, which would require him to "curtail his project of endless 'filtering' and purgation, and delve in the sometimes unpleasant muck of real history" (51).[1] This judgment (properly, in my view) privileges political actuality over theoretical purity. Deconstruction, as Gayatri Spivak has repeatedly underscored, is the prolegomena to politics, and a necessary exercise in

vigilance to make sure your political project does not ossify into
the very oppressive conditions you sought to overcome, but is not
itself a politics, which always involves *choosing* in concrete historical situations. One can appreciate deconstruction while recognizing its limits. If we deconstructively empty out class completely, as
Warley does, we run up against a *political* impasse. When Warley
tries to make a virtue of *not* choosing, of perpetual "hesitation,"
Stanley Fish will cheer, but a Marxist cannot.

Ultimately, however, Warley's investment in a certain curiously
essentialized understanding of "literature"—nowhere interrogated
in the book—underwrites his "hesitation" about "class," I think,
even more than his deconstructive investment in aporia. Defenses
of "literature" are spurting up everywhere these days among academic critics (as well as non-academics), and one should ask
"why?" before joining the chorus. In his introductory chapter, Warley cites Marjorie Garber as a critic who "has complained that the
nearly universal turn to historicism in literature departments has
not only made literary criticism very boring and predictable; it has
also made literature as a unique object of study disappear" (23).
This observation surprised me, since I had read *Use and Abuse of
Literature* without encountering it. Warley does not provide a specific page reference, so it is impossible to know for sure what part
of the book led him to this perplexing conclusion, but he seems to
be referring to Chapter 4, where Garber writes "every [critical] practice is prone to its own excesses, and over time it has occasionally
been the case that the historical fact took preeminence over the literary work. When history is regarded as the 'real' of which the
poem, play or novel is (merely or largely) a reflection, something
crucial is lost, and that something is literature" (158).[2] This passage
is hardly the categorical dismissal of history per se that Warley's
paraphrase suggests since Garber underscores that "excess" is a
hazard of *any* critical practice. Though this "excess" has "occasionally" manifested itself in "historical" approaches, formalism,
too, in Garber's view, produces "a sense of boredom" when it is
overly and reflexively deployed: "the New Critical reading, while
elegant, was at the same time predictable—and limitation led to the
resuscitation and reinvigoration of other critical modes . . . that
depended as much upon context or history as the actual language
on the page" (143). Her point, then, is *not* a dismissal of historical
approaches (on which *Use and Abuse* itself relies), but, rather, a
dismissal of mechanical readings *of any kind.*

Garber, in fact, emphasizes the *historical specificity* of differing understandings of "literature" and "criticism" over time. Unlike "class" for Warley, a literary text can indeed "sit still" (temporarily) for Garber; that is what a reading for her *is* because a*ny given reading* and *any given text* will itself be historically situated—that is, subject to the limits, pressures and possibilities of the moment in which it is made (and in which it has, successively, afterlives)— moments whose social relations and forces it is possible to identify, insert into an explanatory narrative, and judge. Such an approach is even more important for a Marxist critic, who must be invested in reading literature well in order to explore its social mediations and read the world well. If Warley had taken this approach to "class" and "literature," he would have made the former *more* settled and the latter *less* so.

Instead of insisting that "class" means nothing out of fear of "essentializing" it, he could have showed how the texts *we identify as* "literature" *now* belong to politics with "actual" class implications that change over time, as do reading practices and the production of art (and everything else). Class does not remain the same over time, but it is not *impossible* to pin down, temporarily and strategically, in and for any given set of circumstances, either—nor is "literature" a timeless construct that can be taken as a given. Garber, it is true, praises literature for its refusal of definitive answers—an attribute she identifies as its "specificity . . . in comparison with other modes of writing, thinking and research"—but this does not prevent her from identifying very different attitudes toward literature over time. When Warley, extending Garber, treats both literature *and* class as open-ended, he does not pause to ask why this strategy might seem attractive for academics at the moment. One must ask, though, because, *pace* Garber, opening us to questioning is surely *not* restricted to *literature* (the Mona Lisa or the "Goldberg Variations" are not "answers" to anything in a crude utilitarian sense either, and many scientists view their research as generating questions, not answers). Furthermore, just because vocational and utilitarian imperatives are threatening liberal arts does not mean that "answers" are unimportant, any more than it means that literature is the sole antidote. Literature—like class—is a *site of struggle* over (provisional) "answers" *as well as questions*. Garber insists that literature *alone* offers access to a special process of questioning because she seems to believe that this is the only way to save it. To my mind, English professors should, rather, be joining in collective struggle with all the *many* refuseniks of the vocational and the crudely utilitarian.

Because Warley is eager, like Garber, to promote the "primacy of literature," he, too, insists that it (alone!) gives us access to "class." But we can access class in *many* ways—most importantly, in the actual *struggles* of the exploited. While it may be tempting in the face of cutbacks and declining enrollment in English to insist on the superiority of literature—and to promote it (and "class") as non-threateningly "open-ended"—such slippery, fungible concepts have no political purchase. To be sure, this "hesitation" accords well with institutional imperatives to be apolitical. If we stick to the nurturingly, unchallengingly affective, this view holds, we can pack lecture halls once again and live on. I value the Humanities, but I doubt such an approach will save them. Literary studies are under threat from globalizing info-capitalism—most immediately from budget-slashing state legislatures, vocational-training demanding parents and program-closing boards of trustees. To save it, we must directly confront the crude economic imperatives that threaten literature far more than a politically-minded (or any other kind of) critic ever could. While Warley's book provides a necessary corrective to uncritical deployments of "class" in early modern studies, it would need to historicize both class and literature more rigorously to have any *political* purchase in the face of current crises. The Jamesonian imperative—"Always Historicize!"—is as crucial today as ever—even though we have to struggle anew over what it means in the specificity of every now.

Notes

1. Richard Halpern, "An impure history of ghosts: Derrida, Marx, Shakespeare," in Jean E. Howard and Scott Cutler Shershow, eds., *Marxist Shakespeares* (London: Routledge, 2001), 31–52.

2. Marjorie Garber, *The Use and Abuse of Literature* (New York: Random House, 2011).

Index